283
Ark
WAN.24
AC

THE ANGLICAN COMMUNION

A SURVEY

THE ANGLICAN
COMMUNION

A SURVEY

EDITED BY

J. W. C. WAND, D.D.

Bishop of London
Formerly Archbishop of Brisbane

GEOFFREY CUMBERLEGE
OXFORD UNIVERSITY PRESS
LONDON   NEW YORK   TORONTO
1948

Oxford University Press, Amen House, London E.C.4

GLASGOW NEW YORK TORONTO MELBOURNE WELLINGTON

BOMBAY CALCUTTA MADRAS CAPE TOWN

Geoffrey Cumberlege, Publisher to the University

Printed in Great Britain by
Latimer, Trend & Co., Ltd., Plymouth

CONTENTS

v

INTRODUCTION

by the BISHOP OF LONDON

The purpose of this book is to offer a survey of the whole Anglican Communion. A short time ago Canon McLeod Campbell, in his fascinating *Christian History in the Making*, traced the history of that Communion in the course of its formation. We wish to take up the story where he left it, and to present a bird's-eye view of the finished product, or at least of that product at the stage of development it has reached to-day.

It is hoped that the publication will at least be found timely. The meetings of the Lambeth Conference have always been important since their inception in 1867. On more than one occasion they have inaugurated new and striking phases in our history. It is possible that the post-war meeting of 1948 will form no exception. Whether this be so or not a volume of this kind should help members and strangers alike to estimate the present position of our world-wide organization while preparing for further advance.

Also it should help the various branches of the Anglican Communion to know each other better. Such knowledge is all too obviously lacking at the moment. Partly because the component churches are widely separated and are each enclosed within its own national or regional boundaries, and partly because no two of them are exactly alike, it is almost impossible for any one person accurately to know them all. Yet it is vitally necessary that there should be as much common knowledge as possible. Ignorance breeds suspicion and although happily no mutual distrust exists among the various churches of the Anglican Communion at present, it might arise at any time under the pressure of new adventures if ignorance were allowed to go unchecked.

The following survey should thus lead to a more exact and widespread knowledge of what the Anglican Communion is. There will be some gain if it is no longer confused with the Church of England. It includes that Church, but is not identical with it. Nevertheless the confusion exists, and is more pardonable than it might seem at first sight owing to the tenacity with which some of the component churches still cling to the name by which their missionary beginnings were known. In Australia, for instance, the name is retained in both formal communications and in popular speech. So universal is its use that if you wish to ask your way to some local church, you do not inquire as to the whereabouts of 'St. James's', or of 'the parish church', but say 'Will you please tell me where is the Church of England?' and you are shown without surprise to some edifice of greater or less magnificence which is the local representative of our Communion.

Perhaps the easiest definition of the Anglican Communion would be 'the group of churches in communion with the Church of England'. But that would give to the Church in this country a dominating position which it is not anxious to assume. Nor would it allow for those churches with which, though definitely not Anglican, we may be in full communion now or in the future. And in any case it is too jejune and mechanical a definition to afford much insight into the inner character of the Anglican Communion.

The term Anglicanism entered religious phraseology as a result of the course taken by the Reformation in England. That Movement not only separated the Church of the country from Rome and the jurisdiction of the Papacy, it also effected a division between the national church and other bodies which rejected the whole of medieval development in an attempt to get back to the Christianity of the Bible. The term Anglican became descriptive of the national religion after that episode was closed, and it connoted the type of Christianity that deliberately preserved the historic continuity of its faith and organization, while opening its doors to the fresh light shed upon the ancient Scriptures by the New Learning.

The Anglican *Communion* resulted from the combination of this development with the expansion of the British Empire. That expansion involved a carrying of Anglicanism as a seed to produce fresh flower and fruit in many lands. The resultant churches never lost their association with the Church of England, although many of them acquired complete autonomy. It is these churches whether autonomous or not, possessing a common ethos, together with their partners in the British Isles, that are known today as the Anglican Communion.

We may notice in passing that this Communion is 'one of the most powerful forces in the modern religious world'. It is indeed numerically the strongest expression of Christianity among English-speaking people, comprising between thirty and thirty-four million adherents in various parts of the world.

But to return to our attempt to define the Anglican Communion. We may learn more of it if we let the Lambeth fathers speak for themselves. In their Conference of 1930 they described it as follows: 'It is a fellowship within the One Holy Catholic and Apostolic Church, of those duly constituted Dioceses, Provinces or Regional Churches in communion with the See of Canterbury, which have the following characteristics in common:

'(*a*) They uphold and propagate the Catholic and Apostolic faith and order as they are generally set forth in the Book of Common Prayer as authorized in their several churches.

'(*b*) They are particular or national Churches, and as such, promote within each of their territories a national expression of Christian faith, life, and worship.

'(*c*) They are bound together not by a central legislative and executive authority, but by mutual loyalty, sustained through common counsel of the bishops in conference.'

You might perhaps sum this up by saying that the Anglican Communion is a group of national churches and their missions which trace their Catholic heritage through the Christianity of the British Isles and their form of worship through the Book of Common Prayer, and are in communion with the See of Canterbury.

This fellowship of churches manifests so fascinating a variety of organization that it is not easy to say at once what actually keeps it together. In this as in other respects it is very like the British Commonwealth of Nations. Of course there are the same fundamental faith and order, the one Lord, one Faith, one Baptism and one Holy Spirit as a bond of unity. These churches each and all claim to be part of the one Body of Christ. They do not make that claim exclusively, but they have no doubt about its truth as far as they themselves are concerned. However, the very fact that they recognize the possibility of its extension outside their own limits makes it all the more interesting to ask what is their own principle of unity among themselves as distinct from other bodies. What in other words is the precise *differentia* of the Anglican Communion?

In the first place there is no central machinery to hold it together. There is no one head of the Anglican Communion as the Pope is the unquestioned Head upon earth of the Roman Communion. The Anglican churches are truly independent. In this respect there is only a partial parallel between the Anglican Communion and the British Empire. Since the Statute of Westminster the great Dominions have had their independence fully and completely recognized. Nevertheless they can each and all look to the Crown as the symbol of their unity and as the point, so to speak, at which they all meet. The King of England is, as is often said, the King of each of the Dominions separately. To this particular there is no parallel in the Anglican Communion. The Archbishop of Canterbury is recognized as the Senior Bishop, but he has no authority over the autonomous churches and it cannot be said that he is in any sense their Archbishop.

The closest ecclesiastical parallel is to be found in the Orthodox churches of the East which also are autonomous, but even they recognize a certain primacy in the Oecumenical Patriarch of Constantinople, such as is not granted in the Anglican Communion to the Archbishop of Canterbury. If then the Chair of Augustine cannot be likened to the Crown of England or to the Patriarchal Throne of Constantinople, has it no influence in the binding together of the whole Anglican organization?

The answer is in the affirmative. The Lambeth Conferences have emphasized the unique position of the See of Canterbury. These gatherings are summoned by the Archbishop and the invitations sent out are issued by him personally. It is recognized that every bishop actually at work in a church which is part of the whole Anglican Communion is entitled to receive an invitation. Conversely the reception of such an invitation is a sufficient indication that the church in which he works is itself a part of the Anglican Communion.

The Conferences themselves are not authoritative. They have no power to pass canons or to bind rules and regulations upon any part of the Church. Nevertheless they are of great and increasing importance. Matters of concern to the whole Anglican Communion are discussed by them. They pass resolutions indicating their common mind. They even send round encyclical letters which proclaim their views, not only to the churches of their own Communion, but to other churches and to the outside world generally. Although none of this is authoritative, every part of it is of very great importance and may form a very strong 'persuasive precedent'. The matters discussed and the views expressed come before the Synods or Conferences of the various national churches and if occasion so require are translated into canons which will make them authoritative for the particular area concerned. Thus Lambeth has an important part in the exercise of initiative. Much that later becomes part of the church's normal organization has its beginning at Lambeth. But perhaps of greater importance is the simple fact that the Conferences enable the bishops from the four quarters of the globe to meet together. By meeting together they inevitably arrive at some common mind which is bound to be taken as representative of the spirit and feeling of the whole Anglican Communion.

In recent years there has been a Consultative Committee which has carried on the business of the Conferences during the intervals of their sitting. For the most part this Committee arranges the agenda for the Conferences, but it is also able on occasion to carry on negotiations with non-Anglican churches which have been inaugurated by a Conference and left unfinished. But the Consultative Committee, as its name implies, is an advisory body and it cannot commit the Anglican Communion as a whole.

If the central machinery is so lacking in precision what is to be said of the local machinery in each regional church? That is often precise enough, but it differs from church to church, and in the richness of its variety makes a fascinating study. Our object in this survey is to draw out these differences and to make them as easy as possible to grasp.

It will be recognized at once that there is a considerable gulf separating the established Church in England from the disestablished churches in the British Isles, and also from the nonestablished churches elsewhere. An established church is inevitably bound into the common and statute law of the land as a non-established church cannot be. One of the most interesting features of our history is the revelation that Anglicanism, once it was freed from establishment, could not merely survive, but could express itself in new and vigorous forms of life. We owe a very great debt in this respect to clever pioneers like Bishop Gray who developed Anglicanism on free lines in South Africa, and Bishop Selwyn who performed the same service in New Zealand. Nor must we forget the similar work done by White and Pro-

voost in America. This debt is owed, not only by churches overseas, but also by the Church of England itself, which has not been
ashamed to borrow, from the experience of its younger sisters,
methods, fully tested by them, which have helped to free it from
some of the more exasperating trials of parliamentary control.
We may have to notice later certain respects in which the Church
of England has failed to understand the implications of the
arrangements she has borrowed. But that in itself furnishes another reason why it is valuable for us to try to understand the
details of each other's polity as clearly as possible.

It follows from what has been said that the laws by which the
various parts of the Anglican Communion are governed are not
necessarily identical. There is, it is true, a rough and ready
approximation. All accept the Oecumenical councils, and much
of the medieval Canon Law as brought up to date in 1604 is
taken for granted. But many of the churches possess their own
canons which have the same force as the ancient canons. In such
cases clergy at their ordination or institution take an oath to
observe the canons of their own diocese. When a new canon is
passed by the diocesan conference it is duly added to the local
book of canons and thus achieves binding force. In such circumstances it is obvious that the law can vary greatly from diocese
to diocese.

Similar variety is to be found in the methods of appointing the
principal officers. In some cases archbishoprics are attached to
particular sees. In other cases the office belongs to persons quite
apart from their see. In England the diocesan bishop is elected
by a Dean and Chapter on the nomination of the King acting
with the advice of his Prime Minister. In other countries a bishop
may be appointed by an electoral college selected for the purpose
or even by open synod, or else by delegation to some outside
authority such as the Archbishop of Canterbury. In some
dioceses coadjutor bishops have a right of succession, in others
they are merely assistant bishops with no such right. Equally the
rights and status of suffragan bishops differ from country to
country.

Even the forms of worship show a certain variety, though here
the influence of the Book of Common Prayer remains paramount.
Even so it is not always the same revision of the Book of Common
Prayer which sets the tone. In some cases it is the revision of

1662, but in others character and use derive rather from 1549.

Nevertheless in spite of all these varieties, there is a remarkable identity of ethos throughout the whole Anglican Communion and it should be an agreeable task through the perusal of these pages to try to distinguish it and describe it precisely. It will be found for instance that characteristic differences of theological colour cut across national boundaries and reproduce themselves in almost every part of our Communion. Whatever names they go by, high, low or broad churchmen can be found practically everywhere. Their mutual differences help to keep thought alive and fresh, although it must be confessed that there is a tendency on the part of each school to repeat *ad nauseam* its own particular shibboleth, and so to become annoyingly self-conscious.

This unity in variety is the theme to which the following chapters will address themselves. It is hoped that the treatment will not be found too unequal. There has been no opportunity for the various authors to meet, or even to read each others' scripts. However, something will be found in each chapter to answer the kind of question outlined above. In the final chapter it may be possible to group these answers and to give a summary picture of the whole.

THE CHURCH OF ENGLAND AND ITS OFFSHOOTS

by the VERY REV. R. H. MALDEN, *Dean of Wells*

I

The Genesis of Anglicanism

By the end of the sixteenth century the Church of England was in all essentials as it is now, and its future was assured.

The process of reformation, which had begun in 1534 with the Submission of the Clergy, may be considered to have been brought to a close by the publication of the *Lambeth Articles* in 1595.

For the first forty years of Elizabeth's reign it had been uncertain whether she would die upon her throne. After 1598 it was clear that England would never become an appanage of the Spanish crown. Our national independence and the existence of our Church were secure.

Our position was strengthened still further by the accession of James VI of Scotland to the throne of England in 1603. He effected by natural inheritance what Edward I had just failed to achieve by a combination of force and diplomacy more than three hundred years before. We had no longer to fear a stab in the back whenever we were pre-occupied with foreign affairs.

But although the Church of England could now face the future with confidence it did not aspire to be more than its title implies. It was the Church *of England*; not of anywhere else. It was never intended to be more than a local arrangement, as may be inferred from the fact that we did not include earthquakes (*terrae motus*) in the list of natural calamities from which we pray in the Litany to be delivered.[1] It is true that attempts were made to extend our system to Scotland and Ireland as component parts of the United Kingdom, but they met with little success. Archbishop Laud (1633–45) attached great importance to the idea of a uniform ecclesiastical system throughout the British Isles, but his

---

[1] Compare the remarks on the early translations of the Book of Common Prayer into Indian vernaculars on p. 77.

motives seem to have been political rather than religious. No
doubt it would have made the business of government easier.

Our Reformation was a domestic affair. It dealt with abuses
with which everyone was familiar, within a limited area. No one
who took part in it foresaw that the Church of England would
become the centre of a world-wide communion which is not
governed by the Archbishop of Canterbury, but may be said to pivot
upon him. No one could have imagined that a time would come
when principles which we had laid down for our own guidance
would be applied, or at least regarded as applicable, to people
whose antecedents and circumstances are quite unlike our own.
Yet that is what is happening all over the world to-day wherever
a branch of our Communion exists. It is therefore important that
we should understand our system sufficiently to be able to discriminate between those elements in it which are local and acci-
dental, and those which are of permanent value and universal
application. As a preliminary step we must consider the process
by which it has come to be as it is. It is not always clearly understood and is sometimes misrepresented.

The forces which brought the Reformation about had been
gathering for more than two centuries before they took effect.
By the year 1500 it had long been clear that far-reaching changes
in the Church were overdue. During the first half of the fifteenth
century two important councils were held, the first at Constance
from 1414 to 1418 and the second at Basle which dragged on
intermittently from 1433 to 1449. The avowed object of both was
to reform the Church 'in head and members' as the phrase went.
Neither accomplished very much, and as time went on it became
obvious that a violent upheaval of some kind could not be post-
poned indefinitely. The only question was—How and when
would it come? The root of the whole matter was to be found in
the exorbitant pretensions of the Papacy. The story of the rise of
the Papal power is much too long to be told even in the briefest
outline here. It will be enough to say that for a long period the
Papacy had deserved admiration and gratitude. But its claims had
been carried to such a pitch that they had dislocated the system
of the Church. The fifteenth century brought a remarkable increase of knowledge to Western Europe, and the printer and the
paper-maker combined to diffuse it to an extent never possible
before. Men began to ask questions about things which hitherto

they had accepted as a matter of course, and one of these objects of inquiry was the nature and range of the Papal power. Its two chief buttresses and largest sources of revenue were Indulgences (or *Pardons*) and Dispensations. Both these systems were born of the best intentions and had become enormous abuses. Indulgences were designed to help the penitent sinner along the steep and stony path of moral recovery, and ended by almost destroying the sense of sin. Dispensations were found necessary because the Canon Law tried to be impossibly wise and paternal. Breaches of its provisions had to be legitimized and these became so numerous that it was almost impossible to say what the law really did enjoin; and there was always precedent to be found for manipulating it to any extent when important interests were involved. It so happened that Indulgences fired the train in Germany and Dispensations in England. It is sometimes forgotten that Henry VIII's conduct in relation to his matrimonial affairs is less important than the existence of a situation which made it possible for him to act as he did. Once the Papal authority had been challenged in any respect people began to discover that there were other things in the faith and practice of the Church which could only be justified on the strength of Papal sanction, and that this could no longer be regarded as necessarily sufficient. The conscience of the individual had to be taken into account as well.

That, in outline, is the background of all that we did at our Reformation. The claims of the Papacy were rejected as unreasonable and unjustifiable and when the Papal authority fell much else went with it. Besides this, the medieval Church had, as it were, lost its way in a tropical jungle of ceremonial. If the services of the Church were to be edifying and educative they must be made simpler; more intelligible and more nearly uniform. The ordinary Englishman ought to be able to understand and follow what was going on in any church in the land which he might enter. And an attempt to revive personal religion, which had sunk to a very low ebb, must be made. This meant direct frequent and emphatic appeals to conscience.

This is the background of the *Book of Common Prayer* as the two tractates prefixed to it—*Concerning the Services of the Church* and *Of Ceremonies*—declare explicitly.

Neither Prayer Book, Articles nor Ordinal can really be understood without some knowledge of the circumstances in which

B

they took shape. Apart from them we cannot have a true picture of the distinctive characteristics of the Church of England.

The easiest way of appreciating the general outlook of Henry VIII is to consider his attitude towards the episcopate. Everyone who has wished to part company with the historic Church in which he grew up has always decided to have nothing to do with episcopacy. Here Luther, Calvin, Zwingli, Knox, and others who could be named are in complete agreement, however widely they may differ in other respects. Unquestionably they are right. Without trespassing on the dubious ground of *Apostolic Succession*, as many people interpret the phrase to-day, it is quite certain that from the beginning of the third century at least episcopacy has been the core of the Church's system. In times of trouble especially it has displayed a very remarkable power of resistance and recovery.

If it would be too much to say that the Church depends upon it, it is certain that without it the Church would be very different. Henry VIII recognized that the day of the monasteries was done. They had reached their zenith about the beginning of the thirteenth century and had been declining ever since. His method of dealing with them was the worst possible. But he was right in thinking that they could not continue as they were.

If he had wished to break completely with the past he would have dealt with the episcopate in similar fashion. In fact, he did all in his power to extend and strengthen it. Since the Norman Conquest only two new bishoprics had been founded in England, Ely in 1109 and Carlisle in 1133. Henry created six, of which one —Westminster—came to an end after ten years, using monastic churches and revenues for the purpose. (The next addition was not until 1836.) Besides this he drew up a scheme for the provision of twenty-four bishops-suffragan, which meant roughly one for each diocese. These assistants were to take their titles from a place in the diocese which they served, and would therefore have a recognized status. Prior to the Reformation the arrangements for bishops-suffragan had been very haphazard. Sometimes an Irish bishop who found it impossible, or at least undesirable, to live in his own diocese, acted. Sometimes a Friar received episcopal orders, with a titular see *in partibus infidelium*, and went from place to place as might be required, picking up such fees as he could. Henry made an effort to put the whole business on to a proper footing and his scheme showed a real grasp of the situation. Unfortunately full advantage was never taken of it. It would have given England and Wales forty-eight bishops all told: a number which was not reached until the present century had begun, and the population had multiplied nearly tenfold. Probably the financial difficulties proved greater than had been anticipated.

This is not the policy of a man who wished to institute a new religious society on the lines of those which sprang up upon the Continent. But it is exactly what might be expected of a man who found that the entire system of the Church had been brought into complete confusion (to which the monasteries had contributed not a little) and wished to restore it according to its original pattern, and to make it more efficient.

Naturally there was some opposition to these changes, but it never aproached anything which could be called civil war, and the fact that Henry, unlike Richard II, Richard III, Charles I and James II, died in his own bed in one of his own palaces after a reign of nearly thirty-eight years shows that speaking generally he had carried the nation with him. Elizabeth's policy was similar. At the beginning of her reign deaths and deprivations brought the number of bishops very low. If she had wished episcopacy to die out in England she had only to hold her hand for a few years. Instead she had a new Archbishop of Canterbury consecrated by 17 December 1559, exactly thirteen months from the day of her accession, that the vacant Sees might be filled as quickly as possible.

It is probably not too much to say that our Reformation would not have been possible had we not lost our French possessions (with the exception of Calais, which was not much more than a token) almost exactly a hundred years before. It is sometimes forgotten that for nearly four centuries after the Norman Conquest we were a Continental power; sometimes primarily. In 1421 the long drawn out attempt to annex France in perpetuity, which had been inaugurated by Edward III, appeared to have achieved complete and final success. The two crowns were placed upon the head of King Henry VI as soon as he was old enough to receive them. Ten years later our position in France had become hopeless. By the year 1453 we had been reduced to an island power, with all the advantages and drawbacks of the position. No one who faced the real facts could imagine that any resumption of the French adventure would ever be possible. As an island we were on the outer edge of Europe. Our attachment to the European system, of which the Papacy was the centre, necessarily became much looser. We had less to fear or to hope from the Papacy, and were therefore more inclined to look upon its claims with a critical eye. We became less and less disposed to brook interference with our own affairs, especially when they took the form of demands for money, on the part of a foreign power which we felt could do little to promote our interests (if it should wish to do so) and had no very strong claims upon our respect. The outcome was that, owing partly to the statesmanship of Wolsey, which had done much to restore the prestige which the French disaster had shattered, by the year 1534 we felt ourselves to be in a position to defy the public opinion of Europe.

Another feature which distinguishes our Reformation from contemporary movements elsewhere is its corporate character. It is not associated with any great name. Thomas Cranmer played a considerable part in it, not because he was Thomas Cranmer but because he held the highest office in the Church, to which he had been appointed before the changes began. The extent of his personal contribution to the Prayer Book is not known exactly, and his name has never been attached to it. The position of the other great literary monument of the period is similar. The names of the translators of the version of the Bible which appeared in 1611, and may therefore be regarded as a product of Elizabethan scholarship, are of course known but are hardly a matter of common knowledge. No name has ever been associated with it as with earlier versions. It has always been known simply as the version authorized by the English Church.

We have never given our Church any title except the geographical one *of England*, which merely states a fact and does not indicate any particular characteristic. As a description it is almost absurd anywhere beyond our own shores.

Owing largely to this corporate character our Reformation was carried through with a minimum of disturbance and violence, if it would not be true to say with none. It was, therefore, much more religious and less political than any of the Continental reformations, or even than the Scottish one. We have never had a reforming party and the attempts of foreign refugees to create one met with very little success. The whole course of events from 1534 to 1595 was marked by the peculiar combination of respect for law and respect for individual liberty which has always been characteristic of our race, perhaps even before our forefathers had begun to cross the North Sea. That respect is, as I believe, the best contribution which we have to make to the common stock of human civilization. If we have much to learn from other nations, which few people would wish to dispute, we have that to teach them. Our Church is the best and completest embodiment of it which we possess. It is sometimes forgotten that the real point at issue between Henry VIII and the Papacy was—Is the Pope above the Law? Eventually we answered—No.

At this point it may be worth while to touch very briefly on three views of the nature of the reformed Church of England which are widely held. The best which can be said of any of them is that it can be made to appear plausible.

(a) 'The Church of England is merely a variant of Continental Protestantism, which was not allowed to develop fully on grounds of political expediency.'

As has been pointed out above, this theory does not correspond with the facts of history. The Continental systems were the work of individuals. Ours is the outcome of a corporate act. They aimed at creating a new society. Our object was to reform an old one. They were revolutionary inasmuch as they aimed at breaking with the past as completely as possible, and only retained what they found they could not destroy. We aimed at retaining as much of the past as we could, discarding only such developments as we had discovered to be of recent origin, and considered to have proved mischievous. Articles XI and XVII alone are sufficient to show how far we are from either the Lutheran or the Calvinistic system theologically—even if the latter part of the Catechism beginning with 'Why was the Sacrament of the Lord's Supper ordained?' is taken almost verbatim from Calvin's treatise *De Coena Domini*.

(b) 'The system of the Church of England is that of the medieval Church, *minus* the Papal supremacy. That was removed for political reasons which are not operative now. Much went with it, unnecessarily, and might now be restored with advantage.'

To imagine that anything resembling the medieval system

could exist without the Papal supremacy is not unlike proposing
to build a romanesque arch without a keystone; and, it may be
added, without the necessary abutments which were furnished by
the twin systems of indulgences and dispensations.

(c) 'The system of the Church of England is a skilful compromise between two irreconcilable sets of beliefs described
loosely as *Catholic* and *Protestant*. On this theory the principal
duty of an English bishop is to see that neither gets the upper
hand.'

Of course any system which appeals to sound learning, and
therefore refuses to capitulate to extremists of any kind, may
appear to be of the nature of a compromise. It is in reality described better as *via media*; a phrase which Newman used, but
apparently never understood. The difference is this. A compromise is not intended to be permanent by either party. It means
that two people agree, in the interests of peace, to accept something which is not what either of them really wants. Each regards
it as being as much of his own way as he can get at the moment.
Naturally he hopes to get more at some future time. A *via media*
is comparable with a coherent and intelligible system of law in
relation either to anarchy or tyranny. It may be considered to lie
midway between them. But it is not formed by borrowing elements from both, which are in the nature of things irreconcilable.
It is something entirely different and aims at making either
equally impossible. The metaphor of a bridge, which is sometimes employed to describe the position of our Church, is not
really very happy; if only because no one is likely to wish to
make his permanent home upon a bridge. Moreover, a bridge
does not really unite the communities at either end and can be
traversed with equal ease in either direction. An institution whose
raison d'être was to enable wayfarers to travel either from Rome
to Geneva, or from Geneva to Rome, as the case might be, would
not deserve a very high degree of respect or contribute much to
the unity of Christendom.

All that has been said above is part of the history of England
and of medieval Europe. An Englishman may reasonably be
expected to take some interest in it. If he has no knowledge of
it his appreciation of his Church will probably be inadequate.
But he can still accept his Church as part of his national inheritance, together with much else. If he has made his home else-

where he can still value it as part of the English tradition in which he shares. But however strong this sentiment may be in some places now it cannot be permanent. It must diminish with each generation until it has disappeared entirely. At the present day it is by no means universal. In the United States the adjective *Anglican* probably excites a certain amount of suspicion. In South Africa the attitude of a considerable part of the white population towards things English is similar. When we come to deal with coloured races in any part of the world, their general attitude towards us may or may not be friendly. But we cannot commend our presentation of Christianity to them solely or chiefly upon the grounds that it is English. They are not interested in our national history. Why should they be? They are but remotely concerned, if at all, with the forces which brought the Reformation about and can hardly be expected to understand them. Outside our own country it does not matter very much *how* our Church has come to be as it is. What is important is that we should be able to explain *what* it is. We need to be able to separate its essential principles from the local circumstances within which our expression of them took shape, and to show that we have something distinctive to contribute to the Christian inheritance of the whole world. The premises of that contribution will, as we maintain, stand any test, and there is no substitute for it to be found elsewhere. Before proceeding to consider it, a brief sketch of the successive stages by which what began as a domestic arrangement has acquired a world-wide mission will be convenient.

II

The Extension of Anglicanism

The extension of our Communion beyond the seas began as part of what Sir John Seeley described some sixty years ago in the book which made him famous, *The Expansion of England*. In its earlier stages it was not prompted by missionary zeal. Early in the seventeenth century Englishmen began to settle abroad as traders on the continent of Europe and in India, and as colonists in North America. (Newfoundland had been formally occupied by Sir Humphrey Gilbert as far back as 1573, but the whole island did not become British until the treaty of Utrecht in 1713.) Their motive was primarily economic, though religious, political and social considerations played a part. These commercial settlements, of which two of the most important in Europe were at Delft and Hamburg, were supplied with chaplains almost as a matter of course. But these chaplains were not in any sense missionaries. The East India Company was definitely opposed to any attempt to convert the natives, fearing that it would lead to disturbances.

The position in America was somewhat different. A considerable proportion of the colonists had gone there in order to escape from the Church of England as represented by Laud[1] and therefore preferred ministers of their own appointment to its clergy. Laud was at heart a successor of the politician-bishops of the fourteenth and fifteenth centuries. When he held the See of London he was also Lord Treasurer, which meant virtually Prime Minister, and instigated a scheme for extending the Church of England to every part of the world where the English government had, or might acquire, any interest. If it would be too much to say that he looked upon the Church primarily as a powerful instrument of national policy, he would certainly never have hesitated to use it for political purposes. At the same time he proposed to send a bishop to New England 'to keep the Puritans in order'. It may be assumed that the methods contemplated would not have been purely persuasive. In Laud's eyes a bishop who had not power to fine and imprison people who disregarded his godly admonitions would hardly have been a bishop in more than name. Circumstances made it impossible for either of these projects to be carried out. But they appear to have been the origin of the general jurisdiction over the colonies which came to be regarded as inherent in the See of London.

After the Restoration the Church began to take formal account of its responsibilities beyond the seas. In the Preface to the Prayer Book of 1662 it is pointed out that the new service for the Baptism of such as are of Riper Years 'may be always useful for the baptism of natives in our plantations and of others converted to the faith'. There was also a plan for the consecration of Dr. Alexander Murray as bishop in Virginia, and it is said that the letters patent making the appointment were actually prepared. But for some reason the scheme was allowed to lapse.

Henry Compton, who was Bishop of London from 1675 to

[1] Bishop of London, 1628–33, Archbishop of Canterbury, 1633–45.

1713, took a lively interest in American affairs and did all in his power to maintain a steady supply of clergy, but it was impossible that a jurisdiction exercised from a distance of three thousand miles through commissaries could be effective. It was by no means certain that letters written from one side of the Atlantic would ever reach their destination on the other. If they did arrive safely they were necessarily some months *en route*.

An important step forward was taken when the *Society for Promoting Christian Knowledge* was founded in 1697 by Dr. Thomas Bray, who had won fame by the publication of a series of catechetical lectures. He was an enthusiast for religious education, and his original purpose was the distribution of Bibles and other good books amongst the poor in England. He soon extended his scheme to include lending libraries for America and paid a visit to Maryland as commissary for Bishop Compton.

The *Society for the Propagation of the Gospel in Foreign Parts* was founded in 1701. The Archbishop of Canterbury has always been the President, so that it has always stood in a semi-official relation to the Church. Originally the Society was intended primarily for work amongst the colonists, but in 1710 it was decided that preference was to be given to 'the conversion of heathen and infidels'.

In that year Colonel Christopher Codrington left his estates in the island of Barbados in trust to the Society to found a college there. The constitution provided for 'a convenient number of Professors and scholars to study and practice Physick and Chirugrery, as well as Divinity . . . that they might have the better opportunity of doing good to men's souls, while they are taking care of their bodies', thereby anticipating the medical missions of our own time. For some reason the scheme was not fully established until 1743.

During the reign of Queen Anne the question of a bishop for Virginia was raised again, and it is believed that Dr. Jonathan Swift, Dean of St. Patrick's, was considered for the post. It is not clear whether a definite offer was ever made to him, and with the Queen's death on 1 August 1714 the project lapsed. It is interesting to speculate as to what the course of events would have been had he accepted the appointment. Another notable figure is George Berkeley, a distinguished Fellow of Trinity College, Dublin, who is now remembered principally for his philosophic writings, which were of great importance in the Deistic controversy. In 1724 he became Dean of Derry and conceived a plan for a missionary college in Bermuda which he regarded as the best strategic base for reaching any point in the American Colonies. It aroused a considerable volume of interest in England and in 1725 he secured a charter for its foundation together with a promise of £20,000 from the government. He went to America in 1728, but was obliged to return four years later when he discovered that Sir Robert Walpole had no intention of paying the money.

Berkeley was appointed Bishop of Cloyne in 1734, and died there in 1753. His gallant effort has been commemorated in our own day by the foundation of Berkeley College, in the University of Yale, by an American member of King's College, Cambridge.

Many hard things have been said about the failure of the Church of England to provide America with an episcopate during the first half of the eighteenth century. Undoubtedly the outcome of the omission has been very serious. But the fault does not really lie with the Church.

Edmund Gibson, who was Bishop of London from 1723 to 1748 was as deeply interested in American affairs as Compton had been. He did all in his power to raise the standard of the clergy who were ministering to the English settlers and was keenly alive to the need for an episcopate. But the opposition was too strong for him. In the first place, many of the colonists did not want to have a bishop as they were afraid of what was known as 'Prelacy' and of Church Courts. Their attitude shows that the horror and detestation which had been aroused by Laud a century earlier had not died out. Secondly, the governors of the royal colonies, and the proprietors of the proprietary ones, were suspicious of anything which might curtail their powers in matters ecclesiastical, and in many places the vestries preferred to keep the clergy in a humiliating dependence upon themselves, which the presence of a bishop would make impossible.

The Government at home were indifferent and although Gibson was for many years *persona gratissima* at Court he could not overcome their inertia. There was not enough general interest in the question for him to be able to rally public opinion in his favour.

Matters were not improved by a visit about the year 1724 from two non-juror bishops.[1] Naturally they did not conceal what they thought of the House of Hanover, and they seem to have caused some disturbance. Gibson pointed out that the best safeguard against such occurrences would be to send to America some bishops whose orthodoxy and loyalty were above suspicion. But the Government contented themselves with issuing some prohibitions of a general character against intruders. Yet another difficulty was occasioned by slavery. Gibson urged that the negroes should be taught Christianity and given reasonable opportunities for Sunday worship. The slave-owners did not approve of this, thinking that it would make the slaves more difficult to manage, and the negroes themselves thought that baptism was the first step in a design on the part of the Crown to set them free. Gibson's attempts to convince them that they were mistaken were not successful.

In 1763 the Peace of Paris established England as an Imperial power. This led to a general quickening of interest in America and the question of a colonial episcopate was raised again. The need was obviously great and increasing, and it was equally obvious that the Jacobite sympathies of the clergy need no longer be taken seriously, if they existed. But the Crown was still reluctant to issue the customary letters patent and the Archbishops thought that they ought not to consecrate without them. If we are surprised at their attitude we must remember that at that time people thought in terms of law and institutions more than we do now. The events of 1688 were not very remote: there must have been still people living whose parents had remembered them. Moreover, the revolution of that year was not an isolated event. It was the last of a long series of struggles which had begun in the reign of King John, nearly five hundred years earlier, and had vindicated triumphantly the principle that the Law of England is not to be over-ridden or set aside by any person on any pretext for any purpose. It is not wonderful that the Archbishops thought that they must at any cost avoid any action the legality of which could be called in question.

In 1783 Samuel Seabury, a native-born American, came to England seeking consecration. But although the independence of the American colonists had been recognized, the Archbishops

[1] Talbot and Welton.

still thought that they ought not to act without authorization from the Crown, and were unwilling to ask for what they believed would certainly be refused. If that should happen the position would be worse than ever.

Seabury is said to have contemplated approaching the Bishops of Denmark, when it was pointed out to him that there were bishops whose Orders were not open to question[1] nearer at hand, and that they could act without reference to the State because it had no official knowledge of their existence. He was consecrated as Bishop of Connecticut at Aberdeen by three Scottish bishops on 14 November 1784.

It is believed that Martin Joseph Routh, subsequently President of Magdalen College, Oxford, from 1791 to 1854, was to some extent responsible for this solution of the difficulty, though it is not known exactly what part he played. It is a matter for regret that the idea did not occur to anybody fifty, or even twenty, years earlier.

On 4 February 1787 William White and Samuel Provoost, both citizens of the new republic, were consecrated in the chapel of Lambeth Palace as Bishops of Pennsylvania and New York respectively. At the same time Charles Inglis, a British subject, formerly rector of Trinity Church, New York, was consecrated as Bishop of Nova Scotia. From that day to this our communion has expanded steadily until it has become world wide.

The *Church Missionary Society*, which was founded in 1799, has made many notable contributions to the process, chiefly in Africa and Asia amongst people not of European descent.

It would be impossible to attempt even the briefest sketch of the events of the last 160 years here. The results of that process will be described in the later chapters of this book. But two outstanding events may be recorded.

First, the institution of the Colonial Bishoprics Fund in 1841, and second the summoning of the first Lambeth Conference in 1867.

In 1840 Charles James Blomfield, Bishop of London, wrote a letter to the Archbishop of Canterbury (William Howley) in the course of which he said that the time had come for a great effort to be made by the Church of England 'to impart the full benefits of her apostolical government and discipline, as well as of her

---

[1] The status of the bishops of Denmark was doubtful.

doctrines and ordinances, to those distant parts of the British Empire where, if the Christian religion is professed at all, it is left to depend for its continuance, under the blessing of its Divine Head, upon the energies of individual piety and zeal without being enshrined in the sanctuary of a rightly constituted Church, the only sure and trustworthy instrument of its perpetuation and efficiency'. A year later, on 27 April 1841, a public meeting was held to launch the fund, at which the Archbishop presided. By that time the sum of £80,000 had been given and promised. Before the end of the year six new bishoprics had been created, New Zealand (now Auckland), Valletta (now Gibraltar), New Brunswick, Cape Town, Ceylon (now Colombo) and Van Diemen's land (now Tasmania).

As the Bishop of London had acted in accordance with the long-standing tradition of his See, and as the Archbishop had given the scheme all the support in his power, it may fairly be regarded as a corporate act on the part of the Church and the year may be counted as *annus mirabilis* in its history.

On 20 September 1865 the synod of the Church in Canada passed a resolution on the motion of the Bishop of Ontario, asking the Archbishop of Canterbury (Charles Thomas Longley) and his Convocation to summon a general council, or national synod of the Anglican Church at home and abroad, without delay.

Courage was needed to accept the invitation, as a number of Bishops, including the Archbishop of York (William Thomson) refused to have anything to do with the matter. It was suspected that the real motive for calling the conference was to get support for the action of Robert Gray, Bishop of Cape Town, who had recently deposed John William Colenso, Bishop of Natal, for heresy. (It would be out of place here to go into the details of the dispute or of the outcome of Gray's action. The Bishop of Natal denied that the Bishop of Cape Town had any authority over him, as he had been appointed by letters patent,[1] and professed himself ready to have his cause heard by the Queen in Council.) Of the 144 invitations sent out, only 76 were accepted. The proceedings passed off smoothly, and the conference was felt to have been so valuable that it was determined to repeat it at ten-

---

[1] These ceased to be issued after 1863 to colonies which possessed local self-government.

year intervals. Conferences have been held in 1878, 1888, 1897, 1908, 1920 and 1930. Three hundred and eight bishops were present at the last.

It will be convenient to tabulate here the statistics of the Anglican Communion as it stands to-day outside the British Isles, taking its component parts in chronological order, and giving the name of the original See.

1. *America:* Connecticut, 1784.

The Church now has 112 bishoprics including missionary jurisdictions in the Philippines, the Panama Canal Zone, Cuba and the Dominican Republic. When Samuel Provoost was consecrated as Bishop of New York in 1787 his diocese was coterminous with the State. It is said that his first convention was attended by five clergy and eleven laymen. At the 150th anniversary of the foundation of the See there were in the State of New York six dioceses containing 956 parishes with a staff of 1,026 clergy.

2. *Canada:* Nova Scotia, 1787.

There are now twenty-seven bishoprics grouped in four provinces each with its own archbishop.

3. *India* (now *India, Burma and Ceylon*)*:* Calcutta, 1814.

The Church now consists of twelve bishoprics[1] including the new See of Delhi, to which an Indian has been consecrated.

4. *The West Indies:* Jamaica and Barbados, 1824.

There are now eight bishoprics in the province. The archbishop is elected and may be the holder of any See.

5. *Australia*, 1836.

A metropolitical See of Sydney was formed in 1847. There are now four archbishops; Melbourne, Brisbane and Perth having been added, and twenty-one suffragans.

6. *New Zealand*, 1841.

The title of the See was subsequently changed to Auckland which is now an archbishopric. There are now nine dioceses in the province, including Melanesia and Polynesia.

7. *South Africa:* Cape Town, 1847.

There are now fourteen bishoprics in the province and the See of Cape Town is the permanent seat of the archbishopric.

---

[1] Sixteen before the formation of the Church of South India (see p. 93 of this book.)

8. *China.*

A See was established at Hong Kong in 1849 and the Chung Hua Sheng Kung Hui[1] now consists of fourteen dioceses.

9. *West Africa.*

A See was established at Sierra Leone in 1852 and four other bishoprics have been founded since.

10. *East Africa.*

Missionary work was begun in 1861 in the neighbourhood of Lake Nyasa, and there are now eight bishoprics in the region.

11. *Japan.*

A bishopric of South Tokyo was created in 1883 and in 1939 the Nippon Sei Ko Kwai[2] consisted of ten bishoprics. The situation in 1947 is described in Chapter VIII of this book.

Besides these, there are fourteen other bishoprics in various parts of the world, including one at Jerusalem. The total number of bishoprics of the Anglican Communion overseas to-day appears to be 258, all of which have come into being since the year 1783.[3]

III

The Character of Anglicanism

The Church of England as we know it now was the outcome of a series of domestic reforms passed to meet the conditions of a particular locality. It did not contemplate becoming more than the Church of England—or at most of the British Isles. To-day its sound is gone out into all lands. We are, therefore, bound to ask—What is there distinctive in our system which is not at the same time distinctively English? What have we to offer which can be welcomed on its own merits by people to whom the English tradition as such makes no appeal; by people moreover who cannot be expected to take much interest in the history of England or of the medieval Church.

We have said above that our system is the religious expression of two great moral and intellectual principles—respect for law and respect for individual liberty. Because these are real principles they are of permanent value and universal application. It

[1] The title of the Church in Chinese.
[2] The title of the Church in Japanese.
[3] Much of what has been said above about relations with America during the seventeenth century and the first half of the eighteenth century has been taken from Professor Sykes' *Life of Edmund Gibson.*

does not matter in what part of the world or by whom they were developed first. It is obvious that the progress of civilization and the existence of a stable society anywhere must depend to a very large extent upon their maintenance and extension. A presentation of Christianity of which they are the core must be of unique value. Besides, this system is in all essentials the immemorial one of the Church Catholic, freed from a number of abuses which had arisen during a very dark period in the history of western Europe. They all sprang from one root, namely the claims made for itself by the great See of Rome. A time came when we realized that the basis of these claims would not stand investigation and that they must be set aside. When they are gone and the abuses connected with them have been cleared away, what remains? A system which deserves to be called apostolic inasmuch as it is a legacy from the apostolic age. None of the new religious societies which have come into being since the beginning of the sixteenth century can prefer that claim. They may consider that they reproduce certain characteristics of the apostolic age but that does not constitute them its heirs. Our system is simple and intelligible. We expect every one to be able to understand it and to make use of it all. The individual is not supposed to make such selections from it as he pleases and to discard the rest. Yet it leaves him sufficient moral and intellectual freedom to be fully educative. It is obvious that there can be no real education of any kind without trusting the person to be educated with a measure of freedom. The exact amount may vary according to his character and capacity. But the object must always be to increase it as much as possible, because it is only in an atmosphere of freedom that the human spirit can bear its finest fruit. Of course anyone who is entrusted with freedom will make some mistakes. The Church can afford to take that risk, because it knows that no mistake or failure is beyond repair. Here lies the difference between Direction and Education. The two are often confused, especially in relation to conscience. In reality they are poles apart. Direction aims at making mistakes impossible, and is prepared to arrest development to achieve its purpose. Education aims at producing people who are less and less likely to make mistakes as they go on and at helping them to recover when they do. Necessarily neither system is ever perfectly successful. But can there be any doubt which is more consonant with the standard set by Christ? He never would dictate details. He taught men principles, for them to apply and work out for themselves, promising them the help which they would need.

Our method is by direct appeal to the conscience of the individual, which by the sixteenth century had been almost smothered to death by a vast mass of ceremonial. That is written so plainly across the pages of the Book of Common Prayer from cover to cover that it is hardly necessary to give instances. However, the following may be noted.

1. The introductory sentences and the Exhortation, Confession and Absolution which inaugurate Morning and Evening Prayer.
2. The Collect at the beginning of the Communion Office.
3. The use of the Ten Commandments in the Communion Office. Before we proceed to the Divine Mysteries we declare that the moral law is binding upon everyone and that in it God speaks directly to the individual soul. Moral principles are absolute. They are not something which men have devised and can therefore modify at will. They are; and are as they are because God is as He is. *God spake these words*.
4. It is left to the conscience of the individual to decide whether he will avail himself of the ministry of private confession. It is provided but not enforced.

Naturally everyone to whom the exercise of Private Judgment is abhorrent will not find himself at home in such a system as this. But it may be worth while to point out that to decide to forego all private judgment is in itself an exercise of private judgment on the most comprehensive scale imaginable, and with very far-reaching results. If the motive behind the momentous decision is the desire to escape all personal moral responsibility, as far as possible, once for all, can this be reconciled with the standard set by Christ?

We are also alive to the value of the Bible as (*inter alia*) the school and training-ground of conscience—e.g. *the Scripture moveth us in sundry places to acknowledge and confess our manifold sins and wickedness*—and partly for that reason make (I think) more use of it in our services than any other Communion. The Lectionary was arranged to secure that as much of the Bible as possible should be read in church every year, because it was re-

c

garded as a coherent record of the scheme of our redemption. The modern practice of treating it as an anthology, from which passages which are considered likely to prove immediately edifying may be selected almost at will, does not seem to me to have much to commend it.

We are not blind to the dangers which may come from indiscriminate reading of the Bible. We know that it is impossible to prescribe the limits of human perversity and are well aware that it is not difficult to select a text which can be employed to uphold any abuse which anyone finds convenient,[1] or to justify any course of action which he may happen to have in contemplation. But we are quite sure that when the Bible is not known the standard of conscience, public and private alike, will decline. And that is worse.

Besides this, is anyone who does not know the Bible, especially the Old Testament, likely to be able to regard all history as the unfolding of a Divine purpose in which he is called to play a part? It is upon recognition of this that our sense of the meaning and importance of every human life must ultimately depend.

We have always refused to put the Ministry of the Word above or below the Ministry of the Sacraments. We bracket them together. If the scale is ever tilted in favour of either, that is a corrupt practice which traverses the letter and spirit of our formularies.

The Gospel began as something to be preached and as something to be preached it must always remain. If preaching is neglected, or becomes feeble and perfunctory, religion will always decay. On the other hand, we know that preaching alone cannot build up or maintain healthy spiritual life. Divorced from the Sacraments of the Gospel it is apt to sink to the level of arid ethical disquisitions which become less and less effective as time goes on; or else it becomes ultra-emotional. Emotional preaching may lift men to a high level of religious fervour. But in the nature of things it cannot keep them there, any more than a swimmer can remain poised on the crest of a wave. And when they sink back their last state is likely to be worse than their first. The preacher himself is always liable to wander into strange paths in his search for new methods of rousing the emotions on which he depends. The sanity and simplicity of the Sacraments of the Gospel, by

---

[1] Even at one time negro slavery.

which the ordinary acts of washing and eating are raised to the highest religious level, are our best defence against all forms of religious extravagance.

On the other hand, if attention is focused almost exclusively on the Sacraments so that the Word is relegated to a secondary place if not ignored outright, they will be degraded to something indistinguishable from magical charms. The danger of this can never be very remote, and it is so insidious that unremitting vigilance is required to avert it. Nothing can debase all moral standards more rapidly and completely than magic, or if we prefer so to put it, the introduction of the ideas which belong to magic into religion. If the Sacraments themselves are corrupted the very springs of religious life have been poisoned.

Lastly, we recognize the fundamental austerity of the Christian revelation. Truth is always austere and cannot surrender to the demands of popular devotion. The medieval Church fell by being too kind, and by claiming for itself a degree of omniscience which God has not made possible for men. We do not intend to make the same mistakes. We are aware of our limitations and know that justice, mercy, and wisdom can never be combined perfectly in any hands save those of God.

Such, in outline, are the principles of the Church of England. They can be discerned by anyone who will take the trouble to read *all* our formularies from beginning to end, and then to review them as a whole. These principles are the common heritage of the whole Anglican Communion and what it has to offer to the world. Their English dress is only a dress. It can be changed, like any other vesture, to suit new conditions: or, if we prefer so to say, translated into any language. But it must always be remembered that the value of a translation depends upon the success with which it reproduces the spirit of the original more than upon its fidelity to the letter.

THE PROTESTANT EPISCOPAL CHURCH IN THE UNITED STATES OF AMERICA

by the RT. REV. E. L. PARSONS, *formerly Bishop of California*

The American daughter of the Church of England had hard going for a long time after the War of Independence. In six colonies there had been a quasi-establishment of the Church; but there was practically no organization beyond the local parish. The supervision of the Bishop of London was exercised through commissaries who were not always successful. Clergy sent out from England were often of poor quality, although the popular notion that they were all ne'er-do-wells is not true. It was difficult to recruit a native ministry. The long voyage to England was necessary for ordination. Add to all this the fact that the Revolution found, as was natural, many of the clergy, English-born, loyal to the Crown, and one understands why the growth of the Church was slow. It was a small frail child left motherless. Indeed forty years after its organization was completed in 1789 it could muster only about 30,000 communicants, one out of more than four hundred of the population. That ratio has changed. More than a million-and-a-half communicants have brought it up to about one out of ninety, but it still ranks only sixth or seventh among the churches of the land. Whatever place it holds in American life to-day is due not to numbers but to the things for which it stands, and, we may hope, to the quality of its leadership, clerical and lay.

But this small frail child had a heritage; and our first concern is with the terms in which it recognized that heritage. They were framed originally in the correspondence with the English Archbishops which led up to and made possible the consecration of Bishops White and Provoost. Assurance was given at that time that it was the purpose of the newly organized Church to continue loyal to its inheritance, that is to the 'doctrine, discipline and worship' of the Church of England. Three years later, in 1789, this was given its most satisfactory expression in the Preface to the Book of Common Prayer which still stands unchanged. After noting the necessity which the newly acquired national independence had put upon this Church to make certain changes in its liturgy, the preface goes on to say that by a comparison of these changes with the English book it will 'appear that this Church is far from intending to depart from the Church of England in any essential point of doctrine, discipline or worship; or further than local circumstances require'. The words must have been carefully chosen. They indicated the spirit in which the assurance to the English bishops would be carried out. The statement is not legal or canonical. It makes no attempt to define what it means by essential. It expresses an attitude. It means not that this Church is bound or binds itself to accept this or that position of the Church of England but that it does intend to cherish its heritage, to recognize the weight of the tradition it has received and obviously to develop its life in fellowship with the Mother Church.

It should perhaps be noted in passing that our leading canonists have always held that the Canons of the Church of England in force in 1783 are still in force here unless superseded by legislative action. Whether or not that view would be sustained by General Convention, it is quite apparent as one studies the life and work of this Church that it has been little concerned with such canonical questions but always deeply concerned with loyalty to its heritage. The illustrations of this attitude are innumerable. There come to mind at once: the threefold ministry, the liturgical worship, the use of familiar terminology, such as 'diocese', 'parish', 'warden', 'vestry', 'rector' (sometimes with a change of meaning), the still widely prevalent use of the word Church or churchman in the English sense of the term, which is, although we seldom notice it, quite inappropriate to American conditions—these and many others which will appear as we pass in review the various aspects of our church life are daily reminders of the Mother Church.

But none of these included a name and one had to be found. The first appearance of 'Protestant Episcopal' is in a petition (1780) from the clergy of Maryland to the legislature of that state. The Church was obviously Episcopal (even if at the moment it had no bishops). It was definitely Protestant in relation to Rome. The use of the two terms as describing the new organization seems to have commended itself to the churchmen in other states. The informal convention of 1784 used only the term 'Episcopal Church'. 'Protestant Episcopal' however appears in the journal of the first official Convention (1785). It was apparently accepted by general consent without definite action. General Convention has up to this time declined to accept any proposals to change it.

HOW THE CHURCH IS GOVERNED

Turning now to our survey we come first to the organization of the Church. In all its inherited traditions the little Church had few precedents to guide it as it faced the problem of organization. 'Local circumstances' would require an almost completely new type of government. There was to be no established church in the new nation. Each church stood on its own, had its own way to make. In the Episcopal Church substitutes had to be found for the role played by King and Parliament, the Convocations, the Courts and the age-long system of appointments to benefices. The little group (thirty or less) which met in 1786 and 1789 had few precedents to go on; but it did have a long colonial experience in self-government and a realization of the importance of the laity in the councils of the Church. Its members shared, too, the faith which guided the makers of the United States Constitution, many of whom were churchmen. Washington was the most conspicuous. John Jay, the first Chief Justice of the United States, was a member of the Convention of 1786. Bishop White was Chaplain of the Continental Congress during most of the many years it met in Philadelphia. With such background they laid down lines along which the Church has travelled for more than a century and a half; and here is what we have to-day.

The General Convention

At the top is the General Convention. It meets once in three years at a place chosen by the previous Convention. In 1946 it met in Philadelphia; in 1949 it will cross the continent to San Francisco. It consists of the House of Bishops and the House of Deputies. In the former sit and vote all bishops in active service and all bishops retired for age or infirmity, at present 156. It had long been a disputed point whether a vote in the House of Bishops depended upon jurisdiction. The recent conferring of a vote upon suffragan bishops has made it clear that in the mind of the Church a bishop is a voting member because he is a bishop and not as the representative of a diocese.

In the House of Deputies, the Dioceses (at present seventy-four) are each represented by four presbyters and four laymen, the Missionary Districts (domestic and overseas, twenty-eight altogether) each by one of each order. Voting on routine matters is individual. On constitutional and canonical provisions, on such a matter as Prayer Book revision, and when called for by a diocesan delegation, the vote is by orders, each diocese having one vote in each order. Thus for important decisions the General Convention is really tri-cameral. It is a striking illustration of the same 'checks and balances' system which is at once one of the best and one of the worst features of the American Constitution. The two instruments were framed in the same city and represent, as already suggested, the same general attitude toward government. The Convention is obviously a slow-moving body. Its leisurely progress is further increased by the fact that all amendments to the Constitution and to the Prayer Book must pass two Conventions. The 1928 revision of the Prayer Book was begun in 1913.

The two Houses are now on equal footing as regards legislation except that all matters concerning finance originate with the Deputies and it is customary for matters which concern doctrine or worship to be referred for primary action to the Bishops. It is customary likewise for the committees which direct the business of the two Houses to plan together so that on important and especially controversial matters the two Houses will not be debating the same matter at the same time. In 1943 the controversial proposals concerning marriage and divorce were defeated in the Deputies and never came before the Bishops at all. The report of the Commission on Unity came first to the Bishops. In 1946 the order was reversed. The day-long debate on the proposals dealing with Unity took place in the Deputies and the Bishops accepted the Deputies' decision with little modification.

But the Bishops are not a mere co-ordinate body. They do things 'on their own', always issue a Pastoral Letter at the time of General Convention, a letter which the canons require to be read in every parish throughout the Church, ordinarily meet at least once during the triennium and ordinarily speak at that time on some important ecclesiastical or social matter. They have at times missionary bishops to elect, and 'in Council' they confer

with one another on problems of administration and pastoral
care. So much suggests the importance of the role of General
Convention and of the House of Bishops.

The Provinces

Next in logical order, although by no means in importance,
comes the role of the Province. It is already clear from what has
been said concerning General Convention that in the historic
meaning of the term the Church in the United States is one
province. It has no metropolitan; but the Presiding Bishop takes
order for all consecrations and consent to consecration must be
given by the whole Church speaking either through General
Convention or, when that is not in session, through the Bishops
and Standing Committees. Furthermore at every consecration the
bishop promises 'conformity and obedience to the Doctrine,
Discipline and Worship of the Protestant Episcopal Church'. At
ordination priests and deacons do the same. The provinces therefore are such only *in posse*.

Various attempts were made during the nineteenth century to
develop in some of the larger states a kind of provincial system;
but it was not until early in this century, through the initiative
of those responsible for the missionary work of the Church, that
the present plan came into being. The continental area of the
United States was divided into seven (later eight) missionary
departments in each of which the then Board of Missions planned
to have an executive secretary whose task it would be to stimulate
the interest of the dioceses and parishes in his area in the missionary work of the Church and to advise the Board on local
conditions and needs. In 1913 these eight departments were re-
named and partly reconstituted as provinces by General Convention. Each province has a synod of bishops, presbyters and laymen.
a bishop for president, and a provincial council which plans for
meetings of the synod and for any common work the province
may undertake. Some provinces have undertaken to help support
institutions within the province or to carry on some special kind
of missionary or educational endeavour. But the co-operation is
entirely voluntary. No province has any authority over its constituent dioceses.

Each province does however elect a representative to serve on
the National Council, establishes a Court of Review which is a

court of appeal for any clergyman from the decision of a Diocesan Court and has the authority (not always exercised) to nominate to the House of Bishops candidates for vacant missionary districts within the province. As to the future of the provinces it is safe to say that the Church has in no way made up its mind. At the present moment the tendency both in the administrative work of the Church and in General Convention seems to be to regard them as little more than a useful way of developing fellowship, of stimulating work and the like. On the other hand particularly in the larger and more definitely missionary areas there is widespread belief that the province should, and with the growth of the Church must, have increasing responsibility both legislative and administrative.

The Diocese

It has been apparent from what has been already said about General Convention that the diocese has only a relative autonomy. In the beginning it was completely autonomous. Just as the nation was formed by the union of independent states, so the Church was organized out of ecclesiastical groups representing the Church of England parishes in the different states. The Bishops were first designated as of the state rather than of the diocese. The union was voluntary. But it was a real union. Each independent church accepted the 'Doctrine, Discipline and Worship of the Protestant Episcopal Church'. It retained the right to elect its own bishops and carry on its own work in its own way; but it gave to the General Convention the right to determine whether the bishop-elect should be consecrated. It accepted from the Church the Prayer Book and surrendered any right to amend it. It accepted likewise certain constitutional provisions concerning the bishop's administration of his office, the most important of which is the function of the Standing Committee.

The Standing Committee elected by the Convention of the diocese consists in most dioceses of four presbyters and four laymen (in all canonical legislation the term presbyter is used). It is constitutionally a check upon the bishop. Its recommendation is necessary before the bishop can receive a candidate for the ministry or ordain deacon or priest. Its concurrence is necessary in the establishment of parishes. During a vacancy in the episcopate or an official absence of the bishop from the diocese for more than three months it becomes the ecclesiastical authority. It gives consent, as representing the presbyters and laity of the diocese, to the election of co-adjutors or suffragans in other dioceses or to the consecration of bishops-elect. It is officially the bishop's Council of Advice to which he may and presumably does turn when difficult problems concerning clergy or parishes come to him for decision.

The Episcopate

And that brings us to the consideration of the bishop's office. There is really only little to notice for, within the few constitutional restrictions, he exercises his traditional authority, holds in the minds and hearts of the people his traditional position. He does (or at least the Church hopes that he does) all the things which a bishop is expected to do. He speaks for the diocese. He shapes its policies. He is the Ordinary of its institutions. He appoints the clergy in charge of missions (congregations which are supported in whole or in part by diocesan or general Church funds). He must be consulted by all vestries in the choice of a rector but whether or not he has authority to veto a call is still an undecided canonical question[1] It is safe to say however that if he has such authority he seldom exercises it. Parishes consult bishops but they ordinarily make their own choice.

The bishop is of course far more than the administrative officer suggested by such functions. He is Father-in-God, chief pastor, counsellor and guide. He confirms and ordains. He cannot exercise his so-called *jus liturgicum* by altering any of the offices of the Prayer Book but he can and does issue offices and prayers for special occasions and in other ways guide the devotions of his diocese. Whatever his theological position or that of his clergy and people his relation to them is fundamentally sacramental.

In a paper like this, one would like to describe the life of a 'typical' American bishop, but there is no such person. The great urban dioceses like New York or Pennsylvania (Philadelphia) bring the bishop innumerable administrative tasks and as many civic demands. He is not a travelling missionary. An hour's drive will probably take the Bishop of Rhode Island to any parish in his diocese. But the Bishop of Montana has to reach parishes and

---

[1] The Civil Courts have sustained his authority. The Church in General Convention has not acted to clear the interpretation of the Canons.

missions scattered over an area as large as Great Britain and Ireland. The missionary district of North Texas is about the size of England and Scotland. There is no typical bishop. We may however say that the average American bishop is a traveller; within his diocese to know his people, to guide and cheer his clergy, often isolated, lonely and discouraged, outside his diocese to conventions, meetings of the House of Bishops, Synods and the like. He is constantly on the move. He has little time for study, for meditation, for the cultivation of the inner life. And so it may fairly be said that few American bishops are scholars, that most of them have been chosen for their pastoral and administrative capacity and their Christian characters.

A few technical matters must be noted in conclusion. Dioceses incline to elect fairly young men, under fifty, but there is no favoured age. It depends on the man. But General Convention has now decided that all bishops must retire at seventy-two. Neither diocese nor bishop has any option in the matter. A bishop may have the assistance of a co-adjutor who has the right of succession and to whom a field within the diocese is assigned in which he exercises full authority; or of a suffragan who has no right of succession nor any independent jurisdiction. The suffragan however may be elected to his own diocese or to any other. A missionary bishop (who is elected by the House of Bishops) may also after five years of service in the missionary field be elected to a diocese. But although there is no prohibition of translation of diocesan bishops every attempt to make it feasible has so far failed—a custom which may claim the authority of the Nicene Council but is to-day unique among Christian communions, certainly among those that claim to be Catholic. One asks the 'why' of such a position and the one serious item in the answer seems to be that American life is so changing, people are so transient, that it is well to have some Church leaders who stay for life in one place. So thinks General Convention, but one may guess that some day it will change its mind.

The Presiding Bishop

It has been already noted that the Presiding Bishop is not strictly a metropolitan. He has no 'authority' in any diocese but his own; and at present he has not even a diocese of his own. His great authority, and it is very great, lies in the fact that he repre-

sents the whole body of the Church in many official functions and
in public relations, and is also administrative head of the Church's
missionary work with all its ramifications in evangelism, education and social relations.

For well over a century, until it became apparent that through
the formation of the National Council and the consolidation of
the work of the whole Church an authoritative administrative
head was needed, the senior bishop in point of consecration held
the office. Since 1925 the office has been elective. The House of
Bishops elects. The House of Deputies confirms. At first the
elected bishop continued as bishop of his diocese. In 1943 the
then Presiding Bishop (Dr. Tucker) stated to his fellow bishops,
and through them to General Convention, that he could no longer
with a good conscience serve as both Presiding Bishop and Bishop
of Virginia. One or the other task must suffer. The Convention
immediately passed legislation permitting him to resign his
diocese and making such action compulsory thereafter. The
Presiding Bishop is thus a bishop without a see. By courtesy he
has a seat in the National Cathedral, Washington. By courtesy he
will have his Chapel at Seabury House in Greenwich, Connecticut, where he will live. The effort to provide a See permanently
attached to the office has so far failed. He retires not as does a
diocesan bishop at seventy-two, but after the General Convention which follows his sixty-eighth birthday.

The Other Clergy

The constitutional position of the other clergy is easily defined.
Ordination depends upon recommendation by the Standing
Committee and certificate from the Examining Chaplains. After
ordination deacons are under the direction of the bishop. Priests
are free to move not only within their own diocese, but into others.
The bishop, if there are no canonical charges against a priest,
must accept his letter dimissory and, as already noted, must in all
ordinary circumstances ratify a vestry's choice of a rector. The
call being thus completed the rector has tenure. Unless brought
to trial under canonical provision, the pastoral relationship of
rector and vestry can be dissolved only by mutual consent or, in
cases of serious trouble, by the bishop with the advice and consent
of the Standing Committee. Vicars of mission congregations
appointed by the bishop have no 'tenure'. Clergy charged with

canonical offences are by a somewhat complicated process brought to trial in Diocesan Courts. In cases involving 'doctrine, faith or worship' appeal may be made to the Court of Review of the Province which may confirm the decision of the Trial Court or order a new trial. There is no further appeal. General Convention has several times declined to complete the judicial system with a final Court of Appeal; an action or lack of action much disapproved by canonists and many lawyers. The Church has evidently felt that the history of decisions in heresy trials makes it desirable to avoid what may be interpreted as *finality* in such matters.

The clergy are for the most part poorly paid and the present inflation has not brought to them, as it has to some classes, any corresponding increase of salary. Half of them have less (including rectory) than $3,000 a year; three-quarters have less than $4,000. Bus drivers in New York get $3,600, policemen $3,900. It is quite true that expenses in many parts of the country are far less than in New York; it is also true that in many parishes (industrial areas, small towns and the like) even the poorly paid parson will have as much as most of his parishioners. But the general picture is accurate. The pension system carefully worked out on actuarial principles does however afford a measure of security for old age. It is based on salaries. Money is provided by a 10 per cent payment by the parish. The pension becomes available to any priest at sixty-eight; but no retirement age is fixed.

Problems? Plenty of them! How to recruit for the ministry; how to provide adequate support; how to get first-rate men into the rural field and the big missionary areas; how to move men who ought to move; how to get the right man for a difficult task? Problems? Yes! but no doubt no Christian church escapes them. There is also the profoundly important matter of the education of the clergy, but that we shall touch when we come to the matter of education in our sketch of the Church at work.

THE WAY THE CHURCH WORKS

It is something of a task for this body scattered, sprawling over the whole area of the United States, to get its work done. How does it draw together the people in the thickly settled East and those thinly spread out over the vast area of the plains and the Rocky Mountain states? The answer to the question probably

should begin with the somewhat obvious remark that Episcopalians are Americans, and Americans like to travel. Distance
means little to them. The air-age makes travel still easier. They
like also to get together. They have an extraordinary fondness
for conventions and conferences. They delight in passing resolutions, and, quite as important, they have an almost pathetic
confidence in organization. A committee, a board, an association,
a program—that is the key to progress. And the interesting
fact is that on the whole it works. It works because in our organizations leadership comes to the fore. 'Institutions', said Elihu
Root, 'are but means by which and through which personalities
may work.' So in the Church, we organize; we are a bit compla-
cent about it; then we begin to grumble; soon we are sure that
our whole structure must be overhauled; and finally, we discover
that wherever the organization has opened the way to leadership
we do move forward. And here is a sketch of our present working
methods.

The National Council

The National Council is the body to which General Convention has entrusted the administration of all organized missionary,
educational and social work which is felt to be a responsibility of
the whole Church and not merely of interested groups within it.
In 1820 the Domestic and Foreign Missionary Society was
organized, not by a few people filled with missionary zeal, but
by the action of General Convention. The principle underlying
that action was made clear when in 1835, at the time the first
missionary bishops were sent out, General Convention declared
that all members of the Church were *ipso facto* members of the
missionary society. The missionary work has thus always been
regarded as a corporate responsibility. Although during the
ritual controversies of the last century a Church Missionary
Society was formed, it lasted as an independent group only a few
years.

The Church came more slowly to realize that its educational
and social responsibilities were all part of its mission to the world.
But in 1919 most of the many agencies acting on a national scale
were consolidated in what is now known as the National Council.
The Council consists of twenty-eight members; twenty bishops,
presbyters and laity (four women) elected by General Convention,

and eight representatives elected by the provinces. The Presiding Bishop is its chairman and administrative head. Its headquarters are at the Church Missions House in New York, familiarly known by its street number as '281'. It meets at least three times a year; hears reports from its departments of work, makes appropriations and decides policies. It is not however an executive committee of General Convention. It has no authority over any diocese. It is established to carry on the general work of the Church, to lead and to stimulate diocesan and parochial endeavour.

It is to the Council that the Church turns when any special need has to be met. When, e.g., the War was drawing to a close and it became apparent that vast sums would be needed for relief and rebuilding in the mission fields and indeed throughout the world, the Council asked for the sum of three million dollars. It soon appeared that that was not enough. They asked for five. That was not enough and in the end the Church gave over seven millions, 10 per cent of which went to direct relief. The seven millions still was not enough, but it has provided, in addition to immediate relief, for the rebuilding of churches, schools and hospitals in China, the Philippines, and other devastated areas, and for some rebuilding and extension in the homeland.

Before turning now to a sketch of the various aspects and ramifications of the missionary and educational and social work which the chief departments of the National Council suggest, it should be noted that the dioceses and missionary districts have for the most part followed in their own organization the lines marked out by the National Council. Under different names they all have councils, working through departments, advising the bishop, appropriating the funds for diocesan work and promoting through the local congregations the interests of that work. Sometimes, as already suggested, we groan a little. We feel over-organized. 'We' in the parishes (especially the clergy) are deluged with booklets and leaflets of information and advice. We wonder whether any time is to be left for preaching the Word, for the administration of the sacraments, and for pastoral duties. We do not like to see our bishops absorbed so greatly in administration. We do not like to see the Presiding Bishop burdened with such vast business responsibilities when his spiritual leadership is of such moment. We groan and then we stop and think and realize that if our work is to be done effectively in twentieth-century America we must inevitably use highly organized methods. We can always correct over-organization; and if we will it is possible to keep our hearts fixed on the essential things.

We cannot leave the National Council without noting the service rendered in all its fields by the Woman's Auxiliary. The women on the National Council represent the Auxiliary, but it has also its own Executive Board, its own staff headquarters at '281', its provincial representatives, and in every diocese and in most parishes its organized work. It supports women workers in the mission fields. It carries in the parishes the responsibility of educating the women in the work of the Church and does it effectively. Its triennial meeting at the time of the General Convention leads the whole Church in generous, profound and radical Christian thinking on the problems of the Church and the world. Its thank-offering at the Triennial Meeting ($1,635,126.20 in 1946) is an example and a stimulus to the whole body of Church people. It is indeed a God-given Auxiliary to everything good for which the Church is striving.

Missionary Work

There are actually only thirteen missionary districts in what is called the Continental area; although for purposes of administration Porto Rico and the Panama Canal Zone are considered Home Missions within the Province of New York and New Jersey, and Alaska and Honolulu within the Province of the Pacific. The Philippines (now no longer an American dependency) are still reckoned as part of the latter Province. There are ten Overseas missions—in Mexico, Brazil, Liberia, China, and the West Indies. As already noted, missionary bishops have the same status as diocesan bishops in General Convention, but their districts are represented by only one deputy in each order. In the continental area, however, most districts look forward to diocesan standing in the not too distant future. Some are already stronger in numbers and in income than a few of the small dioceses; but to achieve diocesan standing means the building up of endowments and assumption of full responsibility for all current costs. Of late years districts have become very cautious about taking the step. It is obvious that any such achievement lies in the very distant future for a sparsely settled state like Nevada or a frontier community like Alaska.

The gradual achievement of autonomy by churches in foreign lands brings with it a problem of adjustment. American clergy in those dioceses (in China for example) which are missions of the Church in America are in good standing in both the Chinese and the American Church. They hold a dual membership. But as the Chinese Church becomes less and less dependent upon American resources that relationship must inevitably change.[1] At the present moment the Church in the Philippines is not only an American mission; it is altogether dependent upon America; but the time will come when it will no longer need help from outside. Native bishops and native priests do not have canonical standing in the Church in America. Japan has no longer any representatives of its dioceses in General Convention. Some day there will be independent Churches in Mexico and Brazil. Some day Cuba and Liberia will have their own native bishops and other clergy.

One question which faces some of the other Anglican Churches does not exist for this Church. Since all the missions (the exceptions are so few as not to matter) are under the Church and not under a society, questions of 'authority' do not arise. Bishops are elected by the House of Bishops. All appropriations come from the central office, all appointments to the field are ultimately the responsibility of the Presiding Bishop and the Council. Naturally there are often differences concerning policy between a bishop and the Council; questions of appointments to the staff, of distribution of appropriations and the like. It is sometimes hard for those who pay the piper not to want to call the tune. But differences such as these get adjusted and the work goes on with unity of purpose and devotion.

As to churchmanship it seems at the present time to play a rather minor part in missionary work. The old tradition which grew out of a kind of informal agreement during the last century's controversies that the 'Evangelicals' would take the foreign field; the 'High Church' the domestic (a tradition which explains the fact that the dioceses which are predominantly Anglo-Catholic tend to be in the Middle West), is entirely broken down. In the

[1] On the Constitution, etc., of the Church in China (Chung Hua Sheng Kung Hui) see Chapter VIII of this book.

D

domestic field the districts naturally tend to take on the colour of the bishop's churchmanship and that depends on the kind of churchman which the House of Bishops has elected. It is safe to say however that the House of Bishops is pretty conscientious in trying not to send to any particular district a bishop who will upset the prevailing type of churchmanship.

Perhaps it should be added that the budget of the National Council is about three-and-a-half million dollars, which is in addition to what is raised in the missions and takes no account of the sums devoted by dioceses and parishes to missionary work within their own areas.

Educational Work

The educational work of the National Council includes the schools and colleges in the mission field both at home and abroad. St. John's University, Shanghai, with its distinguished record in training leaders of modern China, Iolani School, Honolulu, St. Augustine's College for Negroes in North Carolina, and innumerable others, look in whole or in part to the National Council and its affiliates for support. The Department of Education of the Council is on the other hand a small division whose function is to advise and lead in the more distinctly religious educational field. It counsels diocesan and parochial directors of religious education, issues booklets and leaflets, edits courses for Church (Sunday) Schools, organizes conferences and sends members of its staff hither and yon to stimulate the interest of clergy and laity.

The problems of religious education in America to-day are difficult of solution. The public schools[1] have become secularized to an alarming extent; but owing to the constitutional provisions against the 'establishment' of religion distinctly religious teaching and even the most non-sectarian recognition of religion must depend on the public opinion of any particular state or district. There are great differences, but nowhere in the public school system does religious teaching find a place.

What then is to be done? Most of the American churches accept the public school system, the only notable exceptions being the Roman and some branches of the Lutheran. They (the non-Roman churches and the Jews) feel that the school is essen-

---

[1] In the United States 'public schools' are part of the state system of education.

tial to national unity, to the breaking down of discrimination on ground of creed or race. But they also recognize (and this sentiment has grown greatly of late) that the churches must meet the task of religious training more adequately than in the past. The Sunday school is inadequate. There is growing use of week-day classes both out of school hours and through what is called 're-lease time'; the schools excusing pupils during specified school hours for teaching by their own church or in inter-denominational classes. There is also the effort to bring into social and historical studies in the schools the part that religion has played in human society. In all this kind of work dioceses and parishes turn to the National Council's Department for help.

There is little or no effort anywhere to establish parochial schools such as the Roman Catholics and Lutherans support. But although there are almost no parochial schools for secondary education this Church has been particularly successful in the establishment and maintenance of private schools ('public schools' in England). Over one hundred and fifty are listed as affiliated with or maintained by the Church. All over the country one finds them. Great boys' schools like St. Paul's in New Hampshire and Groton in Massachusetts rival the famous English schools. Girls' schools like Rowland Hall in Salt Lake City or St. Helen's in Portland, Oregon, have pioneered for the Church in the newer areas.

Great success has attended the Church in the private secondary schools, but little success in establishing colleges and universities. Some, like Columbia in New York, founded by churchmen, keep but a tenuous connexion with the Church. Half a dozen have carried forward successfully and are developing notable contributions. It is perhaps not invidious to mention the University of the South at Sewanee, Tennessee; Hobart in New York State; Trinity in Connecticut.

One often wonders why this Church has everywhere fostered the secondary private schools but numbers so few colleges, while the land is dotted everywhere with colleges and universities affiliated with the Methodist and Presbyterian Churches. What is the difference in *ethos* which creates this difference in emphasis? The answer must lie somewhere within the scope of the social backgrounds which distinguish the three groups. One might at a guess say that the concentration of Episcopal Church population in the more thickly settled areas and a larger proportion of families in the upper income class brackets make the older colleges and universities of the east a sufficient resource.

But if the Church has few colleges and universities which it may call its own, its work in the hundreds of institutions of higher learning throughout the land has attained a high degree of efficiency, or perhaps it would be wiser to say that the importance of keeping the Church in close touch with church boys and girls who go to college is now recognized everywhere. The National Council has a division of college work with a staff. Many dioceses have commissions and directors of college work, and in most of the larger institutions there are special chaplains and other workers; at the smaller institutions the local parishes recognize their responsibility. The Church Society for College Work leads in stimulating work. There are groups, clubs, societies of Church students everywhere. There is a national association of Canterbury Clubs, as many of these local groups are called. And finally, in the matter of lay education there has of late been great emphasis upon 'Youth Work'. There is a national secretary. There are diocesan secretaries; there are hundreds of youth conferences, youth services, youth summer schools. Whatever else we do we have not failed to 'organize'.

And here too may be noted the educational influence of Church papers and journals. Three weekly papers, one bi-weekly, the official monthly, *Forth*, besides a number of journals maintained by special groups carry church news to church people. Practically every diocese has its own diocesan monthly, many of which go to every family registered on parochial lists. *The Anglican Theological Review*, the *Historical Magazine* and others less important play their part in educating and in tying together the widely scattered membership of the Church.

The Training of Clergy

We have already looked at the constitutional provisions which govern the ordination and life of the clergy. We have now to turn to their preparation. That is achieved normally at theological schools. There are eleven. The General Seminary in New York is the only one which reports to General Convention and is under the auspices of the whole Church. The others, five on the Atlantic Coast, four in the South and Middle West, one on the Pacific

Coast, have varying degrees of diocesan or provincial status. But all of them are dependent upon their own endowments and their own efforts for support. They vary greatly in character and emphasis and teaching. They tend to carry on the tradition of their founders. One expects Virginia to be evangelical, Cambridge to cherish the liberal spirit of its Broad Church founders, the General Seminary to be 'high', and Nashotah to be Anglo-Catholic. But in these days one also expects that none of these schools will be partisan. Students of all kinds of views will probably be found in any of them. Indeed the hope of increasing unity within the Church is very closely bound up with the capacity of the theological schools to interpret understandingly the various types of churchmanship to one another.

Whatever the emphasis in churchmanship the ground covered by students is determined primarily by the Canons of General Convention. Examining Chaplains, whose appointment rests with bishops and diocesan conventions, must certify that candidates for orders have passed satisfactorily the subjects required by the Canons. Those subjects are obvious: Bible, Church History, Theology, Liturgics and the various fields which are grouped under the general title of Practical Theology. Hebrew is an elective. Greek may be dispensed with and is very frequently. The slight attention given to the classics in our public schools means that occasionally one comes across a priest who can read his Greek Testament but knows nothing of Latin nor of any of the Greek classics. But this is all a change of emphasis, not a lowering of standards.

The theological schools all require a three-year course. Most of them require a B.A. degree for entrance. Before ordination to the diaconate all the requirements for priest's orders must be met (some special exceptions being allowed). Although it is still possible for men who pass the examinations to be ordained without a seminary course, the number decreases steadily. It will certainly be a long time before our clergy astonish the world by their learning as did their English brethren of a past generation. But the standard steadily rises. In that connexion it is worth noting that many of our schools have also affiliation with neighbouring universities and the seminaries of other churches. The universities open libraries and courses. Our own and the other seminaries do the same. Union Seminary in New York (the most influential centre of theological learning in America) has three Episcopalians on its faculty and always some among its students.

The Religious Orders, of which there are listed twelve for men and sixteen for women, although small in number have made distinguished contributions to the life of the Church. They have helped to bring much needed emphasis upon the devotional life and especially to reveal the value of 'retreats' for clergy and laity alike. They have been of great service in educational work by maintaining some of the best church schools. St. Mary's, St. Anne's and the Community of the Transfiguration have well-established foreign mission stations. The Holy Cross has a Liberian Mission. The Cowley Fathers have a Mission House in Japan.[1]

Social questions

Brief notice must be given to one other field of Church activity; that of social relations and social agencies. The National Council's Department of Social Agencies (like the Department of Education) is an advisory body. It leads, stimulates thinking, promotes the work of diocesan and parochial groups, plans conferences; bringing, for example, industrial and labour leaders together. Most dioceses have departments or committees covering the same field of the application of Christian principles to the social and world order.

The Church has also been a leader in the establishment of social agencies. Church Hospitals are found everywhere, as are convalescent homes, homes for old people and for children, community centres, settlements, carried on by dioceses or parishes or by organized groups of church people. In many areas the Church has an acknowledged leadership in this field and it is safe to say that in proportion to its strength no other Christian body has done more for the alleviation of suffering and immediate social welfare. A few years ago at an important Social Work Conference a member looked around and whispered: 'Are they all Jews?' 'Look again,' said his neighbour. 'Well, if not, they are Episcopalians.' We shall comment later on the attitude of the Church towards the economic and social order. But the contribution of this Church to philanthropic and welfare agencies is outstanding.

[1] On the religious orders in the Anglican Communion generally, see pp. 306–8 of this book.

THE WAY THE CHURCH WORSHIPS

The Book of Common Prayer

The dependence of the first American Book of 1789 upon the English Book of 1662 has already been noted. Since that first book there have been two revisions (1892 and 1928). In each the old Preface is reprinted. In each it is quite evident that the variations have to do with 'local circumstances' and the inevitable change of emphasis which comes with the passing years. They do not touch the essential faiths; and indeed as one compares the present American Book with the English Deposited Book of 1928 one detects the same working of the time-spirit. But comparing the American Book after two revisions with the book of 1662 from which it sprang one may note certain very obvious contrasts.

(a) There is some rearrangement. Prayers and Thanksgivings are slipped in before the Litany. The Collects, Epistles and Gospels are placed after the Communion Office. (b) There are many new prayers especially emphasizing the Church's responsibility in civic and social fields, legislatures, courts, education, social justice, other nations. Family Prayer is enriched by a score or more of prayers chosen and adapted from the best sources. An Office of Instruction takes the place of the Catechism although the latter is printed after the Ordinal. There is a complete revision of the Visitation of the Sick; the Marriage Service is greatly shortened by omitting much of the introductory exhortation and all of the nuptial benediction and concluding address. The Baptismal Office is shortened, is somewhat revised and includes two questions addressed to the sponsors. (c) The principle of flexibility and the permission of alternative uses is highly developed, as for example, in the shortening of Morning Prayer if the Holy Communion is to follow. The Confession and Absolution may be omitted and the priest may pass from the Canticle following the First Lesson to the Communion. (d) But the most significant change is in the Prayer of Consecration. Bishop Seabury brought back with him in 1784 after his consecration by the non-jurors in Aberdeen their Communion Office (1764) and the promise to use it (especially the Prayer of Consecration) as the basis for his diocesan use and if possible to secure its adoption in the American Church. He succeeded. Keeping the place of the

Great Intercession as in the English Rite, the Prayer of Consecration follows the Scotch model (words of Institution, Oblation, Invocation). The Scotch and American bishops believed they were coming nearer to ancient usage. They laid great stress on the Invocation. Bishop Seabury was even concerned as to whether the English Rite was adequate! (e) One other variation may be noted. In the Ordination of Priests, the Bishop may use either the form in the English Book or an alternative which omits the first two phrases and substitutes the words 'Take thou authority to execute the office of a priest in the Church of God'.

It will be seen however that in spite of these many variations the substance of the Book is the same. There is no departure from the English heritage in anything 'essential'. The spirit is there. Furthermore the Book holds the same central position in the life of the Church in America that it does in the mother country. The constitution requires its use in the public services of the Church. The constitutional provision merely expresses what is in the hearts of the people. It is true here as in other parts of the Anglican Communion that there is much technical violation of the law by both Evangelicals and Anglo-Catholics. Prayers are interpolated; phrases or words are altered; the 'Anglican Missal' or the 'American Missal' takes the place of the Prayer Book on some altars. But one must not lay too much stress upon these various practices. They represent not conscious disloyalty but what are believed to be perfectly legitimate efforts to enrich the Prayer Book or to correct what seem to their users obvious anachronisms. The great body of the clergy accept the Prayer Book as it is, and the laity being always conservative in matters of the cultus would not have it otherwise.

There is also to-day a very live movement which seeks to modify extreme uses and to unite 'parties' by emphasizing loyalty to the Prayer Book. Such loyalty does not prevent wide diversity in worship. It does make it possible for any loyal churchman to feel at home wherever he may happen to be. Diversity is found almost everywhere throughout the Church. In an Evangelical diocese there will surely be Anglo-Catholic parishes of the most extreme type; and a predominantly Anglo-Catholic diocese will probably find that Church life is made interesting by a specimen or two of radically Protestant churchmen.

Dioceses tend to maintain traditions in worship. We talk of Virginia churchmanship and mean that in that state the average parish has a very simple 'use'. We expect an elaborate ceremonial in Wisconsin. It is ticklish to generalize in a matter of this kind. It is however safe to say that there has been in America as everywhere an increase in ceremonial. Candles are almost universal. Eucharistic vestments, reverences, the sign of the cross, no longer arouse serious antagonism. Yet the ceremonial on such great occasions as the opening of General Convention is simple. Few bishops ever wear a mitre. Pectoral crosses and rings are recent adornments.

What is one to say then, about parties and the party spirit? It is perhaps enough to say that on occasions (perhaps something which happens at the election of a bishop or, as last year, in connexion with proposals concerning Church unity) the Church gets very troubled by its lack of unity. But for the most part it goes along, does its work, worships in unity and assumes that the differences in view are part of human society and that under the guidance of the Spirit of Truth we shall find ways of adjusting conflicting views. So the American Church Union goes on with its Catholic Congresses and its publications. The Episcopal Evangelical Fellowship holds conferences and distributes pamphlets. The Church Congress invites men of both groups to discuss and debate. Other groups are doing the same kind of thing. Most of us enjoy our diversity in spite of the perversity and stubbornness and ignorance of the other side! We sometimes feel as if we were two Churches trying to be one. But when we get on our knees at the altar we know that in Christ there is neither high nor low, neither Evangelical nor Anglo-Catholic but that all are really one.

Under this general head of worship one further point may be mentioned. In the oldest states there are still many lovely 'Colonial' churches. Through most of the Middle and Far West our churches are what is by courtesy called 'gothic'. Some are beautiful, most are quite ordinary. Almost all are furnished in conventional style; altar, choir, pulpit, lectern. In the Pacific South-West the Spanish mission style is popular. Here and there through the country one finds a straight-lined unadorned 'modern' church. There is certainly growing interest in all that concerns ecclesiastical architecture and Church furnishings.

THE CHURCH'S PLACE IN NATIONAL LIFE

Social Responsibility

Whatever may have been the case in the past, no one who knows the facts could accuse the Episcopal Church to-day of indifference towards public affairs. The responsibility of the Church is constantly emphasized. The House of Bishops in its pastoral letters impresses it upon the people. Convention addresses and special Episcopal charges stress it; and many clergy are looked to for leadership in questions concerning the social order. Laymen take their full share in public life. Nine Presidents—Washington the first; Franklin Roosevelt the last— have been Episcopalians. No other religious body can claim so many. The Presbyterians come next with five. In the present Congress, Episcopalians rank in numbers with Baptists and Presbyterians and are exceeded only by Roman Catholics and, at the top, Methodists.[1] In every community enterprise Episcopalians will be found at the fore and among these the women are pre-eminent in leadership and devotion.

Resolutions of diocesan and general conventions are numerous; some are routine, few are startling, and yet on the whole they represent a wholesome and balanced view of the application of Christian principles to the social order. A body like General Convention is not likely to be very radical; but it has supported the reports and work of very forward-looking commissions. The Commission on Social Reconstruction published before the last General Convention a book composed of papers on world and national problems by various leaders. A Penguin Edition had a very large sale. The Convention was not asked to endorse the positions taken in the book; but it did approve the reappointment of the Commission.

One interesting aspect of this whole matter is that the bishops tend to be the most 'radical'. The laity can always be depended on to be most conservative. The bishops begin a pastoral with the words 'Christ demands a new order'. Convention resolutions would be somewhat more indirect in stating that goal. On the

[1] The Roman Catholic population is claimed to be about 24 million. Ours cannot be more than 3 million. The Methodists report 7 million members. But except occasionally in Roman Catholic circles little stress is laid on religious affiliation in politics, although in 1928 Gov. Smith's Roman Catholic faith was a large factor in his defeat for the Presidency.

other hand in some matters the laity seem to be less conservative. For many decades the Church has been dissatisfied with its
canons on matrimony. It has allowed the marriage of the 'inno-
cent party' in a divorce for adultery but under very rigid legal
provisions; neither those holding to the doctrine of indissolu-
bility nor those approaching the problem from other points of
view have been satisfied. Finally at the Convention of 1946 a new
canon was passed with substantial unanimity which seemed to
make clear the Church's insistence upon the Christian meaning
of marriage and at the same time to allow in the matter of re-
marriage some recognition of other than purely legal factors. It
is already clear that there are variant interpretations of its meaning. It may or it may not stand; but the point of interest is that
during all these years of discussion it has been almost always true
that the laity, conservative on economic questions, have favoured
what is called a more liberal position in this matter.

There are many groups within the Church working all the
time on social problems. Conferences under the auspices of commissions or departments, study groups, Church Congress pro-
grams, deal with them. The Church League for Industrial
Democracy spearheads what to many seem radical positions. The
Pacifist Fellowship has continued active through the war. Much
progress is being made in the problems of racial discrimination.
It would take many pages to record the active leadership of
bishops, other clergy and laity *particularly in the South*, in the
struggle against racial discrimination.

The Church's Social Position

But whatever service the Episcopal Church renders to the
common good, we cannot ignore the fact that we are to a very
large extent a privileged group. That would be the verdict of
outsiders. A good illustration lies in the fact that in the older
endowed colleges and universities Episcopalians are likely to
outnumber any other church group among the students. It is
true that in the cities there are many church community houses,
many church agencies working among the less privileged, but
we have, comparatively speaking, little strength in the rank and
file of the labour movement. In spite of the noble leadership of
many of our outstanding missionaries in the opening-up of the
continent, we have also had a certain lack of adjustability to

frontier conditions and we have never understood the meaning
of the revivalist sects. We have tended to think in terms of 'our
kind' of people, a certain level of culture, a certain exclusiveness,
all of which is a perfectly obvious and natural outgrowth of our
inheritance, our liturgy, our historic contacts; but likewise a
handicap in preaching the Word to less favoured groups.

Relations with other Churches

But we have not kept aloof from contacts with other Churches.
We came in 1940 into full membership with the Federal Council
after having worked with its commissions for many years. Bishop
Tucker, for so long our Presiding Bishop, was President of the
Council for four years, and one of our distinguished laymen (Mr.
Charles Taft) is President to-day. It is fair to say that while many
churchmen fought for years against our taking full membership
there are few whether 'high' or 'low' who are not now satisfied.
In the Ecumenical Movement we have had a position of real
leadership. As everyone known, 'Faith and Order' grew from
Bishop Brent's initiative. We have always supported 'Life and
Work' and had our share in bringing those two movements to-
gether in the World Council.

In all matters of organic unity we have had a position of real
leadership since the issuance of the Chicago declaration which
was shortly developed into the Lambeth Quadrilateral. We have
been much criticized because we act slowly. We have been counted
exclusive and unbrotherly; but on the whole other Christians
seem to have believed in the sincerity of our purpose.

A Final Word

If, after reading all this survey of the Episcopal Church, its
structure, its work and its worship, one should ask the question
'What does the Church actually contribute to American life?' any
answer must be hesitant. Any answer will reflect the presup-
positions and perhaps the prejudices of the answerer; but with
that disclaimer of special insight the answer seems to be surprisingly simple and obvious. Apart from the great contributions
made through illustrious citizens whose lives have been nur-
tured in the Episcopal Church, a great host of them from Washington to Franklin Roosevelt and Henry Wallace, the contribution of the Church in the religious life of the nation has been

precisely what one would expect from a church of the Anglican Communion. It is an American version with the American characteristics which we have noted; but it is essentially Anglican. It is a well-balanced Catholicism; Protestant in its love of freedom; Catholic in its love of order; reverent of the past, confident of the future, democratic in its habit. It is this spirit, this attitude towards life, which we Episcopalians have brought with more or less success into the American scene. We have balanced the revivalist sects with our 'quietness and confidence'. We have undoubtedly helped the great Protestant churches to look back into history and discover the continuity of Christian life from the beginning. Where fundamentalism is rife we have opened to troubled youth the vision of a faith which has no fear of science. When the demands of beauty began to be felt, as they were not in America during the long years of pioneering, we have offered our Prayer Book and the beauty and dignity of our worship. As against the authoritarian clericalism of Rome we have set the fact of a corporate life almost as diversified as the total Christianity about us and yet essentially 'united, loyal, integrated, a real freedom and a real order; and always we bring with us the faith that unity is the will of God.

We do fail. We do not always bring this well-balanced witness to the Gospel—our quietness and confidence easily become sloth; our appeal to history, pride of pedigree; our open-mindedness, an indulgent tolerance; our revelation of beauty mere aestheticism; our balanced freedom and order, a boast. But granting the failings and inadequacies it seems true that these are actual contributions which we are making. We do fail, but we may have a reasonable faith that there is no Communion in America which has a greater opportunity to serve the Kingdom of God and to lead American Christians into that unity which is His Will.

III

THE CHURCH OF ENGLAND IN CANADA AND NEWFOUNDLAND

by the Most Rev. Philip Carrington, *Archbishop of Quebec*

Introductory

Up to the moment of writing, the Diocese of Newfoundland had no connexion with the Church of England in Canada. The Newfoundlanders are a sturdy and independent people; they claim that their island is the oldest British community overseas; and until lately they have been accustomed to manage their own affairs, ecclesiastical and civil. Their Bishop took an oath of allegiance to the Archbishop of Canterbury, but his diocese was not a part of the Province of Canterbury, or subject to English jurisdiction.

This situation is (in 1947) in process of being changed as the Diocese has accepted the constitution of the Canadian Church, and will shortly be admitted to membership in it. This will be in the nature of a return. The first Anglican Bishop in Canada was Charles Inglis who was consecrated Bishop of Nova Scotia on Sunday, 12 August 1787, in Lambeth Chapel, for an enormous diocese, consisting of (a) Nova Scotia, New Brunswick, and Prince Edward Island, (b) Upper and Lower Canada, and (c) Newfoundland.

In 1793 Jacob Mountain was consecrated Bishop of Quebec, with jurisdiction over Upper and Lower Canada, now called Ontario and Quebec.

In 1825 the Archdeaconry of Bermuda was created and added to the Diocese of Nova Scotia. In 1839 the Diocese of Newfoundland was created; Bermuda was part of this Diocese, and the Archdeacon of Bermuda (Aubrey Spencer) became the first Bishop of Newfoundland. It was in the same year that Upper Canada (Ontario) was separated from Lower Canada (Quebec) as the Diocese of Toronto, with John Strachan, formerly Archdeacon of Toronto, as Bishop. The Bishop of Newfoundland attended a Conference of the 'Bishops of the North American

48

colonies' held at Quebec in 1851, after which date the island diocese seems to have gone its own way.

The Canadian Scene

In order to understand Canadian problems, it is necessary to realize the great variety in local tradition which has been spread over thousands of miles of territory. There are several Canadas, which have different characteristics, and sometimes even divergent interests. In order to realize their unity, and set up an effective central administration, the various civil 'Provinces' entered into 'Confederation' in 1867, and established a 'Dominion' Government at Ottawa. It is impossible for Canada to be prosperous or strong unless it has a strong central administration. On the other hand, the moment such an administration asserts itself vigorously, the cry of over-centralization is raised in the Provinces, which have very real governmental powers and responsibilities of their own. In this way a tension is created which is always liable to come into play, and constitutes a major factor in Canadian politics.

Starting from the east, we have the Maritime Provinces (Nova Scotia, New Brunswick, Prince Edward Island) which are the cradle of British settlement in Canada. Halifax celebrates its second centenary in 1949, and old St. Paul's Church is only a year younger than the city itself. Nova Scotia is a colony of the American period which failed to secede from the Empire. After the War of Independence it received a flood of 'United Empire Loyalists' from the United States, many of whom were strong churchmen.

Next comes Quebec, which was the centre of the old French regime on the American continent. The city was taken by General Wolfe in 1759, and the conquered territory was ceded to Britain by the Treaty of Paris in 1763. The fifty or sixty thousand French Canadians then living on the shores of the St. Lawrence were treated with great liberality by the British, and have multiplied into five millions, which does not include their descendants in the United States. Under British rule the Roman Catholic Church grew in wealth and power and political influence. Roman Catholics form nearly 90 per cent of the population of the Province; Anglicans may number as much as 5 per cent, leaving about 6 per cent for all other religious confessions. It can easily be

understood that conditions here are very different from those in
the rest of Canada.

Going farther up the St. Lawrence, we come to Ontario
(Upper Canada). The settlement of 'Upper Canada' began in
earnest after the War of Independence, when United Empire
Loyalists from the States founded Kingston and other cities. For
a long time these 'Tory' families exercised a dominating influence in Church and State. Toronto (originally York) was the
see of the first bishop and is to-day the administrative centre of
the Canadian Church.

Up to 1832 (the date of the Reform Bill) the Church of England
in Canada had been a state church. Its bishops were state func-
tionaries; many of its clergy were paid stipends by the government; the 'Clergy Reserves' had been set apart for their endowment; but the tides of immigration which set in after the Napo-
leonic Wars disturbed this state of affairs and threatened the
ascendancy of the great Tory families. John Strachan fought a
great battle to preserve the ancient privileges of the Church; but
he lost. Anglicanism is still strong in Kingston, Toronto, Hamilton, London, and other cities and towns of Ontario; but not so
strong in the country districts where the Methodist preacher had
sometimes arrived ahead of the English parson, and proved the
more mobile of the two. Nevertheless Ontario is the heart and
centre of Anglicanism in Canada. It is still conservative in
character.

The Maritimes, Quebec, and Ontario, make up what is called
'The East' in Canada, and are divided from 'The West' by the
Great Lakes and the thousand miles of unfertile country surrounding them. In church organization, they formed the original
ecclesiastical Province of Canada which was organized in 1862
with a fixed metropolitical see at Montreal. The old Province of
Canada received the Maritime dioceses into membership in 1870,
and so it continued until 1912 when the Ontario dioceses withdrew and formed an ecclesiastical province of their own.

The old Province of Canada served to unite all the dioceses of
'British North America' with the exception of Newfoundland,
which was too far away in the east, and the new dioceses of
Rupertsland (founded 1849) and British Columbia (1859) which
were too far away in the west. Rupertsland at Fort Garry (later
Winnipeg), the headquarters of the Hudson Bay Company on

the Red River, was the first prairie diocese. The episcopate of Robert Machray (1865 to 1904) coincided with the great westward expansion of Canada and the construction of the Canadian-Pacific Railway. The Canada of the prairies was a new phenomenon, unlike anything in 'The East'. Machray's missionaries spread west and north, carving out new dioceses, as far west as the Rocky Mountains and as far north as the Arctic Ocean. C.M.S. missions were established among the Indians and the Eskimos.

The Province of Rupertsland came into existence in 1875 to unify this vast field of missionary endeavour, and comprises the civil Provinces of Manitoba, Saskatchewan and Alberta; it was not long before the question arose of forming a connexion between the old Province of Canada in 'The East' and the new Province of Rupertsland in 'The West'. 'The East' had been supported in early days by government grants and by the S.P.G. (well subsidized by the government up to 1832) and later on by the Colonial and Continental Church Society and other English missionary organizations; but the government grants came to an end, and the S.P.G. grants were progressively reduced. 'The East' was obliged to stand on its own feet and support itself. By the end of the century some of its main centres were wealthy and well-established, though it had (and still has) considerable missionary areas which can never support their own clergy, and have to receive diocesan support. Nevertheless it was clear that 'The East' ought to support 'The West'.

As a result of a desire for unity, and an enthusiasm for missionary endeavour throughout all Canada, the General Synod was established in 1893 by the two provinces which then existed. Archbishop Machray of Rupertsland was elected first Primate of 'All Canada'. The Metropolitan of the old Province of Canada at that time was Archbishop Travers Lewis, who had sat with Mountain[1] and Strachan in the Provincial Synod of 1861, and had moved the resolution in 1865 which led to the formation of the Lambeth Conference. The student of Canadian Church affairs must be careful from now on not to confuse the Metropolitan of the old Province of Canada with the Primate of All Canada.

There are now four ecclesiastical provinces under the General

---

[1] The second of that name.

Synod, and consequently four Metropolitans, either including or in addition to the Primate, who may or may not be one of the four.

(a) *The old Province of Canada*, consisting of the Maritimes and Quebec, has four dioceses, and any bishop is eligible for election as Metropolitan.

(b) *The Province of Ontario*, which separated from the former in 1912, has eight dioceses, and any bishop is eligible for election as Metropolitan.

(c) *The Province of Rupertsland* has ten dioceses with a fixed metropolitical see at Winnipeg.

(d) *The Province of British Columbia* has six dioceses, and any bishop is eligible for election as Metropolitan.

British Columbia is the furthest-west civil province of Canada, looking across the Pacific to Japan and China in the north and to Australia and New Zealand in the south. It is a different land with a different climate. A Londoner who arrives in Quebec is still less than halfway to 'B.C.'. It is a west beyond the west. On 24 February 1859 George Hills was consecrated Bishop for British Columbia. but did not arrive till 1860. The single diocese did not join either of the older provinces, but affiliated with the General Synod in 1893. It has now become an organized province and includes the vast missionary Diocese of the Yukon. The 'North-Western' Territory of the Mackenzie River is part of the Province of Rupertsland and so is the Diocese of 'The Arctic' with its million square miles of territory.

These northern areas constitute a missionary problem of growing complexity; for Canada is beginning to move northwards. Our Church is emphatically a church of the frontiers. Beyond the limits of cultivation, on the Labrador Coast, or James Bay, or the Arctic, or the North-West, or the Yukon, you can be an Anglican or a Roman Catholic or a pagan. There is nothing else to be.

Our late Primate, Archbishop Derwyn Owen, used to ask whether theAnglican Church in Canada had 'spread itself out too thin'. The answer he expected to his question was 'No'. We shall continue to send our missionaries wherever their ministrations are needed. The historical sketch which we have just given shows that the organization of the General Synod was established with this purpose in view.

Government

The problem of government in Canada is how to provide a strong central administration which will also take into account, and allow for, the immense variety which we have tried to suggest in the previous section. The four ecclesiastical provinces of the Church serve to express the local needs and the local feeling. Their powers and functions in relation to the General Synod are not easy to define, and are not identical in each case. There came a time a few years ago when they tended to lapse into inactivity, except when a vacancy in a diocese made it necessary to accept an episcopal resignation, confirm an election, or arrange a consecration. There was a feeling that Provincial Synods were out of date, and that the General Synod should be all-in-all. In recent years, however, there has been a tendency to reinstate Provincial Synods in some degree.

Yet the importance of the General Synod has steadily grown. It consists of an Upper House in which all the diocesan bishops and their suffragans have a seat,[1] and a Lower House of Clergy and Laity who are elected by the various Diocesan Synods. It meets every third year. It is a strong legislative body, though the terms of its constitution protect in some measure the pre-existing rights and powers of bishops, Diocesan Synods, and Provincial Synods.

There is an Executive Council of the General Synod which meets in the intervening years; and it is this body, acting under a special constitution as an Electoral College, which chooses the Primate. Any archbishop or bishop is eligible for the Primacy, and does not resign his see on becoming Primate. No doubt there is an anomaly here, as the Primate may be one who is not a Metropolitan; but the situation is not regarded as final and it is hoped that a better solution for the problem may be found. The alternative proposal at present is that a fairly small diocese may be founded which can be constituted as a 'Primatial See'; this diocese would of course have to give up its free right to elect its own bishop; but the Canadian genius for administration may overcome these difficulties.

The strong point of the present system, which is not likely to be departed from, is that the whole church, lay and clerical,

[1] Retired bishops have a seat, but no vote.

chooses its Primate by a process of representation. It is a natural development from the system by which the whole diocese, lay and clerical, chooses its own bishop. This democratic system is, of course, criticized in certain quarters, but it is unlikely that any well-established diocese will give up the rights which it now possesses in this respect. The diocese knows its own needs, though it may not always know very well the qualifications of all the men who might be available as bishop. The Diocesan Synod accepts the weightiest responsibilities in connexion with the affairs of the Church in its area, and it can be rather forcibly urged that the election of the bishop is not only a piece of primitive Christian order which it has a right to claim, but also a responsibility which must necessarily be associated with such control and management as it has in its sacred and representative capacity. In any case the Canadian Church grounds its organization here, for good or ill, in the judgment of the clergy and people on whom it relies for support.

There are various safeguards which are or may be in operation; for each diocese has its own canon governing this procedure. There is no election, for instance, until a majority has been recorded both by the clergy and the laity; and in some dioceses there has to be a two-thirds majority in each order. The election then has to be confirmed by the House of Bishops of the Province on canonical grounds. In most cases no speeches are allowed at episcopal elections, and in many cases no nominations either; after the celebration of the Communion and other devotional preparation, the Synod constitutes itself, and proceeds immediately to the balloting.

Among the suggestions which have been made for the improvement of the system is the closer co-operation with the Bishops of of the Province from the beginning. Another suggestion is that the full freedom of election should be reserved to well-established dioceses. In the Province of Rupertsland this is already the case, for the Bishops of missionary dioceses are appointed by an Electoral College of the Provincial Synod. The Metropolitan himself is appointed in a similar way.

Missionary and Women's Work

The observer in Canada is impressed by the strength of the central organization of our Church and by its national character.

The unification achieved in and through the General Synod has expressed itself in various ways, the most striking being the M.S.C.C. (Missionary Society of the Canadian Church) which has replaced the various missionary societies which used to exist, serving various areas, and representing different points of view.

This might be the place to say something about religious parties in the Canadian Church. Controversy was at one time very bitter, but, as we have seen, it is the genius of Canada to include varieties in a workable scheme. The old S.P.G. missionaries in 'The East' were often, one supposes, moderate high-churchmen. The first missionaries in 'The West' were sponsored by the more 'evangelical' C.M.S. But the situation is not so simple as that. 'The East' owes much to strong 'evangelical' leadership from Ireland, particularly perhaps in the Diocese of Huron. Parts of 'The West' received missionaries from England of a more 'Anglo-Catholic' colour, in connexion with which we may mention the Diocese of Qu'Appelle. They all served to enrich the Canadian Church, and combined to constitute the General Synod. The original fires of controversy have burned out. Differences still exist; but we no longer divide on these lines in our Synods. Perhaps the provision of a single Missionary Society has been a help.

The M.S.C.C. is the greatest undertaking of the General Synod. One of the sentiments which led to the formation of the General Synod was the consciousness of a huge field for missionary expansion in the west and north. The letters M.S.C.C. mean that the whole Canadian Church is standing behind those dioceses which need support in their missionary work. In addition it supports work in China, India, and Japan. There is no other missionary society in the Canadian Church. M.S.C.C. is simply the Church itself organized for missionary work.

The M.S.C.C. does not, of course, cover all the missionary work of the Canadian Church, because the self-supporting dioceses carry on a great deal of missionary work within their own borders, for which they receive no financial assistance. No survey of this 'home mission' work has ever been made; but it seems likely that the missionary work done in self-supporting dioceses without assistance from M.S.C.C., exceeds the amount of missionary work in the west and north for which grants are given by

M.S.C.C. These dioceses have their own missionary work to consider as well as their contribution to M.S.C.C.

A few statistics may be of interest here. The census allows us about one-and-three-quarter million Anglicans in Canada, compared with two-and-a-quarter million members of the United Church, and five million Roman Catholics. We are distinctly a minority church.

Our own statistics disclose less than a million church members. These effective church members raise every year a 'Budget' for the work of the Church through the General Synod, quite distinct from the financial support needed for provinces, dioceses, or parishes. This income is based on a businesslike system of apportionment. First the estimates are prepared; then agreements are made with dioceses; the diocese accepts its 'apportionment', and allots it to the various congregations; the congregations raise their allotment from the parishioners by means of an envelope system. The money comes back through the congregations to the dioceses, and through the dioceses to the General Synod. The efficiency and goodwill and co-operation which makes this system possible is characteristic of the Canadian people. Ideally it should make an end of 'special appeals', but in reality this is not completely feasible.

In 1943 the General Synod Budget Committee asked the dioceses for $331,000 (in round figures) for all purposes; it received nearly $343,000. In 1944 it asked for $371,000, and received $382,000. In 1945 it asked for $371,000 and received $380,000.

In 1945 the M.S.C.C. received as its share from the 'Budget' about $335,000, which was brought up to about $374,000 by revenue from capital and a grant from the W.A. (Woman's Auxiliary). About $200,000 was paid out in regular grants for missionary work in Canada, about $25,000 for special purposes (Programme of Advance). Over $70,000 was spent on Missions Overseas, which figure it is now hoped to raise to over $90,000. The remainder was required for missionary education, publicity, office expenses, etc.

A word should be added here about the W.A., an official organization for women in connexion with the General Synod. Originally called the Woman's Auxiliary to the M.S.C.C., it was primarily a missionary organization; but its zeal and efficiency were so great that it entered into almost every department of women's work, and in 1947 changed its name to the Woman's Auxiliary of the Church of England in Canada. Its membership in 1946 was 99,537, and it raised $267,000, of which it granted over $130,000 to the missionary work of the Church, devoting the rest to its own special activities. In addition to this the Diocesan Boards of the W.A. give help to missionary and social and educational work within the diocese, and the branches give similar help in the parishes.

Under its own special activities, the W.A. is responsible for training, equipping, and supporting women workers in our various missions at home and abroad. It has its own Pension Fund in which all its workers participate. It provides the clothing for all the girls in some eighteen or twenty Indian Boarding Schools. It also assists with the education of the children of the clergy in the missionary dioceses by awarding forty bursaries annually.

The success of this great organization goes far to explain why organizations of English origin, like the Mothers' Union and the Girls' Friendly Society, do not have the same scope in Canada as elsewhere. The W.A. has developed to fit Canadian conditions, and combines the functions of a parish organization for women, with those of a missionary society. There are also parish 'Guilds' for women whose special function is in many cases the care of the church and its ornaments, or the repair and redecoration of the parsonage. These Guilds are often a great help to the Wardens in financial matters.

The W.A. does an active work among girls. In addition to sponsoring the Girl Guides, it has its own Junior Department, and its 'Girls' Auxiliary' (G.A.) which has recently made great strides, and been reorganized to give a training in Christian citizenship along Girls' Club lines.

Its 'Little Helpers' department for children under seven years old, enables it to keep in touch with young mothers.

The W.A. is not under the direction of the General Synod, though it has the closest connexion with it. Representatives of the W.A. sit in Synod, and have rights as members when subjects which concern them are being discussed. The right of women to sit in the General Synod as representatives of dioceses has not been carried very far. Any diocese which admits women to its own Diocesan Synod, may elect one of these women as its representative on the General Synod. In 1946 the President of the W.A. sat in the General Synod as the first regular diocesan lay delegate of the female sex, representing the Diocese of Yukon.

Other central activities

As the M.S.C.C. took over the work of all the previous missionary societies, so the G.B.R.E. (General Board of Religious Education) took over the Sunday School work. Up to that date (1908) there were several series of Sunday School lessons used in the congregations, representing different schools of thought and methods of education. The provision of a graded system of lessons with all necessary publications has been a large undertaking, which has extended over years, and is naturally in need of constant revision. It is not, of course, compulsory for every congregation to use it; but it is widespread and has no serious competitor.

The G.B.R.E. has a wide field of work both as a church publisher and bookseller, and also in the field of Youth Work. It sponsors the Anglican Young People's Association (A.Y.P.A.) which began as long ago as 1902. This organization has caught on not only in Canada but elsewhere. It has about two hundred branches in Britain.

The G.B.R.E. also sponsors the Boy Scouts, and collaborates with the W.A. in connexion with girls' work and children's work.

In 1945 the G.B.R.E. received over $25,500 from the General Synod Budget, and this constituted the greater part of its income for working purposes; but this does not include the Editorial and Supplies Accounts which concern the work of G.B.R.E. as publisher and bookseller.

The third department of the General Synod is the Council of Social Service (C.S.S.) which received a little over $20,000 from the General Synod Budget in 1945. The work of the Council is largely informative, and it aims through its 'Bulletins' at keeping the clergy well advised on social subjects. It is also the point of contact with many Canadian-wide social service organizations.

The fourth principal department of the General Synod is the Pensions Board. Quite early in its history the General Synod set out to build up a contributory Pension Fund for the Clergy and Clergy Widows of the Canadian Church, that should be actuari-

ally sound. Certain of the older dioceses, however, preferred to
remain on a diocesan basis, so that Toronto, Huron, Ottawa,
Ontario, Niagara, Montreal, and Quebec, stand outside the
General Synod Fund. These dioceses, however, have given
generously to strengthen the General Synod Fund, which is now
declared to be actuarially sound; this is due to the Advance Appeal
which will be mentioned farther on. In 1945 the receipts of the
Fund for the year from various sources were $189,033; 'Disburse-
ments for the year' were $137,385; $50,000 was set aside for
investment.

This record of achievement since 1893 would not be complete
without mentioning that the General Synod has issued a Canadian
Prayer Book (not fundamentally different from that of 1662) and
a Canadian Hymn Book which recently appeared in a new edition.

New activities and new committees of the General Synod are
constantly coming into existence, and we may have reached the
stage where simplification would be beneficial; but the object of
this section is to give the reader a picture of the old-established
regular work of the General Synod. It will at once be obvious
how far the Canadian Church has advanced along the lines of
'official' national organization, to a certain extent excluding competition from some fields. Before criticizing this tendency, the
reader should reflect on the extraordinary variety of the Canadian
scene as pictured in an earlier section of this essay, and the chaos
which might have ensued without the centralization which has
taken place. It should also be remembered that no power exists
by which General Synod can enforce its forms of organization on
the parishes; they have been accepted by a democratic Church,
doubtless because it is generally felt that a measure of centralization and unification is necessary if our Dominion-wide Church
is to be strong.

On the other hand there is a certain amount of protest from
time to time at what seems to be a certain top-heaviness at the
centre. I do not think it can truly be said that we are over-
organized. Certainly the two other principal churches, the Roman
Catholic Church and the United Church, have stronger central
organizations than we. The protests we hear are probably merely
a symptom of that tension between the Dominion organization
and the local governments which we have found to be a feature
of the Canadian problem in general. They may also proceed from

the difficulty that has been found in accommodating the central organization to the old church tradition of provinces and dioceses and to the episcopal system.

The Parish

Passing from the subject of general organization, we glance at the average Canadian congregation, if such a thing can be found.

The average Canadian churchman, when he moves from one place to another, likes to find things much the same. He likes services out of the Canadian Prayer Book, and hymns out of the Canadian Hymn Book. He is prepared to take envelopes, and contribute his share to the finance of the church. The envelope will probably have two ends, a 'white end' for the needs of the local church, and a 'red end' for outside needs including the Diocese and the General Synod. He will undertake to give a regular sum each week, and will bring his envelope to put on the collection plate. If he is absent from church he will arrange to send in his full set of envelopes for the year.

His children will get G.B.R.E. lessons in Sunday School or Children's Church. His older sons and daughters will join the A.Y.P.A.; or if they are a little younger, the G.A., or the Guides, or the Scouts: his wife will join the W.A., or Parish Guild, or both. The religious affiliation of his family will be of more importance to him socially than it would be in England.

If he lives on the outskirts of civilization, his community will receive monthly or fortnightly visits from a travelling clergyman sent by the Bishop. The people will contribute as best they can. There may be a church; more likely the service will be in a school or 'staff-house' or pool-room. The clergyman will stay a night or two, and then go on to the next station.

In a regularly constituted 'Mission' or missionary parish, there will be a clergyman residing at a fixed centre from which he visits two, three, or even more others. There will be regular congregations with churchwardens, and each will undertake to pay local expenses, to contibute a regular sum to the stipend, and to accept an apportionment of the 'Budget'. In most dioceses the clergyman will receive the local contribution to his stipend from the wardens from time to time; but where the 'Quebec System' is in operation, the wardens pay their contributions to the diocesan office, which sends a monthly cheque to the clergyman.

In the case of a Mission, the clergyman is usually appointed by the Bishop or by a diocesan board or by both concurrently.

When a congregation or group of congregations becomes financially self-supporting, and is able to pay the full stipend of its clergyman, in accordance with the diocesan scale, they are usually given a voice in the choice of their Rector; but this varies considerably in different dioceses. In some cases the parish virtually appoints its Rector; in others the Bishop has considerable power.

The country Missions generally have little wooden churches, which are often very picturesque. In the country towns there are larger churches, often of brick or stone. In the cities there are many splendid structures from the unfinished Cathedral at Victoria in the far west to the unfinished Cathedral at Halifax in the far east. These churches are often flanked with vestries and offices, and a large hall with a variety of rooms for Sunday Schools or clubs. The Rector of such a church must have many gifts; he must be as strong as an ox, for his day is one long round of telephone calls, visits, meetings, and services; he must be a good preacher, a good organizer, and a business-man of no mean ability; he must be continually working new laymen and new laywomen into key positions. And yet his chief concern must be for spiritual things; and he must interpret the missionary needs of the Church at large to his city congregation.

These churches are the pillars of the structure. A congregation of this kind has all its own expenses to meet, and in addition it will have an apportionment for the Budget of $10,000 or more. It calls for a broad vision, a well-grounded faith, and the spirit of prayer.

One of the most interesting spiritual features of a big-city church is the observance of Lent and Easter. Often in a big church in a central position there is a mid-day service every day in Lent with an address by a special preacher not lasting more than twenty minutes. In this way the 'down-town church' comes into its own as a centre of quiet but effective evangelism day by day for forty days.

The Diocese

The Canadian diocese varies as much as the Canadian parish. The Bishop of an important diocese with a big city at its centre, has a routine of correspondence which keeps him for long hours at his desk; his administration is a constant burden. The more missionary dioceses, on the other hand, call for constant travelling, by train, motor-car, plane, ship, canoe, and in the winter by sleigh. The Bishop is still the head of a missionary and evangelistic enterprise. He feels the direct burden of providing for the small scattered groups who appreciate so highly the ministrations which are often so difficult to give. He comes into close contact with his clergy and their wives, the churchwardens and other workers, and the conditions of their everyday life.

Most bishops are bound to alternate between the routine of administration with its meetings and correspondence, and the field work with its travel and personal contacts.

The Diocesan Synod meets annually in most dioceses, but less often in a scattered missionary diocese. Each congregation elects a lay Synodsman (or Synodsmen if it is a large congregation). The business of the Synod is to hear Reports, elect officers and committees, approve financial estimates (in most cases) and pass resolutions and canons. The Bishop presides, and the Clergy and Lay Delegates sit together; most votes are decided on the voices; but if a show of hands is called for, the votes of the Clergy and Laity are recorded separately, and the motion must pass in both orders. The Bishop has a veto, but I have never heard of it being used.

The diocese is the real unit of the Canadian Church. Dioceses were established long before provinces. The General Synod is a newcomer. In some cases parishes are older even than dioceses, and where this is the case, as in Nova Scotia, we usually find that the congregation has fairly independent powers to this day. As a rule, the first episcopal establishment had a missionary character, and the present church organization derives from episcopal pioneers whose names and characters are well-remembered. Even when dioceses are subdivided these traditions are not lost. The clergy feel their diocesan loyalty deeply. It is a serious step to change one's diocese, and the transfer cannot be carried out without Letters Testimonial, the issue of which is regulated by a canon of the General Synod.

The ordination of clergy, their appointment to cures, their preferment, and their discipline, are all regulated by the diocese, with some degree of recourse to the Provincial Synod.

The Training of Clergy

The supply, training, and ordination of the clergy depends very largely on the Bishop, who will take advice with his Archdeacons and Examining Chaplains. No canons of the General or Provincial Synods seem to interfere with the Bishop's personal responsibility as to ordination. This is a field in which no unification or standardization has been attempted, though a Commission of the General Synod has recently circulated an interesting Report on the subject.

The various colleges for the training of ordinands are independent corporations. They were established at various dates, and seem for the most part to be fairly independent of the Bishops. All are completely independent of the General Synod. They have however voluntarily agreed to accept the examinations of the General Synod Board for the B.D. and D.D.

The result is that each Bishop is free to lay down his own standards for ordination, and to recognize what college he likes, though circumstances may limit his freedom in actual practice. Some of the colleges have diocesan affiliations; some have a traditional connexion with a special school of thought; some retain a considerable influence with their alumni after ordination, which gives them a strong position in the Church.

The Report issued by the General Synod Commission recommends that a candidate for orders should have a B.A. degree (which takes four years to get in most Canadian universities) followed by two or even three years of theology. Most candidates are unable to pay their way through college, and some are rather over the college age when they volunteer for Orders. The combination of these circumstances often makes it difficult for them to spend seven years in study. This leads to the provision of combined courses, shortened courses, and special courses of various descriptions.

Another limiting factor is that no one now arrives at college with any knowledge of Greek, and few with any serviceable knowledge of Latin, so that the old disciplines can no longer be carried through in the old way.

In Canada, too, there is a tradition of men 'working their way through college', which means getting a job through the long summer vacation. In the case of theological students, this will often consist of a summer's 'experience' in some missionary outpost; few theological students reach the day of their ordination without practical experience of this sort.

In the face of these changing conditions, the Bishop has to make the best decision he can, often giving a good deal of weight to the general form the man has displayed in his 'experience' in a summer mission.

There are too many theological colleges in Canada, with the result that many of them are too small and too poor to have an adequate staff or adequate equipment. And there is still room for a training centre which will take into account all the problems mentioned above, and will develop a positive preachable theology for the average parson, based on sound learning, and integrated with a practical training for the work he is called upon to do.

It is in no way remarkable that Canada has not developed a school of theology. It could not be expected when the Church was still struggling with the labour of expansion and organization, and her scattered colleges were hardly able to supply her needs in ordinands. Even so, individual colleges have reached good standards, and individual men have made their names in theology, usually after 'post-graduate' work in England or the United States. With some degree of consolidation it might be possible to make an advance in this respect.

It may be added that the supply of ordination candidates is usually inadequate to the needs, and that the Canadian Church has always depended on men from the other side of the water whether they come as students or as clergy. We do not, however, take many men from the United States; the current flows south, not north.

We have at present a number of candidates from the armed services in our colleges, and we are informed that they are very promising material; but they are not enough, and they will not be ready for ordination for two or three years.

Relations with other Churches

A word may now be said on the Reunion problem. The geographical factor brings this home to us in a special way. In some areas of Canada our people are settled at great distances from one another and in small groups. Many who are familiar with the conditions think it is impossible to give each of these small groups the ministrations of every type of faith by frequent visits of clergy of each kind. The Romans try to reach them all; the Anglicans try to reach them all; it cannot be said that the others do. There are places where, in spite of all our efforts, we have not been able to do as well as we would like. Sometimes it will happen that one community falls into an Anglican sphere of influence, another into a United, and so on. We have already been obliged to reckon with these conditions, and minister to Christians of other confessions who could not receive spiritual ministrations according to their own rite without unreasonably long journeys. Considerable concessions have been made.

Our Committee on Reunion conferred with representative members of the United Church, and proposed a plan which might meet this problem. Would it be possible for clergy to receive duplicate orders and minister canonically to both sets of people? Could a United Church minister receive Anglican Orders (without denying his present ordination) and an Anglican priest receive United Church orders in the same way? Could such men then serve both types of congregation in these scattered areas?

It is not a blueprint for complete reunion. It is just a Report on a special topic, which has been recommended for study by the General Synod. It will no doubt be discussed at the Lambeth Conference in 1948, and will come before General Synod again in 1949. In the meantime it will be carefully examined from every point of view.

As the Canadian Church has made no decision on the question, and as it is clear that opinions are divided, it would obviously be improper for me to say more at this point. We would like to solve the problem of the scattered congregation. We would like to make a contribution to the work of Reunion. On the other hand, we must make sure that we are on firm ground, and do nothing to divide our Church, or weaken the sound traditions received from our fathers and based on the Bible and Prayer Book which link us with the churches of the Anglican Communion throughout the world.

Recent progress and prospects

I will close with a section on advance in the Canadian Church in recent years.

The period of the depression seemed a dark period for people in Canada, and though the Church responded gallantly to special appeals, her regular year-by-year giving through Apportionments to the General Synod fell from $225,000 in 1929 to $187,627 in 1933. The movement to remedy this situation was already gathering force under the leadership of the present Archbishop of Rupertsland (Dr. L. Ralph Sherman), when the War came with a new challenge. The Church in Canada was not yet independent of help from England. English Missionary Societies, with the utmost generosity, were still sending financial aid to the Canadian Church. At a time when the old country was fighting for her existence and for the freedom of mankind, it did not seem right that this should continue. The Executive of the General Synod met at Stratford in 1940, and following the lead of the Archbishop of Rupertsland, resolved to take this whole burden off the shoulders of the mother-church. The sum of money necessary for this purpose was added to the General Synod Budget and apportioned to the different dioceses. The larger Budget was raised, with increases, through the succeeding years. These new figures have already been given.

There are, of course, a few cases in which societies in the mother-country have desired to continue their help to some part of the mission-field in Canada, and such gifts naturally continue to come. In spite of this, it is true to state that the Canadian Church, at the Stratford Meeting in 1940, assumed all its own burdens, and ceased to be dependent upon the Church in England which had mothered it so long.

There have been further signs of vigour and confidence. The General Synod of 1943 led to the Anglican Advance Appeal of 1946 in which the whole Church set out to raise a sum of $4,300,000 to enable the General Synod to make those advances in various fields which seemed most urgent. The first of these was to set the Pension Fund on a firm basis, so far as it applied to Missionary Dioceses, and the second was to enable the M.S.C.C. to expand its work at home and overseas. The objective of $4,300,000 has been subscribed by the dioceses, and over two million has actually been paid; but as payments are spread over a three-year period, no final figures can be given.

The Advance, however, is not only in the field of finance, and is not to be measured by dollars and cents. The financial appeal was set against a background of Spiritual Advance. The lay committees which were formed in every diocese and district and parish, to undertake this vast nation-wide canvass, had other work as well. During the weeks before Lent there was a house-to-house visitation of all who professed and called themselves Anglicans by laymen and laywomen, to find out where they stood on the subject of church attendance, to offer them friendship and interest, and to invite them to attend their parish church during the Lenten Season. It cannot be claimed that this plan was adopted everywhere; but it was adopted very widely, and leading men and women threw their energies into the novel work of personal visitation; the results, as reported, were most inspiring, and congregations were considerably increased.

With regard to the future of the Canadian Church, I cannot do better than quote a few words from the address delivered by our late Primate at the General Synod in Winnipeg in September 1946:

What is this adventure of the Canadian Church? It is the attempt to build out of the groups of Church of England people scattered over the vast stretches of Canada one organization, which, while it leaves each Diocesan and Provincial entity supreme in its own sphere, yet unites each to all, and all to each, that all may function as one Dominion-wide Church capable, by God's grace, of meeting the difficulties and problems of a country like ours, and of seizing the opportunities with which the modern situation is full.

Canada—our country, our field of work and suffering! What a vision, what a task, what an inspiration! Brethren beloved, I rejoice to have known something of this, to have had a little share in the adventure of the General Synod of the Church of England in Canada under whose auspices we meet, and on whose business we are to occupy ourselves through these coming days, trusting to the merciful guidance and grace of the God of our fathers.

F

THE CHURCH OF INDIA, BURMA AND CEYLON

by the RT. REV. STEPHEN NEILL, *formerly Bishop of Tinnevelly*

Origins

On 31 December 1600 Queen Elizabeth granted a charter to a private company of merchants, bearing the title 'The Governour and Company of Merchants of London trading into the East Indies'. Thus began officially the long connexion of British trade and British authority with the country and peoples of India. In 1614, five chaplains were appointed by the Company. Thus began the mission of the Church of England in India.

One of these first chaplains was the Rev. John Hall, who accompanied Sir Thomas Roe on his embassy to the great Mogul at Ajmere. Within little more than a year, Hall died, and Roe was left lamenting the death of 'a man of a most gentle and mild nature, religious and of unspotted life'. Without delay he wrote in urgent terms to the headquarters of the Company at Surat for the supply of another chaplain: 'Here I cannot live the life of an atheist; let me desire you to endeavour my supply, for I will not abide in this place destitute of the comfort of God's word and heavenly sacraments.' It would have been well if all the English in India had been followers of the simple and unaffected piety of their first ambassador. Unhappily his followers were few. Many of the dispatches of the Company, and the rules put forth for the guidance of the authorities in its factories in India, evince a sincere desire for the glory of God and for good morals among its employees; but action was very far from being equal to aspiration. During the next two and a half centuries, the supply of chaplains always fell far short of the need for them. Englishmen in the army, in government service and in commerce spread far and wide throughout the country. But it often happened that there were chaplains only in the three great presidency cities. Divine service had to be conducted not in churches but in warehouses or business offices hastily converted for the moment to a religious use. In the absence of the chaplain, junior members of the Company's service were required to read prayers for a small fee. Chaplains found it difficult to obtain the respect due to their office and found themselves from time to time engaged in unseemly disputes and contentions with the authorities. Not a few of them became more involved in earthly commerce than in the affairs of the kingdom of God. At times, the natives of the country were inclined to doubt whether the Europeans had any religion at all.

But it would be wrong to represent the situation in too dark colours. For the most part, the chaplains were godfearing and hardworking men. In the face of great difficulties, they maintained at least the minimum of the ordinances of the Church. Under their care, churches were built in the great cities. There was kept before the eyes of men some reminder that the purpose for which man was created was not exhausted by the prosecution of trade and the amassing of the largest possible fortune in the shortest time.

The chaplains were sent out to care for the spiritual welfare of Englishmen; they do not seem to have regarded the proclamation of the Gospel to Indians as falling within their province. It is true that in 1698 the Company passed a new series of regulations, in which it was required that all Ministers appointed to work in India should learn Portuguese and the language of the country, in order 'the better to enable them to instruct the Gentoos in the Protestant Religion'. But, apart from the solitary example of the Bengali boy brought to England by the Rev. Patrick Copeland, and baptized in London on 16 December 1616 by the name Peter (to which later he added somewhat surprisingly the surname Pope), there seems to be no record of any attempt by a chaplain to carry out the regulation and to teach the Protestant religion, or any other, to the inhabitants of India. Nor did any English missionary arrive in India till near the end of the eighteenth century.[1]

Roman Catholic missionaries had been active in India for nearly a century before the arrival of the first English chaplains. From the non-Roman world, the first mission to be established was that founded in 1706 by the King of Denmark in the little

---

[1] The first seems to have been the Rev. A. T. Clarke, B.A., of Trinity College, Cambridge, sent out by the S.P.G. in 1789. He served for only a short time as a missionary, and then transferred to the Chaplaincy service. The famous mission of the English Baptists was founded by William Carey in 1793.

Danish settlement of Tranquebar, on the east coast of India, south of Madras. The king was not willing that the funds supplied by him should be used outside his own dominions; when evangelistic openings were found, as naturally they were, beyond the narrow limits of Danish territory, the missionaries were faced with the difficult problem either of limiting the scope of their work just when it showed signs of profitable expansion, or of undertaking work which they would have no financial means of supporting. They were delivered from their dilemma by the timely aid of the English Society for Promoting Christian Knowledge. This society had been from a very early date interested in the work of the pioneers Ziegenbalg and Plütschau, and had helped them by the gift of a printing press and in other ways. As the work spread into British territory, and permanent stations were established at Fort St. George (Madras) and at Fort St. David (Cuddalore), the English society took over the financial support of these stations, and of the German and Danish Lutheran missionaries by whom they were manned. That part of the Tranquebar mission which was in non-Danish territory was known by the rather misleading title of the English Mission. Thus when the greatest of South Indian missionaries, Christian Friedrich Schwartz, after twelve quiet years in Tranquebar was transferred in 1762 to Trichinopoly, he was described as having 'entered the English Mission service'.

In one respect, however, the title was not a misnomer. As we have seen, the cadre of chaplains was always extremely small. Whenever and wherever British troops or civilians were left without spiritual care, the Lutheran missionaries stepped in, and did their utmost to help them. Most of them had no objection to using the Book of Common Prayer; one of them even made a translation of it into Tamil. Even in Calcutta itself, at a time when there were no resident chaplains, the British community accepted the ministrations of the Swede Kiernander, whose church, built by his own efforts and from his wife's fortune, was for some years after 1771 the only non-Roman place of worship regularly in use in Calcutta.

It cannot but strike an English churchman as strange that in all this long period of more than two centuries the Church of England made no effort to provide an episcopate for the Indian Church. Churchmen at home were lethargic; the general policy of the authorities in India was cordial towards the religions of the country, and most anxious that nothing should be done which should lend countenance to the idea that the government had any intention of interfering with the religious practices of its subjects. It was not till 1813 that, as a result of the ceaseless efforts of Wilberforce and his friends, the Act passed in that year in renewal of the charter of the East India Company included provision for the establishment of one bishopric in India. The relevant section of the Act reads as follows:

And whereas no sufficient provision hath hitherto been made for the maintenance and support of a Church Establishment in the British Territories in the East Indies and other parts within the limits of the said Company's Charter, be it therefore enacted that in case it shall please His Majesty, by His Royal Letters Patent under the Great Seal of the said United Kingdom, to erect, found and constitute, one Bishopric for the whole of the said British Territories in the East Indies, and parts aforesaid; one Archdeaconry for the Presidency of Fort William in Bengal; one Archdeaconry for the Presidency of Fort George on the Coast of Coromandel; and one Archdeaconry for the Presidency and Island of Bombay, on the coast of Malabar; and from time to time to nominate and appoint a Bishop and Archdeacons to such Bishopric and Archdeaconries respectively; the Court of Directors of the said Company . . . shall, and they are hereby required to direct and cause to be paid, certain established salaries to such Bishop and Archdeacons respectively.

This section has been quoted *in extenso* to show the extent to which the extension of the episcopate to India was regarded as an affair belonging to the State and to the Crown, and how little strictly ecclesiastical considerations entered into it.

It did please His Majesty to erect, found and constitute one bishopric for India. On 2 May 1814, he issued Letters Patent, in which it was stated that:

We having great confidence in the learning, morals and probity of our well beloved THOMAS FANSHAW MIDDLETON, Doctor in Divinity, do name and appoint him to be Bishop of the said See of Calcutta, so that the said Thomas Fanshaw Middleton shall be and be taken to be Bishop of the Bishop's See of Calcutta, and may by the virtue of this Our nomination and appointment enter into and possess the said Bishop's see as the Bishop thereof, without any let or impediment of Us, Our heirs or successors.

Bishop Middleton arrived in Calcutta on 28 November 1814. At once he became aware of the difficulties and uncertainties of his position. The Church of England had existed in India for two hundred years, without any regulation or episcopal supervision, except such distant and vague authority as had been exercised by successive Bishops of London. His See was so vast that it was impossible that he should ever encompass it in his visitations. But what pressed upon him most hardly was the complete inapplicability of the parochial and diocesan system as he had known it in England to the situation of the Church in India. He was faced with two classes of ministers unknown in England— chaplains whose nomination and appointment to their stations was in the hands of the Company, an authority which jealously refused to abate in favour of the Bishop one jot of its prerogatives; and missionaries, almost all of them in Lutheran and not in Anglican orders, who were appointed by missionary societies to preach the Gospel to the heathen, and who had not as yet any parochial location or habitation. It was the question of the missionaries which most sorely perplexed him. In a well-known phrase he declared that he must either license them or silence them. The number of chaplains was inadequate, that of the missionaries was annually growing; to refuse to permit the missionaries to minister in English to Europeans where their services were desired would seem to be imposing intolerable bonds on the service of the Gospel. As far as Bengal was concerned, the Bishop never saw his way to a solution of the problem. In South India, the situation was very different; the preaching of the Gospel had been so far successful that large Christian congregations had been built up, and to these the missionaries stood very much in the relation of parish priests. The fact that they were in Lutheran orders only, and had not had episcopal ordination, seems not to have presented any insuperable difficulty to the mind of the Bishop. After his visit to Trichinopoly, reached in the course of his vistation on 28 February 1816, he wrote to the Archdeacon of Calcutta:

The mission at Tanjore pleased me exceedingly. Mr. Kohloff is almost another Schwartz. He attended me to Trichinopoly: and when I came away he pronounced over me a prayer for my future welfare. Looking at his labours, I could not but feel that the less was blessed of the greater. Mr. Pohle at Trichinopoly does equal honour to our mission. He has been a very distinguished man in point of learning; but he cannot in the course of nature have long to live. . . . I stayed at Trichinopoly five days, during which I inspected the mission, consecrated a church, licensed the clergyman, confirmed and delivered a charge to about 100 persons, mostly adults, and preached twice on the Sunday, which in this climate is no small exertion, and leaves one quite exhausted.

The clergyman licensed at Trichinopoly was the Rev. Mr. Pohle, an admirable German missionary, whose name is commemorated in the village of Pohlaiyarpuram in the Diocese of Tinnevelly. It is notable that, though both he and Mr. Kohloff had received only Lutheran orders, Bishop Middleton felt no difficulty in approving of the ministrations, pastoral and sacramental, of both of them, and actually gave his authority by licence to the work of Pohle in Trichinopoly. In neither case did he raise the question of re-ordination according to the Anglican rite.

The policy of Bishop Heber, who held the See from 1823 to 1826, was rather different. On his arrival, he immediately cut the knot by licensing the missionaries, thus recognizing that they were under episcopal jurisdiction though not tied to the work of a stationary parish. But he did desire that those who had not received Anglican orders should do so. There could not but be considerable inconveniences arising from the fact that missionaries who had received Lutheran ordination were not permitted to minister in the Churches ordinarily served by chaplains of the Company. In December 1826, the Bishop admitted to deacon's orders three of the Lutheran missionaries, and also the eminent Abdool Messeeh, who had owed his conversion to Henry Martyn, and who was also at the time a clergyman in Lutheran orders. This action was severely criticized by some, who went so far as to accuse the Bishop of being guilty of such a profanation as attends the wilful repetition of the sacrament of Holy Baptism. To these criticisms, the Bishop replied in a dignified letter, dated 23 December 1825 and addressed to the Reverend Deocar Schmidt:

You suppose that I generally admit ordination by presbyters without a bishop to be valid. I do not admit this. All I said is that, when a Christian nation has, by unfortunate circumstances, lost its apostolical succession of bishops, the continuance of ministers being a thing absolutely needful and essential, those good men are not to be censured who perpetuate it by the best means in their power. And were I to return to Germany, I would as before humbly and thankfully avail myself of the preaching and sacramental ordinances of the Lutheran evangelical church, not doubting that they are a true church of Christ, and that the Spirit of God is with them as, I trust, he is with us also. But though an imperfect ordination may, doubtless, be accepted by our Lord and common Master, and though a church, under circumstances such as I have described, may remain a true church still, it does not follow that, where this supposed deficiency may be supplied, it may not be adviseable for a Minister of the Gospel either to seek fresh orders himself, or to counsel others to do so. And this may be more especially adviseable where his, or their, ministerial utility is likely to be much augmented by a closer union with a church under (what I conceive to be) the ancient discipline.

But it is to be noted also that in South India Bishop Heber accepted the arrangements made by Bishop Middleton. In Trichinopoly, Tanjore and elsewhere, the Lutheran missionaries in the service of the Church of England were left undisturbed in their work, and no suggestion was made by the Bishop that they should be re-ordained.

The dual ministry continued for almost twenty years after the death of Bishop Heber. In 1829, the Society for the Propagation of the Gospel took over the stations maintained in South India by the S.P.C.K., and took over with them the six missionaries who were not in Anglican orders. These men were allowed to continue in their work without re-ordination. The most distinguished of them, Kohloff of Tanjore, the foster-son of the great Christian Friedrich Schwartz, continued at his post until 1844, assisted by a younger missionary in Anglican orders sent out by the S.P.G. It was the rule of that society to send out only missionaries who had received ordination after the Anglican order.

The Church Missionary Society, at the outset of its work in India, was faced by two grave difficulties: the unwillingness of the English Bishops to ordain men for its service overseas, and the unwillingness of Anglicans to engage in missionary service. In consequence, almost all its early missionaries in India were German Lutherans. One of the most distinguished of these was the Prussian, C. T. E. Rhenius, a man of high ability and apostolic devotion, who in 1820 was sent to Palamcottah to open up the work of the C.M.S. in the Tinnevelly area, and who is justly reckoned by the Tinnevelly Church as its second founder. After ten years of work, Rhenius, faced by the problems of what would now be called a Mass Movement, desired himself to ordain some of his catechists, as had been done at their discretion by the older Lutheran missionaries. The authorities of the C.M.S. replied that a practice which had been inevitable in days when there had been no Bishop in India could not be continued after the establishment of episcopacy in India, and that all ordinations for work in their areas must in future conform to the Anglican rule. This decision led to an unedifying controversy, and ultimately to a schism, which broke up the promising work in Tinnevelly for more than three years, and ended only with the death of Rhenius. This unhappy incident had, however, the advantage of making clear the Anglican position; the dual ministry was accepted without question, as it had existed throughout the eighteenth century; but, since all ordinations for the future were to be episcopal, the dual ministry would automatically come to an end with the death of the surviving missionaries and Indian pastors, who, though only in Lutheran orders, had been licensed to minister the word and sacraments in the Church of England. By 1861, the process of absorption was complete, and the Church in India, like that in England, had an episcopal ministry and no other.[1]

It has been necessary to describe in some detail the organization of the dual ministry and its gradual resolution into a single type. This was the most curious and original feature of the life of the Church of England in India; the full facts are not very easily accessible, but are indispensable for a right understanding of the history of the Church.

Development of Self-government

In the Act for the renewal of the Company's charter passed in 1833, provision was made for the foundation of the Bishoprics of Madras and Bombay. Of these, the former came into existence on 10 October 1835, the latter on 1 October 1837. In 1845, Colombo was added to the Indian bishoprics, one of the first to

[1] I am not certain as to the date at which the C.M.S. ceased to appoint Lutherans as its missionaries in India. Perhaps the last appointment was that of Peter Fjellstedt, the distinguished Swede who was from 1831 to 1834 a colleague of Rhenius in Palamcottah, and was later greatly used in stirring up missionary enthusiasm in his own country.

come into existence in connexion with the Colonial Bishoprics Fund. The Indian episcopate was still sketchy; but at least the beginnings of the lines of an Indian province were beginning to appear.

The further development of the Indian episcopate was hindered by endless delays and frustrations. The Act of 1833 had fixed the boundaries of the three dioceses, and no alteration could be made in them without the passing of a supplementary Act of Parliament. With that curious and almost malevolent anticlericalism, which led certain parties in the House of Commons in the high Victorian age to oppose every kind of ecclesiastical legislation, every suggestion of the better ordering of the Indian Church was steadfastly voted down. After much opposition, permission was at last obtained in 1877 for the creation of the bishoprics of Lahore and Rangoon. As neither of these fell within territory which had been under the jurisdiction of the Company in 1833, the constitution of the new dioceses did not involve any modification in the sacrosanct Act of that year. For the formation of the other dioceses urgently needed by a rapidly growing church recourse was had to what may almost be called subterfuges. It was noticed by someone that Travancore and Cochin, being Indian native states, were not properly British territory or part of the dominions of the Sovereign of England. It was therefore possible to take advantage of the Act passed in 1841, in connexion with the formation of the Anglican Bishopric in Jerusalem, which provided for the consecration of bishops and the establishment of bishoprics outside the limits of the British Empire. The Diocese of Travancore and Cochin, to include the territories of these two states only, was constituted in 1879;[1] the first bishop was consecrated on 25 July of that year. The excessive burden which rested on the Bishop of Madras was lightened in 1877 by appointing two Assistant Bishops to supervise the missionary areas of the C.M.S. and the S.P.G. in Tinnevelly. This unsatisfactory arrangement was nowhere else repeated. When the work in Chota Nagpur, still a part of the diocese of Calcutta, had reached the point at which the appointment of a bishop became desirable, yet another arrangement was devised; a bishop

---

[1] In practice, the diocese has also included the tiny settlements of Anjengo and British Cochin, which were parts of the British Empire. Many such adjustments have been necessary in different parts of India.

was to be appointed 'who should receive a commission from the Bishop of Calcutta, and who would exercise ecclesiastical jurisdiction in his diocese by consensual compact'. This method was followed in setting up the dioceses of Tinnevelly, Dornakal, and Assam, and in part that of Lucknow. The arrangement, though from the strict ecclesiastical point of view unusual, worked quite well in practice; the only respect in which these quasi-dioceses differed from the real thing was that, as the jurisdiction of the Archdeacons of Calcutta and Madras had been fixed by the Act of 1833, and could be altered only by Act of Parliament, not even by Act of God, the new dioceses had to forego the inestimable advantage of having Archdeacons of their own.

Anglican churchmanship is an adaptable thing and skilled in making the best of an undesirable situation. The Church made great progress even under the unfavourable conditions of the establishment. But it is not difficult to see that for an increasingly missionary Church to be tied hand and foot by Acts passed in London by a remote and not always well-informed British Parliament could not but be in the highest degree inimical to its well-being. The Church in India was simply part of the Church of England. The Act of 1883 had conferred on the Bishop of Calcutta the title of Metropolitan, which he still holds and alone among the Metropolitans of the Anglican Communion habitually uses, and had given him certain rights and dignities, but had naturally withheld the title of Archbishop, Calcutta still being under the Primacy of the Archbishop of Canterbury. So tightly were the bonds drawn that, when the Book of Common Prayer was translated into the vernaculars, these versions had to follow exactly the order of the Church of England; any part which was translated had to be translated exactly and in full; even such minor concessions as the omission of the 'Forms of Prayer to be used at Sea' in parts of India more than a thousand miles from the coast were technically inadmissible.[1]

Difficult relationships with two governments, that of India and that of England, were not the only factors which made the work of the Indian Church exceptionally difficult and complex. From the beginning of the nineteenth century there were at all times three different classes of ministers: chaplains, missionaries, and

[1] A comparison is suggested with the remark about earthquakes in Chapter I (p. 1).

Indian pastors mostly in the employ of the missionary societies. The chaplains were appointed by the Secretary of State for India; the control of the Bishop over them was limited by the terms of their appointments. The missionaries could not exercise their office without a licence from the Bishop, but their direct responsibility was to the local secretary and committee of their society, and through them to the society in England. It was not easy to see how a direct relation between them and the diocese could be achieved. One of the least happy attempts to secure closer integration was that made by Bishop R. S. Copleston in the early days of his episcopate in Colombo (1875–1903). His proposal was that the English parochial system should be so far introduced that the chaplains should be licensed as rectors, and the missionaries in their area as their curates. It was a well-intentioned but fantastic and unworkable scheme. It is no unfair criticism of one who became in later life one of the greatest and wisest of the bishops who have served the Indian province that this fruit of his early inventiveness was put forth without the least understanding of the situation with which he had to deal. Nevertheless the proposals were pressed with such vigour that all the C.M.S. missionaries in the island resigned. Some time elapsed before harmony was restored. The missionaries were not licensed as curates.

The Church of India not merely had three types of ministers, but had three distinct types of Christians to be ministered to. There were those Europeans who were only temporarily, though often for long periods together, in India; there were the Europeans permanently resident, mostly soldiers and their children who had made the country their home, and the Anglo-Indians, as they are now called, the descendants of unions between European men and Indian women; there were the Indian converts from the non-Christian religions. The interests of these three classes diverged considerably. In many places, there was little fellow-feeling between European and Indian Christians, the latter not infrequently being given, most undeservedly, a bad name by the former. To make a real unity out of these disparate elements was a tremendous task; it cannot be said that it has as yet been finally accomplished.

But grave as were the disadvantages under which the Church in India laboured, the most serious drawback of all was the failure of the Church of England to provide its daughter church with any means of self-government. The Synod of the Church in New Zealand was formed as long ago as 1857; the Church in India had to wait till 1930 before receiving such rights of self-government as made possible the formation of a governing body having genuine synodical authority.

In practice things were not quite as bad as these general statements might suggest. Before 1866, the three bishops of the Indian sub-continent had occasionally met for counsel. From 1873, meetings of bishops took place not at regular intervals, but sufficiently often to make a real series. After the conference held at Nagpur in 1873, certain resolutions were published under the heading 'Resolutions passed at the Conference of the three Bishops'. Such resolutions had weight, but no authority. They carried, that is to say, to the minds of faithful Christians, such weight as belongs to the considered judgment of experienced bishops, deliberating on matters of high import to the Church. But they were simply the expression of the opinion of those bishops; they had no binding power, and none of the bishops could institute any action on the basis of such resolutions, if at any point they contravened or went beyond the ecclesiastical law at the time in force in England.

It was this limitation which made the bishops feel their position to be intolerable and led them to seek such liberty as was enjoyed by the province of New Zealand. In 1877, four bishops agreed to the following resolution:

That the time has come for taking steps to provide a system of synodical action, both Diocesan and Provincial, and that we undertake to ascertain the feelings of the Clergy and Laity of our several Dioceses in regard to the constitution of diocesan Synods.

Six years later, a more decisive step was taken. The bishops assembled in Calcutta set forth a pastoral addressed 'to all people of whatever race and religion in India and Ceylon', in which they set forth their ideas of the task to which the Church of England was called in India, and for the first time, adumbrated the thought of the Church of England in India transforming itself into the Church of India. One passage of this pastoral deserves to be quoted in full:

We do not aim at imposing upon an Indian Church anything which is distinctively English or even European. The Word, the Sacraments

and the Episcopal Ministry—these are unchangeable. They belong to
no age or country. As they met the needs of Europe or of Asia many
centuries ago, they will meet the needs of the India of to-day. But in
regard to the conditions under which these are presented, the Church
adapts herself, and we desire to see her adapt herself more and more,
to the circumstances and to the tempers of every race of men; and
from these, under the guidance of the Holy Spirit, her forms of service, her customs and rules and institutions will take an impress. We
trust that God has given this mission to the Church of England, to
give to India that pure truth, and that divinely appointed order, in
possession of which India shall work out her own spiritual life, bear
spiritual fruit of her own, contribute her own spiritual gifts to the
wealth of the universal church of God.

For twenty-five years nothing further was done, and the idea
of synodical government slept. The Diocese of Colombo alone,
always independent in relation to its larger neighbour, went forward with the formation of a Diocesan Synod, which, though it
had no canonical authority, worked well within the limits of the
ecclesiastical tradition of the time.

But during this quarter of a century, the Church did not stand
still. The number of Indian Christians was steadily on the increase. Mass movements were beginning to bring in the fore-
runners of those literally hundreds of thousands of converts who
have been gathered in in this century. Indians were being ordained to the priesthood in ever-increasing numbers; their
qualifications were rising steadily away from the rather primitive
level of achievement required of the village clergy in the pioneering days. Already in 1869, in what is now the cathedral in Palamcottah, in one day seventeen Indians had been admitted as deacons
and fifteen ordained as priests, probably the largest ordination
yet held in the Church in India. Already Travancore had an
Indian Archdeacon. Time was ripe and more than ripe for an
advance towards self-government and independence.

The next step was taken in 1910. The Bishops decided to
enlarge their meeting by summoning to it clerical and lay representatives. When the Episcopal Synod next met, at the beginning of 1913, the bishops, now thirteen in number, and including
for the first time an Indian, Vedanayagam Samuel Azariah, consecrated Bishop of Dornakal on 29 December 1912, had with
them twenty-two clerical and seventeen lay representatives from

the dioceses of the Church in India. It must be emphasized that this body, though beginning to bear more recognizably the likeness of a Synod, had that character only by courtesy, since, though it could discuss, it could not decide; it had no canonical authority to make any decision which would be in any way binding on the conscience of any member of the Church. Its chief task was, in fact, to consider the next step on the road to obtaining real synodical government for the Church it had been summoned to represent.

The bishops, priests and laity of the Church in India, thus assembled, declared themselves unhesitatingly in favour of synodical government, and of proceeding as far as the legal hindrances permitted in the achievement of it. In the advice presented to the Bishops, the clerical and lay assessors recommended that clerical and lay representatives should be added to the existing Provincial Synod (that title being given to the informal and legally unrecognized meetings of the Bishops). They proposed that there should be sixty clerical and sixty lay representatives (a number not as yet reached in the General Council of the Indian Church, a body the efficiency of which, like that of the Church Assembly (of the Church of England), is in inverse ratio to its size), and that these representatives should be chosen by Diocesan Synods or Conferences. As some of the dioceses had not at that time either Synod or Conference, this proposal contained within itself a suggestion made explicit in the seventeenth resolution of the Episcopal Synod on that occasion that 'in the matter of Diocesan Synods, the synod recommends that each bishop take steps as soon as possible for the formation of a Diocesan Synod'.

The Provincial Council, a body still without legal status or canonical authority, held its first meeting in 1922. Its main concern for the next eight years was to bring about those changes, which would make it possible for the Church in India to govern itself, and under God, to direct its own destinies. This would involve the legal separation of the Church in India from the Church of England, the reconsideration of the position of chaplains appointed to the Indian Ecclesiastical Establishment and of the congregations to which they ministered, and the drawing up of a complete constitution, under which the liberated Church should be governed. In January 1926, the Provincial Council, with a full understanding of what was involved, drew up and passed the following resolution:

That the Provincial Council desires that the legal union between the Church of England and the Church of England in India should be dissolved, and that any enactments necessary for enabling the Church in India to govern its own affairs after that dissolution should be passed.

It would be tedious to narrate all the steps by which the liberty so eagerly desired was achieved by the Indian Church. The Bill to effect the necessary legal changes was introduced into the House of Lords on 10 May 1927. The Indian Church Measure was introduced into the Church Assembly on 4 July 1927, and was passed through all its stages in record time, unanimously approved by the Assembly on 7 July, and laid before Parliament on 25 July. During the next few months, all the further stages necessary to the enactment of the Bill as law were passed through, and on 22 December 1928, the Indian Church Act received the Royal Assent. The Indian Church was free.

But to be legally free is not the same thing as to enjoy freedom. Before freedom could be enjoyed, the Church in India had to complete the framing of its constitution, make arrangements for the holding of its property and settle some outstanding issues arising out of the long connexion of the Church with the State. In the end, the long process was completed on 31 January 1930, when

'we the Bishops . . . and representatives of the clergy and laity of those Dioceses, which together make up the Church of India, Burma, and Ceylon, hitherto known as the Church of England in India and the Church of England in Ceylon, assembled in a General Council at Calcutta on the thirty-first day of January, 1930, in virtue of every authority whether inherent or representative to us respectively appertaining, and in exercise of the above recited power conferred upon the General Council of the Church of India, Burma, and Ceylon by the Measure aforesaid do now adopt and enact the following Constitution, Canons and Rules and each and every Declaration, Canon and Rule thereof.'

To this declaration all the bishops and all the other representatives of the dioceses appended their signatures.

Working of Self-government

The *Constitution, Canons and Rules of the Church of India, Burma and Ceylon* is a work of 327 large pages, foreseeing and providing for almost every contingency which can possibly befall a Church in the course of its life and witness. In its main lines, it follows the same form as the Constitutions of other churches of the Anglican Communion, which have in like manner attained their independence. It is not necessary to do more than draw attention to some features in the life of the Church of India which diverge a little from the general pattern.

The desire of the Church of India to remain faithful to its great Catholic heritage is so often emphasized and safeguarded in so many ways as to make it clear that the legal changes made by the Act of 1928 did not bring into existence a new Church, but simply made possible the efficient organization of what was already an existing Church within the one fellowship of the whole Church of Christ. At the same time, the Constitution makes it clear that independence does not mean spiritual separation and that the Church of India is most concerned to maintain full communion with all branches of the Anglican Communion throughout the world. There is however at one point in the declarations which preface the Constitution a new and significant note; the latter part of Declaration 21 reads as follows:

When the legal connexion formed by Acts of Parliament between the Church of England and the Church in India was removed, the Church in India, Burma and Ceylon gained the rightful freedom of a regional Church within the universal Church to direct its own life and to bear its own responsibilities. This Church aims at accomplishing for India, Burma and Ceylon what the Church of England has accomplished for England. As the Church of England, receiving Catholic Christianity from the undivided Church, has given a characteristically English interpretation of it, so the Church of India, Burma and Ceylon aspires to give a characteristically national interpretation of that same common faith and life.

At the time when this declaration was accepted, the word *national* had not acquired the sinister connotation which is now almost inseparable from it. Even taking the words in the sense which they bore in 1928, it is permissible to wonder whether the framers of the declaration had thought out the full implications

G

of what they wrote, and whether a national interpretation of Christianity is really possible. The excessive isolation of the Church of England from all the larger currents of Christian life over a very long period of its life may serve as a warning of the dangers that may beset the Indian Church, unless the emphasis on national development is fully balanced by an equal emphasis on the necessity of standing within the Catholic Church of Christ.

The organization of the Church, on the basis of its Constitution, is thoroughly democratic. A diocese cannot be recognized as fully organized, until it has a Diocesan Council, consisting of the Bishop, all the priests of the diocese holding the Bishop's licence, and lay representatives, at least three-quarters of whom have been elected by the adult communicants of the diocese. The exact qualification for representatives and voters may vary from diocese to diocese, as each diocese has its own constitution under the Constitution of the Province. In most dioceses, the Diocesan Council is based on a solid structure of congregational, parochial or deanery councils, these again being organized on a thoroughly democratic basis. There are those who hold that in the last fifteen years the Church has been the only democratic body in India, and that not the least of its services has been the education of thousands of Indians in democratic method, procedure and responsibility. The laity have been brought into connexion with the life of the Church at every point.

One of the manifestations of true Christian democracy is the election of bishops by the clergy and laity of the dioceses over which they are to bear rule. The Indian constitution contains provision for various forms and methods of election. That which has been adopted in most of the Indian dioceses deserves description, as avoiding some of the vices almost inseparable from some other methods of election.

Any five members of the Diocesan Council may nominate any bishop or priest of the Anglican Communion as a candidate for the vacant bishopric. One so nominated may not withdraw his name, but may indicate reasons why he is not likely to accept the bishopric if elected.

The clergy and lay representatives then meet in a special session of the Diocesan Council, and, after prayer, proceed to elect a panel of persons, not less than two and not more than four, from among whom the final choice of a bishop is to be made, each member of the council having as many votes as the number of persons to be chosen to the panel, but not being permitted to give more than one vote to one candidate. The votes are then sealed up, and sent to the Metropolitan of the Province, who, with two other bishops chosen by the diocese concerned, counts the votes and arranges them according to the method known as the single transferable vote, thus forming the panel of persons elected by the diocese, from among whom the Metropolitan and the two bishops with him are to make the final selection. It is not laid down in the Constitution, that the bishops must choose the person who has received the largest number of votes, though in practice it appears that they have ordinarily done so. It is provided that 'if only one person shall be found to have received the necessary quota of votes, the Bishops shall not be bound to appoint that person as Bishop for the Diocese, but may themselves choose some other person'.

This rather complicated method avoids many difficulties. It saves the diocese from the frustrating experience of seeing two strong parties fail to secure the election of either of two favoured candidates, and fall back on some colourless candidate, in order that somehow or other the place may be filled. It ensures that a number of names shall be before the diocese. It makes it possible, by the system of plural voting, to secure a much wider indication of the mind and desire of the diocese than is possible when only a single vote is given. On the other hand, there are serious drawbacks. Very great power is put into the hands of the Metropolitan and the bishops who sit with him. It is possible for them to impose on a diocese a candidate who has secured less than 10 per cent of the first votes in the election, and who can therefore hardly be regarded as in any real sense the choice of the diocese. It makes it possible for them, in certain circumstances, to appoint as bishop a candidate who had failed to secure even the minimum quota necessary for his election to the panel, or even to impose on the diocese a man whose name has never been considered by it at all. Nevertheless, of all the methods of election in use anywhere in the world, this is probably that which combines the greatest advantages with the smallest drawbacks.

In any election there is a tendency for the electors to play for safety rather than to adventure themselves on unknown seas. Since 1930, fifteen elections of diocesan bishops have taken place in the Indian Church. In one case only has a candidate who had not previously served in India been elected to the vacant see. In the majority of cases, the choice has fallen on a priest resident and working in the diocese. This inbreeding has its dangers. In a province where the total number of priests is so small, and the tendency to develop a peculiarly Indian outlook is so strong, the strengthening of the episcopate by enrichment from other provinces would seem to be desirable.

Even more disturbing is the reluctance of the Indian Church to elect Indian bishops. In most of the Diocesan Councils, there is an overwhelming Indian majority; on many occasions, Indian candidates have been among those nominated. Yet, of the fifteen elections, one only has resulted in the election of an Indian. This indicates that, in spite of the intense national feeling which has prevailed in the Church as elsewhere in India, Indian Christians have steadfastly refused to allow racial or national feelings to interfere with anything so solemn as the choice of a chief pastor for a church. But this excessive caution and lack of trust in Indian leadership are disappointing. It is only by bearing responsibility that individuals and churches can learn to bear responsibility.

One peculiar feature of the Indian constitution is that the bishops continue to meet as the Episcopal Synod, as well as taking their part, as the House of Bishops, in the business of the General Council of the Church. This arrangement is without parallel in other provinces of the Anglican Communion. The one strong argument in favour of the dual arrangement is the size of India, and the impossibility of frequent meetings of the General Council. Any group of bishops can meet for personal intercourse and mutual counsel; but it is perhaps desirable that in India the bishops should meet with rather more authority than attaches to a private meeting for consultation. The dual arrangement was agreed to only after the bishops had given most stringent guarantees against the use of the Synod to establish any kind of episcopal autocracy. 'They made it clear that the Episcopal Synod would do nothing which the Provincial Council could do; they undertook not to issue any resolutions dealing with matters which would naturally form the substance of normative resolutions of the Provincial Council, unless there was some very urgent reason for action, and even then they would issue resolutions in the form of advice which Diocesan Councils or churchmen generally were asked to act on pending consideration by the General Council.' A further safeguard is found in the canon which requires, that except when the Episcopal Synod meets to confirm the election or appointment of persons to be bishops of the Province, the Metropolitan shall do his utmost to secure the presence of priests equal in number to the bishops as assessors, and of at least four laymen. Though these assessors do not vote, their presence ensures contact between the mind of the bishops and the mind of the Church. But the continued existence of the Episcopal Synod in separation from the General Council does make possible at all times a loss of the due balance intended by the Constitution, and introduces at least potentially an element of episcopal autocracy, against which the other elements in the Church have to be on their guard.

The transition from subjection to independence in 1930 was made so quietly and smoothly that probably the majority of Indian churchmen did not realize at the time that anything important had happened. It was not long, however, before the changes in the situation of the Church began to manifest themselves.

The first of these was in the psychological rather than in the material realm. The use of the name 'Church of India, Burma and Ceylon' began to have its effects on the minds of the Indian Christians, who by this time far outnumbered Europeans and Anglo-Indians in the membership of the Church. They began to feel as never before that this was their Church, something in which they were entitled to exercise the functions of government, for the maintenance of which they must take responsibility, and the growth of which would depend in the main on their exertions.

In the second place, the election of bishops, instead of their nomination by the Crown or by the Archbishop of Canterbury, marked the reality of independence and of responsibility.

Third, the passing of the Act made possible the beginnings of independent liturgical development in the Indian Province. The first Canon of Chapter XXI of the Constitution lays down the following 'guiding principles concerning the development of public worship which the Church of India, Burma and Ceylon sets before itself':

(1) It desires to work towards the development of forms of worship congenial to the nature of the Indian races.

(2) It desires to give opportunity for great liberty of experiment in the direction of such development, but at the same time to safeguard provincial unity.

A wise conservatism has guided the steps of the Province in its progress towards liturgical differentiation. There has been what some would regard as a rather precipitate acceptance of the abortive English Prayer Book of 1928. Certain changes have been permitted in the Communion Service, all tending towards the type familiar in the order of that service in the Scottish Episcopal, (American) Protestant Episcopal and South African Churches. A special liturgy has been sanctioned for Ceylon; in this are blended together, not always quite happily, traditional Eastern, Western and Anglican elements. But none of these changes can be said to bear any relation to a 'form of worship congenial to the nature of the Indian races'.

It is indeed very difficult to work towards any such forms. Indian Christians derive from both Hindu and Muslim backgrounds, and these are so radically opposed the one to the other that any form of worship which is congenial to one is not likely to make any appeal to the other. There is the further difficulty that the vast majority of Indian Christians come from the classes which, through no fault of their own, have been disinherited from the great wealth of Indian culture, and have no intellectual or cultural forms into which the Christian faith can readily be poured.

Nevertheless the new liturgical freedom has been a great boon to the Church. The Diocese of Dornakal has probably gone furthest, under its Indian Bishop, in experimenting with the use of Indian music and forms of ceremonial, though without wide departure from the traditional Anglican framework. Almost every diocese has made a beginning with extra services for the special occasions of the Indian year, and with some modifications in the existing liturgical practice. As every change is loyally reported to the Episcopal Synod, there is a real safeguard for unity, and the possibility of the enrichment of the whole Church by successful experiment in one part of it.

Position of the Church

It is time now to give a brief description of the Indian Province, as it exists at the time of writing, August 1947.

Although it claims the proud title of the Church of India, Burma and Ceylon, this Church is neither the oldest nor the largest nor the best equipped of the Churches which serve God in India. The oldest of all the Churches is the Syrian Church of Malabar, now sadly weakened by its many divisions and by the inward-looking tendency from which it is only gradually beginning to break free. By far the largest is the Roman Catholic Church, which includes probably not less than half of all the Christians in India and has the great advantages of strict unity of organization and strong supplies of men and money from many Western countries. In South India, the best-manned and organized of all missions is that of the English Methodists; in the north, the most extensive and grandiose of Christian projects are those of the Methodist Episcopal Church associated with the Church of that name in America. In comparison with these, the Church of India figures only about halfway down the list in antiquity, numbers and efficiency.

Quite accurate statistics are hard to come by. It is probable that at the time of writing, the Church of India numbers rather more than 800,000 adherents. Though much stronger in the south than in the north, it is represented in all the provinces of British India and in most of the larger native states. It is organized in sixteen dioceses, with three Indian diocesan Bishops, and four Indian Assistant Bishops. Most of the Europeans in the country belong to the Church of India; but a large majority of its members are Indian-born, and with every year the Indian element tends to increase in relation to the European.

Comparatively small though the Church of India is in relation to other Christian bodies, and infinitesimal in comparison to the total population of the country, its influence is not to be gauged by its numerical strength. This influence depends a little, but only to a small extent, on its connexion with the ruling power; this has worked far more to its detriment than to its advantage. The deep influence of the Anglican Communion in India on Christian thought and strategy and on the policies of governments has been due to two facts—that, although both the chaplaincy and missionary work of the Church have at all times been disgracefully undermanned, it has been fortunate in having been served by a number of men of superlative ability and devotion; and also that it has always numbered among its members some laymen who have surpassed the official representatives of the Church in their zeal for the kingdom of God. Space forbids the enumeration of many names. Among clergy and missionaries of eminence, the Indian Church will always remember with gratitude Henry Martyn, saint and translator; Reginald Heber, Bishop; Daniel Wilson, Bishop; George Alfred Lefroy, Bishop; Thomas Gajetan Ragland, Priest; and among Indians, Vedanayagam Samuel Azariah, Bishop; Imad-ud-din, Priest; Vedanayaga Sastriar, poet; Narayan Vaman Tilak, poet; and an uncounted multitude whose names are written in the book of life. Among the laymen, the most memorable group is that which laid the foundations of righteous and Christian rule in north-western India, and also founded many of the early mission stations in that region— the Lawrences, Edwardes, Montgomery, Thomason and a dozen others.

In the twentieth century, the Church is the beneficiary of the immense labour of education carried out by the missionaries in the nineteenth. To some extent all Churches have reaped the advantage, the Anglicans perhaps more than any other body. One of the main features of social change in India in the last fifty years has been the emergence of a large middle class of professional people, doctors, lawyers, teachers, government servants and so forth. Of these, a surprisingly large percentage are Christians and Anglicans. Their profession carries them all over India, so that it is probably safe to say that there is no town of 5,000 inhabitants anywhere in India which will not have its Christian community, tiny perhaps, but existing, though no missionary work may have been carried on within a hundred miles of it. On higher levels, many Anglicans have held positions of great trust and influence in public affairs. There was a time when the Mayor of Delhi was an Anglican clergyman. It is no accident that at the time of writing, one member of the Cabinet of India, the Speaker of the Assembly of a great province, and the minister for local self-government in the Congress ministry of another province, are all Anglican Christians.

But these Christians of eminence are the exception. The base and foundation of the Church of India is the village; the vast majority of its members are villagers, living laboriously and penuriously from the land, and spending their whole lives within sound of the bell of their village church. Many of them come from the depressed classes, and suffer still from the physical and psychological effects of malnutrition, oppression, and the contempt of men no better than themselves. A considerable proportion however, like the hardy Nadars of the extreme south, come from stocks which though not wealthy have never belonged to the depressed class, and from independent tribes, such as the Santals, living in their mountains, and maintaining to a considerable degree the habits and outlook of their free ancestors. These village folk are magnificent material for the Christian faith, rather slow, like other farmers in other countries, in their ways, not for the most part easily stirred, yet loyal, tenacious and devoted, and ready to give undying affection to those who have won their confidence.

The typical community is that in which between a hundred and two hundred Christians live in a village, with perhaps twice that number of non-Christians round them. The centre of the village is the church, perhaps a very simple unadorned structure, built by the hands of the villagers themselves and therefore all the more highly prized by them. Each day, the church bell calls the people to prayer. In 1939, it was ascertained by careful study of figures that in the diocese of Tinnevelly, on an average, 20,000 Christians were attending evening service in their village churches every day. The festivals of the Church are the festivals of the Christian village; at every point the Church leaves its mark on their lives and is woven into their thoughts. This does not mean that every village Christian is a saint; far from it; those who know and love them best have most to lament in their constant failure to live up to what they know to be the Christian way. It does mean, however, that the integration of the Church with the life of the people, which has so largely disappeared in the industrialized West, is still a living reality in the Church of India, and is the foundation on which, in spite of ignorance and poverty, a genuine structure of Christian living can be built.

These village congregations are served by teachers drawn from the village population itself and equipped with a very slender stock of knowledge for their work. These in turn are supervised by village clergy, most of whom have to care for not one village but perhaps a dozen, scattered over a hundred square miles or more. There has been a steady rise in the standard of the Indian clergy. Underpaid, spiritually isolated as most of them are, they carry on their work with a faithfulness that would put to shame many of their brethren in older and better-established churches. But the work of theological training, like all other parts of the work of the Church in India, has been so undermanned and so ill equipped that the standard attained is less than is worthy of the men sent for training, and very much lower than is needed either for the adequate shepherding of the growing Church of Christ or for the presentation of the Gospel to the educated non-Christians of the country. Most thoughtful members of the Church, if asked at what point its work most urgently needs to be strengthened, would probably choose the training of the ministry as having priority over all other needs.

Present changes

Before this chapter is in print, two immense changes will have taken place in India and in the state of the Indian Church.

On 18 August 1947, British rule will cease in India, and autonomy in the form of Dominion status will be handed over to the two Dominions of India and Pakistan. No one can foresee what effects this is likely to have on the Church and its life. It cannot be said that such connexion as the Church in India has had with the ruling power has been to its advantage. Ecclesiastical affairs have been tucked away as a not very important branch of the Department of Defence, and the influence of the authorities has been much more restrictive than expansive. On missionary work the government has at most times looked with a step-motherly eye. The complete separation between Church and State, consequent on the handing over of power, is not likely to cause the Church any serious inconvenience. There are those who fear that, with the departure of the British power, and as the new Indian governments feel more sure of their position, there will be a tendency for them to discriminate against and even to persecute the Christian minority. There have been disquieting happenings in some parts of the country, and the Church must face the possibility that it will have to pass through a period of difficulty, and it may be even of hardship. On the other hand, the majority of Indian

Christians feel that the connexion of Christianity, however vague, with the ruling power has been a grave handicap, and that the ending of this connexion makes it possible for the Church as never before to stand before the peoples of India as the Body of Christ and nothing else.

The second great change will take effect on 27 September 1947, when the four dioceses of Madras, Tinnevelly, Travancore and Cochin, and Dornakal, will leave the Church of India, Burma and Ceylon to become constituent parts of the new united Church of South India. This is not the place either to narrate or to appraise the negotiations as a result of which the new Church will come into existence and the separation of the four dioceses will be accomplished. After many years of thought, prayer and study, the General Council of the Church of India, Burma and Ceylon has given its approval to the separation taking place, and has wished the four dioceses well in their new venture of faith. At the time when the Constitution of the Church was being drawn up, the negotiations were already in progress, and the contingencies which might arise were foreseen and provided for in Chapter XLII *Of Union with other Christians*. There are those who welcome the decision of the General Council, there are others who deplore it. Whichever view is taken, there is no doubt that, under its constitution, the General Council was competent to take the decision allowing the four dioceses to go forth, and to enter on a very different life from that which they had had as integral parts of a province of the Anglican Communion.

The separation is more serious in its effects than might appear at first sight. Although only four of the sixteen dioceses go out from the Church of India, they carry with them nearly if not quite half the membership of the Church, and a very large proportion of the largest and best-equipped congregations. The continuing Province of India, Burma and Ceylon will be only a fragment of what it has been in the past. It will work under difficulties greater than those which have faced it in the past.

But the task which, under the providence of God, it is called to fulfil, is still the same as that laid down for the Church by the Bishops in their first declaration in 1877—to manifest in India a form of Christianity which is free from the rigidity of Rome and from the nebulousness of unhistorical Protestantism, to assert unhesitatingly the claims of the historic faith and the historic ministry, and yet to be so adaptable as to fashion itself according to the needs of the people of India and as the natural expression of their faith, and at the same time to work humbly and patiently for the union of all Christian people in India in one great Church, which shall be in very truth the Body of Christ in India.

V

THE CHURCH OF THE PROVINCE OF SOUTH AFRICA

by the MOST REV. J. R. DARBYSHIRE, *Archbishop of Cape Town*

In a hundred years the Diocese of Cape Town, to which Robert Gray was sent as Bishop by a Church none too soon awakening to a sense of its colonial responsibilities, has grown into a Province of fourteen dioceses occupying the whole territory between the Zambesi and Cape Agulhas, an area of some 960,000 square miles, to which must be added the islands of St. Helena, Ascension and Tristan da Cunha. Of these, two are specifically still styled 'missionary dioceses' namely Lebombo (which is Portuguese East Africa) and Damaraland (which is South-West Africa). The Dioceses of St. Helena and of Southern Rhodesia are also outside the limits of the Union of South Africa. The dioceses of the Transvaal are not so much as mentioned in the life of Bishop Gray and the greatest city of the Province—Johannesburg—did not exist in Bishop Gray's time![1]

Variety and Unity

It is difficult for people in England to realize the vast distances which so great a province involves. Quite recently the present writer journeyed 5,000 miles to fulfil two engagements between Palm Sunday and the Second Sunday after Easter in places so far apart as Tristan da Cunha and Johannesburg. This means that the Province comprises very many types of work among people of many races under at least six different forms of civil government, while for several purposes affecting the Church— e.g. education and hospital work, the four provinces comprising the Union (Cape Province, Natal, Orange Free State and Transvaal) have their own separate administrations. Again, there are two capitals—Cape Town where Parliament annually meets, and

---

[1] The word 'Province', in the title of this Church, is of course used in a different sense from the use of it for the four administrations which comprise the Union of South Africa, and includes dioceses outside the Union.

Pretoria which is the central seat of Government; and from a commercial and financial point of view Johannesburg has all the marks of being a capital city and all the problems that arise in a modern centre of industry.

The work of the Church is concerned with many races: of the African peoples one thinks readily of the Xhosa-speaking Africans in the Cape Province, the Zulus in Natal, the natives of the British High Commission territories; but there are also the native peoples in Ovamboland on the one side and in Portuguese East Africa on the other, and still this list is incomplete. Even of the Coloured people or non-Europeans, as they are more politely called, there are several varieties: those of the Island of St. Helena are distinct from those of the Cape Province. In Cape Town there are many Moslems, known as 'Malays', while in Natal the presence of many thousands of Indians constitutes a particular problem which is gradually spreading to other parts. Europeans themselves are divided into many groups: the Afrikaners who used to speak Dutch but now speak Afrikaans as their normal tongue—these are the people whom Englishmen are used to thinking of as 'Boers' (which really only means 'farmers'), countrymen for the most part, strongly Nationalist in temperament, of descent partly Dutch and partly Huguenot, and almost all members of the Dutch Reformed Church; the British, going back to the 1820 Settlers but, of course, comprising earlier settlers and later immigrants; Jews; Germans (of whom not a few came to this country with noble missionary aims); and numerous other European races. Roughly speaking the Anglican Church works principally among English-speaking Europeans, the native races, the Cape Coloured, the people of St. Helena, the Indians of Natal, many of whom are Christians: and its missionary work is among the still 'red' or heathen natives and the Moslems. One inevitable consequence is that each diocese develops its own particular character and its own body of rules and regulations: those of the Diocese of Johannesburg where most of the natives are 'urbanized' must differ in some particulars from those of the Diocese of St. John's where the native population is rural and still living according to tribal customs in a 'reserved area'.[1]

[1] White people in South Africa are called Europeans though many of them have never been out of Africa and are intensely proud of being South African Nationals. The word is held to indicate purity of stock free from any strain of

Such a variety of work must entail many problems which are enhanced by conflicting racial aims, political ideas, social conditions and even geographical conditions. Before going on to speak of these, however, it is perhaps well to emphasize, and that pretty strongly, that the Church of the Province of South Africa enjoys a real unity of life and worship and is informed with a felicitiously common spirit.

Synodical Government and organization

The causes of this happy condition are various. It is partly due to the fact that though in area the dioceses are huge, the numbers of the parishes and their clergy in each diocese are not too overwhelming for the Bishop to get round on periodic visitations to confirm. The Bishop knows his clergy, sees and is well acquainted with the conditions under which they work, and he meets from time to time most of the faithful laity and finds in their common churchmanship a great bond of unity. The very fact that the Anglican Communion is not the religion 'established by law' in this country—in which no church is 'established'—makes for cohesion. There are, of course, many whose adherence is purely nominal and whose attendance at Divine worship is only occasional, but the fact remains that membership of the Church means more here than it can mean in a country where to be 'C. of E.' so often merely signifies that *no* religious allegiance of any sort is practised. Further, the history of the Church makes for a certain homogeneity of outlook. The support of the Society for the Propagation of the Gospel and of S.P.C.K. has been given generously to all the dioceses, and each has developed along lines that may be called broadly 'Catholic' as distinguished from 'Evangelical' in the party sense. There is not any absolute uniformity of 'use' throughout the Province but it would be true to say that more advanced ceremonial is usual in churches serv-

Native blood. But many Europeans resent the claim of the Native peoples to be called Africans, though that is the logical description to distinguish them from 'Europeans'. The term 'Natives' has become invidious as conveying a suggestion of inferiority, and the term 'Bantu' is little more welcomed. In this article 'European' denotes white people; 'African' the black races. There is no really convenient name for those people who are of mixed race. 'Coloured' is in general use but those who desire to be considerate prefer to say 'non-European'. The term 'Asiatic' is coming into use for the Indian population and very often all Mohammedans are termed 'Malays'.

ing African or Coloured congregations than in those where the congregations are predominantly European. The notion that advanced ceremonial is forced upon unwilling Europeans by a tyrannical and bigoted hierarchy is just not true. More will be said on this point when the South African Liturgy is dealt with. Beyond all question a main cause of the real unity of this Province lies in the Constitution of the Church, which Bishop Robert Gray recognized with true foresight to be necessary, and laboured, in spite of much misunderstanding both in South Africa and in England, to establish. To-day one reads with amazement what so fine a man as Frederick Denison Maurice wrote in 1865: 'I see the Bishop of Cape Town waging a fiercer war against the principle of the Old Testament than Bishop Colenso has done. A thing called a Church, consisting of a Metropolitan and a Synod, a poor imitation of a popedom, is to set aside the glorious traditions of the English Nation which were grounded upon the Old Testament, which were the deliverance from priestly tribunals and a King-Bishop.' The present writer has always revered Maurice as one of the noblest Christians of the nineteenth century, but such a sentence as this reveals a complete ignorance both of the neces-sary difference of a branch of Christ's Church in a land where it is and can only be regarded as 'one of the sects' from the situa-tion in a land where it is established by law, and also a complete misunderstanding of Gray's purpose. A sense of humour was the least conspicuous gift in the make-up of either Maurice or Gray, and perhaps this lack obscured for each of them the understanding that the other was fighting for the spiritual liberty of the Church. To Gray the only safeguard for the Church from anarchy or tyranny—that is from individualism run riot or episcopal govern-ment despotically exercised—was a settled constitution which members of the Church as a 'voluntary association' agreed to accept, and a Synod which comprised the three houses of Bishops, Clerics and Laity. And the constitution which Gray lived to see provisionally accepted in 1870 (but was fully confirmed only in 1876 at the first Provincial Synod held under the presidency of his successor William West Jones) has proved a safeguard against the very things which Maurice dreaded. The very last thing which the Metropolitan of the Province of South Africa could venture to claim is a popedom; and every clergyman and layman in the Province is protected against an exhibition of tyranny on the part of his bishop by the very carefully framed canons providing for the exercise of ecclesiastical discipline. The powers of bishops are as strictly limited as those of anybody else. But the inauguration of a canonical Synod in every diocese and of a Provincial Synod once in five years, of a yearly Synod of the bishops, and of Missionary Conferences also, both diocesan and provincial, has provided occasions when the bishops must meet each other and their flocks in solemn convocation for responsible conference and necessary legislation; while also giving opportunity for churchmen to meet one another regularly and hear important questions debated seriously. The Church of the Province of South Africa is, of course, not unique in this respect. It was in New Zealand that the first synod of clergy since the silencing of Convocation in 1717 was held; but the opposition offered to Gray's proposal to hold a synod, and a little later the whole tragic business of Bishop Colenso of Natal, provoked controversy, and this, culminating in protracted litigation, threw a lurid light on the Cape Town experiment.

It is no part of the present chapter to deal with the complicated, prolonged and unhappy controversies which rendered the work of Gray and his successors so full of anxiety and distress. Suffice it to say that suspicions that no one would dare to vote against the wishes of the President, that he would necessarily pack the Synod with men who agreed with him, have been proved to be quite unfounded. The system has survived the terrific shock it sustained when the deposition of a Bishop, as famous for his missionary zeal as he was notorious for his bold criticism of the Bible, convulsed the young Province like an earthquake. Indeed it may be said that this calamity only made more clear the urgent need of a constitution and regular meetings of Provincial Synod. That the vitality of the system is obvious is shown by the fact that the Provincial Synod of 1945 bestowed on women the right to serve in the house of Laity, if elected—after lively debates in the earlier Synod of 1939 and again six years later— and authorized amendments of consequence to ten other canons which involved practically the entire re-writing of the Canons on Discipline.

As Provincial Synod normally meets only every five years, some business is slow. It is this that has held up the work of Prayer Book revision, as at each stage proposals have been pro-

H

visionally accepted and only ratified after an experimental period
of at least four years.

The procedure at Provincial Synod is as follows. Synod is
always held in Cape Town and is constituted at a solemn Celebration of the Holy Eucharist in St. George's Cathedral; and after a
brief adjournment meets again in the Cathedral Hall for the
President's charge and necessary preliminary business such as the
election of a Prolocutor for the House of Clergy and a Chairman
for the House of Laity. The three houses sit and debate together
unless some special business requires otherwise, but when it
comes to a vote any member may demand a vote by houses. A
programme is drawn up for each day's work so that 'bills' of a
legislative nature are distinguished from reports of committees
or resolutions of one kind or another. It is usual to dispose of
legislation before the presentation of reports. An elaborate code
of 'Standing Rules' regulates the procedure. At the conclusion of
the debates the members repair to the Cathedral where the
promulgation of the Acts of Synod is made and signed, prayer is
offered, and a Te Deum sung, and the President dismisses the
members with the blessing. Perhaps the climate of South Africa
is responsible for the tea intervals in the morning and afternoon,
but these brief periods of relaxation have their own value as
enabling friends from different dioceses to meet and chat. Possibly they serve another useful purpose of helping to keep members in their places during the debates. At any rate the interest
of the members of Synod in the debates is alert and well maintained.

In the endeavour to conduct the business of legislation as
correctly as possible Provincial Synod has adopted the procedure
of Parliament, and this sometimes reduces business to absurdity
or entangles it in difficult complexities. (At one time, at least, a
somewhat similar difficulty impeded the work of the Church
Assembly in England.) In another aspect Synod is much in
advance of Parliament, for in it Africans, Indians, and Coloured
people sit in complete equality with 'Europeans' and contribute
directly to the debates and decisions.

Between Sessions of Provincial Synod, essential business is
carried on by various Boards which meet at least annually, some
even monthly. The Provincial Standing Committee, for instance,
annually budgets for certain Provincial expenses and assesses

the dioceses on their incomes to contribute the required sum. The other Provincial Boards have these functions entrusted to them:

1. The Provincial Trusts Board holds in trust moneys belonging to various dioceses, invests the same and pays an annual dividend to the dioceses. It now administers in various funds £565,585, besides acting as agent of the Colonial Bishoprics Fund in respect of the income of the Archbishop of Cape Town and parts of the incomes of other bishops.

2. The Provincial Board of Education has hitherto done little beyond allocating annually the gift of the Pan-Anglican Congress of 1908 to various diocesan educational institutions, but it has recently established a fine graded system of instruction by post and examination of teachers, who can win the Metropolitan's certificate of proficiency.

3. The Provincial Board of Missions is doing its best work in centralizing and co-ordinating translation into the vernacular of liturgical and theological literature. Besides this, it organizes the Provincial Missionary Conference which meets the year before Provincial Synod. This is not a legislative body though it may prepare matter for legislation in Synod. Its real value is that it brings together Europeans and Africans in debate and fellowship, discusses vital questions affecting Missionary work and acts as a very useful stimulus both to needful activity and spiritual brotherhood. In most dioceses an annual missionary conference exists. There have been those whose missionary zeal tempted them to try to make these conferences miniature Synods; but this is to deny the true character of Synods and such a system of working might lead to a sad separation of African from European congregations.

4. The Provincial Pensions Board was inaugurated at the Provincial Synod of 1915 and was designed to produce in course of time a pension of about £187 for any priest retiring after forty years' service at the age of seventy. As the fund began, so to speak, from scratch, those who were in the service of the Church before 1915 are at a disadvantage. Most of the dioceses do their best to augment the pensions of such priests. The fund began with a flat rate of £9 per annum paid by the diocese on behalf of each priest, but in 1945, in order to secure an actuarially possible pension of higher value, the rate was increased to £18, of which

£12 is borne by the diocese (through the parishes) and £6 by the priest. This introduced a new but not inequitable system of contributions by the priest. The fund now stands at £184,453. There is also a Provincial Fund for the Widows and Orphans of the Clergy which now stands at £104,519. At 31 December 1946, pensions of various amounts were being paid to fifty-seven European and thirteen non-European clergymen, and to fifty-four European widows and forty-nine non-European widows. Each clergyman is expected to contribute £6 per annum to the Fund for Widows and Orphans. Reciprocal arrangements have been concluded with the Pensions Authority of the Church of England, which greatly eases the movement of priests to and from England, and also with the Episcopal Church in Scotland.

Of Provincial Institutions proper there are but two.

1. The Anglican Hostel at Fort Hare Native College in which about 100 students are housed and cared for. They are not all Anglicans but the majority are now members of our Church. The founder and first Warden was Bishop Smyth who gave to the library, as a token of his hopes that the Hostel would serve to produce men with vocations to the Ministry, a complete set of Migne's *Patrologia*. All the students at this college are housed in hostels under the auspices of one or other of the Christian denominations.

2. St. Paul's College, Grahamstown—the theological college of the Church, now happily full of men being prepared for the ministry under the bracing guidance of the Rev. F. C. Synge. This college has always been used hitherto for European candidates alone for various reasons, one being the paucity of candidates from the non-European community whose educational background was high enough for such a college to be an appropriate place for their training. The training of Africans has been sometimes undertaken within the dioceses that sponsored them. St. Bede's College at Umtata in the Diocese of St. John's and St. Peter's College at Rosettenville under the Fathers of the Community of the Resurrection have both done valuable work and enjoy a quasi-Provincial status but are not financed directly by the Province.

The appointment of bishops in this Province is by election, the electors being the clergy of the diocese and representatives of the laity elected for that purpose according to the rules of the diocese.

The elective assembly may delegate their powers, if unable to reach a decision, and may request the Metropolitan to consult with the Archbishop of Canterbury in choosing a Bishop from the Church of England. But the Bishops themselves elect when a vacancy occurs in one of the two 'missionary' dioceses or where in any diocese the number of priests is less than six.

In most dioceses the appointment of the clergy lies with the Bishop. The rights of congregations are variously conserved; generally the Bishop consults the parish before making any appointment. Further, he has a Chapter or a Senate whom he takes into consultation upon this and other matters. In the Diocese of Johannesburg there are indeed two Senates, one dealing with purely European matters, the other with matters affecting Africans. On each of these bodies six members are elected by the Diocesan Synod. All the Bishops have their own commissaries in England through whom they obtain recruits for work in South Africa; there is also a Provincial Commissary in the person of the Director of the South African Church Institute who does invaluable service in this matter, besides being in other respects a most useful and helpful link between the Province and the Church in England.

Finance

The matter of finance has been from the first a perpetual problem of the Church in South Africa. Gray's biography is full of his complaints that he is held back from fulfilling his aims by lack of funds. And to some degree that remains still true. South Africa is popularly supposed to be a very rich country seeing that it produces gold and diamonds. It is true that Johannesburg, where the gold is, has become a vast city and the centre of a strong, well-financed and progressive diocese: the wealth produced by the diamond mines has but little effect in the parishes of the Diocese of Kimberley, and for the rest South Africa is not a land of vast agricultural wealth: the costs of farming are immense and though labour—that is to say non-European labour—has been cheap, that only means that large numbers of those whom the Church serves are dreadfully poor. Yet the work has steadily prospered. It has done so through generous help from overseas. The S.P.G. and S.P.C.K. have been large and most sympathetic benefactors, never dictating policy but supporting the Bishops in their appeals for their dioceses. Most dioceses have also associations in England which support the work in the particular diocese, and in the case of St. John's the Scottish Episcopal Church has for many years provided a block grant for the work and special help to certain districts and other gifts from time to time, besides sending men to work in the diocese. Church dues are collected from members of the Church in most dioceses and the revenue so collected has been increased by many handsome benefactions from keen churchmen. The dioceses vary in this respect. Perhaps (not counting the 'missionary dioceses' of Lebombo and Damaraland) the poorest dioceses are Bloemfontein (where so great a proportion of the population is Afrikaner) and Kimberley (where so much of the area is almost desert). No one can yet tell what will happen in the Diocese of Bloemfontein where rich deposits of gold are about to be opened up. In most dioceses the finance is more centralized than is usual in England. In Southern Rhodesia 'incumbencies' in the sense of quasi-freehold rectories do not occur. In most other dioceses parishes are assessed and pay in to the diocesan office their assessments, from which the clergy are paid monthly or quarterly. In most dioceses the spirit of generosity evoked by the war was reflected in increased giving for church work by churchmen. Two dioceses in particular have succeeded in raising for themselves here moneys which came formerly from S.P.G., thus relieving the Society of part of its responsibility so long borne so willingly. The increase in local contributions has, of course, been counter-balanced by the increase in cost of living, the need of raising funds to supplement pensions, and increased cost of capital expenditure upon buildings.

A tabulated statement of the incomes and expenditure of the dioceses is given in the *Church of England Yearbook*. Here it will suffice to give the latest available figures, stating merely the totals thus:

	£
Diocesan and parochial endowments	31,285
General income from collections, donations, etc.	298,917
Income raised overseas, i.e. in Britain	27,519
Expenditure for capital purposes, education, and works of mercy	61,132

It remains to give some account of the life and work of the Church under the following five heads: its worship and liturgy; its religious communities; its specifically missionary work; its educational work; its peculiar problems. It may not prove possible to keep these points in clearly distinguished sections; but so far as may be, that will be attempted.

Worship and Liturgy

Robert Gray's strong convictions as to the spiritual autonomy of the Church and the obligation laid upon the bishops to be leaders and fathers of their flocks and not merely the agents of any society established for missionary work, led him to look for support rather to the S.P.G. than to the C.M.S. as it was then operating, or at least as he feared it was operating. The association with S.P.G. has remained. The Society has been a most valued and generous source of help throughout the century, and this has influenced naturally the general tone of the worship in the Province. Ceremonial as such seems to have had little attraction for Gray, but his discovery of the very ill-balanced conditions of things obtaining on his arrival in Cape Town led him from the first to build up a strong church life. An interesting monument of it is in the little churches designed by Mrs. Gray, many of which still stand to bear witness to her skill as an architect of simple gothic buildings. Gray himself writes of his delight in having a chapel at Bishopscourt which he made 'as ecclesiastical as possible'. How much this influence was needed can be seen when we read how Mr. Green of Pietermaritzburg found the strongest opposition being taken to two things—the use of the Prayer for the Church after the sermon on Sundays and the taking of a collection!

The principal results of this course of development have been a general tone of sane and loyally Anglican high-churchmanship with more advance in ceremonial in the missions both to African and Coloured peoples. In European congregations there has been less movement in that direction. It is sometimes urged that Europeans miss the opportunity of attending Matins. That is not because there are not such opportunities provided, for in many places they are provided. It is much more probably the case that the South African way of life makes a service of sung Matins at eleven o'clock inconvenient to attend. There are, of course, parishes where Morning Prayer is only said, not sung, a sung Eucharist being the chief service of Sunday.

The Church of this Province was among the first to revise the Liturgy, and the alternative form generally known as the 'South African Liturgy' was authorized by Provincial Synod in 1924. However slow the rest of Prayer Book revision has been, this revised Liturgy has been in increasingly wide use since then. Synod was careful to state in 1924 'its continued loyalty to' the Order in the Book of Common Prayer 'as a sufficient and completely Catholic rite, endeared to multitudes of churchmen by the most sacred associations'. Its use is continued in many churches on Sundays, especially in the older dioceses. The South African Liturgy follows in its order the Communion Service in the Book of Common Prayer very closely. It expands the intercessions in the Prayer for the Church and precedes this prayer with a prayer found in the Coronation Service which is technically a 'secret'. It adds to the Proper Prefaces. In the Canon there is a mention of the Incarnation at the beginning: the 'Epiklesis' occurs after the Words of Institution and the first of the prayers in the Book of Common Prayer after the Communion is inserted in the Canon.

Lighted candles at the Eucharist are in general use—except in some congregations in Natal: the use of vestments is pretty general. Incense is not so commonly used. Most of the clergy are aware of and give due consideration to the fact that some members of their flocks come from parishes in England where a simpler use obtains. And on the other hand many accept and even welcome the rather 'higher' standard of worship generally adopted here. It is a matter of grief to us all that there are a few congregations so opposed to what they believe to be the Rome-ward tendency of the Province that they reject our fellowship altogether, and relying on a narrowly legalistic position maintain that they alone represent the Church of England in South Africa.

Religious Communities

The Church of the Province owes much to the work of the religious communities. Robert Gray with no little courage (on which one of his brother bishops twitted him) brought out with him after his visit to England in 1868 eight ladies to form a kind of sisterhood. Later this Community was replaced by the Sisters of All Saints. In the Diocese of Bloemfontein a Brotherhood of St. Augustine was founded, the last surviving member of which, Fr. Carmichael, has only recently died at a great age. This was replaced by the Society of the Sacred Mission. The 'Cowley Fathers' have worked among Africans in Cape Town and at St. Cuthbert's in St. John's Diocese. The Community of the Resurrection does a splendid work in the Dioceses of Johannesburg, Pretoria and Southern Rhodesia. Three Communities of women have been founded, two by Bishop Webb, the Community of St. Michael and All Angels in Bloemfontein, and the Community of the Resurrection of Our Lord in Grahamstown; one in Natal, the Society of St. John the Divine, by Bishop Macrorie. There are interesting beginnings of community life among Africans, none yet very strong excepting perhaps the Community of St. John at St. Cuthbert's Mission which has eleven professed sisters, four novices and three postulants. Several English Communities of Sisters are at work in other parts of the Province.

Specifically missionary work

Every diocese (with the possible exception of Cape Town and George) has a definite missionary work going on among Africans, and as stated above two dioceses are called Missionary in the special sense that the Church in this Province was active in starting those two dioceses and has been responsible in some measure for their support. Even in Cape Town there is the difficult and often disappointing Mission to Moslems (the 'Malays', as they are called, are regarded as picturesque, and are definitely industrious, and many people fail to see any vital difference between Islam and Christianity, a point which the Moslems are not slow to exploit), and the number of Africans in the Native Mission is on the increase. Missionary work still calls for itinerant missionaries in rural areas, and the missionaries who do that work often live very austere lives, sleeping in kraals and sharing Native food as they 'trek' to numerous outstations from their central mission. In areas where there are urbanized Natives, as in the larger locations, missionary work includes social service, education and medical service. How far Africans coming to the cities and receiving there instruction and baptism return to their tribes in rural parts as evangelists it is not easy to estimate, but quite undeniably this happens to a considerable extent. It must

be realized that in the rural parts it may require great courage,
and entail loss or even persecution still to become a Christian.
One who has visited Zululand or the Diocese of St. John's can
bear witness to the great work going on. The present writer
visited Zululand a few years ago. Bad weather prevented him
from seeing the greatest centre of work there at St. Augustine's;
but on a visit to Mapopoma he was present at a great gathering
of 4,000 persons including the Chief of the Tribe. The service,
a Eucharist, had to be held out of doors. The church, though a
fine one, could not hold such a number. One thousand persons
made their Communion, and in spite of the unfamiliar conditions conducted themselves with such reverence and dignity that
the whole service was carried through without the slightest difficulty. The people knew in what they were taking part, and their
singing, as all African singing, was spontaneous, congregational
and seemly, enriched with the subtle harmonies which an African
congregation seems to know intuitively how to produce. The
Dioceses of Lebombo and Damaraland each have their special
appeal as being scenes of intensive missionary work, of which the
most important stations are St. Mary's Mission, Ovamboland, in
the latter diocese, and Maciene in Lebombo. The large church at
Maciene is actually the Cathedral Church of the Diocese. Lately
the Bishop ordained there a deacon who had been a catechist in
Lourenço Marques, working amongst the Native house boys employed by residents in that city. These boys sent a wholly delight-
ful letter couched in primitive, almost biblical, terms, expressing
their joy that one who had been among the washers of dogs was
to become 'with the soap of the Word a washer of men'.

A special word must be spoken of the work of the Community
of the Resurrection, both in the overcrowded townships of
Orlando and Sophiatown in Johannesburg, and in the Jane Furse
Hospital in the Diocese of Pretoria and the splendid mission of
St. Augustine's, Penhalonga, in Southern Rhodesia. Equally de-
serving of praise is the work of the Society of the Sacred Mission
in Bloemfontein Diocese, especially at Modderpoort and in the
location at Bloemfontein where the 'power house' is a church
of outstanding interest and dignity. Here, as at Penhalonga, the
mantle of Mrs. Gray as an amateur architect seems to have fallen
most happily on the shoulders of the Rev. E. Rose and the
Rev. F. Baker, respectively.

This may be the proper place to insert a brief note on the Order of Ethiopia. Much interest was aroused at the beginning of this century when what looked like a mass movement of Africans brought a number of Xhosa-speaking Natives as a body into the fellowship of the Church of the Province. It was hoped that these people would prove a great missionary force. The hope has not wholly been fulfilled. The movement is necessarily restricted to Xhosa-speaking Africans and has tended to become a separate society within the Church requiring separate worship and to some degree separate organizations, spreading as members of the Order move to new places, but not proving to be a really evangelistic power. The Order remains loyally within the Church. It has a Provincial, a Chapter and an annual Conference. It would like to have a Bishop of its own but has quite loyally accepted the impracticability of this. An access of missionary zeal is to be desired and may come.

One special feature of definitely missionary endeavour deserves mention: the Church Railway Mission. In this a staff of men and women missionaries travel up and down the main railway lines and minister to railway officials and employees in the less populated parts of the vast railway system, baptizing and helping to teach the children of men stationed in parts remote from any parochial organization and bringing a personal contact with the Faith to many otherwise cut off from the Church. The increase in the employment of Afrikaner personnel has rendered our work in some ways less but in other ways more difficult as the English-speaking English Church employees are fewer and more widely separated from each other. It is a happy feature that the co-operation of employees has been secured for this service and a system has been inaugurated by which a quite considerable income for the work is now contributed willingly by the railway servants themselves.

Educational Work

Besides the educational work referred to above among Africans (as at Penhalonga, Modderpoort, St. Matthew's, Keiskama Hoek) and innumerable 'Mission' schools (primary) for both Africans and Coloured, the Province has a proud record of educational endeavour for European boys and girls. No schools in the Union stand higher educationally than Diocesan College,

Cape Town; St. Andrew's College, Grahamstown; Michaelhouse in Natal; and St. John's College, Johannesburg; these being boys' schools comparable to English public schools. Besides, there are fine schools at Bloemfontein (St. Andrew's), St. George's Grammar School in Cape Town and St. Mark's, Mbabane, and preparatory schools in George, Ruzawi, and Windhoek. Girls are equally well looked after, hardly a diocese failing to have provided a good girls' school. If detailed mention of them all is avoided this is only through lack of space and avoidance of making this article a mere catalogue. Briefly, the contribution of the Church to education of all kinds is a great one. One may here mention that at last a Chair of Theology has been founded at Rhodes University College towards the cost of which the Church of the Province bore its allotted share among the contributing religious denominations.

The Church's Peculiar Problems

The overwhelming problem is the racial one. Europeans, as we have seen, form two great divisions. The Afrikaner is not without his sense of responsibility to the African, and the Dutch Reformed Church has to its credit much missionary enterprise and philanthropic effort. But it holds tenaciously to the conviction that by divine ordinance the Africans belong to an essentially and permanently inferior race, and can find a possible solution of the racial question only in the policy of segregation of races. The British tradition is not so, but it has to be confessed with no little shame that apart from those whose faith is strong or who are profoundly humanitarian in outlook there is a deplorable tendency among some of British origin to allow themselves to acquiesce in exploitation of the Natives and avoid any serious responsibility for their welfare, through the desire for cheap labour or sheer racial prejudice. The problem is even more acute in some respects when it comes to the treatment of the Coloured or 'non-European' section. These have already adopted, inherited and cling proudly to a European way of life, but they are frustrated by the prevalence of colour prejudice, and in their frustration sometimes act so as to provoke an access of the prejudice that they rightly resent. With the adoption of universal compulsory education the situation may prove in some ways less tense, but in another it may be rendered still more difficult. White skilled labour is afraid of being ousted by cheaper Coloured labour. The main difficulty is social. Many Europeans have no desire to promote education among the Coloured people. It seems to them only to enhance the danger of miscegenation—an ominous word full of dread. The Church has a real difficulty to meet in this situation. It is paralleled by the problem of the Indians in Natal, themselves a proud and sensitive community. To carry on our work at all while trying to be true to the principle that in Christ's Church there can be no place for colour prejudice involves all manner of delicate situations. To some we appear to encourage the dreaded miscegenation: to some of the Coloured people we appear to deny in practice what we preach in principle. Perhaps a clear-cut policy is out of the question. The future is obscure. We can but go on trying to be as true to our Christian faith as we can be, and as generous to a sorely tried section of the community as possible. At present the number of loyal Anglicans among the Coloured people is very great. Some are tempted however, to look to some secular ideology for their deliverance. It must be acknowledged that for many people this plight of the Coloured people is of little interest compared with that of the pure Africans. The former are less romantic, fewer in number, and (what many forget) they have been largely robbed of what the Cape Ordinance of 1829 appeared to guarantee them in respect of their citizen rights.

The case of the Natives is complicated. Historically they are only the first of the conquerors of South Africa. Before them the Bushmen and the Hottentots were here. Superior as the many tribes of the Bantu are to these perhaps aboriginal peoples and possessed as they are of elaborate tribal customs, rituals and rich languages, they are hardly qualified to be masters of southern Africa. Their methods of farming, if left to themselves, are wasteful. Their kraals are primitive. The European when he discovered South Africa could not avoid claiming ownership of the land. A situation thus arose which provided inevitable tension, even wars. Into the history of this it is not possible here to enter. No one could pretend that their eventual conquerors have given them always a square deal, and as time has gone on this failure has become more and more apparent; but it is unfair to past and present governments to talk as if the Europeans in power had never made any attempt to govern them fairly, or protect at all their interests. No elaborate civilization develops without some measure of injustice, and the result is always that champions of one ideal contend against the champions of another. The negrophile can remember only the failures of government, the politicians tend to exaggerate what government has already done in the interest of the Natives.

There are some features of the attitude of Europeans to Africans that appear utterly indefensible: there has been a continuous stream of repressive laws and regulations, hampering the life of the African peoples at every turn, more especially the notorious 'pass laws' which inflict on the most ignorant and helpless section of the community restrictions that are bewildering and irritating. Equally unjust it seems that Africans should be taxed without receiving any adequate representation in Parliament. Unjust it is that hitherto Government has done so little, so culpably little, to promote adequate health services and education. It ought surely to have been possible to employ Africans in industry and the mines and in domestic service without so breaking up their tribal and home life. It is surely unjust that on the one hand any strike of Native employees is under any conditions illegal, but, on the other, that in the case of a grievance or dispute arbitration is only granted, if ever, at the mere pleasure of Government. When the Natives were compelled to live in 'locations' it ought not to have been the case that well-run Native Townships, decently laid out and equipped with a sufficient provision of sanitation, should be the rare exceptions (as at Pietermaritzburg, Port Elizabeth and Cape Town); that should have been the normal thing. In the mine compounds the men employed are well cared for, their health is carefully watched; but one is left with the suspicion that this care is really taken chiefly in the interest of the mine-owners, not of the employees. For the men are herded in artificial conditions exposing them to vice and going against all their age-long tribal customs. They eventually go back to their reserves unfitted for their agricultural avocations. It is with real thankfulness that those who have the interest of the Africans at heart learn that the largest company formed to operate the new mines to be opened up in the Orange Free State have asked the Director of the Institute of Race Relations to carry out a scheme whereby the Natives employed shall be housed with their families and their traditional modes of life disturbed as little as possible. There are other signs not less hopeful. A health scheme to embrace all Natives is being begun. New projects for extending education are afoot. What had been left almost entirely to the missionary societies and the churches is now to become by a gradual process part of the State's direct concern. In the opinion of the present writer the worst disgrace to Africa is the fact that it has been possible for individual employers of Native labour to exploit the African so shamelessly as in far too many cases has been done. In many places excessively long hours of labour render their lives a burden. Their ignorance is sometimes exploited by unprincipled traders who take advantage of their weakness for drink to fuddle them and then cheat them. Of course there are just and honourable traders but there are too many who are the reverse. This cannot be laid directly to the responsibility of Government. It is the result of a selfish public opinion that a Native as such has no human rights. Even among church people there are to be found those who fear that common worship will lead to social complications.

But when all is said that can be said of the white man's failure to do his African brother justice the fact remains that the Native races are not being stamped out, that they are not a cowed and miserable people. Many earn good money. Many have become wealthy. Education is not wholly denied them, and both in their reserves (as in the Transkei) and in the centres of industry (as in Johannesburg) they carry themselves not as slaves or wretchedly as having lost all joy in living. They have been amazingly patient under many provocations and their congenital sense of humour has carried them through many difficulties. They have not shunned the dangers inherent in aping the white man's way of life. To many it is a fine thing to go to be employed in a great city.

It is not easy to speak of the future. There is without question a growing distrust of the white man, a growing desire to be independent, and this is manifesting itself even in the churches. In the Church of the Province many Africans are impatient to see an African consecrated to the episcopate, and agitation in this matter flares up from time to time. The Church has not withheld positions of responsibility from Native priests and in more than one diocese canonries have been bestowed upon Native clergymen. Canonically there is no bar to prevent the election of an African to the episcopate. But although the Church can justly be proud of the number of faithful African priests in its service, none yet has proved to be so outstanding as to be clearly fit for that high and most responsible office. A hundred years is a short time in the history of a church: it may be that events will move swiftly in the coming years to give far more responsibility to the Africans. The chief barrier to be overcome is the pride and prejudice of Europeans.

As these pages are written the Church is preparing to observe the one-hundredth anniversary of Robert Gray's consecration. We do not forget, but are definitely putting out of the foreground of our remembrance, the unhappy controversies that Gray and his successors had to experience: rather, as the Dean of Johannesburg put it, all our thoughts are concentrated on thanksgiving, saying with grateful hearts 'what God hath wrought!'

THE CHURCH OF ENGLAND IN AUSTRALIA AND TASMANIA

by the RT. REV. F. DE W. BATTY, *Bishop of Newcastle, N.S.W.*

The Australian Church had no very auspicious beginning. It seems to have originated in what could almost be described as an afterthought. Those responsible for manning and equipping the fleet of ships which brought the first batch of convicts to Australia forgot to provide much that was needed for the bodily welfare of their charges. For the welfare of their souls they made no provision at all. Shortly before the fleet sailed it was discovered, by the great William Wilberforce, that no chaplain had been appointed to accompany it. But for that discovery the fleet would have sailed without any minister of religion, and without any of the apparatus for religious worship. There was only just time to repair the omission; but it was repaired to the extent of providing one clergyman—Richard Johnson—and one Bible to cater for the spiritual needs of nigh a thousand souls, seven hundred and fifty convicts and two hundred soldiers, and to lay the foundation of church life in the new colony of New South Wales.

For the first three years and more Johnson laboured alone. Reinforcements were slow in coming, and very few in number. At first the tiny band of priests had no real superintendence, except the nominal superintendence of the Bishop of London, to whose diocese by an Order-in-Council of Charles I they belonged. The first improvement in this regard was effected when the Diocese of Calcutta was created in the year 1814, to include all the territories within the Charter of the East India Company. As these expressly included Australia and Tasmania, the Anglican Christians of those two countries thus became, for the first time, really part of a diocese. This was brought home to them ten years later when, in 1824, Australia was constituted an archdeaconry in the Diocese of Calcutta, and a resident Archdeacon, Thomas Hobbes Scott, was appointed to its charge. He was succeeded by William Grant Broughton, who held office as Archdeacon until 1836, when he was consecrated to be the first Bishop of the new diocese of Australia. The progress made by the Church under Broughton's episcopate (1836–54) was so rapid, and so great, that already in 1841 it was possible to create a separate see of New Zealand, in 1842 to create a separate see of Tasmania, and in 1847 to divide the one huge diocese of the Australian mainland into four dioceses, Sydney, Melbourne, Adelaide, and Newcastle. Since then the process of development and subdivision has continued, until to-day there are twenty-five dioceses, organized in four provinces, coterminous with the States of New South Wales, Victoria, Queensland, and Western Australia, with the Dioceses of Adelaide, Tasmania, and Willochra as independent autocephalous dioceses. The fifteen priests of 1836 have become the seventeen hundred of 1947.

The Australian Census Acts invite, but do not require, citizens to state the religious denominations to which they profess allegiance. According to the latest figures available (those of the Census of 1933) about 80 per cent of the population was willing to furnish this information. The figures show that the Church of England is by far the largest religious denomination in the Commonwealth. In Tasmania its professed adherents number roughly 52 per cent of those who profess and call themselves Christians, in New South Wales and Western Australia, just 50 per cent, whilst the proportions in Victoria, South Australia and Queensland are slightly lower. In the Commonwealth as a whole the proportion is roughly 44 per cent. These figures are in no way surprising when one considers the predominantly British character of the population. It is generally computed that about 95 per cent of the population of Australia are British in origin. Great Britain is still spoken of affectionately as 'The Old Country' and 'Home' even by those who may never have visited it.

Organization

At the beginning of its episcopal history the Australian Church was organized in a single province, of which the Bishop of Sydney was the Metropolitan. The Letters Patent constituting the three dioceses created in 1847 provided that the bishops of the new sees 'shall be subject and subordinate to the Bishop of Sydney as Metropolitan in the same manner as any Bishop of any See within the Province of Canterbury in our kingdom of England is under the Metropolitical See of Canterbury and the Archbishop thereof'. And this arrangement was voluntarily preserved after it became known that with the grant of self-government to Australia the Letters Patent had no longer any legal force. The Bishop of Sydney still remained the Metropolitan of Australia, and was subsequently given the rank of Archbishop, and the title of Primate.

At the beginning of the present century it was decided, in accordance with a recommendation of the Lambeth Conference, to divide the one Province of Australia into the three Provinces of New South Wales, Victoria and Queensland, each comprising the dioceses falling within the territorial boundaries of their respective States. Later a fourth Province, that of Western Australia, was created. Because the States of South Australia and Tasmania still lack the number of dioceses required for the formation of a Province, the Dioceses of Tasmania and the two South Australian dioceses, Adelaide and Willochra, remain extraprovincial and autocephalous.

The creation of these new provinces at once created a difficulty of organization. It was the general desire that Sydney should continue to be the seat of the Primacy. Considerations both of history and of geography gave point to the desire. But there was also a general feeling that if the occupant of the Sydney See was to be the permanent chairman for the whole Australian Church, and its official spokesman, then in some way, and to some extent, the whole Australian Church should be associated with the business of his election. But it is hard for bodies corporate, as for individuals, to accept limitations on powers which they have previously possessed. The Diocese of Sydney found it so hard as to be impossible, and its spokesmen openly admitted that they would rather lose the Primacy than part with their right to elect their own bishop, unimpeded by any outside influence or votes. It was accordingly arranged that when the office of Primate became vacant, the bishops of Australia should elect as Primate one of the Metropolitan bishops. In 1909 the choice fell by the narrow majority of one vote on the Archbishop of Sydney (Dr. Wright). On the next occasion in 1935 the choice fell, again by a majority of one, on the Archbishop of Perth (Dr. Le Fanu). In 1947 the Archbishop of Sydney (Dr. H. W. K. Mowll) was chosen.

The office of Primate is one of great distinction, but of very little direct power. The Primate can, at his own discretion, summon the General Synod to meet at such time and place as he may deem fit. He receives the resignation of a fellow-Metropolitan, or of the bishop of an autocephalous diocese; and a diocese which desires to appoint a coadjutor-bishop must satisfy him that provision has been made for the payment of an adequate stipend. Apart from these prerogatives, it would seem that he has no direct power at all, though his indirect influence as Chairman of the House of Bishops can be very great indeed. During Dr. Le Fanu's Primacy the practice was inaugurated of summoning the Bishops to a three-days Conference in the spring of every year. The practice is so obviously desirable, and so practically beneficial, that it is likely to become permanent.

In its organization the Church of Australia follows traditional lines. It has its diocesan synods, in which the clergy and elected representatives of the laity meet under the presidency of the bishop. There are variations in the manner of representation of the clergy. In some dioceses every ordained person, bishop, priest or deacon, holding the licence of the bishop of the diocese, is *ex officio* a member of Synod. In others only the beneficed priests; in at least one diocese all the priests are full members of Synod, but deacons, though invited to sit in Synod, can neither speak nor vote. The legislative acts of a diocesan synod do not become effective until they have received the assent of the bishop who thus has virtually a power of veto over all legislation.

There is also a Synod of each Province, which is summoned to meet every three years, and a General Synod which meets every five years under the presidency of the Primate. In these Synods there are two Houses, the bishops forming one, the representatives of the clergy and the laity forming the other. The number of clerical and lay representatives summoned for each diocese is calculated in proportion to the number of its clergy. The method of their election is left to the discretion of each diocese. They are normally elected by the Diocesan Synod. It is frequently argued that it ought to be compulsory for the representatives of each order to be elected by the members of that order only. It is felt, not unreasonably, that since the representatives of the laity outnumber the representatives of the clergy in any Synod, in most cases by as much as two to one, it will be their vote which determines the election of the clerical representatives, who will not, therefore, necessarily represent the choice of the clergy. This method of election has been voluntarily adopted by some diocesan synods, but has not yet been made obligatory for all. Considerable weight naturally attaches to the deliberations of these bodies; but they have no real legislative powers. They can initiate legislation, but cannot bring it into effect. Their acts are binding only on such dioceses as accept them. The Church does not govern the dioceses, but the dioceses the Church. This is clearly an inversion of the rightful order. The synodical pyramid may be an admirable one, but according to the well-known epigram of a former Bishop of Sydney, the pyramid is poised precariously upon its apex.

This consideration has played a real, though subordinate, part in the movement for the obtaining of a Constitution for the Church of England in Australia. At present it has none. Indeed it is not even entitled to its rightful name. Its official designation is not 'The Church of England in Australia' but 'The Church of England in the Dioceses of Australia and Tasmania'. This title, regrettably enough, more accurately describes the present constitutional position which has long cried out for reform.

The Question of Autonomy

The main motive of the movement for constitutional reform is the desire to secure spiritual freedom for the Australian Church. At present it is in the unenviable position of being the only particular or national church of our Communion which has not claimed the right to order its own spiritual life, and to determine its own law of worship. Originally its organization was created by the British Sovereign. By issuing Letters Patent Queen Victoria created the original Diocese of Australia, and the Dioceses of Sydney, Melbourne, Adelaide, and Newcastle, into which it was later divided. But with the granting of self-government to the Australian Colonies these Letters Patent ceased to have any operative force, and no more were issued. The question immediately arose as to what, in these altered circumstances, was the legal relationship of the dioceses of the Church of England in Australia to the Mother Church in England. Various opinions were held on the point, but it was not until the beginning of the present century that any precise definition of the situation was obtained. In the General Synod of 1905 a Committee was appointed 'to consider what is the legal nexus of the various dioceses in Australia and Tasmania with the Church of England in England; and to obtain legal opinion in the Commonwealth and in England; to consult with the Archbishop of Canterbury; and to report to the respective bishops in the dioceses of Australia and Tasmania'. A 'Case' was subsequently prepared and submitted to very eminent counsel in England and in Australia. The opinions of counsel, when they were given, left the matter in no doubt at all. The Church of England in Australia is not a free and self-governing body. It does not possess those powers of spiritual self-determination to which Article XXXIV declares every particular or national Church to be entitled. From a purely legal viewpoint it is rigidly bound to adhere to the laws and formularies of the Church of England in England as determined by the English Parliament, and interpreted by the English courts. 'The Anglican Churches in Australia and Tasmania', said the English counsel, 'are all organized upon the basis that they are not merely churches "in communion with" or "in connexion with" the Church of England, but are actual parts of that Church'.

The wording of that statement deserves careful notice. It has sometimes been mistakenly asserted that counsel described the Australian dioceses as being actually parts of the Church of England. They made no such assertion, and it would not have been true if they had. What they did say was that the Australian churches were 'organized upon the basis . . . that they are actual parts of the Church of England'. And that, of course, is true, and is the source of our present legal disabilities. Because in process of time the title 'Church of England' has acquired a denominational significance, and a quasi-adjectival force. By applying it to themselves and accepting gifts and bequests to be used for purposes in conformity with that designation, the Australian dioceses had automatically—and possibly quite unwittingly—become subject to the laws of the Mother Church, and powerless to vary them, except at the risk of forfeiting their trust property. That the risk was no imaginary one has been proved by the still-recent 'Wee Free' case in Scotland.

The General Synod of 1916 appointed a committee of bishops, priests and laymen to examine the position revealed by counsel's opinion, and to report as to whether or not it could be considered permanently satisfactory as a basis for church fellowship in Australia. If the answer to this question were in the negative, the committee was instructed further to report as to what, in their opinion, would be a satisfactory basis, and what steps should be taken to secure it. This committee reported in 1921 that the existing legal position was not satisfactory, and set out 'two strongly contrasted courses of action' which might be taken to deal with it. One possible course would be to draft a Constitution for the Church, with revised standards and formularies. The other would be simply to retain the existing standards and formularies, but to obtain from the Australian Parliaments the right to revise and vary them as occasion might demand under adequate safeguards. The Committee recommended the latter course. There was also, however, a Minority Report, signed by five members—all of them resident in the Diocese of Sydney. This Minority Report criticized the Committee's Report, mainly on the ground that it would leave the way open for the Church to make such drastic alterations in its standards and formularies as would completely alter its character, and, in effect, set up a new Church in place of the old.

A Draft Determination embodying the recommendations of the Majority Report was submitted to the Synod, and secured a second reading by a unanimous vote in the House of Bishops, and by large majorities of clergymen and laymen in the House of Representatives. In view, however, of the strong opposition of a minority, it was decided to proceed no further with the measure, but to make another effort to secure unanimity in a matter of such vital moment to the whole Church. It was ordered that the Committee's Report should be submitted to the dioceses, and, meanwhile, that a Central Committee should be appointed 'to receive the suggestions from the respective dioceses, to correspond with such dioceses, and to co-ordinate and codify such proposals as may be received, and finally submit to the dioceses a uniform document which, in its judgement, most clearly expresses the common mind of the Church in Australia'. Under the leadership of the late Bishop of Bathurst (the late Dr. G. M. Long) and his Chancellor (the late Sir John Peden) the committee executed its commission. The result of its labours was laid before the General Synod of 1926 in the form of a Draft Constitution, which, in one edition after another, has been under consideration by the Church ever since. The labours and discussions of more than twenty years have so far failed to secure its adoption. It has twice been accepted by the General Synod, but it has subsequently failed to secure, or to retain, the necessary number of diocesan acceptances. The Draft has always provided that no approach can be made to the State Parliaments for the necessary amendments of our Church Property Trust Acts until the Draft has been accepted by at least eighteen of our twenty-five dioceses, two of them, at least, being metropolitan sees.

It will naturally be asked why it is that the Australian Church has been hesitant to take a step which would seem to be so clearly indicated, and so definitely in accordance with the principles of the Church of England, amongst them the basic principle of ecclesiastical nationalism, which made the Reformation possible. There have, of course, been criticisms of the Draft Constitution on points of detail. And since these criticisms have been not merely different from one another, but actually the opposite of one another, it is tempting to infer that the Draft does justice to all legitimate divergencies of view. There can, however, be no doubt as to the main reason why the Draft has not, as yet, secured unanimous approval. It is the fear of certain minorities in the Church lest in a Church constituted as it would be under the Draft Constitution, their distinctive witness should be submerged. This belief finds expression at both ends of the ecclesiastical scale. It is, quite certainly, groundless. In every recension of the Draft the rights of minorities have been scrupulously safeguarded. But fears and suspicions persist, largely because of traditions and loyalties inherited from the past. The contributors to the present volume have been told that one of its objects is to ascertain how far Anglicanism is 'one religion or two or more rival religions, constituted by party traditions and loyalties'. This question, therefore, must now be posed in reference to the Church of England in Australia.

Churchmanship

All the main types of Anglican churchmanship, Anglo-Catholic, 'Central', Evangelical, and (to a very limited extent) Liberal, are represented in the Australian Church, which came to self-consciousness at a period when opinions were very sharply divided in the Church at home. The first Australian bishop was consecrated three years after the launching of the Oxford Movement. Its next bishops were consecrated two years after Newman's secession to Rome.

Dr. Broughton, the first and only Bishop of Australia, was what would nowadays be called an old-fashioned high-churchman. He held strong sacramental beliefs. He had a discriminating sympathy with the Oxford Movement, assenting cordially to its general principles, whilst finding some of its propaganda—notably Tract XC—somewhat difficult of digestion. His general attitude was expressed in a letter dated October 1837. It was addressed to a correspondent who had written to him about one of Newman's sermons. He writes:

'Your introduction of his [Newman's] name reminds me to say that if I might make choice of my fellow-labourers they should be from his school. They take, I think, the most just and comprehensive view of the true constitution of our Church, and of its actual duties in the present state of the world; and it is amongst the young men brought up in their principles that I should expect to find that temperate and professional ardour which appears to me the first requisite for a man doing his duty well, and finding his chief support and reward in the consciousness of doing it.'

Dr. Broughton's successor in the bishopric of Sydney and the primacy of Australia (Dr. Barker) stood on the opposite side in the Tractarian controversy. He was a man of conspicuous energy and ability. During his primacy of twenty-six years the work of the Church in Australia was greatly extended and consolidated. Seven new dioceses were created; the Synod of the Diocese of Sydney was formed; and later the General Synod of the Australian Church. St. Andrew's Cathedral, Sydney, was completed and consecrated, and more than two hundred new churches were built. A theological college was founded, and the finances of the Church were ably reorganized to meet the situation created by the withdrawal of government grants. It is from him too that the Diocese of Sydney has inherited the tradition of strong evangelical churchmanship which still gives it a special tone and character. This tradition finds expression also in some other dioceses, but in Sydney it is markedly predominant.

As to how far 'party traditions and loyalties' are divisive in their influence it would be difficult to estimate. Certainly they do nothing to make friendship impossible, or even difficult. Nowhere do the representatives of the other Australian dioceses receive a more cordial or hospitable welcome than in Sydney. The Diocesan Church House is at the disposal of any pan-Australian Committee which desires to make use of it. Three times every year it welcomes the members of the Australian Board of Missions; every five years it acts as host to the General Synod of the Australian Church, and lavishes hospitality upon its members.

Friendship, however, is no real substitute for fellowship, and it must be admitted that 'party traditions and loyalties' do tend to prejudice the possibility of complete fellowship within the Church as a whole. Apart from the failure to achieve an autonomous constitution, in some departments of its work, notably that of religious education, it has not been found practicable for the Church to function through a single organization; side by side with agencies representing the whole Church there have to be other agencies particularly designed to give expression to the Evangelical point of view. There is also to be observed in some quarters that curious differentiation, to which the Archbishop of York has recently called attention, between the bishops regarded distributively and 'the Bishops' regarded collectively. Individual bishops are treated with friendliness, courtesy, and respect: their utterances may be quoted with approval. It is, however, otherwise with 'the Bishops' as a body. 'They were asked to trust the Bishops,' said an enthusiastic lady speaker at a meeting held soon after the General Synod of 1937, 'but *could* they trust the Bishops?' The question was clearly one which, according to the Latin grammars would have to be introduced by the particle '*Num*' as expecting the answer 'No!' The expectation was not disappointed.

Such a viewpoint is doubtless confined to a minority, and probably to a decreasing minority. There are those on both sides of the party arena who opine that the divergencies of belief which create our divisions are far less serious than is sometimes supposed. It has more than once been suggested that round-table conferences should be held at which controversial issues could be resolutely faced, and differences possibly resolved. Hitherto it has not been found possible to arrange for such conferences, but those who desire them will continue to give voice to their desires. It would mean a very great deal to the Australian Church if any time and energy which is now being wasted on either side in partisan recriminations could be conserved for the cause of the Kingdom of God. It is being increasingly felt, especially amongst the younger members of the Australian priesthood, that it is time we ceased squabbling about what the Church did, or did not, mean to do in England in the sixteenth and seventeenth centuries, and gave our attention more exclusively to the question of what it means to do in Australia in the twentieth. Two things will be needed before this desirable goal can be achieved. One is the success of the movement for Australian church autonomy. The other is the development of a more distinctively Australian Church consciousness. For this latter development we must look to the Theological colleges.

Training for the Ministry

For some years past the Australian Church has been almost entirely dependent on its own resources for the recruitment of its ministry. The flow of volunteers from overseas which, up to the end of the first decade of the present century, was fairly constant, has now almost entirely ceased. Importations are nowadays rare, and are mostly only made to fill a bishopric, or some other key position in the Church. It is hoped that presently the need for even such importations as these will wholly cease, and that it will be possible to fill such posts with men of Australian birth and training. The importations have certainly served the Church well in the past. So much is unmistakably shewn by the choices of electoral bodies. Three of the four archbishops, and eleven of the twenty-one diocesan bishops are of English birth and training. The fourth archbishop is of English birth, but Australian training. It should be added that of the episcopal importations only one was imported direct to fill a bishopric. The rest had served in the ranks of the Australian priesthood for a longer or shorter period before their elevation to the Bench. Two of the arch-bishops and eight of the diocesan bishops had served in one or other of the Bush Brotherhoods.

None the less, it is clearly to be desired that, as soon as it is practicable, the Australian Church should provide itself with leaders as well as followers from its own ranks. And there are signs that it is beginning to be able to do so. All of the last five appointments to the episcopate have been of men with Australian experience, three of them being also men of Australian birth and training.

The oldest and largest theological college in Australia is Moore College, which was established at Liverpool during the episcopate of Dr. Barker, and has since been moved to Sydney. Like Wycliffe Hall at Oxford, or Ridley Hall at Cambridge, it stands for a distinctively Evangelical tradition. It has been served by Principals of first-rate scholastic attainments, and has always been able to command the services of an adequate and competent staff of teachers. It usually acquits itself with distinction in the annual examinations of the Australian College of Theology. Another college which embodies a similar tradition, but is of much more recent foundation, is Ridley College in Melbourne. At the other end of the ecclesiastical scale is St. Francis' College, Brisbane, which has come to be increasingly identified with the Anglo-Catholic type of churchmanship. It too has been well served by its principals and staffs, and has a distinguished record of examination results. St. John's College, Morpeth, serves the six country dioceses of New South Wales, and is governed by a council consisting of the bishops of those dioceses. Occasionally it attracts students from dioceses outside the province of New South Wales. In no way does it suffer by comparison with the other colleges, and it has an 'ethos' of its own. If Moore College is the Wycliffe Hall of Australia, and St. Francis' Brisbane the Ely, Morpeth can fitly claim to be the Cuddesdon or the Wells. A similar character might be attributed to St. Barnabas' College, Adelaide.

An important development in the field of theological education and training for the ministry took shape this year (1947) with the establishment near Adelaide of a branch of the Society of the Sacred Mission. The Kelham Fathers have come to Australia in response to an almost unanimous invitation from the Bench of Bishops. It is the opinion of very many that their coming will be a definite and considerable help in raising the standard of training for the Ministry. The pains they take in selecting candidates for training, the careful observation which enables them to reject at any stage a candidate whose vocation there is reason to doubt, the proved success of their syllabus and scheme of training, and their own example of self-forgetful service, lead many of us to believe that the products of their college are likely to be of high quality.

That there is room for their particular kind of work is proved by the fact that they had more than two hundred applicants for training when it became known that they were ready to open their doors. Of these some seventeen—all that there is room for until the college premises can be enlarged—have been selected, and are now at work.

The place of the General Ordination Examination in England is taken in Australia by the Th.L. Examination of the Australian College of Theology. The standard of this examination is fully as high as that of its English counterpart, and with fewer and fewer exceptions it is made a *sine qua non* for ordination by the Australian bishops. It is becoming increasingly common also for bishops to insist on the matriculation examination of some recognized university as the entrance examination for postulants for Holy Orders. The Kelham Fathers are particularly insistent on this, arguing, convincingly enough, that if God is calling a man to the ministry, He is likely to have furnished him with sufficient brain-power to enable him to survive a general educational test of at least matriculation standard. If he fails under such a test, it is a reasonable inference that his vocation is to some other occupation. In some dioceses—notably the Diocese of Goulburn, a serious effort is being made to increase the number of candidates who have proceeded to a degree in Arts at some univerity. At St. John's College, Morpeth, it is possible for a student who has passed the matriculation examination of the Queensland University, and, as an external student, has passed in two Arts subjects whilst under the college roof, to complete the remainder of his degree course piecemeal after his ordination. It is not claimed that this is of equal value to a degree obtained through residence at a university, but it has shewn itself in practice to be a substitute of no inconsiderable value.

Post-ordination study is also encouraged by means of the more advanced examination conducted by the Australian College of Theology. This is called the Th.Schol. or Scholar in Theology Examination, and is intended to require a standard of scholarship equivalent to that required for a B.D. degree in London. It is a really valuable examination, and it is matter for satisfaction that so many young priests are willing and eager to submit themselves to it. The college offers a still higher diploma, that of Th.Soc., or Th.D. This diploma is awarded to candidates of approved academic record and standing, who present a thesis written on a subject which has previously been approved by the Council of Delegates, and judged by the Council to be of sufficient merit. The standard is reckoned to be that of an examination for a Doctorate in Divinity, and in judging the thesis the delegates are assisted by expert opinion from overseas.

In recent years there has been a tendency in some quarters to question the inclusion of Greek as a compulsory subject in the curriculum for Th.L. Those who wish it to be compulsory only for students who seek honours, argue that it is a waste of time, which could be put to much better use, to require students with no aptitude for languages to acquire a smattering of Greek, of which they are unlikely to make any use once the examination is over. Those who press for the retention of Greek as a compulsory subject argue that no one can rightly undertake the ministry of the Gospel, if, through ignorance of the language in which its title-deeds were originally written, he is denied access to the greatest commentaries upon them. They also argue on general grounds that no one can really master his own language if he knows no other. And they adduce the further argument, already mentioned above, that inability to master the study of Greek may well be an indication that a man's vocation is not to the Ministry. There is strong feeling on both sides of this controversy, but so far those who advocate the retention of Greek have had their way.

This controversy will serve to illustrate one real ground for anxiety concerning the future of the Australian Church. The shortage of man-power and the constant demands for church extension do undoubtedly tend to contentment with less than what ought to be the minimum standard of qualifications, and to an increase of the Ministry in quantity at the expense of its quality. Such a policy, if it were generally pursued, would be suicidal. If the Church were to fail altogether to win and hold the intellectual classes for the Christian faith, its whole cause would be in jeopardy. Yet such failure is more than probable unless the ministry can be adequately reinforced with a constant supply of men with converted hearts and awakened and well-trained minds. It is moreover obvious that if such reinforcement is not forthcoming the Australian Church will be hard put to it to find its own leaders from amongst the rank and file of its own ministry. The urgency of this matter is already gaining recognition in some quarters. It is greatly to be desired that the recognition should become general.

Church and People

In the larger centres of population, the pastoral work of the Australian Church does not differ in any essential respect from the work of parishes in England. The services of the Church are the same. The use of the English Prayer Book is obligatory. The use of one or other of the English hymn-books, though not obligatory, is universal. The same organizations are at work— C.E.M.S., G.F.S., Mothers' Union, Guild of the Servants of the Sanctuary, Guild of St. Barnabas for Nurses, etc., as in England. The duty of pastoral visitation is observed at least as fully as it is in England, and, in most cases, the parish priest knows his people well, and is known and trusted by them. He lacks the official status which establishment gives to the parish priests of England, but, if he is the right sort, he gains an unofficial status in the community which can be of even greater value. He is looked to for a lead in public affairs, and is not infrequently elected to office in public or semi-public bodies.

All this is true to an extent of parishes in the country. But there the factor of distance comes in to effect some important differences. Much of the time of the parish priest is occupied in travelling between the various centres (of which there may be as many as ten or more), in his parish. He will almost certainly be in his parish church at least once every Sunday, and he will certainly aspire to be there more than once if the demands of other centres allow of it. A typical timetable of a parish priest in the country might be an early Eucharist at, say, 7.30 a.m. in the parish church, Eucharist at two other centres at 9 or 9.30 and 11 respectively, Evensong at a country centre at 3, and in the parish church in the evening. But there are some parish priests who would consider this timetable an easy one, and who are accustomed to fit in six, or perhaps even seven, services every Sunday. In a parish with many centres it is customary to have some services on week-days as well. Undoubtedly the demands of a country parish upon the physical, mental and spiritual energy of the parish priest are very great, but they are usually fulfilled with cheerfulness and zest, and meet with an encouraging response.

As is well known, the great bulk of the population of Australia inhabits a comparatively narrow belt of country, bounded by the surrounding seas, and fitted by nature to be exploited by more or less intensive cultivation. Here are the larger centres of population, and here are the closely-settled country districts just described. But the annual rainfall diminishes both in volume and in seasonal regularity in ratio to the distance from the coast, until in the centre of the continent a stretch of country estimated as roughly one-fifth of the whole area, is completely desert. Nearly another two-fifths is arid' country, which can be used only for sheep and cattle 'runs' of vast dimensions.

In this 'outback' area, where distances are huge and settlement is sparse, the pastoral work of the Church naturally presents difficulties of an unusual kind. It is country to which the parochial system is clearly unadapted and unadaptable. But where was any alternative to the parochial system to be discovered? It is to the everlasting credit of the Church of England in Australia that it found the answer to that question in the system of what are known as Bush Brotherhoods. The system originated in the heart and brain of Dr. Westcott, the great Bishop of Durham, and was worked out by him in consultation with three other great churchmen: Canon Body, the great Missioner, Mr. Winnington-Ingram (afterwards Bishop of London), the Head of Oxford House, and Nathaniel Dawes, who had recently been enthroned as the first Bishop of Rockhampton.

The scheme was for the establishment in one of the larger centres of the district to be served of a Community House, to be recognized as the occasional home of a company of priests who would spend the bulk of their time in visiting the vast districts of which they had the oversight, but would return at stated intervals to the Community House, there to spend a period of perhaps a week or more in fellowship, conference, and prayer. This, in rough outline, is the scheme which was inaugurated just fifty years ago, when, in July 1897, George Halford, one of the ablest and most trusted of Dr. Westcott's parish priests, arrived in Longreach, there to be instituted to the charge of a parish which was twice the size of England. The scheme was greatly blessed of God, and greatly welcomed by the people to whom the Brothers went. Its pattern was subsequently copied at Dubbo (New South Wales), at Charleville in Southern Queensland, and in the Diocese of North Queensland and elsewhere. It has attracted to its service many men of high ability and great spiritual force. As has been already stated, two of the Australian archbishops (Brisbane and Perth) and eight other bishops, gained their first experience of work in Australia in one or other of the Bush Brotherhoods.

Another most successful effort to cater for the spiritual needs of the 'outback' is represented by the Bush Church Aid Society, which has its headquarters in Sydney, but has its agents at work not only in New South Wales but also in South Australia, Victoria and Western Australia. It provides parish priests to take charge of great areas for which it might otherwise be difficult for the bishop to make provision. It maintains school hostels for children coming from distant places to centres where greater educational facilities are available. It maintains two hospitals, four nursing services, and two 'flying doctors', who, with the help of a professional pilot, bring immediate medical and surgical aid to patients who might otherwise have to wait days for a doctor to reach them. It also conducts a Mail Bag Sunday School, sending out to isolated families leaflets to be used in the religious instruction of their children. Although the Society stands for a distinctively Evangelical point of view, its series of instruction in preparation for Confirmation is used by many besides those who would claim adherence to their viewpoint. For its work, no less than for that of the Bush Brothers, Australian churchmen can truly thank God.

In one important respect the clergy, in common with ministers of other denominations, become the servants of the State. At the request of the bishop of the diocese they are licensed by the Registrar-General to perform marriages, and become subject to the provisions of the Marriage Acts. They deal with the Registrar-General's department, generally through a local Registrar, and have to supply a copy of the marriage certificate within a specified period, to enable the marriage to be duly registered. They take statements of particulars from the parties to a proposed marriage, and are virtually furnished by the State with the powers of a Commissioner for Oaths for that purpose. Any false statement made to them in this connexion is regarded by the State as an act of perjury.

This statement of particulars given upon oath is the only safe-

K

guard which the State requires to ensure that the conditions of a valid marriage obtain. In at least one State (Victoria) three days' notice of an intended marriage is required: in other States no notice at all is required, and it is competent, but not of course compulsory, for the parish priest to celebrate the marriage directly the particulars have been furnished to his satisfaction. Therefore, in order to comply with the Church's requirement that every marriage for which banns have not been called, must be by special licence, all the clergy in some dioceses, and a great number of the clergy in others, have to be appointed by the bishop as Surrogates for the issue of Marriage Licences.

The Church's Finance

The older dioceses in Australia have endowments derived partly from grants of land made from the State in the early days, and partly from generous private benefactions. But these endowments have been made mostly for specific central purposes. For the support of its ordinary pastoral work, the Church depends mainly upon the freewill offerings of the faithful. In general these are most generously given, and wherever the work of the Church is being faithfully done, support for it is readily forthcoming. The 'Envelope System' of Church finance is very commonly used for securing regular contributions towards the payment of the Rector's stipend, and the general maintenance of the Church's work. In many parishes in Australia, as in England, it is used (by means of a double envelope) to raise the parish quota for the missionary work of the Church. In most parishes these direct contributions are supplemented by various indirect money-raising efforts of the familiar types. This dependence of the parish priest for his stipend on the goodwill of his people has its advantages and disadvantages. It can certainly furnish him with a clear indication as to the value which is set upon his services, and perhaps also as to the extent to which he is regarding and fulfilling his obligations, and can thus act as an incentive to activity and efficiency. On the other hand, it does invest the laity with a power which could be used to 'starve out' a man who had become unpopular, either by reason of unfaithfulness to his duty, or, perhaps, even of an unappreciated faithfulness in the delivery of his message. It is to the credit of both clergy and laity that this power is hardly ever used.

In the older dioceses the stipend of the Bishop, and at least part of other central administrative expenses, can be met out of income from endowments. In dioceses of more recent formation, such expenses have to be met to a very large extent by means of a levy on the parishes, calculated on a basis of percentage on the parish income, or on the amount it pays for its Rector's stipend. The cost of Provincial Synods, and of General Synod, is met by a levy on the dioceses, calculated on a scale proportionate to the number of their representatives, which, in turn, is determined by the number of their licensed clergy. In the computation of the cost of holding these Synods, the travelling expenses of members attending them are taken into account. So also are the travelling expenses of members attending the meetings of Committees which may have been appointed by the Synod, as well as the expenses of the Committees themselves.

The Church and Education

In Australia, as in England, the Church was the pioneer in the field of education. All schools were originally denominationl schools, which gradually secured increasing recognition and support from the Government. This denominational system held the field till 1848. Then the State began to take a share in the work, and for thirty-two years a dual system—state and denominational —was in operation. In 1880, under pressure from public opinion, the Government of Sir Henry Parkes finally withdrew all state aid to denominational schools. Since then the Church of England has virtually withdrawn from the field of primary education, while continuing to maintain secondary schools for both boys and girls, and residential colleges at the universities. The schools enjoy a deservedly high reputation for the quality of the education they impart. They have given to Australia some of its most highly esteemed public men. They have not been so successful in providing the Church with candidates for its Ministry, or in swelling to any noticeable extent the ranks of the Church-going laity, and they are frequently criticized on that account.

The University Colleges are also doing most valuable educational work. None of the Australian universities are residential. The denominational colleges are therefore rendering a service of indispensable importance by providing students with collegiate life and tutorial help with their studies. In the training of men for the Ministry they are an asset of great actual value, and of still greater potential value to the Church.

In primary education the Church takes full advantage of the opportunities provided by the various State governments for the giving of religious instruction. The word 'secular' as applied to education has never been interpreted in Australia as ruling out general religious instruction, but only as debarring the schools from themselves providing dogmatic or polemical religious teaching. And the Education Acts in most of the States accordingly provide for the giving of 'simple Bible teaching' in the school curriculum, and also for the right of the representatives of the various denominations to give religious instruction to the children of their own denomination in school hours. Both these provisions are subject to a conscience clause. The value of these opportunities necessarily varies with the capacity of those who use them, but there can be little doubt that in general it is both real and great. It will become greater still when we are wise enough to insist that all candidates for the Ministry shall be trained in the art of teaching.

The Church's Missionary Work

The real test of a church's life is its zeal in the cause of Christian Missions. It is a test which the Australian Church need not fear to face. A great Archbishop of Brisbane (St. Clair Donaldson, afterwards Bishop of Salisbury) was accustomed to say that Australia was destined to be a great missionary base, and Brisbane to be the Antioch of Australia. A glance at the map will explain his meaning. Geographically Australia is ideally qualified to be one of the principal evangelists of the Southern Hemisphere. She is rising nobly to her responsibilities.

The missionary work of the Australian Church is carried on by two main agencies, the Australian Board of Missions, and the Church Missionary Society. The latter was the first in the field, and it has a splendid and honourable record for missionary service, generosity and zeal. The Board of Missions dates from 1850, when at a meeting of the six bishops (Sydney, Melbourne, Adelaide, Tasmania, Newcastle, and New Zealand), it was decided that the Church as such should organize itself to undertake missionary work amongst the aborigines of Australia, and the people of the islands adjacent to its shores. The two organizations thus stand respectively for the view that the Church as a whole should be its own missionary society, and for the view that missionary enterprise is likely to be most effectively carried out by voluntary societies within the Church. Powerful arguments can be adduced on either side. On the one hand it can be argued that a task which was committed to the Church as a whole should be carried out by the Church as a whole. On the other hand it can be argued, in the words of Dr. Max Warren, that 'a Church so widely and properly pre-occupied can only discharge her missionary task, as historically she has best succeeded in discharging it, by treating it as the specialized function of those within the ranks who have felt laid upon them the divine constraint'.

That both views are strongly held in Australia is proved by the figures relating to missionary contributions. The Missionary Budget for 1947–8 is for a total of just over £100,000. Of this sum it is expected that C.M.S. will raise £56,000, and A.B.M. £44,000. The dioceses which are predominantly C.M.S. in sympathy are Sydney, Melbourne, and Tasmania. These three dioceses between them are expected to contribute very nearly £50,000, or half the total missionary budget of the whole Australian Church, to the work of the Church Missionary Society. It should be noted that the dioceses in which C.M.S. interest predominates include the two largest centres of population in Australia. The Diocese of Sydney alone is said to contain more than a quarter of the total Anglican population of the Commonwealth.

The Australian Board of Missions is elected every five years in connexion with the meeting of General Synod. Its Chairman *ex officio* is the Primate. Its membership is composed of bishops elected by the House of Bishops, and certain representatives of the respective Provinces, clerical and lay, elected by the representatives of the Province in General Synod, the bishops of missionary dioceses, and representatives of the Church Missionary Society. It meets normally three times a year, generally in Sydney. It gives its support to the aboriginal missions on the Australian mainland, to those in the islands of the Torres Straits, to the New Guinea Mission, for which it is mainly responsible, and to the Melanesian Mission. Its outlook is not however limited to the Pacific area, and in the past it has sent missionaries to China and to Japan. Immediately after the close of hostilities in the

Pacific war a young priest of the Australian Church (the Rev. Frank Coaldrake) offered his services through the A.B.M. to the Nippon Sei Ko Kwai, and is now at work in Japan.

The Church Missionary Society also takes its share in the evangelization of the Australian aborigines, and is doing effective work amongst them. Its outlook is as world-wide as that of its parent society. Its special responsibility is the Diocese of Tanganyika, whose first two bishops (Dr. Chambers and Dr. Wynn Jones) have both served in the ranks of the Australian priesthood.

Missionary interest in Australia was greatly stimulated by some of the experiences of war-time. Australian soldiers, many of whom, if they had thought of Christian missions at all, had thought of them sceptically and even derisively, were suddenly confronted with the astonishing results of missionary enterprise. Expecting to find, in New Guinea for instance, untutored savages or perhaps some slightly contemptible 'rice-Christians', they suddenly found themselves in the company of great-hearted Christian gentlemen, who helped them, when they were well, with all the courage of a man, and nursed them, when they were wounded or ill, with all the tenderness of a woman. The verses written by a Canadian-born soldier who was serving with the Australian forces deserve to be better known than perhaps they are. Here is an extract from them:

> Bringing back the badly wounded,
>   Just as steady as a hearse,
> Using leaves to keep the rain off,
>   And as gentle as a nurse.
> Slow and careful in bad places,
>   On the awful mountain track,
> And the look upon their faces
>   Makes you think that Christ was black.

Evidence such as that it is impossible to gainsay, and it may be that the whole attitude of Australia towards its missionary obligations has been permanently altered by suchlike experiences of the transforming power of the Christian gospel.

Attempts have been made from time to time to co-ordinate the work of the two great Australian missionary organizations, and to minimize the danger of competition, and one day this great desideratum will be achieved. Since 1916 representatives of the

C.M.S. have sat on the Board of Missions as representing a recognized missionary agency of the Church. A Determination passed by the General Synod of 1945 constitutes a Missionary Council on which both organizations can be equally represented, and in which general questions of missionary policy can be jointly discussed. This may well prove to be the greatest step towards effective co-ordination which has yet been taken.

So ends our survey of the Australian Church. It is perhaps the best note on which such a survey could be ended. For if it be true, as undoubtedly it is, that the best index of a Church's life is its zeal in the missionary cause, then the Australian Church is unmistakably alive, and can face the future without misgiving.

VII

THE CHURCH OF THE PROVINCE OF NEW ZEALAND

COMMONLY CALLED THE CHURCH OF ENGLAND

by the MOST REV. C. W. WEST-WATSON, *Archbishop of New Zealand*

This is the official title of the Anglican Church in New Zealand. Its first bishop, George Augustus Selwyn, landed at Auckland 105 years ago. In 1857 the constitution of the Church was agreed to in old St. Stephen's Chapel which still looks out over the beautiful harbour of the Queen City. Two bishops, Bishop Selwyn and Bishop Harper of Christchurch, were present that day. When Selwyn left New Zealand in 1867, five bishoprics had been founded, three in the North Island, Auckland, Waiapu and Wellington, and two in the South Island, Christchurch and Nelson. With the Province was associated the Missionary Diocese of Melanesia, constituted in 1861 under the martyr, Bishop Patteson.

The Diocese of Dunedin, making the third diocese in the South Island, was not constituted until 1871, and since then only one diocese has been added, that of Waikato, formed of the southern portion of Auckland Diocese, and constituted by General Synod in 1925. Our additional Missionary Diocese, that of Polynesia, was associated with the Province in 1923.

The Dioceses

The seven dioceses of the mainland are extensive in area, ranging from 8,000 square miles to 30,000 square miles. The North and South Islands are of approximately equal area, but, whereas in earlier days their population was about equal, the development of large areas in the North Island has led to a shift of population. Twenty years ago the ratio of population was three to two. To-day the North Island has a ratio of two to one. The total population of New Zealand is about one-and-three-quarter million, of which 120,000 are Maoris. Ninety per cent of the total number are of British extraction. Census reports show that 41 per cent enter themselves as Anglicans, the three other most numerous Communions being Presbyterians 26 per cent, Roman Catholics 14 per cent and Methodists 9 per cent. Two-fifths of the population are located in the four main centres: Auckland 250,000, Wellington 200,000, Christchurch 150,000, and Dunedin 80,000.

The supervision and administration of the large scattered dioceses was, till recently, a matter of much difficulty and some adventure. Roads and tracks were in many places only negotiable on horseback, and the flooding of creeks and rivers was all too common. With the advent of motor traffic, metalled and surfaced roads have multiplied and creeks and rivers have been bridged. Air travel has now made communications easier. Whereas a journey from Dunedin to attend a General Synod in Auckland by train and steamer used to occupy some forty-eight hours for a distance of 900 miles, the journey can now be accomplished by air in eight hours.

The oldest of the dioceses is Auckland, originally covering the large area in the north of New Zealand which was left to Selwyn when Waiapu and Wellington Dioceses were constituted for the rest of the North Island. Selwyn himself always retained his original title of Bishop of New Zealand and Metropolitan, but his successor, Bishop Cowie, became the first titular Bishop of Auckland. In this diocese the earliest missionaries worked, and here are the oldest historic church sites and buildings, and the Selwyn tradition is strong. Close to the city is St. John's College, a Provincial Theological College founded by Bishop Selwyn and justly proud of its unique little chapel. There are eighteen parishes and thirty-three parochial districts, with 114 clergy, fifteen of them of the Maori race. The Cathedral is a fine timber structure, but a large legacy has been left for the building of a new Cathedral in permanent materials. With the growth of the city and the opening-up of new areas for cultivation a subdivision became advisable, and the southern portion of the diocese was in 1925 constituted as the Diocese of Waikato with Hamilton as its see-town.

The second diocese to be formed in New Zealand was that of Christchurch, including the central third of the South Island, most of the Canterbury Plains, and extending across the Southern Alps to take in a long stretch of the west coast; and also including the Chatham Islands some 500 miles off the east coast. Christchurch was designed to be an Anglican settlement, and the 'first four ships' brought the founders to Lyttleton in 1850. The fine stone cathedral in the centre of the city witnesses to their design. The spirit of these founders, affectionately remembered as the Canterbury Pilgrims, is still an inspiration to the diocese. The Cathedral was endowed by them, and is the only one in New Zealand without parochial responsibilities. Bishop Harper, an old friend of Bishop Selwyn, came out to be the first bishop in 1856. There is a very fine stone church in Timaru, the second largest centre in the Diocese. Christ's College, the earliest public school in New Zealand, was also founded by them, with an 'Upper Department', which has since grown into 'College House', a university hostel and training centre for ordinands. There are now twenty-five parishes, thirty-four parochial districts, with sixty-nine clergy.

The Diocese of Wellington was created in 1858, and covers a large area to the north of the city with its other large centres in Palmerston North, in a central position, and Wanganui, 100 miles up the west coast. The district had been settled with a view to commerce and agriculture, with the result that there was no early and strong ecclesiastical tradition as in some other dioceses. In spite of this the Diocese made its own tradition and has grown to be one of the most important and best manned in the country. The fixing of the capital in Wellington in 1865 gave it an added importance. There are now twenty-one parishes and forty parochial districts with seventy-three clergy. There are also five Maori pastorates, with at present three licensed clergy. The Cathedral is the old timber church of St. Paul, but the last bishop, Bishop Holland, secured a magnificent site for a permanent building, and raised a considerable sum of money towards its erection. Palmerston North has a beautiful church built in brick.

In the same year (1858) the Diocese of Nelson was formed to include the northern portion of the South Island. Nelson, a very early settlement, created a city by Queen Victoria in 1858 because of its cathedral, is the see-city, but mountains and rivers separate the various towns and districts. On the west coast, Greymouth and Westport are mining and shipping centres, and Blenheim, a farming centre on the north-east coast, is the other largest centre. The Diocese includes the very beautiful Marlborough Sounds. The first portion of a new cathedral in grey marble has been erected on the commanding site occupied by the old cathedral in Nelson. Despite difficulties of communication, there is a strong diocesan life and tradition. The population is not large, but there are five parishes, twenty-nine parochial districts, and twenty-five clergy.

One year later (1859) the Diocese of Waiapu was created, covering the north-eastern portion of the North Island. It has a great tradition of the work of the early missionaries and includes the famous Maori centre of Rotorua. The See is fixed at Napier on the west coast; Hastings is the largest centre of population and has a large church which calls up memories of an abbey church in the homeland. There are no large centres of population, and the Bishop until recently had long months of difficult travelling every year. Communications have improved vastly of recent times, but the work is of necessity less centralized than in any other diocese. A fine cathedral in brick was built in Napier in 1886, but it was completely destroyed by the disastrous earthquake in 1931, after which a temporary building was erected. There are eleven parishes in the Diocese, seventeen parochial districts, and fifty clergy.

The area of the Diocese of Dunedin, covering the southern portion of the South Island and Stewart Island, was administered for a time by the Bishop of Christchurch, but in 1871 it was formed into a diocese with its centre in Dunedin. The settlement was originally distinctively Presbyterian, and the Presbyterian Church took a leading part in the founding of Otago University, which is now one of the constituent Colleges in the University of New Zealand. Anglicans are in a minority, but have built the nave of what will eventually be a very fine cathedral in a striking position in the centre of the city. Selwyn College, where students of the university reside and ordinands are trained for the ministry, is also an Anglican foundation. There are fifteen parishes, fourteen parochial districts, and thirty-two clergy in the Diocese.

The Diocese of Waikato, constituted in 1925, has its see-town in Hamilton in the Waikato, one of the most fertile farming districts in New Zealand. The fine church rising above the town makes a striking cathedral. The Diocese also includes the 'King Country' with a large Maori population. A good deal of this country is rough and difficult. Beyond it the Diocese extends over to the west coast where the central town is New Plymouth, with its beautiful stone church built in early days. Nearby some of the battles of the Maori Wars were fought and the memorials to the fallen are a conspicuous feature in the church. Mount Egmont with its snowy cone dominates the district. There are five parishes and twenty-six parochial districts as well as five Maori mission districts, with forty-four clergy, one of them a Maori.

The different dioceses grew up for the most part around settlements from the Old Country, and developed their different ecclesiastical outlooks. One of the tasks of the Church is to achieve a common policy and common action. Each diocese has its own Diocesan Synod which meets annually. The Province has its General Synod which only meets once in three years, as in Selwyn's day, though plans are being discussed for more frequent meetings and for ways of bringing the whole Church into closer touch with its proceedings. Only the bishop, three clergy and four laity from each diocese attend, so that the proceedings of General Synod are apt to have a certain remoteness from the parishes. The Diocesan Synods are the real centres of church life, as is inevitable when the early settlements grew up with so little mutual contact possible. There the bishop, all the clergy and an equivalent number of laity meet together annually. The primary purpose of Diocesan Synods is to legislate for the diocese, subject to the canons and to resolutions of General Synod. But questions of the day are also discussed, and in addition to the Synod service and sermon, devotional gatherings often form part of the programme. In earlier days the meetings of Synod were prolonged and many social gatherings took place, as the Synod time was generally also the annual holiday time of the clergy. More strenuous times have led to concentration on business, and Diocesan Synods rarely last more than four or five days. Occasionally a woman member has been elected, but very rarely.

General Synod

Each of the Diocesan Synods sends the bishop, three clergy and four laity to General Synod. The Missionary Dioceses have a somewhat smaller representation. No woman member has yet been elected to General Synod. The Constitution of General Synod owes very much to the vision and foresight of Bishop Selwyn. It has had its influence on Church Assemblies in England, and also on the constitution of the Nippon Sei Ko Kwai in Japan. The laity have an effective voice in the proceedings, in which the consent of all three Orders is necessary for any decision.

The meetings are held in rotation in the various dioceses and normally last about ten days. The Church has its own canons in which certain clauses are defined as fundamental. But an Enabling Act was passed through Parliament giving certain liberties so long as the doctrinal foundation is maintained. A curious survival is the reference to 'The United Church of England and Ireland'. The essential business of General Synod is legislative and financial. At meetings of General Synod canons are amended or added to, and a levy made on the different dioceses by agreed percentages to meet the necessary provincial expenses. The 'power of the purse' really rests with the dioceses, and there is an urgent need for an adequate Central Fund to enable the Church as a whole to have some more freedom of manoeuvre without the appeal to the parishes through the dioceses.

Between the meetings of General Synod executive power rests with the Standing Committee of General Synod, which generally meets once a year, but can be summoned more often if necessary.

The Primacy

One result of the way in which the Church has grown up from local centres is that the Primacy has never been attached to any fixed see. Shortly before Bishop Selwyn left New Zealand it was agreed by General Synod that General Synod should elect one of the bishops to be Primate. There are obvious disadvantages in the removal of the administrative centre from place to place, and proposals have been made for fixing the Primacy in the capital city, Wellington, where the Archbishop would be in touch with the central authorities, and in a central position. Headquarters of government and commercial departments are being increasingly centred in Wellington, and it may be that the Primacy will eventually be fixed there also. At present the advantages of the sharing in the Primacy by the various dioceses seem to outweigh the arguments for a fixed see. Primates have been elected from Auckland (one), Christchurch (three), Wellington (one), and Dunedin (one).

It was only in the General Synod of 1922 that it was decided that the Primate should be styled 'Archbishop', so that there is no long local or official tradition behind the title, and diocesan rights and prerogatives are not prejudiced.

Parishes and Parochial Districts and the Clergy

It should be explained that 'parishes' are centres where parochial life has been so developed that parishioners have been able to assume general financial responsibility for the support of the ministry. 'Parochial districts' are centres where such a position has not been attained, or where diocesan help is necessary. Speaking generally, the 'parishes' are in the towns and the 'parochial districts' are in the country. These districts often contain many centres, and services are held in small churches and schoolrooms over a wide area. The work entails considerable expenditure of physical energy, and the ability to drive a motor-car long distances sometimes through difficult country. One of the postwar problems is the provision of motor-cars for the clergy now that prices have risen to such a height. Sometimes the cars are the property of the parishes, sometimes they belong to the clergy themselves. In the latter case the purchase of such cars entails a burden of repayment over years, and is a heavy tax on the already small incomes. Clerical incomes vary in the different dioceses, but those of 'parishes' rarely exceed £400 per annum (with a house) and those of 'parochial districts' might vary from £250 to £350 (with a house). Strenuous efforts are being made to raise the incomes of the clergy in order to keep pace with the rising cost of living, and something is being done to raise central diocesan funds. Endowments are few and small, Christchurch Diocese being the most fortunate in this respect, owing to the enthusisam of its early founders. In the cities the Church is faced with some extensive municipal building schemes, and this entails the raising of further central funds both to help over-burdened parishes and also to found new 'parochial districts'.

For many years General Synod has been planning and working for a Provincial Pension Fund for clergy, and considerable progress has been made in this direction. At present the three northern dioceses and the Missionary Dioceses have a fund of their own, while the four southern dioceses have their own diocesan pension funds. The clergyman and the parish each pay an annual amount into the fund, the amount paid by the clergyman increasing according to his age at the date of joining the fund. The retiring age is sixty-five, and few of the clergy continue their work much longer, for the conditions of work are more exacting than in most English parishes. On retirement a beneficiary would, speaking generally, receive some £5 per annum for each year of service in the diocese, his widow receiving proportionately less. The rise in prices, and the difficulties of housing, have made the problem of retirement more difficult, and, at present, the clergy have to pay their Social Security tax as well as their pension contribution. This entitles them at present to a small sum in addition to their ecclesiastical pension, but in some twenty years this additional sum should, by annual increases, amount to £75 per annum.

Of the clergy themselves approximately 60 per cent are of New Zealand birth and training, most of the remainder having come from England or Australia. The Church of the Province conducts its own Central Ordination Examination, and awards a Diploma of Licentiate in Theology to those who reach the required standard. A good many of the clergy have also taken the degrees of B.A. or M.A. of the New Zealand University. Some have taken what is known as the Melbourne B.D. degree, which entails considerable scholarship. Recently the University of New Zealand has included in its curriculum a B.D. degree, for which the Churches are to supply the teaching. It is probable that this will supply the aim for post-graduate study in the future. Many of those who have come from outside New Zealand also hold university qualifications. Some of the younger clergy avail themselves of opportunities for short periods of service in England, which proves of great value to their work. Isolated as the Province is, contact with England and the help of clergy coming from the homeland has proved most valuable. Links with England have been and are much closer than with any other country, though, with the growing feeling of a Pacific solidarity, it is not improbable that links with our Church in other Pacific lands will be closer in the future. The last war made it clear that the fortunes of Australia and New Zealand are linked with those of the islands of Melanesia and Polynesia to the north which served as a defensive screen and, occupied by American and British troops and ships, protected New Zealand from a Japanese invasion. The idea of a 'South Pacific Zone' is becoming more definite, and our obligations to that Zone will become more definite too. Air travel has brought us closer to the branches of our Church in Japan, China and the North American mainland, and it would be strange if in future years the Church in New Zealand did not develop more intimate relations with those Churches. The Primate in 1947 accepted an invitation to visit the General Synod of the Episcopal Church in Japan.

Educational work

The New Zealand Church very early in its history undertook educational responsibilities for both Maori and 'Pakeha' (as the Maoris call the white people), along with other Churches. The idea of state responsibility had not developed, and, indeed, the governments of early days were too sketchy to undertake any such detailed administration. When, however, a central Government was established in place of the former provincial governments, an education policy was steadily developed, until the whole country was provided with educational opportunities extending from the primary school to the university. This was a natural and necessary development, since the churches were not able to cover the ground, and there was the danger of denominational rivalry. When the Primary Education Act was introduced in 1877, the system was declared to be 'free, secular and compulsory'. There has been some difference of opinion as to whether the word 'secular' was to be interpreted as meaning more than 'nondenominational', but in practice it has been taken at its face value and, in spite of energetic and organized efforts by the Church, religion has been excluded from the curriculum. The Roman Catholic Church educates the vast majority of its children in its own primary day schools. The Church of England has just a few of such schools, but finds it difficult to staff and maintain them at a standard which will compare with that of state institutions. There has, however, grown up a system of voluntary teaching, given at times not included in the statutory curriculum, which is generally known as the 'Nelson System'. Clergy and ministers and other voluntary teachers give instruction on biblical and non-denominational lines for half an hour a week, generally in the school buildings. This is felt to be quite inadequate from the point of view of the churches, but most of the clergy make use of the opportunity not only of teaching scripture, but of getting to know the children, many of whom do not come to Sunday

School or get Christian teaching at home. The work and the travelling often involved are, of course, a considerable tax on the time and energy of the New Zealand clergy.

In regard to secondary education, the State has established an admirable and most efficient chain of high schools, and technical schools throughout the country, where the secular bar is not held to operate, and in many of them religious teaching is given by members of the staff. Alongside these schools, partly as a result of early benefactions and partly as a result of more recent foundations, the larger churches maintain many secondary schools both for boys and for girls throughout the country, and make through them their most valuable contribution to education. Church of England secondary schools are generally under diocesan management, but sometimes under Anglican boards of governors. There are such schools both for Maori and Pakeha, though some Maoris attend Pakeha schools and vice-versa. The rising standards of salaries, maintenance and food, present great problems to such private schools as have no endowments, but the churches place a high value on them, and will make a great struggle to maintain them. The Education Department is sympathetic, and our schools are visited and reported on by Government inspectors. It should be said that there are excellent Anglican preparatory schools for boys, generally in private hands.

New Zealand University is composed of four University Colleges, one in each of the main centres. The main contribution of the churches to student life is through students' hostels for men and women in certain centres, of which work a further development is most desirable. It is much behind the point reached in Australia, where some of the denominational hostels are almost on the lines of colleges at Oxford and Cambridge. The churches are also developing a system of Student Chaplains in the various centres, who, though unofficial, are making a valuable contribution to the spiritual side of student life. The general situation is much like that in the newer universities in England, where the Church is rather at the circumference than the centre, and finds it difficult to make its contribution, or to arouse church people to the importance of using every opportunity to minister to the spiritual life of the student world.

L

Maori and Pakeha

The life of the New Zealand Church is intimately bound up with its fellowship of Maori and Pakeha, and the problems of their relationship are some of the most urgent which press for solution. In the early missionary days Maori Christians far outnumbered all others, and the prospects for a great Maori Church seemed most hopeful. The rush of immigrants from Europe and the unfortunate Maori Wars changed the whole outlook. Political differences obscured the religious issue. Maori schisms such as the Ringatu and Hau Hau movements carried off many Christians who were not deeply rooted in the faith and order of the historic Church, and had not realized its real emphasis. Mormon missionaries secured a large following, and are still working energetically to-day. More recently the Maori prophet Ratana, who had powers of spiritual healing, founded a Church of his own, with bishops and clergy, which has deeply divided the Maori people. At first the religious element in the movement was strong, but it has become more and more political and a means of expressing the nationalist aspirations of the Maori race. The Anglican, Methodist, Roman Catholic and Presbyterian Churches, however, still include large numbers of Maori people in their membership. The dioceses which include the bulk of our Maori churchmen are Auckland, Waiapu and Waikato. There are a fair number in Wellington Diocese, and a small number scattered over the South Island.

The Maori people went through a period of deep discouragement after the Maori Wars. Chivalrous and generous themselves, they felt deeply that the Pakeha had taken unfair advantage of their simplicity, and grievances, mostly about the sale of lands and the appropriation of lands, rankled in their minds. The Pakeha indeed had often been impatient and inconsiderate, and had failed to understand the intricacies of Maori communal ownership of land. The Pakeha believed in fixed settlements and development of land. The Maori was accustomed to temporary and casual cultivation, and to freedom of movement in a land which for centuries he had looked upon as his own. More and more the Maoris became a small minority in a growing Pakeha population, and, with loss of hope, the race declined rapidly in numbers. There were many who thought that it was only a matter of time till the Maori would be merged in the Pakeha race, and

who discouraged long-term planning for a Maori people. Happily
a change took place during the present century, largely owing to
a 'Young Maori party' led by Sir Apirana Ngata, and consisting
largely of Maoris educated at Te Aute College, an old-established Anglican secondary school for boys of Maori race. This
movement brought the Maoris more into line with modern
methods of agriculture and encouraged Maori people to take
advantage of educational opportunities to qualify themselves for
the professions and for industry. Hope revived in the race, and,
whereas in 1900 their numbers had fallen to some 60,000, they
number to-day about 120,000. Many are full-blooded Maoris:
many are of mixed race, but 'live Maori'. Maori lore and traditions are being revived, and members of the race are taking important positions in Parliament and in the life of the country.
The achievements of the Maori Battalion in the recent war have
won the gratitude and admiration of all New Zealanders, and
have revealed great gifts of leadership in the Maori race. The
ancient grievances are being rectified, and there is hope that unhappy memories will be laid to rest. One thing must be said, and
that is that any talk of a colour bar is grossly exaggerated. Intermarriage brings no reproach. Whatever our domestic differences,
Maori and Pakeha stand together as New Zealanders towards
those outside our boundaries. We have lived together, fought
together, played together, laughed together. We are 'one people',
as Governor Hobson said to the Maori Chiefs at Waitangi in
1840.

All this history has, of course, had its bearing on our church
life and problems. On the one hand there are those who feel that
the Maori Christians should be absorbed in the main stream of
Church life, and take their place in its leadership and counsels
as they prove themselves worthy and competent. The aim should
be that Maori and Pakeha should minister interchangeably to
congregations of the different races. Distinctions of race should
not be encouraged in a Church where all are 'one man in Christ
Jesus'.

On the other hand, many Maoris and Pakehas feel that the
Maori's small numbers will be lost in the huge Pakeha majority,
and the special contribution which he should make will be dis-
sipated. He will be practically unrepresented on church Synods
and committees, and his voice unheard. For the present it may

be better that, where there are considerable numbers of Maoris, the Maori congregations should be ministered to by Maori clergy until Maori leadership is developed and standards of churchmanship strengthened. At present more would be lost than gained by premature fusion. It is worth noting that four Maori members are elected to Parliament by special Maori constituencies, and that the Education Department appoints special Inspectors of Maori schools.

These same problems affect the question of the usefulness of schools specially maintained for Maori boys and girls.

Some twenty years ago these two points of view came into conflict in General Synod when the question of forming a Maori diocese was under consideration. Finally it was resolved to consecrate a Maori suffragan bishop in Waiapu Diocese, who might be commissioned by other bishops to visit and help Maori churchmen in their dioceses. Such a plan has its obvious difficulties in regard to dual control, and, if it has not solved our difficulties, it has at any rate given to the Church in Bishop F. A. Bennett, first Bishop of Aotearoa (the Maori name for New Zealand) an honoured and beloved member of the episcopate. The main difficulties in regard to fusion at present are not really those of language or colour or even different standards of education, but a deeply ingrained difference of cultural background, and of psychological approach. It may be some time before our life together in New Zealand gives us a common background.

At present Maori pastorates are organized in the North Island dioceses, administered by Maori clergy working alongside Pakeha clergy. In the past many of the Maori clergy have been inadequately supported and have had to supplement their incomes by other work, but this is being rectified. There is, however, an urgent need for more intensive work among those Maori people who have lapsed from the Church or who have joined sects or movements which have no spiritual future. The need for such work is impressing itself on our Maori Christians, and there is hope that they may be able to appeal to their brethren more effectively than the Pakeha. There is also an urgent need for the encouragement by the Maori leaders of suitable and able young men to offer themselves for the ministry of the Church.

The Church is justly proud of its secondary schools for Maori boys and girls, some of them of early missionary origin. Many scholars are supported at these schools by Government grants, and there is an increasing number of Maori young people who are training there with a view to devoting themselves to the service of their own people as teachers and nurses.

Much will depend on a wise and sympathetic treatment of the problem of the Maori Church in the coming years. Diocesan boundaries make a unified treatment more difficult, and it has also to be remembered that tribal distinctions and traditions among the Maori people are still to be reckoned with. They are strangely reminiscent of the clan spirit of the Scottish Highlands. But some way must be found for the enrichment of our Church by the spiritual gifts and possibilities of this attractive, generous and gifted people.

Youth work

The Church of this Province has given a good deal of thought to its youth work in recent years, and is making great efforts to reach the large numbers of children of its nominal adherents who are untouched by its present organizations, and to retain others who drift away after Sunday School age. Sunday School work receives much attention, and three dioceses have full-time Sunday School organizers. There is also a Church Mail Bag School, which has over 1,600 members. There are a few church primary day schools and kindergarten schools, and most clergy give some scripture instruction in out-of-school hours in the state primary schools. Some twenty-five years ago an indigenous movement grew up in the Anglican and other churches, called the 'Bible Class Movement'. Anglican Boys' Bible Classes and Girls' Bible Classes, with religious, social and recreational activities, grew in numbers till eventually Dominion-wide central councils were formed, and annual summer camps arranged. Recently boys' and girls' unions have been amalgamated into one 'Anglican Bible Class Union'. There are also in some parishes branches of the Girls' Friendly Society; in some, troops of Boy Scouts and Girl Guides, generally open troops, are established. This movement has taken a deeper hold in some dioceses than in others. In a few there are Boys' and Girls' Brigades. A few years ago the feeling that our youth work was too fragmentary led to the inauguration of a new movement, the 'Young Anglican Movement', which was intended to be inclusive and was modelled on a successful experiment made in the Diocese of Goulburn in Australia. Circumstances, however, are different in New Zealand, and, though in some dioceses the new movement has become the central youth organization, in others the Bible Class Movement continues vigorous. In many parishes 'Youth Fellowships' have been developing mostly for young people of seventeen and over.

Of late years the different dioceses have set up Youth Councils, and a Youth Council for the Dominion links all the various efforts together.

The Government is taking a very active interest in the development of the youth of the country, and there have been fears that the Sunday work of the churches might be interfered with by a call to attend week-end camps. These fears have not been realized, and the churches have been glad to find the Government cooperative, and also to avail themselves of training courses for youth leadership provided by the State. Leadership in youth work, as in other departments of church life, is one of our most pressing problems, and in some dioceses camps and conferences have been arranged for the training of leaders.

Much depends on what part the churches can play in the youth work of new Community Centres, and on whether we can supply leaders who are equipped not only for the athletic and recreational demands of such centres, but are also capable of spiritual leadership. The changing 'set-up' of community life requires constant watchfulness lest new methods should be overlooked and new opportunities missed.

The Church Army

In 1931 a team of Church Army Captains and Sisters came from England to pay an exploratory visit to New Zealand. They travelled round all the dioceses holding missions, and eventually received invitations from sufficient dioceses to justify the Church Army establishing itself in this country. A suitable building having been offered on generous terms by Auckland Diocese, headquarters were established in that city, and Captain S. R. Banyard, C.A., who had led the visiting team, became the first Director. Here a beginning was made in the training of men and women candidates. During the war the Church Army gave yeoman service in the manning and staffing of huts for the troops in various camps in New Zealand. A hut was also maintained in

Maadi near Cairo, and a small team of Church Army workers
were with the troops in the Middle East. At present a hut is
worked through Church Army at Kiwa, the New Zealand hospital centre in Japan. The training centre in Auckland, now known
as Carlile House, is being developed for the training generally of
women church workers, as well as of Church Army Sisters. A
Mission House for work amongst the Maori people has been
established at Waimate North. The help of Church Army Captains and Sisters is being increasingly valued in social work and
in the parishes; indeed the demand outruns the supply. All the
dioceses now co-operate in welcoming the Church Army, which
has recently been formally constituted and incorporated.

Men's work

There are various parochial organizations, Men's Groups, etc.,
but the only Provincial men's organization is that of the Church
of England Men's Society. An effective Dominion Conference is
held annually, and vigorous efforts are being made to increase the
number of parochial branches. At present there are sixty-eight
such branches. There is room for a real advance in the concentration and direction of the potential effectiveness of our church
laymen, but it has to be remembered that as churchwardens and
vestrymen they play an essential and important part in our church
life. Where endowments are so few, the responsibility of raising
funds for stipends and church maintenance entail considerably
heavier tasks than in most English parishes. The laymen also
render invaluable service as lay readers, both diocesan and parochial. Where country parishes have so many centres to be served,
and often at such great distances, the help of lay readers is
specially important, and both clergy and people are greatly
indebted to them for their services.

Women's work

The Mothers' Union is well established in all the dioceses of
the Province. There is a Dominion Council and also Diocesan
Councils. The earliest branch was formed in Avonside Parish,
Christchurch, in 1886; and there are now 9,380 members in the
Province, the largest branches being in Auckland, Christchurch,
Wellington and Waiapu. The Mothers' Union is one of our
strongest organizations, and plays a most important part in our

church life. In various centres Junior Branches, Fellowships of Marriage and Open Groups have been formed. The Union took part in the recent world-wide 'call' to re-dedication and re-affirmation.

There are two Religious Orders in New Zealand, the Community of the Good Shepherd in Auckland, and the Community of the Sacred Name in Christchurch. The former developed out of a 'Streets and Lanes' Mission in Auckland, the latter was inaugurated as a community of deaconess sisters, but, since 1917 no sister has been made a deaconess.

Deaconesses have been ordained in Christchurch and Waiapu Dioceses. One is still working in Waiapu Diocese, one (from abroad) is working in Wellington Diocese. In Christchurch the Director of Sunday School and youth work and one of her assistants are deaconesses, and one deaconess is working in a parish.

New Zealand does not seem to provide as large a field for the recruitment of women with a vocation for leadership in church life and activities as England. In other departments of our national life women are taking an increasingly prominent place, and it is to be hoped that our churchwomen too will respond to the urgent call for leadership and initiative in women's work and youth work.

An attempt was made in Christchurch to provide a training house for women church workers, but there were not sufficient candidates to justify the continuation of the experiment. Recently arrangements have been made for the training of women candidates for work as deaconesses, missionaries, youth leaders, etc. at Carlile House, our Church Army training house in Auckland. Training will be on lines similar to those of the inter-diocesan syllabuses in England. The General Synod in 1946 asked for a Commission to report on the advisability of appointing an inter-diocesan council for the regularizing of the training and employment of women church workers.

Chaplains to the Forces

Before the World War the only regular chaplain supplied by the New Zealand Church was a Naval Chaplain, with headquarters at Auckland. The mobilization of forces at home and their despatch overseas made heavy calls on the Church for chaplains for sea, land and air forces. Altogether seventy-eight chaplains were mobilized for army work in New Zealand, with the Middle East Force, in the Pacific, or on transports, seven being Maori clergy. One chaplain was killed, and two were wounded. Three were awarded the D.S.O., three the M.C., one the C.B.E., two the M.B.E., four were mentioned in despatches, and one received the U.S. Bronze Star. Four chaplains were mobilized for the Royal New Zealand Navy, of whom one died on active service. Eleven were mobilized for the Royal New Zealand Air Force, of whom seven were on active service in the Pacific, one being awarded the M.B.E.

Army chaplains are at present under the Adjutant General's Department, and are appointed after nomination by a Dominion Chaplains' Advisory Council on which the various churches have representation. Such nominations are made in a proportion roughly corresponding to the numerical strength of the denominations. Since the war there is still a call for chaplains, and the Chaplains' Advisory Council continues to function. Three of our clergy (one Maori) are serving with the New Zealand Brigade in Japan, three with the Navy and two with the Air Force. The number who will be required permanently will depend on the outcome of plans for Empire defence and the contribution which New Zealand will be called on to make.

Various Chaplaincies

There are branches of the Flying Angel Mission in Auckland, Wellington and Dunedin. In Auckland and Wellington, the largest ports, there are whole-time chaplains, and in Christchurch and Dunedin one of the parochial clergy acts as Port Chaplain. Arrangements for the welcome and help of Church of England immigrants are under discussion.

There are City Missions in Auckland, Wellington and Christchurch, under the charge of a clergyman in the first two cases, and in Christchurch under a Church Army Captain. Ministrations in public hospitals and mental hospitals, as well as in prisons, are provided for either by a special chaplain (who may be a clergyman who has retired from active parochial work) or by one of the parochial clergy.

Foreign missionary work

The Church of New Zealand owes its origin to the historic missionary labours of Samuel Marsden and his band of Church Missionary adventurers for Christ in what was then a difficult and dangerous sphere. It strives to repay something of its debt by sending its own missionaries to other lands. The early obligation to the Church Missionary Society has never been forgotten, and the N.Z.C.M.S. has a vigorous life and maintains missionaries in China, India and Africa. The arrival of Bishop Selwyn in 1842 brought an immediate missionary responsibility of its own. For some reason the borders of his diocese were defined so as to include a large area of Pacific islands to the north of New Zealand, and the Bishop initiated a vigorous evangelistic and educational work later handed over to Bishop Patteson when a Diocese of Melanesia was constituted in 1861. This Mission is naturally regarded as a primary call on the New Zealand Church, though substantially supported in England and also helped by Australia. It includes missions in the Solomon Islands, New Hebrides and Santa Cruz, islands prominent in the recent Pacific campaign. In 1921 the Diocese of Polynesia, including missions in Fiji, Tonga, Western Samoa, and the Cook Islands, was also associated with the Province of New Zealand. Missionaries are also sent to the S.P.G. Diocese of North China and supported in their work there. The Jerusalem and the East Mission is financially assisted.

In earlier years each mission raised its own funds and conducted its own propaganda campaigns, but in 1922 an important new system was introduced. A Board of Missions was inaugurated, in which the various missions were co-ordinated. This was a step towards the Church becoming its own missionary society and facing up in a corporate capacity to its missionary responsibilities. The committee of each mission annually prepares and presents to the board a budget of its needs for the coming year. After examination and approval of these budgets, the board, after allowing for working expenses and any other calls on its funds, arrives at the total sum required, and calls on each diocese to provide a share of the whole, assessed on an agreed proportionate basis. The dioceses in their turn apportion their quota among the various parishes. Most parishes gladly contribute their quota, some provide more, some less. But, year by year, the total sum

asked for is provided and even exceeded. Elasticity is secured by
freedom to earmark contributions for special missions, which are
reckoned as part of the parochial quota. Experience proves that
such earmarked money rarely, if ever, exceeds the total amounts
asked for by any Society, and does not upset the system. The total
budget asked for last year amounted to £25,000 and £27,700 was
contributed, of which Melanesia receives £9,000 and C.M.S.
£8,000. At present the budgets are being stepped up by £1,000
each year, with a view to reaching a total of £30,000. A sum of
£10,000, made up out of annual budget surpluses, has now been
laid aside in order to stabilize the amounts required for missionary budgets in case of any financial depression or unexpected loss
of income.

During the war a sum of well over £30,000 was raised for
restoration of war damages in the co-ordinated missions, and for
advancement of the work of the missions after the war.

The Board has from time to time supported a missionary or
missionaries of its own, but it is not a 'sending' society. Its task
is to consider claims of work, to provide finance and to direct propaganda. Visiting missionary agents and missionaries on furlough
work under direction from the Board, and though their message
naturally concerns their own work, their appeal is for the funds
administered by the Board. The Board has a General Secretary
and office in Wellington, and a bi-monthly leaflet, *The Reaper*,
with news of outstanding missionary interest and information
about the missionaries from New Zealand supported by its funds.

This missionary method has proved a benefit to all the co-
ordinated societies, and is now well established. It has eliminated
much overlapping and is giving to churchpeople a sense of the
unity of their missionary opportunities and responsibilities.

Co-operation with other Communions

As a result mainly of the World Conferences in Edinburgh and
Oxford in 1937, the Anglican Church has taken part in the formation of a National Council of Churches in New Zealand, which
has its organizing secretary and office in Christchurch. The
Council has its local branches in various centres, and has co-
ordinated a Youth Council which had been in existence previously. There is also a women's sub-committee which is very
active. The Council has no power to make pronouncements on

behalf of the churches except when authorized by them to do so, but appoints commissions or organizes conferences which produce reports for the consideration or action of the constituent churches. In 1945 a representative and largely attended 'Life and Work' Conference was held in Christchurch. In 1947 a 'Faith and Order' Conference with a membership of 160 was held in Wellington. By these conferences the churches in New Zealand are trying to keep abreast with the work and thought of the Ecumenical Movement. Through the work of the National Council, the churches have been discovering the wide field of work which opens up for common consideration and action without trying to arrive at premature solutions of their differences, and there has been a real growth of fellowship.

Six places as members in the forthcoming Amsterdam meeting of the World Council of Churches have been allotted to the New Zealand churches, with alternates, and the Anglican Church has nominated a delegate.

The emergencies of the war led to the formation of a central 'Inter-Church Council on Public and Social Affairs' in Wellington, on which the Roman Catholic Church is represented as well as the Anglican and other Churches. This Council has proved a most valuable one in presenting a united Christian attitude on many matters submitted to it or taken up by it. Especially it has been able to represent to the Government the Christian reaction to proposed plans or policies, and also to bring matters which call for action or amendment to the notice of Ministers of State. Recently the Council was approached by the Government with a view to the appointment of representatives of the churches to take part in a conference on aid to Britain. The Government has also asked the Council to arrange for the appointment of representatives of the churches on local committees with regard to the reception of immigrants.

The Anglican Church is represented on the National Missionary Council of New Zealand, and on the 'Bible-in-Schools League' which was formed to support Parliamentary action for securing the inclusion of Bible teaching in the curriculum of primary schools. Attempts to secure the passage of such a bill were unsuccessful and the League is at present engaged in furthering the 'Nelson System' of voluntary religious teaching, previously mentioned.

VIII

THE ANGLICAN COMMUNION IN THE FAR EAST
(CHINA, JAPAN, KOREA)

by the REV. MICHAEL BRUCE, *formerly Assistant Chaplain of Shanghai
Cathedral and Secretary of the S.C.M. in China*

The Churches of China and Japan are autonomous provinces,
the Diocese of Korea is under obedience to the See of Canterbury. Whereas at first sight it might seem therefore a simple task
to survey at least the ecclesiastical organization of the area, the
situation is in fact most complex. For example, within the
Church in China (the Chung Hua Sheng Kung Hui), the Diocese
of Eastern Szechuan is staffed by Anglican members of the China
Inland Mission, but this Mission itself is not Anglican but undenominational: the bishops of the dioceses of American origin are
members not only of the House of Bishops of the C.H.S.K.H.,
but also of that of the Protestant Episcopal Church in the U.S.A.
The Missionary Society system in England results in a series of
differing relationships between mission and diocese and also in a
difference in 'colour' between dioceses, owing to the differences between their parent societies.

The Church in Japan (the Nippon Sei Ko Kwai) owing to the
much smaller territory which it serves, and to its decision to adopt
the principle of self-support, might be thought to be at a stage
of relationships which would be simpler to describe; but in the
first place it is too soon for the new arrangements to have their
full effect in cross-fertilizing and unifying the diverse traditions
of the original missionary society districts. Secondly, during the
war a part of the Anglican population entered, and a part did not
enter, the Union of Churches, which was founded under considerable nationalist pressure. The resulting schism created problems which are happily well on the way to solution, but clearly
no survey would be complete which did not give some account
of this.

The Diocese of Korea is the most homogeneous of the three
areas covered by this chapter, but it differs considerably from

either of the others in the tradition of its churchmanship and clearly calls for separate treatment.

It seems wise therefore to treat the three areas separately and to confine any general conclusions with regard to the Far East as a whole to a final summary.

CHINA
(CHUNG HUA SHENG KUNG HUI)

Introductory

The Chung Hua Sheng Kung Hui (Holy Catholic Church in China) was recognized as an autonomous province of the Anglican Communion by the Lambeth Conference of 1930. It came into being in 1912 as a result of the work of a conference of representatives of the Anglican dioceses in China. In view of the size of the country and the vast population, a quarter of that of the whole world, it seems probable that as the Church grows, it may prove advisable to divide the Church in China into a number of distinct provinces, co-ordinated, as are the two provinces in England, by some central organization of the whole Church. The immediate need however is for the development of a Christian statesmanship which will see China as a whole and plan for the development and extension of the Church in that light. This makes it unlikely that any division into provinces will take place in the near future. At the present time Church and province are co-extensive. The need for a greater sense of the unity of the province came particularly to light during the war. In 1943 those bishops who were not interned wrote:

The Chung Hua Sheng Kung Hui is the child of at least twelve distinct missionary societies.[1] Long years of generous giving by these missionary societies, their great variety, and their willingness to co-operate have been our strength in the past, and give us to-day a deep sense of security and fellowship. But in these days of supreme crisis, we believe this great diversity of godfathers and godmothers may

[1] The National Council of the Protestant Episcopal Church of the U.S.A., the Church Missionary Society, the Society for the Propagation of the Gospel, the China Inland Mission, the Church of England in Canada, the Australian Board of Missions, the Australian C.M.S., the New Zealand Board of Missions, the Church of England Zenana Missionary Society, the Dublin University Mission, the Society for Promoting Christian Knowledge, and the Bible Churchmen's Missionary Society.

prove a source of weakness. For they each have a special interest in China, and have not continually before them the full picture of the disaster that war with Japan has been to the young Chinese Church. Moreover, the Sheng Kung Hui has so far no central office or officers. We are a federation of dioceses, under a chairman, with widely differing relations to missionary societies and most unequal financial support. . . . Of the Anglican Communion throughout the world we ask the following:

1. A continuation of constant prayer on our behalf.
2. A succession of young men and women, who will come to work for fifteen to twenty years as associates of the Chinese clergy, as teachers in universities and schools, and as doctors and nurses in our hospitals.
3. A full recognition that, like the Church of England or U.S.A. or Canada, or any other, we need a central office, central planning, central funds; so that help, for example, for Fukien or Shantung, is not limited by the fact that they are the fields of particular missionary societies, but additional help can be made available in personnel or funds from other parts of the Church.

Of the seven bishops who were signatories of this statement, four were Chinese and two of these were diocesan bishops.

A national office has now been set up with Bishop Y. Y. Tsu as its General Secretary. The growing desire, while maintaining close ties with the missionary societies, to be able also to act as a united province and to speak, when occasion arises, from province to province, without intermediary, was witnessed to by the call for help which resulted in the 'Archibishops' Appeal for the Church in China'. This request for help was addressed not to any missionary society, but to the Church of England as a whole, for the need it sought to meet was not that of the field of any one missionary society, but of the Church of China as a whole.

Organization: General

As in other parts of the Anglican mission field there is thus a double organization, on the one hand the fourteen dioceses of the Chung Hua Sheng Kung Hui into which the original missionary beginnings have grown, on the other, the missionary organization which still continues. There are links between certain missionary bodies and certain dioceses and several dioceses draw their foreign support from one mission only. Fukien, Chekiang, Kwangsi-Hunan, Western Szechuan, and Hong Kong are linked with the

Church Missionary Society; North China and Shantung with the
Society for the Propagation of the Gospel; Hankow, Anking and
Shanghai with the Episcopal Church of the U.S.A.; Honan with
the Church in Canada; Eastern Szechuan with the China Inland
Mission. The Bible Churchmen's Missionary Society, besides
contributing to the work of the Diocese of Eastern Szechuan, has
its own area, with its own sub-synod, in the Diocese of Hong
Kong. The other missionary societies and boards with work in
China have no areas of their own but contribute assistance within
the framework of the various dioceses.

There are, however, two areas which do not stand in the relationship just described to any foreign-based missionary society.
The work in these areas is the missionary work of the Chung Hua
Sheng Kung Hui itself. When the General Synod of Anglican
dioceses and missionary districts in China was organized and the
C.H.S.K.H. was born, as its first united act a domestic mission
was planned. A canon was passed according to which the Church
acknowledges that the responsibility for missionary work rests
upon every member of the Church, and upon the whole Church
in its corporate capacity. It lays upon every congregation the
obligation to make at least one annual offering for the missionary
work of the Church, and requires the ministers and lay officers
of each congregation to use 'all diligence to secure the funds
required by the Board of Missions for the spread of Christ's
Kingdom, at least to the amount of the apportionment for the
year'. The canon also provides for the General Synod to meet as
the Board of Missions at each of its triennial meetings and for a
committee to carry on its work in this respect between synods.

Shensi, probably the poorest and most backward area, was
chosen as the mission field. Missionary work was started in 1916.
No foreign workers are employed, nor has any foreign missionary
society any share in the work. The first bishop, the Rt. Rev. Shen
Tzu Kao, was appointed in 1934, and the second the Rt. Rev.
Newton Liu in 1947.

The capital of Shensi, Sian (the Ch' Angan of those days) was
the city where the Nestorian missionary Alopen started his work
in A.D. 635. There could have been no more fitting response to
the challenge of its new status on the part of the C.H.S.K.H.
than to start its own missionary work in the place where the first
mission to China faded out after 200 years of apparent success,

through being still not sufficiently Chinese to withstand a wave of anti-foreign persecution.

The missionary zeal of the Chinese Church is also witnessed to by the opening up of new work along the Burma Road during the war, when foreign help was not available and Chinese resources were strained to the uttermost. The opportunity presented itself: it was taken. Work in this area has now been organized into the Missionary Diocese of Yun Kwei, with its own bishop.

The Church's Work

Most chapters of this book have begun by describing the provincial and diocesan organization of the Church in the area concerned, going on from the various provincial and diocesan institutions to the work of the individual bishops and their clergy, and the Church's educational and social work. It would be possible to adopt this order in the case of the C.H.S.K.H. but it is perhaps more realistic in view of the vast area of China, the variety of missions engaged, and the difficulties of communication, to begin with the work in 'the field' and go on to the synodical organization which has been erected on the basis of this work. Besides the pastoral and evangelistic work and the clergy and lay workers who carry it on, it is necessary to speak also in China of schools and hospitals and their staffs as part of the Church's work.

In all the categories of clergy and lay workers, teachers, doctors and nurses, Chinese workers now outnumber the Europeans; for example, the Diocesen of Chekiang has four European clergy, including the Bishop, and twenty-nine Chinese clergy. The Diocese of Honan has four European clergy and sixteen Chinese clergy including the Bishop. The greatest preponderance of Chinese over Europeans is in the category of teachers. European men teachers seem to be almost non-existent. Most dioceses have some European women teachers, but these are a very small minority. Head teachers are by law all Chinese, except in the British Colony of Hong Kong.

To the Europeans mentioned above should be added in some dioceses a few other European lay workers: a diocesan treasurer in one case, a business manager of a hospital in another. The dioceses of American origin add to the list social workers, secretaries and

M

laboratory technicians. The number of Europeans in general is at present reduced owing to the war. European clergy, for example, in Eastern Szechuan are reduced from fifteen or twenty to five, including the bishop, and in Shantung, from seven to three.

The inclusion of teachers in the category of the staff of the Church and of missions raises a question of missionary policy. The Bible Churchmen's Missionary Society has, of set policy, laid down that 'this Society shall under no circumstances provide secular education above the primary stage for non-Christians'. The Society opposes the theory, which it would regard as specious, that a legitimate approach for the missionary to a non-Christian Society is to provide general education for non-Christians in the hope of influencing the minds of those who have not yet 'grown old in heathenism' in a Christian direction. On the contrary (it quotes from the American missionary, Judson):

'The first profession of the religion of Jesus must, by necessity, expose the disciple to obloquy, reproach and persecution. No one can suppose it to be the will of God that all these are first to be borne by little children. Besides, the influence of the heathen parent will be more powerful over his child than that of the Christian school-teacher. Hence, while schools diffuse knowledge, improve the intellect, hasten the progress of civilization, and therefore are benevolent and philanthropic, they are not the missionary work which Christ committed to his disciples. That they have done good who can doubt? But, as a means for converting men, that they have fallen very far below the simple preaching of the Gospel is, I think, beyond question.'

The view here expressed is in marked contrast to that which at present governs the work of most of the missionary societies and dioceses in China, where education is regarded as an important handmaid to evangelism. The contrast is particularly great in regard to the work of the American Church where a great deal has been done in university education, many prominent non-Christian Chinese having received their college training at St. John's University, Shanghai. It is beyond question that many Chinese have been converted during their student days at Christian colleges; but on the other hand an experienced student worker has given it as his opinion that the opportunity to-day is at least as great in government schools and colleges as in those which are sponsored by missionary agencies. The need for specifically religious workers in the field of Chinese student life as a whole is of immense importance. At the same time the most recent news from China stresses the strategic need to strengthen the Christian staff of Christian middle schools. Where there is a sufficient moral preponderance of Christians amongst both staff and students to make the school or college in a real sense a Christian family the influence can be very great. A great friend of the present writer owed his conversion to the fact that having been educated in a Christian college and having then gone to teach in a government college, he felt miserable in the latter and returned to join the staff of the Christian college at the first opportunity. It was borne in upon him that the different family atmosphere in the Christian institution was not due to the people concerned being inherently nicer, but that they were in some mysterious way made a family. In this fact he saw Christianity in action, and this led him to the serious study of the Christian Faith and so to baptism.

A similar situation arises in regard to medical work. Modern medical work in China is largely the product of the work of Christian missions. There can be no doubt of the great service that has been rendered to suffering humanity. But with the great increase in government medical services it becomes increasingly important to be clear about the true place of medical missions. Are they to be regarded merely as a voluntary adjunct to state medical services which fill a gap until the State is able to undertake the whole field? Are mission hospitals to be regarded as a valuable 'convert-catching' device, and therefore to be kept as clear as possible from any secular medical service? Both of these approaches fall short of a truly Christian attitude.

While Christianity is no substitute for medical efficiency, and while medical missions should always set the highest standard of professional integrity and skill, yet the essential fact is that Christian doctors and Christian nurses do their work, not merely as a means of earning a living, nor merely for the sake of bettering the physical lot of mankind, nor merely for the sake of attracting men to the Church, but simply because those who love God have an inescapable obligation to reveal His love to men, and to dedicate their professional skill to this purpose. Staffing statistics are no guide in this case. The real questions involved have no relation to figures.

The matter may be summed up by two quotations from a pamphlet of the Bible Churchmen's Missionary Society:

If ever the missionary is tempted to think that the Gospel by itself is not enough, and that without medicine or education or some other aid the message is ineffective, it would be far better to scrap all these aids and to rely only on the armour provided for the Christian warrior. He goes forth, armed with the Sword of the Spirit, and his feet shod with the preparation of the Gospel of Peace.

The skilled medical worker, as well as that great army of non-professional missionaries who are impelled in heathen lands to do all they can to relieve physical suffering, find in so doing a way into hearts that have never seen the love of God in action before.

Medical work forms an essential part of the work of the Sheng Kung Hui in every area, and an increase of staff both foreign and Chinese is desirable in all of them.

The Missionary and the Chinese Contributions

To the work of the Church, the missionary bodies and the local membership of the Church each contribute (a) workers (Europeans and Chinese respectively), and (b) money—or sometimes, in the case of the Chinese contribution, its equivalent in kind.

The war with Japan and the enormous inflation which has accompanied it has had the effect of making it particularly difficult for the local community to contribute adequately in money to the expenses of the Church. It is reported, for instance, from Fukien that $30,000 is now needed to buy what $1 would buy in 1936, and that the £ stands at about $86,000. While contributions from overseas have therefore maintained a large part of their purchasing power, the value of local endowments and fixed money incomes has almost vanished.

The way in which the local and the missionary contributions are integrated together varies from diocese to diocese; what follows is based on recent correspondence with a number of representative informants in various parts of China. Before the war it was probably true that all parts of the Church were making efforts to increase the percentage of local financial support. In spite of inflation it is everywhere reported that these efforts continue and are even being increased; thus it is said that in the Diocese of North China in 1937 less than 10 per cent of the support of Chinese clergy and native workers was raised locally, whereas the figure is now 25 per cent. It is also reported from the same diocese that the whole of the 'salaries' of Chinese workers are paid by local funds, but owing to the inflation they receive also a 'maintenance allowance' from funds supplied by the mission (in this case the S.P.G.).

The policy of the S.P.G. in China, as elsewhere, is to make a block grant to a diocese, and the use of the money so granted is solely determined within the diocese. Details of the work are of course reported to the S.P.G. and each diocese is expected progressively to assume more and more responsibility for its own support. Similarly, all workers sent out by the S.P.G. work under the direction of the bishop of the diocese and there is no missionary body in the field distinct from Diocesan Conference or Synod. The area supported by the Canadian Church forms a single diocese, Honan, and here also the use of money sent out is determined in the diocese.

In the dioceses connected with the C.M.S. it is reported that 'apart from missionary salaries the use of money sent out by the Society is determined in the field chiefly by bodies in which there is a large Chinese majority'. The amount of self-support naturally varies according to the conditions of the people. In Fukien all parishes contribute to a central Diocesan Fund to which a contribution from the Society is added: Chinese clergy and catechists live on rice locally provided, together with an allowance from this fund. In Chekiang, it is reported, the parish clergy are supported by their own people, apart from one or two poorer parishes, but catechists are largely, though not entirely, supported by mission funds. Schools and hospitals are also reported to receive small grants from the C.M.S. but to be virtually self-supporting. In the C.M.S. areas too the appointment of workers is largely controlled by diocesan bodies under the bishop, but in Chekiang the appointment of missionaries is determined by a Local Conference, i.e. a C.M.S. body, which works in consultation with the diocesan authorities. In some cases where, as in Eastern Szechuan, the parishes are expected to pay the stipends of their Chinese workers, they also have a considerable say in their appointment. In Chekiang it is reported that parish clergy are appointed by a board representing the diocese, the District Church Council, and the parish, the chief word lying with the parish.

The China Inland Mission and the B.C.M.S. have a somewhat different relation to the diocesan system from the other missionary bodies. The C.I.M., which is an undenominational body, has a headquarters in Shanghai which plays a part, in consultation with the Bishop and the diocesan committee, in determining the use of money sent out from England as far as the Anglican members of the Mission are concerned. The non-Anglican members of the same Mission (who are of course not under the jurisdiction of a bishop) work in a different area. But the theoretical and legal position here is clearly different from what it is in the dioceses connected with purely Anglican societies.

The B.C.M.S. work in South China forms a part only of a diocese and the Bishop is not, as in the case of the C.I.M., a member of the Mission. Under the B.C.M.S. a Field Council, consisting of missionaries only, decides the use which is to be made of money sent out by the Society, and the annual budget of each mission station is 'supervised and passed' by the executive committee at home; but since the War Area Church Councils have been introduced on which both missionaries and Chinese Christians sit, and it is intended that these should deal with all matters except those concerning European missionaries only. In the past Field Councils engaged and allocated Chinese workers, but it is now reported that this will in future be done by Area Councils. At the same time it is said that the local Church has agreed to pay half the 'rice allowance' of the Chinese clergy from July 1946, and the whole of it from July 1947. This particular mission is financially independent of the diocese in which it works.

Whatever the exact relations in the matter of finance and appointments, all workers, Chinese or foreign, in the Church promise as a condition of appointment in the Church to obey the Constitution and Canons of the C.H.S.K.H. Each diocese sends delegates to the General Synod and these naturally include both Chinese and European workers connected with all the various missions.

The dioceses supported by the Episcopal Church in the U.S.A. have a position of their own. It is reported that 'the use of money sent out is determined by the Church in America'. On the other hand, missionaries from America are appointed to work under the bishop, who has 'complete freedom to decide what assignment they receive in his district'. In this connexion it must be re-membered that, as is explained in Chapter II, these dioceses rank as Missionary Districts of the U.S. Church in exactly the same way as (for example) Alaska, or even the Missionary Dis-tricts within the continental U.S.A. Their bishops and delegates sit in the General Convention of the U.S. Church, and it is the Board of Missions appointed by this Convention under which they work. Although decisions may be taken in the U.S.A., therefore, the relationship is different from that between a Chinese diocese and a British missionary society. Besides being represented in the General Convention, these dioceses are also full members of the General Synod of the Chinese Church.

The Constitution of the Church

The constitution of the C.H.S.K.H. establishes a General Synod and Diocesan Synods and so integrates the dioceses into a province, but this is as far as the provincial organization goes. There is no metropolitical see; Canon VI states that the Chair-man of the House of Bishops 'represents the C.H.S.K.H. in communications with the authorities of other Churches', and he is recognized by Lambeth as a Metropolitan.

The General Synod is composed of all bishops, retired bishops having no vote, and of four clerical and four lay representatives from each diocese. It meets triennially, but after 1937 no meeting was possible until 1947; it will meet again in 1950. Canon V pro-vides for a standing committee to act between its meetings. As has been mentioned above, it is provided that at each triennial meeting the General Synod shall also meet as the Board of Missions of the Church. In this capacity it appoints the bishops of Missionary Districts and otherwise supervises their affairs.

The canons lay down that every diocese shall have a Diocesan Synod and give it authority to elect the bishop of the diocese by a two-thirds majority of each order, a clerical and lay. Such elections must be confirmed by the General Synod and the Diocesan Synod may refer the whole election to the House of Bishops. Canon XI provides for a Standing Committee of the Diocesan Synod with powers to act on its behalf between meet-ings.

Other subjects dealt with in the canons include the ordination of deacons and priests (minimum ages twenty-one and twenty-four respectively), and the declaration required from the candidate of loyalty to the doctrine, discipline, and worship of the C.H.S.K.H., etc. Canon XXIV establishes the principle that Christian marriage is indissoluble. A marriage according to the law of the land entered into before the parties to it become Christian is recognized as indissoluble after their baptism. A marriage between a Christian and a non-Christian may not be solemnized by the Prayer-Book rite, and may only be solemnized at all if the non-Christian promises to be baptized after marriage.

Canons XVII and XVIII provide for the discipline of bishops and clergy, and church courts are set up.

Training of the Clergy

Bishop Shen, formerly of Shensi, has been asked by the Church to take charge of the Central Theological School, which is temporarily situated in Shanghai. Most clergy, however, are trained in local Union Theological Colleges, where distinctively Anglican teaching is given as well as the training the students have in common. In general a minimum of three years is required for candidates for the ministry. Catechists have a two-year training. In the dioceses of American origin the course for the clergy is four years combined with college. There is a growing sense of the importance of getting a predominantly university-trained clergy, but this is still largely a hope. Selected clergy have visited Great Britain, Canada and America for further study and experience. The Church in the U.S.A. has been particularly alive to the value of this.

The subjects taught cover the usual curriculum. Under the heading of Church History, the history of Christianity in China from the seventh century is included in most instances, but not in all. The omission, where it exists, seems to be a serious deficiency. A purely Western approach to this subject is unimaginative when there are so many lessons to be learnt from the story of early Christian missions in China.

More than one informant questions whether training in liturgiology or morals is adequate. This criticism comes from within the ranks of those responsible for teaching and may therefore be taken as an earnest of improvement.

Canons XVIII and XIX lay down that the bishop shall cause candidates for the diaconate and priesthood to be examined in:

1. The Bible in general.
2. Two or three specially selected parts of the Old and New Testaments.
3. The History and contents of the Book of Common Prayer.
4. And further in three or more of the following subjects as the Bishop shall appoint:
    (*a*) Systematic Theology.
    (*b*) Church History and Ecclesiastical Polity.
    (*c*) Pastoral Theology.
    (*d*) Preaching.
    (*e*) Christian Evidences.
    (*f*) Christian Ethics.
    (*g*) Principles and Methods of Religious Education.
    (*h*) Social Application of Christianity.
    (*i*) Church Finance and Bookkeeping.

Doctrine

The Preamble to the Constitution and Canons of the Chung Hua Sheng Kung Hui binds the Church: to accept the Scriptures of the Old and New Testaments, to believe them to contain all things necessary to salvation and to be the ultimate standard of faith; to profess the Faith as summed up in the Nicene Creed and the Apostles' Creed; to hold to the Doctrine which Christ our Lord commanded, and to the Sacraments of Baptism and the Lord's Supper which He Himself ordained; to accept His Discipline according to the Commandments of God, to maintain the ministry of the Church which they have received through the episcopate in the three orders of Bishops, Priests and Deacons, which orders have been in Christ's Church from the time of the Apostles.

The dioceses supported by C.M.S. and C.I.M. are of the 'Evangelical tradition'. It is interesting that a missionary from one of them reports that the bishop and many others, partly owing to the effect of pressure from the 'Little Flock' are 'turning in a Catholic direction' and feeling the need to stress 'the importance of Church Doctrine—Church: Bishop: Priest: Eucharist: Confirmation: Baptism'. This does not of course imply any departure from the positive notes of the Evangelical tradition. The North China dioceses would claim a Tractarian tradition. A witness to the solid foundation of this tradition and its independence of foreign support is the fact that during the war, when

the bishop and all foreign missionaries were interned, the daily
Eucharist at the Cathedral was maintained by the Chinese clergy
as a matter of course. The dioceses of American origin are of
mixed churchmanship. The B.C.M.S. is one of the smaller missions in China, but both because of the fruitful nature of its
evangelistic work in the area it serves and because it is an integral
part of the Anglican Communion in the Far East, its distinctive
theological approach deserves separate consideration in this
chapter.

'The Basis' of the Bible Churchmen's Missionary Society contains the following articles:

Belief that the Lord Jesus Christ is the only Priest and Mediator
between God and Men, and that the direct access of the Soul to God
is through His precious Blood without the intervention of any sacrificial priesthood.

Belief that the Theories of Sacerdotalism concerning the mechanical
conveyance of grace in Baptism, Confirmation, the Supper of the
Lord, and Ordination, whether these be professed in doctrine or implied in ritual, are 'grounded upon no warranty of Scripture, but,
rather, are repugnant to the Word of God'.

Belief that a sacrificial priesthood has no place in the Ministry of
the Church of Christ, but that such Ministry is for preaching, teaching, pastoral oversight and administration.

The contrast between this and the position of the Diocese of
Korea is of crucial importance in any survey which seeks to deal
honestly with the comprehensive character of the Anglican Communion.

Worship

The following survey is based on replies to a request for information concerning worship, apart from services primarily intended for inquirers.

The Dioceses of C.M.S. origin mainly use translations of the
Prayer Book of 1662 in the local dialect. In one diocese they also
make use of the North China Book, and the Yangtse Valley Book
(see below) for mandarin-speaking congregations, and all books
contain the American Prayer of Consecration as an alternative, but
it is rarely used. In another diocese the American form is also
printed and the clergy are encouraged to use it on occasion. In at
least three dioceses the 'Visitation of the Sick' is omitted and the

form of Absolution therefore not included. Auricular confession is exceedingly rare. The Prayer Book rite is always used for the Holy Eucharist. 'Theoretically', writes a missionary of one diocese, 'we use Mattins and Evensong as well as the Holy Communion, but Mattins is always shortened and in many places the service is normally not from the Book of Common Prayer at all, but a sort of "Free Church Service" '. The bishop of another diocese writes, 'We have no other forms of service, only the Prayer Book, but in some country churches the Prayer Book is not used in the afternoon. There are hymns, reading, exhortation and extempore prayer.' Services of local origin are included in some Prayer Books, e.g. a memorial service for use in cemeteries at Easter, but the material of these is largely translations, not original Chinese.

In the northern dioceses, of S.P.G. origin, while there is no doctrinal change from the Book of Common Prayer, there is no section of the Book which has not been changed by omissions, additions and emendations. The North China Prayer Book is thus more than a simple translation. For example the Eucharistic rite has restored the dismissal of the unbaptized; there are alternative Consecration Prayers; either that of the American (standard) Prayer Book, or the English 1662 prayer followed by the Prayer of Oblation. In either case the Lord's Prayer follows before the Communion. The Visitation of the Sick is included. Auricular confession is not compulsory but is used. Besides the services inluded in 1662, the book includes a Form for Receiving Catechumens, and a Seven Day Cycle of Prayers for use at home. Some of the prayers translated are not to be found in any other Prayer Book. Prayers composed by Chinese are also included, e.g. in the Marriage Service.

Apart from the Prayer Book, there are printed and authorized forms for use in marriages when the Prayer Book Service cannot be used, and for encoffining and other burial and memorial services. Non-liturgical Christmas and Epiphany Services are used in addition to the Prayer Book Services, and in home worship, school chapels, and mothers' union services, non-liturgical forms are also used.

In the dioceses of American origin a translation of the American Book of 1928 is used, with the State Prayers locally adopted. This also applies to C.H.S.K.H.'s own Missionary District of Shensi.

The Diocese of Honan, supported by the Canadian Church, uses a Prayer Book which is substantially a translation of that of 1662. The form of Absolution in the Visitation of the Sick is included. A prayer for the President and National Government is substituted for the prayers for the King. There are some original Chinese prayers. At prayer and bible study meetings hymns, extempore prayer, Bible-reading, short addresses, discussion or instruction are used, but no written form of service. Forms of service are prepared each time for special occasions: e.g. National Day, Thanksgiving, and at the discretion of the priest for the wedding service of a Christian with someone who is not yet baptized, and for the burial of an unbaptized close relative of a Christian.

Eastern Szechuan (C.I.M.) uses a translation of the Prayer Book of 1662, but the State Prayers are new compositions, as are also a number of prayers for special occasions. The Visitation of the Sick with its form of Absolution is not included. The Eucharistic rite is that of 1662. Apart from the Prayer Book there is a printed form for worship in the home, but it is not much used, hymns, Bible-reading and extempore prayer being more usual. A correspondent writes: 'Generally speaking in a diocese that is largely rural, it is advisable and practical to hold only one fully liturgical service on Sunday. This is in the morning usually. In the afternoon there is either a service, mainly liturgical but considerably shortened, or else a Sunday School which includes adults as well as children. It is not possible to hold evening services owing to lack of electric light, and also due to the fact that country people often have to walk eight or ten miles to their homes.'

Prayer Book Services (1662) are the only services in regular use in church by the B.C.M.S. in Eastern Szechuan and South China.

A draft of a new C.H.S.K.H. Prayer Book is being prepared for the General Synod in 1950. At least one diocese is likely to produce a new book of its own before then.

Relationships with other Denominations

The general comment on relationships with other denominations from all parts of China is 'very friendly'. Relationships with some of the more peculiar sects are strained by their tendency to 'poach'. Relationships with the Church of Rome are of course limited, as elsewhere, by doctrinal and canonical factors on the Roman side, and a typical report is that there is no co-operation except in regard to some social activities, famine relief, U.N.R.R.A., etc. Co-operation on this level has however in many instances been close, friendly and effective. Beyond this, however, one missionary writes that in his diocese they have friendly relationships with Spanish and German members of the Dominican Order, that his bishop is a close friend of the Roman bishop: they exchange notes and impressions, treat each other and pray for each other as if in practice, if not in theory, fellow-bishops. The Anglican bishop was invited to the enthronement of his Roman brother and provided with a seat of honour.

The main organ of co-operation with non-Roman Christians is the National Christian Council, on which the Church is fully represented. In student work the Church co-operates with the Student Christian Movement and the Y.M.C.A. The Church also co-operates in Christian universities and hospitals and in some Union Theological Colleges (see above).

The extent to which there is co-operation with other bodies probably varies very little, except according to opportunity in the different fields, but the attitude towards co-operation varies radically. There are some who co-operate easily because they do not think that the theological differences between Christians are really very important. They may desire reunion both for the sake of practical efficiency and because they know that the unity of His children is the will of God, but as they do not regard the theological differences as very important, so likewise they cannot regard their solution as a very urgent matter. There are others who can only co-operate within strict rules, because they regard differences as of fundamental importance. They desire unity because they know it is the will of God and feel that it is worth endless care and trouble to strive to find our unity in truth without any compromise. They regard differences as important because they passionately desire unity in truth. There are others again who earnestly desire reunion on theological grounds, whose attitude towards co-operation is less strict, because their theology does not in fact raise the same points of difference. The difference between the three types by no means always follows 'party' lines.

JAPAN
(NIPPON SEI KO KWAI)

Organization: *The Outcome of the War*

The Nippon Sei Ko Kwai (Holy Catholic Church of Japan) was constituted in 1887. It was the outcome of the missionary work of the Protestant Episcopal Church of the United States, S.P.G., and C.M.S. The Church in Canada subsequently also played a part. Tokyo and Osaka were founded as 'Japanese dioceses' in 1923 and are purely urban; South Tokyo and Kobe were 'S.P.G. dioceses' though with areas of C.M.S. work in them—large areas in the case of Kobe. Both are predominantly rural. Kyushu and Hokkaido were 'C.M.S. dioceses', both prevailingly rural. Mid-Japan was the 'Canadian diocese'. North Kwanto, Tohaku and Kyoto were 'American dioceses'. In 1940 the Church became self-supporting and all but a very few missionaries returned home, as the Japanese authorities demanded the severance of all ties which implied dependence on the West either for leadership or money. Though moving slowly in the direction of self-support the Church was not really ready for so sudden a change. It survived financially through the War years by spending its capital. After the War the Church decided to adhere to the decision made in 1940, but to ask for temporary help from its sister provinces. The House of Bishops wrote as follows:

While we have no thought of going back upon the declaration of autonomy already made, we shall hold it in abeyance for the time being in view of the abnormal inflation and for the sake of rehabilitating the Church, and hereby appeal to the sister Churches of England, America and Canada to renew the friendly relationships so unhappily interrupted during the war and to help us both spiritually and materially.

We realize that before making such a pronouncement we should first seek the consent of the Church in General Synod, but we have been compelled by the urgency of the situation to make this appeal forthwith. We trust that our clergy and people will understand our mind, and that, without injury to the spirit of self-government and self-support, they will exert every effort for the rehabilitation of the Church.

Financially this help is being provided in the proportion of 50 per cent from the American Church, 35 per cent from the Church of England (S.P.G. £15,000, C.M.S. £10,000), the Canadian Church 15 per cent. The money is to be used:

(a) For providing temporary places of worship and parsonages, sometimes combined, where these have been destroyed.

(b) To provide salaries for the bishops for a temporary period of six years. They are to be paid at a rate of 10,000 yen a year, which compared with 6,000 yen for pastors leaves a very narrow margin for their added responsibilities in hospitality and other expenses.

(c) To provide for the training of the clergy. The salaries of five professors are being provided for ten years.

The Church in Japan is anxious for help from abroad in personnel. Four liaison officers represent the mother churches in Japan, one from Canada, one from the United States and two from Great Britain. The last-named, though one of them is a former S.P.G. missionary and one a former missionary of C.M.S., both represent the Church of England as a whole. The Japanese Church will invite other workers for specific jobs.

Early in 1940 the Japanese Diet passed a bill for the control of religious organizations. Though Christianity only represented one half per cent of the population,[1] it was listed, along with Buddhism and sect Shinto, as one of the recognized religions. The Nippon Sei Ko Kwai recast its Constitution and Canons in the prescribed form for application for recognition under the new act. Application for recognition was made and refused. In the meantime an amalgamated body had been set up including almost all Christian denominations apart from the Church of Rome. The Society of Friends and the Salvation Army both entered it. By December 1941 this new body and the Church of Rome had been recognized. Some advised the entry of the Nippon Sei Ko Kwai into the amalgamated body, holding that there would be sufficient liberty within it for the Church to maintain its own life. The official attitude of the Church was however to continue to work for recognition, but this was never granted. In

---

[1] The pre-war figures for our own Communion were 43,000 nominal members, 28,000 active members, 17,000 nominal communicants, 12,000 active communicants.

March 1942 the Nippon Sei Ko Kwai ceased therefore to exist as a legal denomination. Individual congregations had to seek for local recognition. The Constitution of Nippon Sei Ko Kwai was suspended, the holding of Synods was no longer legally possible, but the majority of the Church felt that they could hold together despite this blow to their corporate existence. Some of the leaders of the Church suffered imprisonment for their stand.

About one third of the Church, three bishops out of nine and roughly corresponding proportions of other clergy and laity, decided to enter the amalgamated body. Some of these did so because they believed the new body to be a genuinely good arrangement, but the majority did so, because, in view of the Government's refusal to grant the Church separate recognition, they saw no other means by which the corporate life of the Nippon Sei Ko Kwai could be maintained. The three bishops consecrated seven others in order to maintain the episcopal succession within the united body. The Anglicans who entered the new body carried on with their accustomed worship without change.

Shortly after the surrender of Japan the Occupying Powers annulled the act of 1940. Christians were again free to organize themselves as they wished. The House of Bishops revived the Constitutions and Canons as revised in 1938.

Practically all[1] those who joined the amalgamated body have now been received back into the Nippon Sei Ko Kwai. Osaka, the one diocese that had joined the union *en bloc*, has been received back *en bloc*. A Liturgy of Reconciliation was used. The Japanese bishops' own words on this matter deserve to be quoted:

As the three historical orders which Nippon Sei Ko Kwai respects are not local orders but belong to the Universal Church, there should be no doubt or obstacle whatever in the appointment and continuation of such. For that reason we are making use of a Liturgy of Reconciliation for those clergy who desire to return. Some there are who hold that these should be re-ordained, or that they should be degraded to a lower order by way of probation; but the bishops are unanimous in considering it to be an important point that the origin of the present amalgamation lay in the war and in the national policy and so think that it is suitable from the religious point of view to make use of a liturgy. The liturgy we use is based upon one hitherto used in the case

---

[1] Some of these consecrated bishops after the schism, however, have not yet returned.

of those who had been unfaithful to the Church and its important point is regret for separation from the bishops and for joining the amalgamation. Other points do not apply, such as the holding of heretical theories or acts of rebellion against the Lord. We consider wrong only the said separation from the bishops and the joining of an amalgamation of churches that have no bishops. We desire them to return to Nippon Sei Ko Kwai as clergy to do pastoral and missionary work with all their strength. All the bishops believe that, if only this understanding is reached, a return into our fellowship is possible. Sometimes, however, when those who are about to return look at the liturgy, they find difficulties in the choice of the Scripture lessons and in the wording of the prayers and say that the treatment is harsh; but the wish of all the bishops of Nippon Sei Ko Kwai is rather to demand that the cause of the schism during the war be corrected. That we are not insisting upon the details of our liturgy of reconciliation is clear from the fact that we have left the question of the way of using the liturgy to each diocesan to decide. We claim that for the sake of the Church and for his own sake each one who desires to return should make use of the liturgy.

Schismatic Bishops

As regards the recent and secret consecration, by the three bishops who joined the amalgamation in accordance with the national policy during the war, of seven priests who had gone with them, all the bishops of Nippon Sei Ko Kwai are united in the following opinion concerning their treatment. While those consecrations were conducted in accordance with the Prayer-book of Nippon Sei Ko Kwai and, following the rule of the whole, by three bishops, yet we must not fail to recognize that they were deficient in the following respects:

(*a*) These schismatic bishops do not hold any jurisdiction as bishops.

(*b*) They did not receive the assent of all the bishops of Nippon Sei Ko Kwai to their consecration.

(*c*) Their consecration was not accompanied by the public, and necessary, prayer of the Church.

Although for the above reasons it is clear that the aforesaid seven persons are not bishops of Nippon Sei Ko Kwai, they and others are, in the meanwhile, being reconciled. There is theological controversy as to the validity of their consecration and so the House of Bishops, although it has it in its power to make its own decision, will, if necessary, request that a special committee of the Lambeth Conference study the matter, believing it to be of great importance for the future. On this understanding, therefore, we extend a welcome to these seven persons to return as priests.

N

Conclusion

The bishops of Nippon Sei Ko Kwai, led by the Holy Spirit, hereby express their purpose and opinion with regard to the several problems that have arisen in connexion with the schism which our young Church has had to face for the first time. Our desire is that, now in these days when the oppression has been lifted, each one of those clergy brought up with us in Nippon Sei Ko Kwai, shall not look to his own future from his own standpoint, but shall return in all earnestness to the bosom of his mother Church and imbibe his fill of her love. We desire that those who have come to us at such a dangerous time as this as representatives of England, America, and Canada should encourage us and, once more, help on its way the Church that has been able to maintain unity and peace for the past eighty years.

It is good to be able to record that in the reconciliation representatives of the mother churches played their part. It would, I believe, be in accordance with the wishes of the Japanese Church and the other representatives from the mother churches who accompanied him, that special tribute should be paid to the memory of the Rt. Rev. Samuel Heaslett, former Presiding Bishop of the Nippon Sei Ko Kwai. He had himself suffered imprisonment, but knew no bitterness. The same faith, patience and charity which upheld him in prison were bent towards assisting in the reconciliation of the schism in the Church he loved so well.

Including the liaison officers mentioned above, there are about twenty missionaries in Japan at the present time, engaged in pastoral and educational work and nursing (England 8, Canada 3, Australia 1, the rest from U.S.A.). The Church used to employ Japanese doctors, evangelists, Bible women, teachers, nurses, orderlies, etc., as well as clergy. The war has made such heavy inroads into personnel and finance that the ranks are sadly depleted. About half of the clergy are now engaged in secular work in order to provide support for themselves and their families. There are seven Japanese bishops, over two hundred clergy, mostly in priest's orders; a few catechists, mostly candidates for Holy Orders; and a few women catechists.

Since 1940 the Church has been entirely self-supporting. The temporary rehabilitation grant mentioned above is the only money being received from abroad. Missionaries are now to be sent out to the House of Bishops, who will allocate them to their spheres of work. Appointments of all Japanese clergy and workers are made by the bishop of the diocese with his advisory committee. The Province is supreme and autonomous. Help from other provinces is rendered at the request of the House of Bishops. In the case of the Church of England the two liaison officers are financed on her behalf by C.M.S. and S.P.G.

Canon Law

The Canons cover the election of bishops; diocesan organization; the acceptance of candidates for ordination; the requirements for their training and testimonials before ordination; catechists; the qualifications which must be fulfilled before a 'congregation' reaches the status of a 'church'; the duties of pastors; the duties of vestries; district councils, their constitution and duties; the Board of Missions, its composition and functions; marriage; discipline of clergy and bishops; the Prayer Book and Articles.

Training of Clergy

A three years' theological course is required of candidates after their university training. The Canons lay down the following subjects of examination:

(1) The Bible in general.
(2) Two or three specially selected parts of the Old and New Testaments, if possible in the original, or in English.
(3) The Prayer Book of the Nippon Sei Ko Kwai, together with its history.
(4) Systematic theology, the three Creeds, the Articles.
(5) Church history and government.
(6) Pastoral theology.
(7) Christian evidences.
(8) Christian ethics.
(9) Preaching.
(10) Logic.
(11) Psychology.
(12) Sociology.
(13) History of Philosophy.
(14) New Testament Greek.

Provided however that the Bishop, with the consent of the Standing Committee, may exercise power of dispensation as to these subjects from (5) onward.

There are seven men and three women in training at the Central Theological College at the present time.

A few Japanese clergy have visited Great Britain and America for study, either before or after ordination.

Doctrine

While differences of doctrinal emphasis are probably as great in Japan as in other parts of the Anglican Communion, the training of all clergy at the Central Theological College[1] makes for a spirit of unity. The Constitution states that:

The Nippon Sei Ko Kwai accepts the Scriptures of the Old and New Testament, and believes them, as given by inspiration of God, to contain all things necessary to salvation, and professes the Faith as summed up in the Nicene Creed and the Apostles' Creed.

The Nippon Sei Ko Kwai teaches the Doctrine which Christ our Lord commanded, and ministers the two Sacraments of Baptism and the Lord's Supper which He Himself ordained, and also His Discipline.

The Nippon Sei Ko Kwai maintains the three orders of Bishop, Priest, and Deacon, which have been transmitted from the times of the Apostles.

Worship

There is a Standard Prayer Book for the whole Province. This is a cross between 1662 and the American Prayer Book. It contains alternative Consecration Prayers; that taken from the American Prayer Book includes the Epiclesis and the Prayer of Oblation. The Absolution in the Visitation of the Sick is that of 1662, with permissive use of the Absolution from the Holy Communion. There is an appendix including Propers for a commemoration of the Foundation of the Nippon Sei Ko Kwai, for the Emperor's birthday, new year, harvest, thanksgiving, etc., together with forms for family prayers, for the admission of a catechumen, for the licensing of a catechist and prayers for missionary work. There are few prayers of local origin included, apart from adjustments in the royal prayers. As well as the Prayer Book, a translation of Sext and Compline has been issued by the Church. The Episcopate issues special forms of service

[1] Since the above words were written, news has come of the opening of a theological college of the Evangelical tradition at Osaka.

and special prayers for various occasions. Many manuals of prayers have been issued by the Church, including a book of 'Prayers for the Dying and Dead' compiled by a Japanese priest. This contains a form for Holy Unction and a memorial service. It is widely used. Forms for such occasions as the blessing of a new house are also provided.

Relationships with other Denominations

The Church has no official relations with other denominations. It was represented on the National Christian Council before the setting up of the amalgamated body referred to above. The present writer has no information as to whether the National Christian Council has been or is likely to be revived. Friendly co-operation with other denominations is common; the extent of it varies with the diocese and even with the city or town.

THE DIOCESE OF KOREA

Organization

As long ago as 1916 it was contemplated that when the Church in Korea had grown larger it would be split into several dioceses, which would together form a province. Troubled conditions, which at the present time take the form of the country being divided into Russian and American spheres, have not made growth easier. The Church in Korea is therefore for the present a single diocese, like others in a similar position, in obedience to the Metropolitical See of Canterbury.

The staff of the Diocese is chiefly Korean and Japanese.[1] At the present time the European staff consists only of the Bishop and two priests, though there are six vacancies.

The 'Fundamental Declaration' of 1916 quotes the following from the Lambeth Encyclical Letter of 1908: 'All races and peoples, whatever their language or conditions, must be welded into one Body, and the organization of different races living side by side into separate or independent Churches, on the basis of race or colour, is inconsistent with the vital and essential principle of the unity of Christ's Church.' Thus while the Korean-

---

[1] Repatriation of Japanese nationals has now taken place. The Japanese bishop who officiated during the War, together with three priests, has been repatriated in consequence.

speaking and Japanese-speaking elements in the Church are to some extent separately organized for administrative purposes, they are firmly held together in one diocese with one Synod under one bishop. There is a large measure of self-support in the Diocese, Korean and Japanese clergy and workers being mainly supported by their own people. The use of money sent out by Missionary Societies, apart from the salaries of European staff, is decided by the Diocese, subject to approval by the societies when the annual grants are made. The Bishop makes appointments and decides upon the spheres of work of the clergy and others employed by the Diocese. He is advised by the Diocesan Conference which considers recommendations sent up by Deanery District Conferences.

Constitution

The Diocese is governed by its own Canons and Constitutions, which are promulgated by the Bishop in Synod.

Training of the Clergy

The clergy have a theological training which covers the normal subjects of Old and New Testament, Doctrine, Liturgiology, Morals and Church History; Far Eastern Church History is included in the last named. Men catechists pass through a theological training with a view to ultimate ordination. There is also a course for training girls as catechists.

Doctrine

According to the undermentioned Declaration of 1916 the Diocese holds fast to the Doctrine of Christ handed down by the Apostles and embodied in the three creeds, and holds fast to the Old and New Testaments as interpreted by the tradition of the Holy Catholic Church, as the ultimate standard of faith and morals; accepts the Apocrypha as proper to be read 'for example of life and instruction of manners', holds fast to the sacraments, honouring in the first place, as generally necessary to salvation, the two great sacraments and next to them 'those five commonly called sacraments'.

To go to confession once a year is laid down as one of the six rules of the Christian life. The Fundamental Declaration of 1916 says that 'the power of binding and loosing sinners . . . is by

Divine Appointment in the hands of the Bishops and Priests of the Church' and that the penitent is absolved by the priest in virtue of the authority committed to him by Jesus Christ Himself. On the Holy Communion the catechism teaches that 'Jesus personally dwells in the consecrated bread and wine; if we receive these we receive the Body and Blood of the Living Lord, the food of eternal life' and that the Holy Communion is a sacrifice in which the Church offers the Body and Blood of Jesus, the same sacrifice as 'our Lord wrought on the cross and ever offers in heaven'.

On Holy Orders, the catechism teaches that they have come down 'in succession since the time when the Saviour gave them to the Apostles' and that 'only a bishop in the Apostolic succession has authority to administer the Sacrament of Holy Orders'.

Worship

The Korean Prayer Book is substantially a translation of that of 1549, but the Funeral Service is based on the 'Green Book' of 1926, and in the Eucharist the Prayer for the Church precedes the Sursum Corda. Full directions are given in the rubrics for a simple ceremonial of either Low or High Mass. The modifications of the rite for a Requiem Mass are also given.

A GENERAL SURVEY

The 'Cardinal differentia' of the Anglican Communion in the Far East

Replies to a questionnaire, sent out to correspondents covering the whole field of Anglican work in the Far East, show a wide measure of agreement that the 'Cardinal Differentia' distinguishing the Anglican Communion, on the one hand from the Church of Rome, and on the other hand from the non-episcopal bodies, is to be found in the following six points:

(a) An open vernacular Bible.
(b) The Creeds.
(c) The Sacraments.
(d) The threefold Ministry.
(e) A vernacular Liturgy with a common basis in the Book of Common Prayer.
(f) A distinctive attitude to freedom and authority (e.g. Article XXXIV).

The only frankly negative reply comes from Japan, whence a missionary writes 'No! there are others who are with us in (a), (b), (c) and (f)'. This is balanced by three other missionaries to Japan who simply write 'yes' to all six points. (e) is excepted in several replies from other parts of the field and (d), of course, we share with the Roman Catholic and Orthodox Communions. Despite the wide agreement therefore, it might seem that in fact there is no cardinal differentia. The comment of a bishop from a pronouncedly 'low Church' diocese in China may help to explain the apparent confusion of the evidence. He writes:

(*a*) An open vernacular Bible distinguishes us from the Roman Church; (*b*) our *emphasis* on the Creeds, distinguishes us from non-episcopal bodies; (*c*) we are distinct from both Roman and non-episcopal bodies in our teaching on the Sacraments; (*d*) our adherence to the threefold Ministry distinguishes us from non-episcopalians; (*e*) this distinguishes us from both those who use the Latin unreformed liturgy and those who use none; (*f*) our attitude to liturgical freedom distinguishes us from the Roman Church, just as our insistence upon authority makes us different from non-episcopalians.

In parts of China however the Church of Rome has a vernacular Bible on sale. Only one of my correspondents (from North China) seemed to be aware of this. The Chung Hua Sheng Kung Hui Constitution omits the Athanasian Creed. Many, though not all, of the non-episcopal bodies use the Creeds. As the bishop quoted above says, our emphasis on them is distinctive. With regard to the Sacraments the majority of non-episcopal bodies baptize and observe some form of Holy Communion. But in some non-episcopal bodies baptism is commonly regarded as merely a method of initiation and rarely as 'a death unto sin and a new birth unto righteousness'. The existence of original sin is quite commonly denied. On the other hand in some few sects baptism is repeated. More orthodox views are however widely held. It would take too long to go in any detail into the differences in doctrine regarding the Holy Eucharist, but in general, a much greater stress is laid upon it in our Communion throughout the Far East, than non-episcopal bodies lay on their Communion Services. It is celebrated every Sunday, instead of only occasionally. The reverent consuming at the end of the service of the consecrated elements (when not reserved for the communion of the sick) distinguishes the Anglican Communion from those with a receptionist doctrine, who set the elements aside out of common use and therefore return (what in Anglican terminology would be) the consecrated elements to common use when the service is over. The doctrinal difference here is considerable; the practical difference is immense. The ordinary Anglican layman would regard the receptionist practice as grossly irreverent, though of course with their doctrine it is not so.

In regard to the lesser Sacraments the Anglican Communion in the Far East is distinguished from the Roman Communion, except in the instance of Korea, by not demanding auricular confession. The use of confession is so rare over wide parts of the field that it probably does appear to the ordinary non-episcopalian observer as an important distinguishing mark, though the giving of authority to forgive sins in the Ordinal is doctrinally a distinguishing mark of great importance, and would be recognized as such by non-episcopalian theologians.

Confirmation is probably ordinarily regarded as merely the Anglican form of admission to adult membership of the Church, but it would be regarded as a distinguishing feature of our Communion, not only within the Church itself, but also by the more discriminating of our Christian brethren.

The threefold Ministry is commonly accepted by my correspondents as being the feature of our Communion which most strikingly distinguishes us from non-episcopal bodies. Whatever the form in which they verbally express their beliefs, Anglicans throughout the Far East *act* according to the principles of the Preface to the Ordinal, as though they believed episcopal ordination to be essential. No one is accounted to be a priest, or permitted to exercise priestly functions, unless he has been ordained by a bishop. Interestingly, none of my correspondents mention the Methodist Episcopal Church in China, which has an episcopal organization without the Apostolic Succession. It would seem that, whatever differences of doctrinal emphasis may exist, it is commonly realized in our Church in the Far East that episcopacy as we have received it is not merely a matter of ecclesiastical organization.

Several of my correspondents point out that some of the non-episcopal bodies have a book of common prayer and one mentions that the Church of Rome uses the Chinese language for parts of the Mass and for other services.

Some other distinguishing features have been suggested. The existence of married clergy is mentioned by one man as an important distinction from the Church of Rome. On the other side, the existence of celibate Religious Orders within our Church distinguishes us from the non-episcopal bodies. There is no men's Order as yet in China, but the Cowley Fathers have worked in Japan, and there are two women's Orders in China.

A correspondent from a diocese of C.M.S. origin writes:

'I would add "Catholic Tradition"; consider e.g. that *all* Anglicans and almost *no* non-episcopalians emphasize Easter Communion (others have theirs on Maundy Thursday). There are a variety of small signs of this kind which set us off from others, which are found here as well as in England.'

A missionary from North China writes with regard to the 'Cardinal Differentia':

'I incline to think that both Roman Catholics and other bodies would, if asked the questions, stress the ordered reverence of our worship, the atmosphere of spirituality in our services, and the faithfulness which (they feel) characterizes our pastoral care.'

Finally, it should be pointed out, that no correspondent of any ecclesiastical colour has questioned that the six points listed are characteristics of the Anglican Communion. The questions raised have all been in regard to how far they are characteristics which distinguish us from other denominations.

Conclusion

This survey has dealt chiefly with organizational and constitutional questions and only touches lightly on doctrinal matters. It is however in the realm of doctrine that the real issues lie. In some instances these lie behind the divergences the survey reveals, in other instances they are masked by surface agreements. An identity of organization however is of no importance unless there is also unity of doctrine, on the other hand unity of doctrine can be accompanied by a wide variety of organization, without the latter having any great importance.

The main issues before the Anglican Communion in the Far East are doctrinal. It is doctrine that will determine whether it remains a corporate entity growing into a fuller sense of unity, or breaks in two. It is doctrine that will determine whether parts of it coalesce prematurely with other bodies, or whether it remains faithful to its traditions and serves the true cause of reunion. Above all, it is doctrine that will determine whether it can, or cannot, fulfil the evangelistic task that lies before it: a task unparalleled in any other part of the world, in the combination of the immensity of its scope and the openness of its opportunity. Practically a third of the population of the world is in the area covered by this chapter and the doors are wide open.

IX

THE CHURCH OF THE PROVINCE OF THE WEST INDIES

by the RT. REV. JOHN DAUGLISH, *formerly Bishop of Nassau*

The Background

The group of islands known as the British West Indies has often with a great measure of truth been called the Cinderella of the British Empire. They were courted when they were wealthy but when poverty came were left deserted. Yet those who have lived there in any one of the colonies, tried to understand their many problems and to alleviate their distress, know the meaning of nostalgia. The beauty of the coral beaches with the marvellous colouring of the sea beyond, ranging at times from emerald green to a deep purple, has a haunting loveliness; while in this volcanic belt there is the rich vegetation of the tropics to remember: but within this beauty there lurks danger. The West Indies have known bad earthquakes. Ferocious squalls spring up all of a sudden; but the giant which is dreaded is the hurricane which bursts its way through forests, strips the trees of their leaves, throws to one side houses and churches. As it advances the atmostphere grows tense with something so evil that it seems to belong to an unredeemed part of creation. All this must be taken into consideration as it makes for poverty and social instability.

This chapter is not intended as history but rather as a description of the present. All the same it is quite impossible to understand to-day, without saying something of the past.

When Columbus on 12 October 1492 made his landfall off an island in the Bahamas, and named it San Salvador, an evil day dawned for the West Indies. In one way or another the Spaniards managed to eliminate the indigenous race they called Indians (to the end of his days Columbus thought he had reached Asia) either by slaughter, by infecting them with disease, or by sending them down the mines.

Just a hundred years after Columbus landed Britain comes into the West Indian slave market and the discredit belongs to an

English sailor. The traffic grew and grew, and large fortunes were made by English and Scottish merchants dealing in the horrid game. H. A. L. Fisher in his *History of Europe* says that it has been computed that between 1680 and 1786 well over two million slaves were brought to British Colonies, while the planters called for still more. Britain herself did not cease from slave dealing till 1830.

It is well to ponder what this means to the West Indies. The wretched negroes mostly from West Africa were torn away from their tribal sanctions and were, as slaves, human cattle. A husband could be sold away from his wife, or a child from its mother. They could not testify in the law courts. For a long time they were forced to breed but denied legal wedlock. Thus they began to think of themselves as an inferior race. Meanwhile the slave owners were importing an alien race with an alien culture and imported them in such amounts as very greatly to outnumber the Europeans, as they do to this day.

At last the slaves were freed. On the eve of the great day many negroes climbed a hill and singing hymns waited for the sun of freedom to rise. But in the light of the sun they did not find the glory they hoped. What they did find was embittered planters and themselves thrown into the labour market having to accept what small wage the planters chose to offer. Many a man and woman wished themselves in slavery again where there was at least food and shelter. The planters were recompensed for the loss of the slaves, but for the newly-made freemen very little was done. It is arguable that the method of release was as bad as the enslavement.

The sins of the fathers have been visited on the children. The fathers had built up a servile state with a comparatively small number of white men owning their servants. When this was abolished the white man became poor and the ex-slaves poorer. Their poverty must be seen to be believed. When in the last war the United States took over, as they did elsewhere, an air-force base in the Bahamas, they called for labour and the coloured men came in. To the astonishment of the troops they found most of the volunteers were so ill-nourished that they simply could not do their work. Those wise and practical Americans fed them with nourishing food and sent their medical officer to look after them. This is only one case out of very many. There is still alarming malnutrition among the negroes.

Anglican Origins

When the Society of the Propagation of the Gospel (founded 1701) sent missionaries to America and Canada who had in view the white settlers, till then deprived of the services of the Church, they found the Red Indians and at once began evangelizing with real success. So far as is known an S.P.G. missionary named Joseph Holt was in 1712 the first Anglican priest to go to the West Indies and took his way to Barbados. Thereafter there was a steady trickle of clergy and schoolmasters. Some did not stay long; some died of yellow fever. It is on record that one schoolmaster threw up his job and became a privateer.

The man who has left an indelible mark on the Church in the West Indies was a layman, the great General Codrington who, making his will in 1703, left all his estate in Barbados to S.P.G., and when he died the Society, after some legal trouble, entered into possession. To-day Codrington College, Barbados, is being reconditioned as a theological college for white and coloured ordinands.

The clergy sent out by S.P.G. did not confine their ministrations to the Europeans, but went freely among the slaves teaching and baptizing. There were no confirmations because there was for long no bishop. From the days of Joseph Holt in 1712 it took over a century and constant pressure from S.P.G. to persuade the Crown to nominate one. At last in 1842 a bishop was consecrated in England for Jamaica and in the same year another for Barbados.

By this time the colonies were settled down under their Governors. There was not though, indeed there could hardly be, any cohesion among the various colonies. Moreover there was no desire for it.

British Guiana and Antigua got their bishops in 1842: Nassau (Bahamas) in 1861,[1] Trinidad in 1872, British Honduras in 1883, the Windward Islands in 1927.

On 28 August 1880 the Archbishop of Canterbury signed the Instrument authorizing the foundation of the Province.

---

[1] The Bahamas are for Colonial Office purposes not in the West Indies. This seems strange if Columbus is remembered. Their civil constitution is different from that of the West Indies proper. It should be added that Nassau, apart from church affairs, does not wish to be in the West Indies.

Having obtained provincial rights and the recommendation of the Lambeth Conference and the consent of the various West Indies dioceses, the Bishops of Jamaica-cum-Honduras, and Barbados- cum-Windward-Islands, of Guiana, and of Trinidad, solemnly decreed the West Indies Church to be constituted into the Province of the West Indies 'as a branch of the Church of England in full union and communion with the said Church'.

In 1883 they started to draw up the canons of the Province. These have been reprinted and amended six times, the last time in 1930.

Provincial Status

In Canon II. 2 it is ordained that the Primate shall be chosen by the bishops out of their own number, and this rule has continued to this day. Indeed it has become the fashion to elect the most senior bishop. Surely this is a source of weakness and might do serious harm. It can be admitted that the Province has been fortunate in its Primates, but such a rule unduly restricts the range of choice. It ought to be possible to choose an Archbishop from the whole Anglican Communion. It would of course be necessary to provide him with a stable see, just as Canterbury is always the see of the Primate of All England. With good will it might be possible to carve out of one of the existing dioceses a new diocese, endow it and provide a church as his cathedral. He would then be free to travel and visit the dioceses in his province.

The usual conditions demanded for a grant of provincial status is that the province should be self-supporting. Perhaps in 1883 the state of the West Indies was better than it is now. Neither Nassau nor the Windward Islands nor Antigua can do without help from outside to-day. These are among the very poor islands. It would however be unfortunate to exclude any of the colonies. At this time in their history vital changes in their constitutions are coming. The Province as a whole must be anxious. The Colonial Office is spending, not before it was due, large sums for the erection of schools. These cannot be denominational. The Church has her schools and of course wants to keep them, so that the people may be brought up in the Faith: but it is very evident that the Church cannot compete with the State. Unless the policy has recently been changed, the State in the person of the Colonial Office wishes to co-operate with the Church and will help the church schools financially, if the Church can provide an up-to-date school. Already in Nassau the Church under the leadership of that energetic American Bishop of Nassau, Spence Burton, has in being a school with an adequate teaching staff and buildings. The purpose is to give both primary and secondary education to Negro children. Presumably the Government gives a grant.

Synodical Government

The Provincial Canons of the Church in the West Indies provide among many other things that after a bishop has declared his submission to the authority of the Provincial Synod he then proceeds, whether consecrated in the West Indies or elsewhere, to a declaration that he 'will pay due honour to the Archbishop of Canterbury and will respect and maintain the spiritual rights and privileges of the Church of England and of all churches in communion with her'.

There is a canon 'Of the discipline of a Bishop', another 'Of a Provincial Court of Appeal' (consisting of the Primate and two other bishops). The last clause is 'any expenses incurred on account of expert legal advice shall be borne by the person or persons desiring it'.

The Province as a whole seems to be well disciplined and orderly. Probably the reason is, while due deference is paid to the opinion of the Primate, the government is synodical, and every diocese has its own synods. The canons of the Diocese of Nassau are worth study. They are largely the work of the wise and far seeing Bishop Addington Venables (1863-86). It was during his episcopate that the civil government ceased subsidizing the Church, a step which has been taken by the civil governments in at least seven of the eight dioceses. The eighth, Barbados, seems to be in process of suffering the same fate. It fell to Bishop Venables to form the canons. When he produced them a very stormy meeting took place and the Bishop was insulted. He immediately without a word walked out and took passage to England to get advice. When he returned he prescribed the same canons, which were accepted by a big majority. It is due to him that when the Diocesan Synod elects a bishop the procedure is that two Houses are formed. Only the clergy are allowed to submit names, but to secure an election there must be a two-thirds majority in each House. He also provided that when the Synod was called together, all voting should be done by the three Houses and that there must be a majority in each. The House of Bishops is composed of the Bishop. This rule obtains to-day and in his day it was a wise precaution. All this of course was approved by the Province.

The loss of the civil subsidies has reduced the West Indian dioceses to great poverty and the blow is still felt. All the same it is likely that if to-day a poll was taken among the bishops and clergy, with the laity, they would not go back to the Establishment. The freedom they now enjoy within the Province has been the making of the Church. It has certainly grown in stature and in public respect.

Worship and Work

The worship of the West Indian Church is founded on the Book of Common Prayer. One diocese at least has been given permission to use the 1549 Book and uses now right through its whole length the same rite and the same ceremonies. This is of great value when ministering to the unlettered. They find the same thing in all the churches and it fosters a sense of solidarity and serves to integrate the people. This is written not about the educated coloured people but about the illiterate, of whom there are many, living in settlements and far from a town. The coloured people really do love their church and its services. They have never lost their sense of the nearness of God. To the more remote islands with a number of settlements a priest is sent if one can possibly be spared (most of the dioceses are badly understaffed), who will live in one of the settlements, to the real delight of the inhabitants, and visit the others. It is a lonely life. He may not see a white man for long periods. These good priests do a wonderful work and are kept to it not only by a sense of being needed, but by a sense of reparation to these poor folk for the scandal of slavery. They not only minister the sacraments but do a bit of doctoring, patching up quarrels, and generally acting as a father to them. The Church has great influence and in this way does a work of charity which no other body does so well.

It must be remembered that in addition to the negroes, who are in the great majority, there are in some of the islands other nationalities—East Indians, Chinese, and in the mainland dioceses

o

of British Guiana and British Honduras indigenous West Indians, each one presenting a difficult problem.

Finance

If it be asked 'How is all this financed?' the answer is manifold. A casual glance at the list of West Indian dioceses in *Crockford* is sufficient to show how small is their capital.

S.P.G. has since her foundation fostered the Province of the West Indies, and quite recently has raised the sum of the Block Grant and at the request of the bishops launched an appeal for money. The truth is that the Church in the West Indies lives from hand to mouth. Most of the dioceses by maintaining diocesan societies in England raise money to be forwarded to the Bishop. Most bishops think this a bad way but the only one. Indeed it presses very hard on a bishop home on furlough when he is supposed to have a holiday. In fact he gets next to none. He has to travel all about the country trying to raise money, and goes back to his diocese more tired than when he left. This is bad for him and for the diocese. However, when the bishops all come home for the Lambeth Conference, they will meet S.P.G. and it is to be hoped that a better plan may be contrived.

There is another source of financial support which comes from the coloured people. Poor as they are, they try every year to give a little even if it is only a copper or two: and it is good for them to feel that they really do contribute to keep the Church alive. In some of the towns there is a regular system of church dues which they can easily pay. If they are so poor that they cannot give, their priest will know and excuse them. There is a church largely attended by the negroes, which as a matter of course pays its dues and also keeps the rectory in repair and provides a telephone. Their standard of churchmanship in this respect is far higher than obtains in England.

In all that has been said there has been no intention of pretending that the West Indian Church is spotless. There are indeed terrible breakdowns which almost break the heart of a priest. The sexual morality is in places very bad. The uneducated negro seldom has his emotions under control.

Staff

The West Indian Church is manned mostly by priests from

England, young men with some experience of parish life, if possible. The number of coloured priests is steadily increasing. Some of these have gone to England for training but most to Codrington College, Barbados. Soon all West Indian ordinands, having reached a certain standard of schooling, will go there. If a degree is required they will go to the new university, yet to come into being.

There is another grade. When from poverty or lack of priests the bishop cannot send a cleric, the local coloured catechist comes to the front. He is not highly educated, but can read Mattins and generally do his best for the people. Even the unpaid ones are usually splendid. They form the bulwarks of the Church. Should they be left for as long as a year, the priest when he comes finds the church going and the Sunday school at work.

The clergy who join the Province as priests are recruited in a somewhat haphazard way. The first to be approached is probably S.P.G. and then the commissaries. If they have no suitable man at hand the bishop has to wait until someone volunteers to come out and very often that means a long delay and congregations left without a pastor. When, if ever, he does get his man, he probably keeps him at hand for some time before sending him to an outpost. If the priest has come out to take charge of a church in a city, he inducts and institutes him in the ordinary way. Again probably, the city priest has some security of tenure, but the outpost men are under the charge of the bishop who can move them about as necessity demands.

The Spirit of Unity

Should anyone ask if in the West Indies there is any enmity between those who glory in the name of Catholic and those who rejoice in the name of Protestant, the answer is No. If in fact it has happened, it must have been kept very quiet. Neither is there racial hatred. It is true that some negroes say they dislike the white people, but this is not really so, though they may dislike some white folk. There was a riot in Trinidad some years ago which might be called racial. The truth of this is that for one reason or another the negroes started rioting and when they do that there are likely to be indiscriminate brick-bats.

It has been shown how happily the West Indian Church works under its provincial Canon Law. Can one envisage the whole

Anglican Communion under one? Perhaps it could be done in a dream—which would turn into a nightmare. How little, till quite lately, did the clergy and laity of England take note of Canon Law! Recently canons have been debated in Convocation and some tentative canons have been drawn up, and at once there have come ominous questions about getting them through Parliament. It does not seem possible for an endowed and established Church to draw up canons similar to those suitable for provinces both unendowed and unestablished. After all is said, it will not be formal canons that can preserve unity in the world-wide Anglican Church, but the great affirmations of the Creeds, the same Bible, and very largely the same language and the Book of Common Prayer, to which must be added a mystical respect for Canterbury.

Conclusion

At the close of this chapter the writer craves permission to lapse into the first person to tell a true story. It begins strangely enough with Miami in Florida. That city is a mushroom one built with amazing skill on what was within living memory a swamp. There was a call for much labour, and a number of coloured people went across to get the wages. Among them was a large percentage of the congregation of St. Agnes' Church, Nassau. In Miami they found themselves without a church and set themselves to get one. With a good amount of outside help they met with success. They named the church after St. Agnes and when I visited them they had a finer church than the much-loved original one. Though it would have been to their advantage to become naturalized Americans, they stubbornly refused as they wished to remain British. At the time of my visit their Rector was a Bahamian-born priest.

The next scene was in Chicago when I found myself attending a very large meeting of bishops in the Western hemisphere. As I entered the hall, two American bishops came up to me and having verified me as Bishop of Nassau said, 'What we want to know is, how is it that you in the Bahamas have such success in dealing with the negroes and we in the Southern States make such a mess of it.'

Well, I had known that Americans are very courteous and kind to their guests and like paying compliments, and thought no more about it. It was again brought to my mind later, when I read an article in an American Church paper on, I think, 'The Church and the Negro'. In it the author wrote of the small number of confirmations in the Southern States and of the large number in Miami, and said, 'If you ask me why there is such a big number of candidates for confirmation in Miami, I can only answer "The Bahamians are there".'

Let me add that this story would never have been told, had I not known that the same sort of thing has happened in other parts of the West Indies. It is a deserved tribute to the coloured adherents of our Church and to the whole Province of the West Indies.

X

THE MEDITERRANEAN AND THE NEAR AND MIDDLE EAST

by the REV. W. A. WIGRAM, D.D.

The Bishopric of Gibraltar

It was in the seventh and eighth centuries that scattered groups or 'colonies' of English began to settle in the countries bordering on the Mediterranean. They went there at first purely for commercial reasons, and the 'English Khan' at Aleppo where all the English merchants lived together, with their families, can be seen to this day. It was so built as to be defensible against a mob, and —as the English took their religion with them—it had its own church and chaplain from the beginning, and its own school for children born there. It was the same in the more military colony of Tangier, where Thomas Ken was chaplain. These colonies were English, and the Church recognized, even if it sometimes neglected, its duty of spiritual care of them. All were counted as in the Diocese of London, just as all English children born on all the seven seas were parishioners of Stepney. Like colonies grew up in Smyrna and Constantinople, and though there the foreigners now lived in any convenient houses, yet the Turkish 'Capitulations' allowed them, like all other foreigners, to manage their own affairs under their 'consuls', and even to refuse admittance to Turkish policemen. This system was not abolished till the year 1914. The colonies multiplied, particularly when travel was easier. Folk went to them, and especially to the South of France, for health and winter warmth, and in 1840, a bishop, who took his title from one of the two tiny British possessions in the Mediterranean, was found necessary for the scattered communities. His cathedral is at Gibraltar, with a second 'Collegiate Church' or cathedral at Malta. Thus the first *raison d'être* of the Church of England in those lands was, to give spiritual care to English who had settled, and often built their own churches, in those lands, and brought their clergy, all round the Mediterranean. Soon, a further need developed. It was felt to be needful

to give a true idea of what Anglicanism and the Church of
England stood for, to those various churches with which Englishmen came in contact, in order to secure friendly relations with
them if possible, and hope of understanding in the future.

Naturally, the church standards and ideas of the various
chaplaincies of the Diocese varied, with those of the home
societies that supported them, and the habits of the English
residents. Thus they presented a fair picture of their Church, of
real underlying unity with much surface diversity. 'The Church
of England', said a Greek friend to the writer, 'drives her carriage
with a loose rein!' As regards other churches, where the contact is
with Roman Catholics, 'friendly relations' in an official sense
there can be none, for Roman principles forbid it, but only, perhaps, personal friendships between individual chaplains and
Roman priests. In lands that are Orthodox and not Roman, like
Greece and the Balkan peninsula, for example, there has of late
years been much more friendship. Specially is this the case in
Constantinople. 'How is it', said a Roman priest who called upon
the Patriarch Joachim there, 'that you can be so friendly with
those Anglicans, and not with us? Would submission to the Holy
Father be impossible for you? I can assure you that you would
receive a Father's welcome from him.' 'When my Brother of
Rome', said the Patriarch, 'is content to be one of the Patriarchs
of the Church, I will be the first to acknowledge him as first
among them.' In that lies the explanation of the whole position.
The Anglican saw the Greeks as friends. In Greece, there are
historic reasons that facilitate close contact between the Anglican
and Orthodox Churches, and the higher level of general education
among the Orthodox there makes personal friendship and understanding easier.

Steps towards an Orthodox recognition of Anglican orders,
and consequent intercommunion, have been taken on both sides.
Several of the fifteen or more 'autocephalous' churches that together form the Orthodox Communion—for example, those of
Jerusalem, Constantinople, Cyprus, and Rumania—have recognized English orders as 'historically' valid, and 'fully as good as
those of Rome, of the Old Catholics, or of the Armenians'—
these being a typical 'Separated Church'. This is not, to the
Orthodox, the same thing as recognition of the 'validity' of
Anglican sacraments (though it allows the hope that they are

'valid for us'), and still less is it intercommunion, though it is a step towards both. Those can only follow full recognition of the orthodoxy of Anglican doctrine. That we hope for in the future but it is not attained yet.

Naturally a diocese like that of Gibraltar, consisting as it does of a number of scattered 'colonies' in various independent States, in which only the Rock of Gibraltar and the island of Malta are British territory, and which are inhabited and occupied by churches not in communion with the Church of England, is of an anomalous character, and open to many jibes. Some of these come from exalted quarters. 'I believe I have the honour to be in your diocese,' said the Pope of that day to Bishop Collins of Gibraltar. 'It is true, your Holiness, and the honour is shared by your Holiness' brother of Constantinople,' said the Bishop. Some say that the existence of the 'diocese' is a glaring departure from Catholic custom. Actually, like many things in the Church of England, it has grown up naturally in the attempt to carry on Catholic customs as far as possible, after Catholic unity has been broken up by causes not all of our creating. Territorial unity, and 'one church, one bishop' is undoubtedly the old ideal, but that broke down in the East with the christological disputes of the fifth and following centuries, and has never existed since. A divided Christendom is a sad fact, and an ancient. Then those who were conscious of a national and spiritual union among themselves formed those 'Nestorian' and 'Monophysite' churches that still exist, as distinct from the Greek, whose claim to an overlordship, based on the fact that the capital of the Empire was the Greek city of Constantinople, the 'Orientals' resented. The inchoate national feeling that resented this foreign dictation found expression in religion, and used any theological formula that happened to be rejected by the Greek ecclesiastical authorities as their slogan of independence. Thus there grew up that 'Millet system' to which we refer below, starting among the Christians of Sassanid Persia in the fifth century, and continuing in Turkey till our own day. These various national churches had each of them its own episcopate, and though they all lived interlaced with one another, the bishops among them had, each of them, jurisdiction over his own people, and was out of communion with all others.

When Rome began to form 'Uniate' churches in those lands in

the crusading and later ages, she wisely accepted this position, and the Uniate churches ('Maronite', 'Chaldaean' and 'Syrian Catholic') developed on these lines, each with its own rite and episcopate, though all subordinate to Rome, and all with jurisdiction interlacing in a way bewildering to a European though perfectly natural to an Oriental. There might be, for example, in Mosul or in Jerusalem, several episcopal jurisdictions, some of Roman obedience and some not, each one superintending his own people. The state of schism was an evil, but this was an adaptation to circumstances that made the best of a bad condition of things, which nobody could alter.

When the English authorities established the Bishopric of Gibraltar, they neither knew nor cared about this state of things, but in setting up an episcopal system based on a national church feeling as distinct from a territorial one, they were really following a precedent established in other lands rather before St. Augustine came to England. Once established, this type of episcopate tended to grow, as we see in the 'Bishopric of Northern Europe', and the first offshoot from it was the 'Bishopric of Jerusalem', or the 'Jerusalem Bishopric', which had a somewhat stormy history of its own.

The Anglican Bishopric in Jerusalem

Jerusalem has always been a centre of pilgrimage, at least from the days of St. Helena onwards; even in later days, Crusaders described themselves as 'pilgrims', and liked to think that they carried arms merely for needful self-defence. The pilgrimage habit is a human instinct, more marked perhaps at certain periods of development, but Christian men have always sought to visit

> Those holy fields
> Over whose acres walked those blessed feet.

When the Crusades were done, Russian pilgrimages soon began, and great hostels arose, in Jerusalem and elsewhere in Palestine, permanently occupied by an ever-changing crowd of devotees. With modern days came greater facilities for travel, and with the divisions of the Church, there were always crowds of those who were not under the jurisdiction of the church of the land, so that care for their needs meant the permanent presence of clergy of all confessions. Pilgrims being always, unfortunately, inclined to disorder, and apt to stumble over unfamiliar regulations, these clergy had to be of a status that they might respect and obey, to avoid disorders that might be dangerous to all. Hence, when every variety of church had some authority of its own there, the feeling was natural that England and the Church of England could not be 'out of it', and the question of her relations with the Oriental Churches was bound to come up and be important, at a point where all of them had their sanctuaries and representatives. Hence the 'Jerusalem Bishopric' of the Church of England. Its beginning was somewhat ill-omened, and this had results on its story. It owed its origin to the Chevalier Bunsen of Prussia, one of those high-minded and doctrinaire enthusiasts for universal peace, who have a way of ignoring all difficulties, and all other folks' ideas. Having influence with King Frederick William IV of Prussia (who was more of a religious sentimentalist than a modern Prussian statesman is apt to be), he persuaded that monarch, about the year 1840, to take up the idea of an Anglo-German bishopric in Jerusalem. This was to weld all Protestants in the East together and to 'form a centre of enlightened Christianity in those lands'. In the future, it was to lead to a union of English and German Christianity on an episcopal basis; to a protectorate over all Protestants in the East like that claimed by Russia over all Orthodox; to a restoration of the Jews to Palestine (which seems to have been Lord Shaftesbury's suggestion), and finally to a definite check to the political aims (real or supposed) of Russia in those lands.[1] No wonder men thought—wrongly—that the Bishopric was to be political and proselytizing. The Bishop was to be alternately English and German, appointed by the Crown in each case, but receiving orders and consecration from the Church of England. High-churchmen definitely disliked the scheme, and the acceptance of it shattered Newman's failing belief in the possible catholicity of the Anglican Church. It was supported, however, by Archbishop Howley, and by Bishop Blomfield of

[1] Chevalier Bunsen's real knowledge of the state of things he hoped to improve may be gauged by the fact that he really believed that the Bishop thus appointed would be 'the first successor in Jerusalem of James the Brother of the Lord'. His knowledge stopped with the New Testament, and the existence of any other body of Christians in those lands did not come into his purview. His scheme did not lack nobility, or vision of a limited kind, but while it might perhaps have been possible in the seventeenth century, much water had run under the bridges since then.

London. The first Bishop (Michael Alexander, an Israelite by birth, an Anglican priest, and professor of Hebrew and Arabic at what is now King's College, London) was consecrated in 1841. Archbishop Howley made it clear that any proselytizing from the Orthodox Church was most definitely not the object of this foundation, and that the man appointed was to be Bishop *in* and not *of* Jerusalem.

A perverse fate followed the scheme, for the two English bishops appointed under it both died soon after consecration, while the only German selection, Bishop Gobat, lived and flourished for an episcopate well beyond the common lot, lasting for thirty-three years (1846–79). Himself a most benevolent and well-intentioned man, he 'habitually violated'—we quote Archbishop Benson—Archbishop Howley's instructions against any proselytizing from the Orthodox Church, for he was quite unable to understand why he should not, as his own conscience bade him, receive Christians from an 'impure' into the 'only pure' form of Christianity, or why the authorities of the 'impure' church should have any honourable reason to object. 'How can we refuse to accept men who wish to leave their errors and come to us?' was his position. His school, two English churches, and the Protestant Cemetery in the 'Old City' are still features of Jerusalem, and a certain number of native clergy in Anglican orders still minister to Protestant Church of England congregations, composed of converts or children of converts from Orthodoxy and Judaism. These were supported (morally, not financially) by the local Mission of the Church Missionary Society, who were officially engaged in the evangelization of Moslems, but had to admit that converts from Islam were almost unknown. The founding of this small Protestant body was not a happy result of Bishop Gobat's work, but it still remains as a legacy of it. The fact is that it often happens in the East that such a body is started by foreign help, most usually out of converts from some one of the native Christian churches: it attains a certain size, and then ceases to grow, though the descendants of the original seceders may remain in what has now become to them the faith of their fathers. Further, the writer feels that, magnificent though the record of the C.M.S. is in other lands, and in its work of the conversion of the heathen to Christ, yet a task like that in Palestine that required sympathetic dealing with an ancient church, with a long history that had formed it, and a theology and tradition of its own, for which its martyrs had died, and was to them the truth, was not the 'métier' of this very great society. It was not in human nature that the authorities of the Orthodox Church in the land should welcome such an effort, and a letter from the Orthodox Patriarch of Jerusalem, Nicodemus, expresses his feelings. 'You English say that you desire unity, but you act in a way that is not consistent with that idea. Your C.M.S. Mission was established to convert Moslems, but it really only unsettles and detaches our people. It is no good to wish for unity and to send us men who break up the congregations of the Church with which you wish to unite. Your Archbishop says he disapproves, but it seems that he has not the power to stop it.' It was a painful conflict of two parties, both of them composed of most conscientious men— though neither could see that in the other—and it did not bring the understanding between Anglicans and Orthodox, desired by the best men on both sides, any nearer. Of course there were faults on both sides—but the ancient church has a right to the careful consideration of the newcomer.

In 1879 Bishop Gobat died, and his successor, Bishop Barclay, followed him only two years later. There was then a general feeling both in England and in what was now the German Empire that the 'fancy Anglo-German Church' of Bunsen's vision did not work, and in fact, though the English Crown Princess Victoria of Germany was anxious to continue the scheme, her husband the Crown Prince Frederick declared that 'it has produced no spirit of unity, and is of benefit to neither church', so that Germany withdrew, definitely, from co-operation. An interval followed, 1881–7, during which those trained under Bishop Gobat continued to work as their consciences dictated, and there was nobody who had any right to control them. Increased friction with the Orthodox naturally followed, and yet a bishopric in Jerusalem was felt to be right and necessary, and in 1887 Archbishop Benson decided to recast and restart the scheme, and to work it on 'non-proselytizing lines', such as those on which he was working his then newly established Assyrian Mission. There was much anxiety and some opposition among high-churchmen, voiced by Canon Liddon of St. Paul's, but this naturally came to an end when it appeared that not only was the Patriarch Nicodemus of Jerusalem anxious that there should be a Bishop of the Church of England in that centre—if it was only to keep the clergy of that communion in order—but was also anxious that Canon Liddon himself—whom he had met and liked—should be the man.[1] The new Bishop (Blyth) had no easy row to hoe. Many of his clergy and people had been brought up in the idea that proselytizing was almost a duty where the Orthodox were concerned, and indeed the conduct of many of the priests of that communion was such as to encourage this error. The clergy who followed this line were supported by the C.M.S. who had been their leaders and overseers during the vacancy, and a line adopted on conscientious motives was hard to abandon. The acceptance of Anglican Confirmation by those baptized— and so simultaneously confirmed—in the Orthodox Church had come to be regarded as a definite repudiation of Orthodoxy and acceptance of Protestantism, and therefore Bishop Blyth set his face most definitely against it. There was a time, now happily over, when the adherents of the C.M.S. seemed to think of themselves as belonging to a different church from that which worshipped at Bishop Blyth's new Cathedral of St. George, and even the fact that the Cathedral worship was most strictly according to the Book of Common Prayer did not prevent this unfortunate way of thinking. Gradually, however, owing largely to the saintly character of the Bishop, things changed for the better. The C.M.S. leaders were devoted Christian men who could see facts, and they came to see that the proselytizing policy did not produce the results that they desired far more than any party triumph. Thus gradually both Gibraltar and Jerusalem came to look on their dioceses as not just extensions of the Church of England in lands where she must always be an exotic, but as points where that Church came into contact with others with whom they could hope for friendly and even fraternal relations, and that the care they naturally gave to their own people must be carried out side by side with that duty. Some of the C.M.S. workers even came to regard themselves as co-operators with the Orthodox clergy.

The Diocese of Egypt

Much the same holds of the newer See of Egypt, which was till lately a part of the sphere of the Bishop in Jerusalem, but which is now, for convenience of administration, separated from it.

[1] J. O. Johnston, *Life and Letters of H. P. Liddon*, p. 354.

Here, the problems of the diocese are the same as in Palestine, but the elements of those problems are somewhat differently compounded. There is a far larger English colony, of a character both mercantile and transitory, for in days of peace the number of winter tourists in Egypt was naturally large. There has also been, up to the present, a considerable military element, in the British Occupying Force. That is however likely to be removed altogether, or at least to be limited to certain small districts. There is also a native Church, though in this case it is not 'Orthodox', as in Palestine, but of the national 'Coptic' variety. Coptic, by the way, really means 'Egyptian' being like our word 'gypsy', a rather far-fetched corruption of that name, and it dates from the day when the whole native population of the land was Christian of a fiercely national type, counted as heretical (Monophysite) elsewhere, while the followers of Islam were still an invading and conquering minority. The invaders have now largely become Egyptian, and the power of Islam has reduced Christianity to a minority. That minority is far more conservative—some would say more 'hide-bound'—than any other of the Oriental Churches, and at a lower level of education than most. As it was only from it that the Church of Abyssinia drew such culture as it had, the position of the latter was naturally lower. Further, the Coptic Church is at present in a doubtful political position. Egypt has just asserted her right to independence and to self-government as a civilized state; but that does not make Moslems regard Christians as their equals, or as entitled to more rights than they choose to allow; further, like many states in her position, Egypt is by no means ready to grant to others once under her control the liberty that she has claimed for herself, and is apt to be very suspicious of any over-friendliness between her Christian subjects and the English. In that land civil law may say one thing and religious law another, and the religious law—the Shariat— be the one by which men live. Copts may well find here an additional reason for being very conservative, and for clinging to their ancient rights and ways, that date from the days of the Arab Khalifs and were acknowledged by the Turks in their days of rule. One may hope in future for such friendliness as confidence in the intentions of our Church has won with, for example, the Orthodox Greeks, but the natural obstacles to be overcome will take time, and sympathy and patience are needed.

North Africa

In North Africa, outside Egypt, there is even less to be done at present. Once the African Church was one of the great churches of Christendom. Now no Christian Church of ancient date is left in existence, and we find only ruins of ancient fabrics and the remains of baptisteries that their 'cistern-like' structure has rendered indestructible, to remind us of the communion that produced Tertullian, Cyprian, and Augustine. Nothing of Christianity but the fiery character that produced the Donatists and 'Circumcellions' of old seems to have survived in the religion of the native people, where it now takes form in the most fanatical type of Islam known. Conversion seems an impossibility at present, and only example and education seem possible. That a certain number of Protestant missionaries, often of the Church of Scotland, do provide; and it is provided also by the Fathers of Cardinal Lavigerie's order, those 'White Marabouts' (as the Arabs call them) who show the Roman Catholic Church at its finest. All that the Church can do at present is that purely philanthropic and educational work that may in God's good time lead to a better understanding, on the part of the Sons of Islam, of the Christianity that at present they do not try to comprehend, but which their ancestors once accepted with exceptional zeal.

The Lesser 'Separated' Churches of the Middle East

In the Middle East, as in Egypt, there exist other ancient churches, in Syria, Iraq, and Iran, and the Church of England has to do with them. They are known now as the 'Assyrian' and 'Syrian' Christians. They stand accused of teaching the ancient Nestorian and Monophysite heresies.[1] Actually, they are Christians of Semitic stock, representing the old Syriac-speaking Christianity that produced and used the 'Peshitta' version of the Scriptures. Having a strong national feeling, they resented being managed by Greeks, much as our own fathers resented being managed by Italians, and when doctrinal disputes arose, they inclined to take the side that the Greeks condemned.

---

[1] The 'Monothelite' heresy also found a national *point d'appui* here, in the 'Maronite' hillmen of the Lebanon, and this schism lasted long enough for the clans concerned to join up with the invading Crusaders in 1100, and so, keeping their ancient rites but acknowledging the supremacy of the Pope, to form the first of the 'Uniate' churches in communion with Rome.

Those of them that dwelt in Iraq or Mesopotamia (now called 'Assyrians') had another reason for doing this. Being subjects of the Sassanid Persian Empire, which was then fanatically Zoroastrian in faith and the standing enemy of the Roman, they were liable to persecution as Roman sympathizers in each of the periodical wars between the two, and so naturally wished to show that they were not the same sort of Christian as the Roman, and need not be massacred every time the Shah-in-Shah and the Emperor had a quarrel. Hence they were allowed to administer themselves as a 'Millet' or subject race under their own patriarch (the name comes from an Arabic word, meaning 'language', each such race having its own), and when divisions arose among them the right was extended to all such divisions among Christians. This was what came to be called the 'Millet System', when Arab and, later, Turkish rule displaced that of Persia and continued the custom.

Thus, when councils among the Greeks were laying down the law—with some over-enforcement of technical terms—about the 'Nature' and 'Person' of the Christ, it was impossible to enforce their decisions among the Syriac-speakers who found in the dispute a field on which to fight the battle of their national life. Rivalry among the various Patriarchs—a term then coming into use—aggravated the disputes and made them incurable, though as far as doctrine went they could easily have been healed, but for the technical terms which each party used in differing senses. Both sides believed fully in (a) the real and complete divinity, and (b) the real and complete humanity, and (c) the true personal unity, of the Christ, though it was difficult to say (as it is for us) exactly what 'personality' may be. As for the terms in dispute, it is true that the Assyrians (so-called Nestorians) disliked calling the Blessed Virgin by the title 'Mother of God', because in their Syriac language the only possible rendering of the Greek 'Theotokos' inevitably suggests 'Mother of the Godhead'. Yet, instructed theologians of that church readily admitted and admit that there is an interpretation of the term that means no more than 'Mother of Jesus Christ our Lord and our God' a formula that their fathers accepted readily and they use to-day, and that contains all that the word 'Theotokos' guards. What they fear, and Nestorius feared, was a doctrine of the Alexandrine schools that suggested that the manhood of Christ was in any way incomplete or different from ours, save as regards sin. Developments in Alexandria showed this was no idle fear. These questions are alive enough to-day to make it needful to understand them. It must be remembered that if this Church did not accept the council of Ephesus it did accept that of Chalcedon, which stands in its *synodicon* to-day. The writer once translated the 'Second Letter of Cyril' (the document that gives the doctrinal decision of the council of Ephesus) to 'Nestorian' theologians, and was immediately asked: 'From which of our writers did you take this most excellent document?'[1] This church then is certainly not what we mean by the term Nestorian, and we know to-day that it is very doubtful whether Nestorius was either.

As regards the Church known as 'Monophysite', we own that members of it refuse to speak of Christ as 'in two natures' (φύσεις), seeing that to them the term φύσις does not mean 'nature', but something very much more like 'person'. They will, however, and do, assert that He is 'of' (ἐκ), two natures and *in* two *ousiai* (ὄυσίαι) and that He is *homo-ousios* with the Father as God, and *homo-ousios* with us as Man, and that eternally; so that we may affirm that they are not what the term 'Monophysite' means to us. An Athanasius could have reconciled both disputes, had another such saint ever appeared. One of the churches of their communion is the martyr Church of Armenia, who have altered the original text of the Creed of Nicaea as it was issued by the council—a thing that, as all theological students know, every church has done more or less—to make it quite clear that they believe in the reality and eternity of the humanity assumed by our Lord at the Incarnation. 'He ascended *in his own body* to Heaven' is how they make the phrase run, and it was in the face of that that they were accused of holding that His Humanity was not real. As regards our relations with these Eastern Churches, in 1911 our Eastern Churches Committee, now embodied in the Council for Foreign Relations, resolved that if any of the Oriental Churches of whose christology there was doubt, could accept the

---

[1] In some of their hymns, as in some of ours, there is incautious language, but we have never found any (and it has been our duty to examine them to satisfy doubters) as 'Nestorian' as a stanza in the *English Hymnal*, No. 20:

'Behold the great Creator makes Himself a house of clay,
A robe of virgin flesh he takes, that he will wear for aye.'

The language of their Liturgies is admittedly orthodox.

P

'christological versicles' of the *Quicunque Vult* (viz. verses 29–
37) as expressing what they taught about Christ, that would be
ground enough for allowing intercommunion with them (see
Lambeth Conference Report, 1930, p. 144). This confession of
our Faith has the great advantage of being authoritative for
Westerns and yet never fought over by Easterns, though it is
recognized as an orthodox confession by them.

These terms were accepted at once by the Assyrian Church
authorities, among whom the 'Archbishop's Mission' had been
working for twenty-five years, but before anything was done by
us, the 1914 War, and its after-consequences for the whole
Assyrian people, prevented any action on our part and reduced
the Church to a scattered remnant. Still, that is where our formal
relations with that Church stand to-day, so that it would seem
that any isolated communicant of the Assyrian Church has the
right to approach our altars as a guest of ours. The Armenian
Church takes up the same position. That appears to be an adequate summary of our relations with those Christian communities.

Conclusion

As regards missionary work in Islamic Lands, the writer
must own that he has no personal knowledge of such work in
lands purely Islamic, such as Afghanistan; on that then we pronounce no opinion. Where however (as in Iraq) Moslem and
Christian live side by side under Mohammedan rule, it is to be
feared that missionary work directed towards the Moslem cannot be carried on with any profit, till Islam must respect the
religion of Christianity, as shown to it by its own subjects. At
present, they do not so respect it, and though it is true that
it is centuries of Islamic misgovernment that have made that
attitude natural, the fact remains. Hence, it seems to the present
writer, that only educational and medical work is useful at present
for those of that faith, for the raising and educating of the Christians of the East is a needful preliminary to any direct missionary
work on Islam, in those lands. Yet, attempts to proselytize from
any Christian church—as our experience in Palestine tells us—
do not work out well and the fact that the Church of England is
known not to proselytize from them, on principle, is a condition
of her being able to help and to do good to Eastern churches at

large. Because that principle is known to be hers, the Orthodox and all 'Easterns' can meet with Anglicans on a footing of real friendliness, and can discuss points of difference with intent to find agreement, if possible. So, for example, the Orthodox have been able to feel that even if our 'Articles of Religion' (which after all were drawn up with an eye to our domestic quarrels only), do need explanation and re-statement before they can be approved, if produced as a general statement of our faith to-day, yet the teaching of the Book of Common Prayer is the same as their own. Therefore they can allow their sons to accept, at Anglican hands, the education that they feel they need.

It is on these lines that, we are convinced, the Church of England may come to an understanding with all the Churches of the East that may lead in the future to a real spiritual union, and so (we quote an Orthodox Professor of Theology), 'the ancient authority of the Orthodox, and the scientific method of the Anglican, may form a totality that may be the central body of a renewed and truly Catholic Church'.

XI

TROPICAL AFRICA

by the REV. R. W. STOPFORD, *formerly Principal of Achimota College*

Introductory

The continent of Africa presents so bewildering a variety of races, languages and customs, of different stages of material civilization and of forms of government that all generalizations are hazardous and no conclusions can be anything but tentative. From the mangrove swamps and coastal savannahs of West Africa to the mountains of Kenya and the luxuriant vegetation of the Rift Valley there is every type of geographical scene in which the only common feature is the general poverty of the land. The Bantu races are different from the negroid peoples of the west and in every area the tribes show marked variations of language, custom and belief. The political differences, though less marked, are very real; the French system differs from the Belgian and the Belgian from the Portuguese, and all are unlike the British. Even in the territories under British rule there are variations of policy; while white settlement constitutes a major problem in Kenya no European holdings are permitted in Nigeria or the Gold Coast. But everywhere there is rapid change. Tropical Africa, under the stimulus and direction of European powers, is living in two generations through five hundred years of European history. As a result there is tension everywhere, between the progressive youths and the conservative elders, between literates and illiterates, and between two ways of life which are fundamentally opposed to each other. In many parts the African is rapidly becoming conscious of his subordinate status and 'nationalism' is in the air, and the problems of economic development and social and political change are increasingly complex.

It is against this background of infinite variety and rapid change that the Anglican Communion in Tropical Africa must be studied. It comprises the dioceses of the Gambia, Sierra Leone, Accra, Lagos, and the Niger in the west, Uganda, the Upper Nile,

Mombasa, Zanzibar, Masasi, Central Tanganyika, Nyasaland and Northern Rhodesia in the centre and east, with Mauritius and Madagascar off the east coast, all originating from the missionary activity of the Church of England, and there is also on the west coast the Diocese of Liberia which forms part of the American Episcopal Church. All these dioceses are of comparatively recent origin and their growth shows the same rapidity which marks the political scene. The Diocese of the Niger, which had in 1900 only 1,730 members of whom 313 were communicants, had by 1945 grown to 214,984 members and 39,721 communicants. In Elgon, where there were no indigenous Christians at all in 1900, there were by 1937 1,300 Anglican churches and 150,000 adherents. Such expansion has brought with it peculiar difficulties of organization and administration, still further complicated by the prevailing low standard of education. And to the diversity of Africa itself the Church has added the lack of uniformity of the Church of England. The three major Anglican societies at work in Tropical Africa, the Society for the Propagation of the Gospel, the Church Missionary Society and the Universities' Mission to Central Africa, have their own distinctive ecclesiastical traditions and policies. There have been times indeed when it has seemed to the Africans as though the various dioceses were not part of the same Church; Lagosians resident in the Gold Coast, who were brought up in the tradition of the Diocese of Lagos, have even wished to have a congregation of their own apart from the Diocese of Accra, and men have been known to describe themselves not as 'Anglicans' but as 'C.M.S. Christians'.

But the differences between the dioceses must not be exaggerated. In spite of all the varieties of usage and the outward marks of differing emphasis the Anglican Church throughout Tropical Africa is clearly one. The fundamental outlook and temper are the same in the various parts, there is a general agreement on basic policy, there is a common loyalty to the See of Canterbury and the Mother Church. The differences are only those which exist within any diocese in England; the unity is that of the Church of England as a whole. The differences are perhaps more apparent because they are seen in isolation, for the individual dioceses have a uniformity within themselves which is unknown in England. Because they are each the result of the work of one missionary society they have a 'monochrome' character which undoubtedly makes for strength and efficiency. It may indeed be questioned whether something has not been lost which is of the essence of Anglicanism—a rich variety and a comprehensiveness which possess that unity in diversity so dear to the mind of St. Paul. But when provinces come into being they will themselves exhibit a variety of use which will be valuable as a corrective.

The Growth of Self-government

In the growth of every diocese there has been the same purpose—'to build up a native church, increasingly self-governing and self-supporting'. Bishop Hine, addressing his clergy at Likoma in Nyasaland in 1899, used words which could apply to any area in Tropical Africa: 'What this Mission (the U.M.C.A.) has always proposed to aim at is the building up of a native church . . . native in the true sense of the word; the church of the people of the land, irrespective of European influence and adapting itself to the special circumstances of the race and country in which it exists.' That objective has been pursued with varying degrees of emphasis and in different ways, but two main methods can be distinguished. The Church Missionary Society, following the principles laid down by Henry Venn, has sought to build up an indigenous church life from the bottom and to introduce 'into the Native Church that elementary organization which may give it "corporate life" and prepare it for its full development under a Native Ministry and an indigenous Episcopate'. Other societies have started with the diocese as the unit and, as it were, have worked downwards in the development of self-governing institutions. Both methods have proved successful, and though there have been periods when some of the European missionaries have seemed indifferent or even hostile to African ways and have adopted an excessively paternal attitude, the main aim of building up a native church has never been forgotten. It was only eight years after the foundation of the Diocese of Sierra Leone in 1852 that the Church Missionary Society formed the Sierra Leone Native Pastorate Church, the first indigenous church in any mission area. Even when, as in Southern Sudan, distances and difficulties of transport defeated the first plans for full diocesan organization the diocese was brought into existence again as soon as possible.

In most dioceses the organization has been developed rapidly on British lines, with parochial and district councils, rural deaneries, archdeaconries and assistant bishops where necessary. The first Synod of the Diocese of Zanzibar was summoned only twenty-three years after the first beginnings of the Universities' Mission, and though this Synod was very small it was of great value in building up the life of the diocese. The determination of the young dioceses to work towards self-government was shown clearly by the summoning of meetings of clergy and laity even though they were very few clergy and virtually no lay men or women. Bishop Trower told a gathering of clergy and mission agents at Likoma in 1903: 'We are not, I suppose, strictly speaking, meeting in a Diocesan Conference. But rather we are a gathering of clergy and lay missionaries meeting to discuss objects of interest and moment in the work and organization of the Diocese for our mutual benefit and for the assistance of the Bishop in his responsible task of direction and government. The Conference imposes nothing. It passes no resolution. And yet its value, I believe, is very great.' In a few dioceses such as Accra and the Gambia there has yet been no development beyond this stage, but these are now the exception. Almost everywhere there is some central body, whether it is called a Synod or a Diocesan Council, which includes clergy and laity, African and European, and which discusses and advises upon questions of importance for the life and work of the Church.

The development of these central councils has not been without difficulty, for the missionaries have sometimes been divided in their loyalty between Mission and Diocese. Bishop Tucker of Uganda had to overcome considerable opposition in creating the Synod of Uganda. The first draft constitution in 1898 was withdrawn because the missionaries objected that the Africans were not sufficiently educated to take an effective part. When the Bishop brought forward the draft rules in the following year only the non-controversial parts could be enforced because no agreement could be reached whether the missionaries should be included. It was not until 1907 that the Church of Uganda received its full constitution, and even then the Europeans only came in with some safeguards for their position as missionaries of the Church Missionary Society. Time has shown the vision and statesmanship of Bishop Tucker, and the experience of many dioceses has justified his policy. In his Memoirs the Bishop gave at some length the reasons for that policy and one quotation may serve to indicate the nature of the early difficulties and the underlying reasons for the insistence upon the value of a central Council:

➤ In training native Christians in the art of self-government it is a tremendous mistake to hold aloof from their organization, and this for the simple reason that if the work of the European missionaries is carried on outside the limits of the Native Church there must be an outside organization. In that case the native Christians will not be slow to realize that the outside organization is the one which really settles whatever questions may be under discussion in the Church, and that their own organization is more or less a sham. Let [the missionary] therefore throw in his lot absolutely with the native, identifying himself as far as possible with their life, work and organization. Let him submit himself to the law and canons of their Church. As the Church gains in strength, in knowledge and in wisdom the body of missionaries will diminish in number (it was never regarded that their position should be a permanent one), their voice in the councils of the Church will become less and less loud, until at last the missionary element will disappear altogether and the Native Church will stand alone.[1]

In this Bishop Tucker was faithful to the policy which Henry Venn with his prophetic vision had stated in 1851:

Regarding the ultimate object of a Mission, viewed under its ecclesiastical result, to be the settlement of a Native Church under Native Pastors upon a self-supporting system, it should be borne in mind that the progress of a Mission mainly depends upon the training up and location of Native Pastors; and that, as it has been happily expressed, the 'euthanasia' of a Mission takes place when a Missionary, surrounded by well-trained Native congregations under Native Pastors, is able to resign all pastoral work into their hands and gradually relax his superintendence over the Pastors themselves till it insensibly ceases; and so the Mission passes into a settled Christian community.

The questions discussed in the various Synods and Councils show how real is the part which they now take in the work of the Church and include matters both of order and faith. In 1903 the Synod of Zanzibar was considering Public Discipline, the Mar-

---

[1] Tucker, *Eighteen years in Uganda and East Africa*, vol. i, p. 241.

riage Laws, continuity of work and the Native Ministry. The Synod of Uganda in 1928 had as its main topic 'union with other dioceses', and in 1930 'Christian Marriage'. In general the Synod can only advise the Bishop and cannot dictate to him, and bishops, like Frank Weston of Zanzibar, have not hesitated to refuse to act as the Synod has advised. Nevertheless the bishops have always worked through their Synods and have thought it wise to refer to them almost every important issue, and the influence of the Synods, even when they exist only in a rudimentary stage, has been greater than that of most Diocesan Conferences in England.

Diocesan Constitutions

Although some form of synodical government is general in Tropical Africa not every diocese has a formal constitution. Legal constitutions exist in the Dioceses of Uganda, Central Tanganyika, Sierra Leone, Lagos and the Niger, which are similar in form, and Madagascar is governed by a constitution written in Malagasy which is substantially the same as that of the Diocese of Cape Town. A draft constitution for the Diocese of Mombasa was discussed in January 1947. The dioceses founded by the Universities' Mission, although they attached great importance to the early summoning of Synods and the formation of Cathedral Chapters, have not set up formal constitutions, possibly because the level of African education has not been so high in their areas as in other parts and because they have had few European residents to assist in the deliberations. The Diocese of Northern Rhodesia has prepared a draft constitution which has been passed by the Synod and awaits the approval of the Archbishop of Canterbury.

These constitutions define with great care the position of the diocese as part of the Anglican Communion. The importance of this justifies quotation at some length. The Fundamental Provisions of the Uganda Constitution are as follows:

1. The Church of Uganda doth hold and maintain the doctrines and sacraments of Christ, as the Lord hath commanded in His Holy Word and as the Church of England hath received and explained the same in the Book of Common Prayer, and the form and manner of making, ordaining and consecrating of Bishops, Priests and Deacons, and in the Thirty-Nine Articles of Religion, and further it disclaims

for itself the right of altering any of the aforesaid standards of faith and doctrine.

2. Provided that nothing herein contained shall prevent the Church of Uganda from making at any time, after the establishment of a Provincial Synod, in which the Church of Uganda is represented, but not sooner, such adaptations and abridgements of and any additions to the service of the Church as may be required by the circumstances of the Church of Uganda.[1]

The Constitution of Sierra Leone states the same principles more briefly:

The Church planted in the Colony of Sierra Leone, mainly through the instrumentality of the Church Missionary Society, is a genuine branch of the Church of England, so far as it holds its orders, doctrines and general forms of worship, but in all matters of discipline and order shall be governed and maintained in accordance with the Articles following, so that nothing be done repugnant to the terms of the existing Charter.[2]

The more recent constitution of Central Tanganyika, on the other hand, is more explicit in its Fundamental Declarations:

1. This Church, being a part of the One Holy Catholic and Apostolic Church and in communion with the Church of England in England, will ever remain and be in communion with the Church of England in England and with national regional or provincial churches maintaining communion with that Church, so long as communion is consistent with the solemn declarations set forth in this chapter.

2. This Church doth receive all the canonical scriptures of the Old and New Testaments as being the ultimate rule and standard of Faith given by the inspiration of God, and containing all things necessary to Salvation.

3. This Church doth hold and will continue to hold the Faith of Christ as professed by the One Holy Catholic and Apostolic Church from primitive times and in particular as set forth in the Creeds known as the Nicene Creed and the Apostles' Creed.

4. This Church will ever obey the commands of Christ, teach His doctrine, administer His Sacraments of Holy Baptism and Holy Communion, follow and uphold His discipline, and preserve the three orders of Bishops, Priests and Deacons in the sacred ministry.

5. This Church doth retain and approve of the Book of Common Prayer and the doctrines and principles contained therein and will

---

[1] Lowther Clarke, *Constitutional Church Government*, pp. 393ff.
[2] ibid., p. 412.

not in any revision of the Book of Common Prayer or otherwise make or permit any alteration which would change the character of this Church as shown by its assent to this as well as to the other solemn declarations aforesaid.[1]

It is interesting to compare these statements with the Fundamental Provisions in the draft constitution for Northern Rhodesia which read:

1. Pending its incorporation in a separate province of the Anglican Communion, the Diocese of Northern Rhodesia has its place as a missionary diocese of the Province of Canterbury in full communion with the Church of England. It receives and maintains the Christian faith as taught in Holy Scriptures and the Creeds, and administers the discipline and sacraments of Christ as in His Church He has commanded and as the Church of England has received the same. Subject to the canonical jurisdiction of the Metropolitan, the Church of the Diocese has power through its Bishop in Synod to authorize such variations in its rules, rites and ceremonies and to make such decisions in regard to the presentation of doctrine as are permitted by authority in the Anglican Communion and are consistent with the historic faith and practice of the Church Catholic.

2. The Church of the Diocese of Northern Rhodesia proclaims the equal value of all men in the sight of God, and in its membership and government allows no discrimination on grounds of race.

It will be noted that all these constitutions assert the connexion with the Church of England in unequivocal terms and that two emphasize the Holy Scriptures and the Creeds. There are important differences in the extent to which the dioceses claim freedom to alter rites and ceremonies; Northern Rhodesia assumes that there will be such variations, while Central Tanganyika is concerned to limit changes and to preserve the Book of Common Prayer. The constitution of Uganda makes the power to vary the services depend upon the formation of a province.

The various constitutions achieve a very considerable measure of self-government. They make provision for the meeting of a Synod or Council to consider questions affecting the life, work and administration of the Church in the diocese, for a Standing Committee, for Diocesan Trustees to hold property and for the setting up of various Boards, including generally a Board of Finance. But in one respect no diocese is completely self-govern-

---

[1] *East and West Review*. Vol. xii, No. 3, p. 76.

ing because throughout Tropical Africa the appointment of Bishops is vested in the Archbishop of Canterbury as Metropolitan. He may take counsel with the Missionary Society responsible for the diocese concerned, and in some cases the diocese has the right to make representations. The Bishop of Nyasaland stated in 1924 that 'the members of Synod have now the right to an expression of opinion at any vacancy in the Bishopric',[1] and the draft constitution for Northern Rhodesia provides expressly that 'when a vacancy shall occur in the See a Board shall be summoned to receive and consider any communication concerning the vacancy from the Metropolitan. The Board shall consist of the Metropolitan's Commissary, the members of the Cathedral Chapter, three representatives of the House of Clergy and three representatives of the House of Laity'.

As Synods, Councils and constitutions have been developed so the systems of administration have become more elaborate. The organization of the Diocese of the Niger may be taken as typical of that of the larger diocese. The unit is the District, containing between twenty-five and sixty-five churches under a Superintending Priest with one or two assistants; each church has a catechist and a church committee. The Districts are grouped into Archdeaconries with an average of thirteen Districts in each, and there are in every Archdeaconry a Board of Education and a Location Committee. At the centre is the Bishop with two Assistant Bishops, and the Diocesan Council composed of all the clergy, delegates from each district and a few nominated members. The organization of the Diocese of Uganda as set out in its constitution is similar. Villages, each with a church and a parochial committee, are grouped into Districts, and these in turn are grouped into Rural Deaneries; the Rural Deaneries form part of Archdeaconries which have various Councils. The Diocesan Synod meets every other year for a whole week. All communicants, male and female, form the electorate for the various Councils and for the Synod. An interesting feature in Uganda is the existence of a Women's Central Conference and Women's Conferences in every Rural Deanery, District and Sub-district.

It may be that the English model has been followed too closely. As Bishop Kitching has pointed out, 'the European method of making decisions by vote of the majority is foreign to the African'.

[1] Bishop of Nyasaland's Letter, 1924.

This difficulty is present in all constitutional developments in British Africa, in political as well as in ecclesiastical affairs, and it is open to question whether in Church or State sufficient use has been made of African institutions. There is also some truth in the criticism that 'for the most part expansion has been in breadth but not in depth' and that behind the facade of self-governing institutions the effective government of the Church is still largely paternal and in European hands. But there can be no doubt that, as Sir Arthur Cook has said of Uganda, 'the whole proceedings are an invaluable lesson of law and order and an education in themselves to the members of the Church'. Visitors to Diocesan Synods and Councils have been impressed by the quality of the discussions and the evident sincerity and enthusiasm of the Africa members. In this respect the Church has blazed a trail which the Governments are following, though very slowly. The day may come when the Africans themselves will wish to modify the ecclesiastical organization and to bring it more in line with African traditional ways; they alone can do this effectively. But the courage and vision of European leaders have provided a training in democratic self-government which will not only make such modifications possible but will also prove to have been of material assistance, at least to the British territories, in their progress towards their avowed aim of securing political self-determination for the African peoples.

The Question of Provinces

It is perhaps surprising that though much progress has been made towards the creation of self-governing churches in the various African dioceses no provinces have yet come into existence. There have been various reasons for the delay in bringing about what has long been desired by the dioceses themselves, at least in East Africa. Differences in doctrinal outlook, lack of formal constitutions, fears of the peculiar difficulties created by the immense distances which a Metropolitan of East or West Africa would have to cover have all played their part. It can also be argued that the development of provinces before the dioceses have really become 'indigenized' may postpone rather than accelerate the effective transfer of authority in the Church to the Africans themselves. Bishop Heywood of Mombasa has also called attention to an interesting reason for African opposition to the idea of a Province of East Africa: 'From the African side the most powerful hindrance in Kenya has been the dread that provincial organization in the Church would lead to some form of local government in the State which would deprive them of the protection of the British Crown and the Archbishop of Canterbury'[1]. A proposal for an East African Province was made in 1927 which came to nothing, but the idea was never abandoned; in 1937 the East African bishops, following the example of the West Indies, proposed to set up a Provincial House of Bishops as an embryo province, but this proposal came to nothing. Then the bishops, meeting together in 1943, passed the following resolution: 'In view of the increasing need for consultation on the many problems and matters of common interest we, the Anglican Bishops of East Africa, reaffirm our desire for a province as agreed by all the dioceses in 1927 and endorsed in the Pastoral Letter of the East African Bishops in 1937. Both the Archbishop of Canterbury himself and the last Lambeth Conference have urged us to form this province with no undue delay.' It is possible that, in spite of the difficulties of the War and the many problems of post-war reconstruction, an East African Province may soon become a reality. The formation of a Province of West Africa was discussed at a Conference of Anglican Bishops at Lagos as far back as 1906 but no decision was reached.[2] The question was again considered at a similar conference at Lagos in 1944 at which the Archbishop of Cape Town was present and agreement was reached on many points of detail. Here again it is not impossible that a Province of West Africa may come into existence within a few years. The experience of other areas leaves little room for doubt that the Anglican Communion on both sides of Africa would benefit from the introduction of provincial constitutions. Until provinces exist the dioceses cannot be fully self-governing and cannot become true churches of the country. There is force in the objection that undue haste may delay the ultimate assumption of responsibility by the Africans, and that the general level of education is still too low to ensure that there will be enough Christians capable of dealing with the wide range of provincial affairs. On the other hand it can be answered that Tropical Africa is advancing so rapidly that the real danger is that the insti-

---

[1] *East and West Review.* Vol. ix, No. 1, p. 34.
[2] S.P.G. *Annual Report*, 1906.

tutions of the Church may lag behind. Education is developing with such speed, under the stimulus of the Colonial Development and Welfare Act, that university colleges are being created in the Gold Coast and Nigeria and at Makerere in East Africa, and there is no reason to fear that there will be a shortage of educated leaders. The situation to-day is comparable with that which Bishop Tucker faced in Uganda; the success of the Constitution of the Uganda Diocese is an indication that the risk of precipitancy is worth taking.

Canon Law

In contrast to the chaotic condition of Canon Law in the Church of England, many of the African dioceses have a definite set of canons which, in accordance with the freedom which they enjoy within the Anglican Communion, they have drawn up for their own use. The conditions of church life in Tropical Africa did in fact make some clarification of Canon Law essential. To take but one example, it is not easy to enforce Christian rules of marriage in an area where polygamy is regarded as natural. Feeling on this subject is so strong that in Nigeria a schismatic church grew up which followed the general use of the Church of England but allowed polygamy. The pagan African has his own marriage customs and his moral laws, which are strictly enforced by tribal authority, but these are not in accordance with Christian teaching. The Church has therefore to define her position and to make rules for discipline which are free from ambiguity. As early as 1903 the Synod of Zanzibar found it necessary to discuss Marriage Laws and to pass Acts of Synod on the subject. On all moral questions there is the same need for definition of the Church's position and she must speak with one voice; as Bishop Trower once told his clergy 'we want in all our work to have order, system and a strong sense of trust and responsibility'. New canons and alterations in existing canons are normally made in Synod and when passed are sealed by the bishop as 'Acts of Synod' and are binding on all the clergy of the diocese. In general the Canons of the Church of England are regarded as valid unless specifically changed or replaced; this is stated in the constitution of the Uganda Diocese: 'Until the Diocesan Synod shall agree upon Canons and Constitutions with reference to the ministry and worship of the Church of Uganda, and so far as any such Canons and Constitutions shall not apply, the Canons and Constitutions of the Church of England with regard to any matters not specifically ordered in these presents shall obtain so far as the same may be applicable to the special circumstances of the Church of Uganda.' One diocese may profit by the experience of another but there is nothing like an agreed body of Canon Law for Tropical Africa. It is probable that one of the first tasks of the new provinces would be to draw up provincial canons; such a measure of systematization would be a real source of strength to the Church.

The Missionary Societies and the Dioceses

Reference has been made to the relationship between the various missionary societies and the African dioceses, and on this question it is impossible to generalize. The Society for the Propagation of the Gospel leaves the direction of affairs mainly to the bishop of the diocese; a block grant is made to him which he administers, and the missionaries work under his direction. The Church Missionary Society in the past tended to exercise a more direct control from London over the missionaries in the field; and there is still in each diocese in which it works a C.M.S. secretary or representative, and a C.M.S. standing committee, usually presided over by the bishop, which is responsible for the posting of missionaries, and for their personal well-being. There are also in some areas conferences of the missionaries which meet to discuss questions of missionary policy and organization, but except at a very early stage in the development of a diocese these bodies have no power to make any decisions for the Church in the diocese. Where a diocesan constitution exists the Society makes a block grant which is administered by the diocese, but the missionaries are paid by the C.M.S. representative. The Constitution of the Diocese of Western Equatorial Africa,[1] carried into the constitutions of the dioceses of Lagos and the Niger into which it was divided in 1919, provided expressly that the interest of the Church Missionary Society in land, houses and churches should not be affected. Though in theory this might suggest some kind of *imperium in imperio,* in practice the Society has always done everything in its power to encourage the growth of diocesan self-government, and its missionaries identify themselves whole-

[1] Lowther Clarke, op. cit., p. 415.

heartedly with the local church. The difficulties which Bishop Tucker had to overcome in Uganda no longer exist in any area; there is still a strong sense of loyalty to the Society and a consciousness of being members of a great 'family', but this does not in any way conflict with loyalty to the bishop and the diocese. The Universities' Mission disowns the title and status of a 'Missionary Society': it regards the bishops in its area as the representatives of the mission which exists mainly to secure for them adequate support, and the bishops are responsible for all the missionaries, both clerical and lay. Bishop Trower of Nyasaland defined the position as follows: 'No member of the mission is to refuse any work or employment which he may be desired by his bishop to undertake, and all are understood to give their whole time and ability to its service.' The draft constitution for Northern Rhodesia provides that all clergy licensed in the diocese, and all lay officers including lay members of the Universities' Mission shall be required 'to make a declaration accepting the constitution and obedience to the Canons of the Synod and to all rules and regulations enacted by it in accordance with the constitution'.

The Training of Clergy

One of the essential conditions of a church that is of the people is that its clergy should be drawn from its own people, and in every diocese great attention has been paid to the building up of an indigenous priesthood. In some cases Africans from one diocese were among the first missionaries in another field. The mission which Samuel Crowther led to the Niger in 1884 was staffed partly from the Sierra Leone Church, and the Elgon district was evangelized with the help of a number of priests from the Church of Uganda. Such help was always regarded as merely temporary, though the Church of the West Indies has continued the active support to the mission to the Rio Pongas in West Africa which it helped to initiate in 1855. The development of a Native ministry is inevitably slow in areas where there is little or no education, and in most parts of Tropical Africa the Church has had to begin with creating elementary education. The first baptisms in the Diocese of Zanzibar took place in 1865, but it was not until 1879 that the first African was made deacon, and the first African priest was not ordained until 1890. But the process once started generally develops rapidly and European priests

Q

form a minority in almost every diocese in Tropical Africa at the present time. In the area for which the Universities' Mission is responsible there are now 77 ordained Europeans and 107 Africans; in the Diocese of Uganda there are only 16 ordained Europeans as compared with 111 Africans while of the 72 ordained men in the Diocese of the Niger only 6 are Europeans. For some years the Bishop of Accra was the only European in orders on the staff of his diocese. The development of an indigenous episcopate has, however, been very much slower. Samuel Crowther is the only instance of an African diocesan, and though there are four African assistant bishops in West Africa to-day the first consecration of an East African did not take place until 1947.

The rapid expansion of the African ministry has been made possible by concentrating some of the best of the Europeans in the theological colleges and, to some extent, by not insisting upon a high standard of education or lengthy training for ordinands. Practically every diocese has one or more theological colleges of its own, for differences of language have made concentration of training impossible, though Fourah Bay College in Sierra Leone has given a fine training to men from all parts of West Africa. As the dioceses have developed, the standards of theological training have been raised and great care has been given to the building up of the devotional life of the students. Most candidates for ordination have had a considerable period of service as teachers or catechists, and, though this has tended to make the average age of the clergy unusually high, it has the advantage that a man's character is well known before he is accepted as a candidate and his vocation has been thoroughly tested. The system of training used by the Diocese of the Niger is a good example of what is common practice in many dioceses. After completing Standard VI in a primary school a youth may be employed as a 'Local Helper' for several years, taking Sunday school classes and some services, and he is then sent to the training college at Awka for a two-year course, at the end of which he may become Third-Class Catechist in charge of a group of six or seven churches. After two years or more of this work he returns to Awka for a further two years' training and becomes a Second-Class Catechist with a wider responsibility. If his work is satisfactory after two years or more he goes again to Awka for a course of one year and becomes a First-Class Catechist. After serving for a period in this capacity he may be selected for the divinity course which is also held at Awka and after one year's study is made deacon. His ordination to the priesthood may come after two years as a deacon. It will be seen that before a man can become a priest by this means he must have had at least ten years in the field and six years of training. Teachers who have passed through the four-year courses of teacher-training at Awka may become First-Class Catechists after ten years and are then eligible for training for ordination. Great importance is attached to the association of the training of teachers, catechists and ordinands side by side in the college at Awka, which also holds each year refresher courses, lasting a week, for clergy and catechists. The medium of instruction throughout is English, for the difficulty of obtaining books in translation, especially on theology, makes the use of the vernacular languages incompatible with a reasonable standard of academic training.

The Work of the Clergy

In every diocese the bishop is solely responsible for the location of the clergy, though in some cases he may delegate this power to an Archidiaconal Board, and he can move clergy from one charge to another as he thinks fit. Private patronage does not exist. In the early days of the Sierra Leone Church a few African clergy claimed the right to the 'parson's freehold' and a summons of ejectment against them failed,[1] but this is now past history and no such 'freehold' is recognized in Tropical Africa to-day. In matters of discipline also, as a general rule, the bishop is the final authority. The Sierra Leone Constitution provides that 'in all judicial proceedings' the Church Council, consisting of nine members of whom four are laymen, shall 'sit as assessors with the bishop', and in Uganda there is a detailed succession of appeals from Sub-District Councils to the Diocesan Council.

It must be remembered that a priest in Tropical Africa has to serve a parish which is geographically very much larger and may contain many more church members than any parish in the British Isles. There is an instance of an African priest being responsible for no less than 157 separate congregations,[2] and though this is exceptional there are many Superintending Priests in charge of Districts or Pastorates who have to care for fifty

---

[1] *Sierra Leone Messenger*, July 1946.
[2] *East and West Review*. Vol. ix, No. 2, p. 40.

villages with no more than two ordained men to assist them. It is
remarkable that with a limited background of training and education, for graduate priests are rare, such men give the splendid
service that they do. They have to work in conditions of physical
difficulty and often of mental and spiritual loneliness which give
little or no time or opportunity for reading and study. It is for
this reason that the dioceses are concentrating upon the improvement of theological training. Moreover, the standard of education
throughout Tropical Africa is rising so rapidly that there is a
grave danger that the African clergy may, through no fault of
their own, lack the intellectual equipment which their congregations, especially in the towns, will require. Some dioceses are
considering new methods of recruiting clergy and it is clear that
provision must be made for theological training at the university
level. It is encouraging that in one at least of the university
colleges now being established there is a proposal for a Faculty
of Theology and that the theological work carried on at Fourah
Bay College for over a century may be developed. The Church
was the pioneer in education and has anticipated the development of self-governing institutions in the State; it would be tragic
if she were now to fall behind the educational level of the people
in the intellectual standards required in the clergy. And something more than a higher academic standard is required. In West
Africa, in particular, the Colonial Governments have adopted a
policy of sending large numbers of students on scholarships to
Great Britain to gain wider experience and a broader outlook.
The Church has been able to do little in this way, mainly because
such scholarships are costly. A few priests have been able to study
at English theological colleges and to gain parochial experience
in England; a priest from the Gambia recently served on the staff
of Liverpool Parish Church with great success. It is in the interest
of the whole Anglican Communion that such 'secondments'
should become part of the policy of every African diocese and
that many more scholarships should be provided.

Worship

As the aim in every diocese has been, and still is, to foster the
growth of a truly native church it might have been expected that
the worship of the Church would have developed something of
an African character. Comparatively little, however, has been

done. In some dioceses there have been modifications of the Book of Common Prayer, but these have usually been in the direction of a return to the use of the pre-reformation Church in England. Such changes have been made by Acts of Synod or by bishops at the request of their Synods. In the Universities' Mission the aim has been to lay down a 'uniformity of practice and a maximum standard of ritual'. The cathedrals, on which so much care and thought were lavished by the early bishops, have done a great service to the dioceses by setting standards of worship which have influenced even the poorest mud-walled churches of the remote villages. But on the whole, though the worship makes use of the vernacular languages, it remains essentially 'English', and there have been very few developments of a vernacular worship such as are common in India or China. There are obvious reasons for this. Africans in a pagan condition have a strong religious sense but little or no tradition of communal worship. The fetish grove has no ceremonies which compare in splendour with those of the Chief's court, and what ceremonies there are do not commend themselves to Christian adaptation. Missionaries in earlier days lacked the training in anthropology which would have helped them to understand and to adapt customary rites; it is only fair to add that some of the best work in African anthropology has been done by Christian missionaries, but they have been few in number. Because the Europeans found difficulty in distinguishing between the evil and the good in African customs they tended to condemn them all. In West Africa Christians were forbidden to take part in tribal dancing because some dances are degrading in character. But it is the Africans themselves who can best give an African quality to Christian worship and the majority of African priests have been cut off from their old tribal ways by their training and their close association with Europeans.

There are now signs of change. The Bishop of Masasi has made valuable experiments in Christianizing puberty rites and initiation ceremonies and many of the better-educated African clergy are alive to the urgent need for witnessing to the universality of Christ by the Africanization of Christian worship. African music, with its rich store of harmony and spontaneity, could be used more; it is sometimes a painful experience to hear hymns translated into the vernacular sung to the old tunes of Dykes and others, when there exist local tunes which could be used with great effect. But valuable work is being done in the Diocese of Lebombo in using African music and in Northern Rhodesia a group of Africans from a village congregation has recorded vocal and instrumental African music for the B.B.C. St. Mark's College in the same diocese has produced a song book 'for educated Africans' which contains some purely African tunes, and St. Matthew's College at Keiskama[1] has printed a large volume of African traditional melodies. In West Africa there are some Christians actively engaged in utilizing the rich store of tribal music for the service of the Church, and at Achimota College in the Gold Coast many interesting experiments have been made, including the use of 'talking' drums in a religious service. Here and there use is made of African details such as the substitution of elephant horns for the Sanctus bell at Kumasi in the Gold Coast. It is a sign of a new attitude also that at Idunda in Nyasaland the teachers and church elders recently decided that certain African dances should be allowed at festivals of the Church.

What is true of worship is unfortunately true also of Church architecture. The cathedrals, with the outstanding exception of that at Nambirembe in Uganda, have nothing of an African character. The larger churches are generally 'Victorian-Gothic' in style and are totally unsuited to a tropical climate. The village churches are often primitive buildings of 'swish' or sun-dried brick with thatched roofs, and these at least are at home in their surroundings and do not suggest some alien importation, but the village congregations are always ambitious to substitute corrugated iron for thatch and concrete for brick or mud. Tropical Africa has no architectural style of its own for in the past both the skill and the materials for permanent buildings have been lacking. The Church has a great opportunity to help in the creation of an architecture which will reflect the spirit of the country but there are yet few signs of any desire to do other than make a pastiche of Byzantine, Romanesque or Gothic, or to adapt the prevailing style of Government buildings.

Finance

A Church which has its roots in Africa must be not only self-governing but also self-supporting, and here the dioceses have

[1] In the Diocese of Grahamstown (see Chapter V, p. 109).

been faced with the grim fact of African poverty. No diocese has achieved full self-support and all rely, more or less, on financial contributions from England. The Universities' Mission in 1945 made grants to the dioceses totalling £78,200; in the same year the African congregations, apart from paying parochial expenses, contributed only £3,763 to diocesan funds. The position in the Masasi Diocese is described as 'still very unsatisfactory as to self-support. In 1927 the Synod told the bishop that he was justified in asking for one shilling a head from each communicant but we have never come within even distant sight of that goal'. One reason is that given by Archdeacon le Fleming: 'Undoubtedly the idea is still very prevalent that a body called "the Mission" is a corporation with untold wealth at its disposal, in exactly the same way as most people all over the world regard "the Government".' There is a clear connexion between self-government and self-support for it is in those dioceses where democratic church life is strongest that there appears to be the greatest willingness to give freely for the support of the Church. In the Diocese of Uganda no less than one hundred African clergy are described as 'supported by native church funds' and in the Diocese of the Niger the contributions made by African congregations in 1945 amounted to £133,000 as against £14,292 supplied by the Church Missionary Society. But poverty is probably still the main cause for it is in the more prosperous territories that there is the greatest willingness to give.

It is difficult to determine whether the financial dependence on England has had a cramping effect on the Church in Africa. It is certain that the Missionary Societies have not used the power of the purse to dictate policy to the growing dioceses; it is not so clear that the Africans themselves do not think that their affairs are controlled to a large extent from London. Lack of self-support has not meant any lack of freedom but it has a damaging effect psychologically. Some African clergy in one diocese expressed the view that it was because they 'were not trusted' that they were not allowed to control the expenditure of the block grant made from England, but this diocese was one in which there was no self-government. And so long as any area feels that the Church, like the Government, is a kind of fairy godmother who will come to the rescue in any difficulty there will be no proper sense of responsibility. But there are dangers in reducing financial aid from England before the African Church is fully able to stand on its own feet. In 1908 the Church Missionary Society decided that the annual grants to the Sierra Leone church should be reduced as that church was sufficiently well established to stand by itself and take over the work of evangelizing the tribes of the Protectorate; the result was a period of rigorous restriction from which, it is said, the diocese has hardly recovered to this day.

The Church and the Land

Tropical Africa is, and will continue to be, predominantly an agricultural area, though some measure of industrialization is to be expected in the near future. The great majority of its inhabitants live in villages though the superior attractions of urban life have tended to draw the educated youths into the towns. A Church that is truly of the country must of necessity concern itself both with the needs of rural life and with the problem of the drift into the towns, and many dioceses have made this an important part of their policy. This is particularly marked in the Diocese of the Niger where it has been realized that 'in the African mind there is an element of sacredness about the land which produced his food, and the connexion between worship and farm work to him is obvious. It is perfectly natural that the Church should take an interest in helping the farmer to make better use of God's land.' This diocese has a Department of Rural Activities which gives instruction in agriculture and rural science to pastors, catechists and teachers, supervises rural science work in the primary schools, and takes an active part in various projects for rural betterment, including even the distribution of seeds, fowls, and rabbits. With the active help of the Nigerian Government an Inter-Mission Rural Training and Demonstration Centre has been set up. It is an indication of the real interest of the African Christians in the improvement of village life that in one district the Church Council has set up a Sanitary Committee to make periodical inspections of churches, schools and teachers' houses to make sure that they are maintained at a proper standard of cleanliness. Because the Church is recognized as deeply interested in the welfare of the villages it is trusted and respected and is no longer regarded as an 'alien' element in the life of the community. The Church of England has become more conscious in recent years that the country parish presents special problems and opportunities; in its efforts to make a fuller contribution to village life there is much that it can learn from the experience of the Church not only on the Niger but in practically every diocese of Tropical Africa.

Educational Work

The Church of Christ has always recognized that since Christianity is concerned with the whole of man's life it is part of her task to assist in the improvement not only of man's spiritual nature but also of the supply of his mental and physical needs. The Church provided schools and hospitals long before the State began to assume responsibility for the health and education of the people. In Tropical Africa the Christian Church, including the Anglican Communion, led the way in providing education and medical services, and the same spirit which led to the foundation of grammar schools and universities, of hospitals like St. Bartholomew's and almshouses like the Charterhouse, has been active in every African diocese of the Anglican Church. The Commission on Higher Education in West Africa in its Report of 1944 bore witness to the value of the work which the Church has done: 'It is a very remarkable thing that even to-day, if the educational institutions conducted by the religious bodies were suddenly to vanish the greater part of education in British West Africa would practically disappear. It is a simple historical fact that save for the Churches, now largely Africanized, no one so far has seriously tackled on the grand scale the sheer hard work of West African Education.' Though in British territories and elsewhere the State is now planning a vast expansion of education and health services it still looks to the Church for help and assistance, and all the dioceses give a very considerable part of their energies to education. Thus the Masasi Diocese has three training colleges, nine junior secondary schools, two industrial schools, 438 primary schools, and 101 sub-grade schools, and has on its staff 558 trained African teachers and 43 European educationists. The figures for the dioceses of Uganda, Lagos and the Niger are considerably larger.

It is sometimes objected that the provision and oversight of the schools take up far too much of the time and energy of the clergy and prevent them from fulfilling their primary task of evangelization. The Anglican Communion seems alive to the danger though it is convinced of the great opportunity which its educational work affords. It is possible to detect a distinctive quality in many of the Anglican schools, though to say this is not to imply any criticism of the admirable work done in education by other Churches. The Anglican schools have a common character which testifies to the essential unity of the Anglican Communion in Tropical Africa; they are working out a philosophy and practice of Christian education from which other countries have something to learn. School buildings in Africa are often only thatched huts with walls of mud, or even no walls at all; their equipment is pitiably inadequate; their teachers are sometimes only partially trained, often underpaid and generally overworked. But the education given in many of these schools is first rate in quality and the schools themselves examples of worshipping communities as a Christian school ought to be. There is, in most dioceses, an effective and friendly working partnership with Government in educational work; Government makes very considerable financial contributions to the cost of running the schools, and the Church contributes a quality of life which is vital for the proper development of the African peoples. So long as the Church remembers that her task is primarily to 'help people to grow into the disciplined service of Jesus Christ', and not merely to produce more literates or gain more passes in the School Certificate examinations, her educational work will continue to be what, for the most part, it is to-day: an integral part of her Divine mission.

Church and State

In no part of Tropical Africa are the Anglican dioceses in any sense 'established'. The Colonial chaplaincies which existed in West Africa in the early days of British influence have disappeared and the Anglican Communion now enjoys no privileged position even in British territories. Nevertheless its co-operation is welcomed by the various Colonial Governments, not only in education but in the whole field of social betterment. Some dioceses include within their jurisdiction areas under the control of other powers. The Gambia extends over a considerable part of French West Africa, and Masasi and Lebombo include large tracts of Portuguese East Africa; the district of Ruanda in the

Diocese of Uganda lies in Belgian territory and the Diocese of Madagascar is entirely under French control. In these areas the Church has sometimes experienced difficulties. The Moçambique Company was hostile to the Universities' Mission in its early years and even to-day peculiar problems confront the Diocese of Lebombo. The French and Belgian Governments have been distinctly unfriendly at certain periods as when the French authorities closed the Anglican school at Konakry. The problem was perhaps most acute when the Universities' Mission was working under German rule in East Africa. But the Anglican Communion has consistently taught loyalty in political matters to the 'powers that be', while at the same time insisting upon the right to spiritual freedom; by its attitude it has shown convincingly that it is not, as was sometimes suspected, an agent of the British Colonial Office. At the present time it is fair to say that the Anglican Church has the confidence of all the Governments of Tropical Africa.

Not only have other Powers suspected the Anglican Communion of being under the control of the British Government, but Africans themselves have accused it of undue subservience and of failing in courage in denouncing abuses and evils, among which are instanced colour discriminations and economic exploitation. A few individual missionaries may have provided some justification for such criticisms but they are certainly not true of the Church as a whole. The Church has denounced forced labour, has taken a strong line on the 'Colour Bar', as Paragraph 2 of the draft constitution for Northern Rhodesia shows, and has worked constructively and energetically for the social betterment of the African peoples. As has been said already, the Church in several dioceses has shown the way in democratic institutions, and individual missionaries have been the strongest champions of African rights, even to the extent of becoming suspect to Government. But it is right that the Church should enter into partnership with the various governments in all that concerns the people, provided that in so doing its spiritual freedom and independence of action are not endangered. It has never been part of British policy to try to dictate to the Church in Africa. There is a growing appreciation by British officials of the value of the work of the Church, as there is equally an increasing willingness on the part of the clergy to co-operate with the State. And there is much personal friendship between officials and clergy, both African and European. Many British officers, by their example and willing help, have rendered great service to the Church in Africa. Mr. Martin Parr, formerly Governor of the Equatorial Province of the Sudan, expressed well the need for co-operation when he said in 1944: 'The great framework of ordered administration which has been built up in Africa by British Rule is the scaffolding within which the missionary societies may build the solid edifice of a Christian Church. Without that scaffolding there can be no building; without the building the scaffolding is but an empty mockery.'

Conclusion

Within the limits of one chapter only a brief and incomplete survey of the Anglican Communion in Tropical Africa is possible, but it is sufficient to indicate that it has a character of its own and is yet a microcosm of that great Church which has developed throughout the world from the Church of England in England. The Church in Africa has made full use of the freedom which is enshrined in Article XXXIV and it has developed a rich variety of expression, but it has never wavered from its adherence to the principles which distinguish the Anglican Communion from other Churches. Throughout the dioceses there has been the same reliance upon the Scriptures, the same acceptance of the historic Creeds and episcopate, the same dependence upon the Sacraments of Baptism and Holy Communion. There are extremes but they are no greater than those which are to be found in England, and there is perhaps a greater sense of the essential unity of all parties within the Anglican Communion. The unhappy controversies which followed the first Kikuyu Conference are buried with the past. In the strong African sun the finer distinctions of colour cease to be perceptible but the contrasts of light and shade stand out more starkly. So it is with the Anglican Communion in Africa; for all its diversity it is one Church. It becomes, year by year, more African in character and leadership, and when the provinces are established it will develop into being the Church of the people of Africa as the Church of England is of the English people. In the process some of the present differences of emphasis may disappear, but the end of formal dependence will not mean any loosening of the ties which bind it to the See of Canterbury and to the whole body of the Anglican

Churches. The Church in Africa has great resources of faith and zeal and vigour and in the years to come it will, more and more, make its own distinctive contribution to enrich the life of the Anglican Communion, and, through it, of the whole Church of Christ.

XII

THE EAST INDIES

by the RT. REV. B. C. ROBERTS, *formerly Bishop of Singapore*

Introductory

A glance at the map of South-east Asia will indicate the importance of the Malay Peninsula and the massive island of Borneo, which stand like bastions at the entrance into the Pacific Ocean and guard and control the approach to the territories of the Far East. Several centuries ago the cultivation of the spice trade in this area excited the attention of European nations, and Portuguese, Dutch and French made it a hunting-ground for points of vantage. Britain did not, however, become directly and responsibly involved until the early days of the nineteenth century. The first infiltration had been marked by the establishment of a trading-post at Penang in 1786 under the auspices of the East India Company. Thirty years later Stamford Raffles, who had been charged with the administration of Java and Sumatra, detected the strategic and commercial possibilities of Singapore and, with more conscious and deliberate imperial purpose, founded the Colony which was later to be incorporated in the Straits Settlements and to dominate the political scene in the whole Malay Archipelago and beyond. After a brief interval another pioneer adventurer named James Brooke, inspired by more personal motives, set out in 1838 to explore the neighbouring island of Borneo and was led by an unexpected chain of events to respond to an appeal from the native rulers of Sarawak for protection and to assume the role of a benevolent despot, which continued in his line until the deliverance from Japanese occupation in 1945. Thus British influence in one form or another became diffused on both sides of the channel and was further extended in the course of the century by the acceptance of a British Protectorate over the Malay States of the mainland and by the granting of concessions to the North Borneo Company to claim a jurisdiction, similar to that of the East India Company,

over the tract of coastland eastward of Sarawak which came to
be known as British North Borneo.

Anglican Origins and Organization

This brief recapitulation of pregnant history is important because it has appreciably influenced both the character and the
task of the two dioceses of Labuan and Sarawak and of Singapore,
which have evolved out of this background. The origin of British
tutelage over the mixed races, languages, religions and cultures
of these countries has in each case imparted a romantic flavour to
ecclesiastical development, and their political and economic progress has largely shaped the responsibilities which the Church
was called to meet and the opportunities which presented themselves for missionary expansion. In spite, therefore, of sharply
distinctive features between them, it is a plain statement of fact
that the beginnings of the Anglican Church's work in both areas
derived from the advent of Christian rulers, who encouraged and
welcomed the appointment of chaplains and missionaries and
made generous and far-sighted provision for their livelihood. In
Malaya the first obvious necessity was the supply of spiritual
ministrations to the British community of officials and civilians
who were despatched or attracted to the new outposts of Empire,
and a resident clergyman arrived for this duty in 1814. On the
other side, James Brooke was more concerned with the welfare
of the indigenous people than with imperial connexions and commercial interests, and consequently his invitation to the Church
to enter this field was based on a more evangelistic outlook. Yet
by 1848 he too had secured the services of an English priest in the
person of the Rev. F. T. McDougall, who as pastor and doctor
collaborated closely and courageously with the white rajah in his
beneficent experiment and seven years later became Bishop of
Labuan.

These initial lodgments were inevitably primitive and oppor-
tunist and the successful transplantation of Anglican tradition
depended upon a single representative or a handful of men. But
for purposes of perspective and comparison it is well to remember
that India, China and Japan, which have grown to the status of
self-governing provinces, only received their first Anglican
bishops in 1814, 1849 and 1866 respectively. And, whatever may
have been lacking in ecclesiastical equipment and apparatus, the

basic principle of Church administration was observed in the assignment of these two offshoots to the jurisdiction of the Bishop of Calcutta. The episcopal system was thus stretched with some elasticity to cover a new situation, and Bishop Wilson and his successors are known to have paid a series of visits to Malaya and one at least to Kuching, while Bishop McDougall was himself consecrated in Calcutta and stands on record as the first colonial bishop to receive episcopal orders outside the United Kingdom.

The introduction of a local bishop in 1855 marked a notable stage in consolidation and conformity to the inherited pattern, and it was followed by a process of adjustments by which Singapore was added to the Diocese of Labuan and Sarawak in 1881 under Bishop Hose, and was eventually constituted as a separate diocese in 1909 with Bishop Ferguson-Davie as its first bishop. Both territories were thus separated ecclesiastically from India, as Singapore had been governmentally in 1867, and became missionary dioceses owing allegiance to the Archbishop of Canterbury. This relationship, which is entirely congenial and healthy from the point of view of spiritual affinity, provokes uncomfortable questions of administrative convenience. The Archbishop, with all his personal sympathy and official prestige, is too far off to exercise a more than nominal oversight and too burdened to be accessible to frequent consultations. For these reasons tentative schemes have more than once been launched for the formation of a province in south-east Asia, even reaching as far afield as Polynesia and Honolulu, and no doubt the structural framework will sooner or later be completed by an amalgamation of this kind, bringing both wider experience of diversity and stronger defences of cohesion to the aid of each individual unit.

Peoples and Languages

Meanwhile, however, the growth of such ecclesiastical organization as exists had been accompanied by secular changes which greatly increased the demands upon the resources of the Church. With the exploitation of its rich deposits of tin and with the successful importation of the rubber tree, Malaya rapidly assumed a leading place among colonial possessions in the volume of its trade and commerce and made corresponding demands upon neighbouring countries for the supply of the necessary labour to foster its production. The disinclination of the easy-going Malays to harness themselves to the wheels of industry forced the authorities to look to India and China for the human ingredient, and hence arose great streams of immigration from west and east which eventually swelled to such proportions as to outnumber the natural inhabitants and to dilute the consciousness of nationality and citizenship. Here therefore, and to a lesser degree in Borneo where life remained simpler and more sheltered from the pressures of Western civilization, the Church found itself faced with an extraordinarily mixed population, a large section of which, and even the majority, consisted of immigrants, including the small British community, and amongst whom the Malays, with all the rigidity of Moslem converts from animism, were least susceptible to Christian influences. The Chinese and Indians not only proved to be more responsive by temperament and disposition to the message of the Gospel, but had also in many cases encountered the work of Christian missions in their own original homes so that they offered a parallel claim to that which we are accustomed to label as the care of 'our own people overseas'. The multiplicity of languages however—for neither Indians nor Chinese are anything like homogeneous in this respect—made it evident that the task of shepherding and evangelizing this host of strangers could be done more effectively by ministers of their own kith and kin than by European clergy, and steps were therefore taken to build up an Asiatic staff either by enlistment from the appropriate areas or by recruitment of local candidates for training in recognized centres. By these methods a multi-lingual ministry has been created which functions with smooth harmony and with little appreciable difference of status, though each constituent element naturally concentrates on its own sphere of operations. Some variety in standards of living is inevitable, and distinctions of language set limits to completely free intercourse. But the saving grace that separation is along linguistic rather than racial lines is demonstrated by the fact that many English-speaking Indians and Chinese, as well as sprinklings of other nationalities, will customarily attend the services in English churches, and it is by no means unknown for Europeans with a knowledge of the vernacular to return the compliment by frequenting the worship of their Tamil or Cantonese brethren.

R

Unity in Diversity

This happy interchange not only betokens a welcome catholicity of spirit, but also presupposes an instinctive family likeness between the principles and usages of the diverse strands which compose the Christian community. The resemblance itself, and the general satisfaction which it promotes, are rendered the more striking by several circumstances. First, the English colonist is notoriously nostalgic and is eager to find in the Church abroad an exact replica of the familiar Church at home. But in the mass the European population of Kuala Lumpur or Jesselton is drawn from all shades of ecclesiastical colour, which cannot be equally reproduced in a single available place of worship. Nevertheless, the fundamentals are so secure and the common observances so recognizable that impatience over superficial variations is seldom displayed and contentment with the adopted standards usually prevails. Secondly, the similarity persists in the worship of the Asiatic congregations in spite of the devious routes by which it has converged upon the peculiar conditions of Malaya or Borneo. It has already been pointed out that the mission congregations have drawn their nucleus from an earlier experience of Christian tradition in India or China, and the Asiatic ministry has for the most part been trained in the theological colleges of those countries. There is the further complication that, unlike the centuries-old heritage of English Christianity, the faith has in these Eastern lands only supplanted within living memory a congenital adherence to one or another of the Oriental religious or philosophical systems, or to a vacuum of sheer paganism. Springing from such a variety of antecedents and nourished in such different schools, the churchmanship of these two dioceses might have been expected by all human calculations to show a much greater degree of confusion and instability than is actually the case. There are disparities of emphasis and inequalities of conviction, and Labuan and Sarawak has probably achieved a more uniform type of teaching and ceremonial, and at a higher level, than Singapore. But the resultant effect is that the extremes are less widely spaced than in England itself, and that the *odium theologicum* finds little room to assert itself.

How are we to account for this somewhat remarkable and enviable state of affairs? It has assuredly not been artificially engineered by the passing of all the clergy through one mould; for neither diocese has yet been able to establish its own theological college on a permanent basis, and a promising venture in this direction, started some years ago by the Community of the Resurrection in Kuching, never came to full fruition. Moreover, the condition of life-long service for European chaplains in a tropical climate is the exception rather than the rule, and, although many examples of praiseworthy endurance could be quoted, the general expectation of limited tenure is bound to militate against undisturbed continuity. The explanation must be sought on the human side in the common material and instruments which are the constant equipment of the Anglican ministry and which are everywhere identified with the fellowship of the Mother Church.

The Scriptures

First amongst these virtually uniform elements must be placed the Bible: for in every quarter to which the Anglican Communion has spread, the new Christian company, like their Moslem brethren, has become a 'people of the Book', and Malaya and Borneo are no exception to this experience. So the same evolving history of God's purpose, the same story of Redemption, the same picture of apostolic witness and authority, circulates among all; and, although the external medium has been adapted by translation into a variety of languages to meet the understanding of a complex of races, the inward substance remains unchanged and proves its inexhaustible vitality by producing the promised fruits of the Spirit wherever it penetrates. Experience has shown, however, that the Holy Scriptures by themselves are no mechanical and infallible guarantee of unity. Not all the versions which have been rendered in the course of the centuries are of equal merit and trustworthiness, and, even where the reproduction of the original has been most faithfully achieved and where the language employed has been most pliable to unfamiliar ecclesiastical terms and delicate shades of doctrinal meaning, differences of interpretation have at the worst been magnified into occasions of schism, and, even when stopping short of organic separation, have been responsible for the promotion of parties and factions within the one body. The number of communions and sects operating in the Far East as elsewhere are evidence of the extent to which inconsistent values attached to the written word have, amongst other causes, created disharmonies, and it could not therefore be logically claimed that the consistency of the Anglican unit in Malaya and Borneo is solely attributable to the common possession of the Bible.

Worship

There is, however, a companion volume accessible to Anglicans, the Book of Common Prayer, which is both the outcome of their native genius and the standard of their characteristic order and worship. This printed page has also spanned the world and has been reproduced in many tongues, of which the Chinese, Tamil and Malay versions current in Singapore are typical examples. It would be too much to assert that its directions are universally followed with strict exactitude. Such deviations and neglects as are tolerated or authorized in the home Church may have their counterpart overseas, and the occasional resort to other uses, as, for instance, the Scottish Liturgy in the Diocese of Labuan and Sarawak, has been permitted. But in general form the Prayer Book effects a greater homogeneity and commands a more comprehensive loyalty than might have been expected when it is remembered that its acceptance, involves the attunement of Eastern minds and temperaments to ceremonies and rituals which, however Catholic in essence, are undoubtedly Western in expression. No doubt the time will come when even the smaller and less developed branches of the Anglican Communion will feel the urge, and we shall encourage them, to clothe the structure of divine worship in their own idiom, while preserving its fundamental qualities. But in the preparatory stages no incongruity is observed, and the habitual conformity to one pattern of congregational use does palpably contribute to the solidarity of the diocesan family, as well as to the sense of fellowship with the whole Anglican society. It keeps constantly before the consciousness of diverse sections the regular and shapely flow of prayer and sacrament; it illustrates the unremitting care of the Church for all her children from the cradle to the grave, without discrimination of colour or dignity or wealth: it unfolds the mystery of salvation in the recurrent rotation of the changing seasons and in the appointed sequence of Scripture readings: it inculcates by symbol and precept those doctrinal conceptions which overflow from the

Creeds into the formulation of prayers and praises. Thus the articulation of devotion and the direction of faith derive their inspiration from a single model, the adoption of which not only stamps a positive impression upon the response of the worshippers but also proclaims and presupposes the availability of an accredited ministry, embodied in the threefold and recognizable order of bishops, priests and deacons.

Episcopate and Clergy

It has already been noted that, from the very early days of the Church's entry into these territories, its guidance and control were placed under episcopal supervision, and that, with its growth to fuller stature, the episcopate, though remaining representative of the Mother Church and the governing race, became more closely identified territorially with its spheres of influence. Here was a notable step towards the visible recognition of likeness to and kinship with the Anglican heritage, and at the same time towards the provision of a local focus for the cohesion of the diocesan flock. And, while the office and person of the Bishop have in these new environments earned the acknowledgement, which they have held at all times and everywhere, as the emblem of unity in faith and order, in no respect has the episcopal tradition been more apparently reflected and sustained than by the conferment of the lower orders of the ministry through Ordination, and by the endowment and dedication of the laity through the laying-on-of-hands in Confirmation. The latter rite with all solemnity and appreciation is a commonplace of parochial life at every episcopal visitation, and even more sharply than the administration of Baptism brings into relief the reality of corporate membership and obligation in the one body. For reasons which have been explained the admission of candidates to Holy Orders is a comparatively rare occurrence. Where a diocesan staff numbers no more than twenty-five or thirty clergy, replenishment is naturally more limited and gradual than that to which an English diocese is accustomed, and a considerable proportion of these replacements is still sought ready-made from other lands. But the vocation to the ministry has already begun to grip Asiatic aspirants in both dioceses, and when, after prolonged training or more suddenly under the exigencies of war, these first-fruits have claimed and justified the sacramental action of the Bishop, the very infrequency of the Ordination service has added to its impressiveness and significance and touched an intensity of association with the practice of the wide-spread brotherhood.

Finance

At a lower level than these liturgical links economic factors have also had their place in fostering a mutual interdependence between the different sections of the Church's constituency. The work started and has continued without any substantial benefit from endowments, and, with the exception of a few Chaplaincies to which Government grants have been assigned, the English-speaking congregations have not unhealthily been thrown back upon their own resources in the shape of systematic freewill offerings for the maintenance of their ministers. These charges, under circumstances which impose a high cost of living and include periodical passages to and from England and furlough allowances, are unusually heavy; but they have been borne in a spirit which manifests a welcome sense of responsibility and self-reliance and which normally looks for no reinforcement from the home Church. It is otherwise, however, with the Asiatic membership which is largely drawn from the poorer classes of the community. Their individual generosity is often worthy of comparison with that of the European, and they are not ignorant of the ideal of self-support as the ultimate objective to be attained for their own sake as well as that of their unconverted neighbours. At present this standard has seldom been exemplified, though the enforced isolation under Japanese occupation provided a powerful stimulus towards it and a new discovery of sacrificial capacity. The balancing of accounts has been secured in Labuan and Sarawak, and to a lesser degree in Singapore, by the supply of paid workers and money from missionary societies in England, and the fact that S.P.G. is practically the only outside agency operating on behalf of the Church of England in these fields has incidentally exercised another influence in the direction of the unification of policy and character. But in Singapore this subvention of mission work has been supplemented by the organization of a Diocesan Association, which, under the management of a Diocesan Council, administers the funds available for general purposes, and, by a system of quotas adjusted to the capacity of the several parishes, is enabled to apply the superfluity of the better equipped to the needs of the less favoured. The importance of these exchanges is not merely that they help to effect a financial equilibrium and to mobilize reserves on a diocesan scale for expansion, but that they afford a concrete and unmistakable witness to the principle of 'bearing one another's burdens' and to the interweaving of interests and responsibilities between the compartments of the one family.

Self-government

To label these devices therefore as purely mechanical expedients would be less than justice, for they spring out of an integral appreciation of Christian fellowship. But another way in which such organization ministers to the process of 'growing together' and sharing the riches of Christ must not be overlooked. It is doubtful whether the Church in these countries was ever 'established' in the legal sense, and it certainly ceased to be so as soon as independent legislatures were evolved. The earliest form of church government, apart from the authority of the Bishop, was an imposition of trusteeship, and this system was superseded in Malaya by the institution of elected Church Committees, mainly modelled on the lines of the Parochial Church Councils in England. These bodies function in almost every congregation, European and Asiatic, and are granted considerable powers of decision, as well as a voice in the appointment of their pastor. Each of them is represented on the Diocesan Council, and from time to time the clergy meet separately for informal conference with the Bishop to discuss and plan the welfare of the whole. At the outbreak of war in the West a constitution for a formal Diocesan Synod of Singapore had been completed and published after several years of diligent study and consultation with experts in England, and in the preparation of the scheme great care had been taken to safeguard the spiritual equality of all the racial groups and to secure the adequate participation of every self-contained unit, in spite of the disabilities of language, numbers or influence. A change in the episcopate, however, and the swift onset of the Japanese invasion, hindered the Diocese from becoming committed to this experiment, and it would be premature to judge how far it may be suited to the altered conditions of the post-war scene. There are some evidences that Asiatics are occupying a more prominent position in the councils of the Church than they formerly did, and that even the simplest groups have, under the pressure of external events, developed a far greater measure of initiative and self-respect. An English missionary, who had previously held the post of Superintendent of Chinese Missions, and whose writ ran throughout the Diocese, stated, after his return from release, that his commission had been rendered superfluous by the ability with which the Chinese clergy and laity had met the test of the crisis in conducting their own affairs. These signs of growth and advance are to be heartily welcomed; but their strength and vigour make the problem of co-ordination more, rather than less, urgent, and while the recent substitution of the term 'vicar' for 'chaplain' as the title of the English clergy is intended to facilitate inter-relationships within the circle of the parishes, the larger consolidation will also be required to compact the forces of the Diocese and to provide the prerequisite for the future formation of a province.

The Diocese of Labuan and Sarawak has certainly not been less productive than Singapore in the fruits of evangelization and in the cultivation of faithful churchmanship. But in the sphere of organization, it has been handicapped by the very advantages of its seclusion and by its slow and laborious communications. It is not so long ago that its two Archdeacons of Sarawak and British North Borneo were commonly reported to be unknown to each other, even by face, and the Bishop could only pass from one part of his diocese to another by taking a circuitous route through Singapore. With these impediments, it is scarcely surprising that a general assembly of the clergy was an unheard-of event until quite recent years, and that, consequently, the evolution and direction of policy have lingered more permanently in the paternal hands of the Bishop than in other overseas dioceses, where distances are more easily bridged. But the advent of increased air services to these parts may well revolutionize the prospect and open the door to a unity of a more constitutional and wider-based kind.

The future outlook

Both dioceses are interested, as has been suggested above, in the vision of an inclusive province and each will have its own treasures, as well as its common tradition, to bring into it.

Whether the nucleus will be found in the immediate neighbourhood, or in the further reaches of the Pacific, remains to be seen.
But, in either event, it will be incumbent upon the dioceses
themselves both to strengthen their own composite structure and
to exploit the virtues and gifts which are inherent in their fertile
varieties. The emphasis which has been attached to the ubiquity
of Anglican characteristics may have given the impression of a
stagnant and slavish imitation, which allows no free play to
nnovation and obscures the potentialities of enrichment, as the
Spirit of God 'baptizes' the instincts and skills of other cultures
into the service of the one perfect and universal kingdom. It is
true that individual Asiatics have not rarely become so permeated
with the English presentation of the faith and its accessories that
they are jealous and suspicious of any departure from it. When
the opportunity came about ten years ago to build two new
churches in Singapore, primarily for the use of Indian and
Chinese congregations, a plea was raised, and officially sanctioned, to introduce for the first time Indian and Chinese styles of
architecture. Not a little controversy followed, and two curious
features of the situation were that a Chinese architect was chosen
as the designer of the Indian building and that some of the more
educated Chinese themselves vigorously, but unsuccessfully, opposed the abandonment of the gothic mode in the construction
of their own church. Such protests are no more than passing
incidents, and they are paralleled by the proverbial and not un-
natural reluctance of native Christians everywhere to import into
the Christian context any custom or symbol which is remotely
tainted with heathen associations. But the exquisite and enlighten-
ing treatment of religious subjects by Indian and Chinese artists
and the arresting figures fashioned in wood and stone by the
African sculptor demonstrate the wealth of imagination and insight which are waiting to be released and which may be uniquely
concentrated and intermingled in such an area as has been
described in this chapter.

As compared with the birthplace and nursery of Anglican
Christianity, Malaya and Borneo are large in size, sparse in
population and young in experience, but immensely suggestive
of strategical possibilities. Buttressed by the self-governing
Provinces of India and China on either side of them, and embrac-
ing within themselves the confluence of tides of immigration

from these and many other quarters, they give substance to the
dream of a truly Catholic body, worshipping in unison across the
barriers of language and colour and origin, and consecrating their
varied apprehensions and talents to the single purpose of herald-
ing the universal reign of Jesus Christ. Already the intimations
of this destiny begin to appear at the altar and in the activities of
Christian service, and, if these dioceses have made good their
claim to be authentic outposts of the Anglican tradition, the
parent body owes it to them to undergird their mission with more
discerning prayer and more abundant succour, so that the investment of spiritual capital may fructify prolifically to the enrichment of the world-wide household of God.

XIII

THE DISESTABLISHED HOME CHURCHES

by the REV. C. B. MOSS, D.D.

I

THE EPISCOPAL CHURCH IN SCOTLAND

History

The Church was planted in Scotland by St. Ninian in the fifth century, and St. Columba in the sixth. St. Ninian came from Southern Britain (not yet England), St. Columba from Ireland. The diocesan system was introduced in the twelfth century through the influence of St. Margaret, the English wife of King Malcolm III. Until 1472, when St. Andrews became an archbishopric, there was no Scottish metropolitan; the thirteen bishops elected one of their number as chairman, called 'conservator'. He was not elected for life. In 1560 the medieval Scottish Church was swept away by a revolution, led by John Knox and the 'Lords of the Congregation', and the Reformed Church, modelled on Calvin's institution at Geneva, was set up in its place. Every link with the past was broken, as is shown not only by the formal language of the Reformed Confessions, but also by two important features of the new ministry. (1) For the first twenty-one years there was no laying-on of hands at all at ordination. What has always been regarded as the essence of the Reformed ministry is the call of the congregation. Calvin and Beza had no other ordination. John Knox had been a priest before the Reformation, but he repudiated his priesthood: his only ordination to the Reformed ministry was the call of the congregation at St. Andrews. (2) Bishops and priests of the unreformed Church were only admitted into the Reformed ministry by a fresh ordination, in Scotland as elsewhere. It was bitterly complained by the Puritan party in England that priests ordained in Queen Mary's time were not compelled to accept any fresh ordination, whereas men who had received Reformed ordination on the Continent were compelled to be ordained by a bishop. It was not so in Scotland.

For one hundred years the Reformed Church was on the whole Calvinist. The old sees remained, and were from 1572 occupied by superintendents with the name, but not the authority or the functions, of bishops. In 1610 King James VI had three of them consecrated in England (but not by the archbishops, so that the Scottish Church might be independent). They consecrated bishops for the other Sees. In 1618 the Articles of Perth, which prescribed Confirmation, kneeling at Communion, the observance of Christmas, Good Friday, Easter, Ascension Day, and Whit Sunday, and private Baptism and Communion for the sick, were unwillingly accepted, but widely evaded. In 1633 Charles I gave Edinburgh a bishopric, which it had not had before. But though it had two archbishops and twelve other bishops, the Scottish Church was otherwise entirely Calvinistic. For instance, it had no liturgy: the order for Communion in use had no provision for consecration. The premature introduction of a liturgy and canons by royal authority, following the King's attempt to recover some of the stolen church lands, led to another revolution and a return to pure Calvinism. However, this attempt to press Catholic practice on a Calvinistic nation by royal authority had permanent results. An 'episcopal' party became strong, especially in Aberdeen and the North: and the liturgy which had been refused became a basis for future development.

At the Restoration, fresh bishops were consecrated in England, and the Church in its modern form began. The existing ministers were not, as in England, required to accept episcopal ordination: but the General Assembly, which had been suppressed by Cromwell in 1653, was not allowed to meet, and the Church was completely controlled by the Crown. There was still no liturgy, and 'episcopal' services differed little from presbyterian services.

At the Revolution, all the Scottish bishops felt bound to keep the oaths they had taken to King James VII. William of Orange, therefore, allowed the bishops and their clergy to be driven from their homes and sometimes stripped even of their clothes by fanatical mobs, and placed the control of ecclesiastical affairs in the hands of a small body of ministers who survived from the time of the Great Rebellion. Thus the bishops and those who remained faithful to them lost everything. But in the northern half of Scotland there was not one Presbyterian minister, and it was some years before all the northern churches were seized by the Presbyterians. Severe penal laws were imposed on the 'Episcopalians', because they were loyal to the exiled Stuarts.

During the seventeenth century, the struggle to restore Catholic doctrine and practice in Scotland was also a struggle to subject the Church to the royal supremacy: the Calvinist system was democratic and republican, but it was also intensely anti-Catholic and intolerant. It was impossible to compromise with people who regarded the observance of Christmas and Easter, or the baptism of a dying baby, as rags of Popery: still more with people who were pledged, as the Covenanters were, to allow no religion but their own, not only in Scotland but also in England and Ireland, and would obey no government that had not pledged itself to the same intolerance. The Revolution separated the Catholic from the Calvinist elements in the Church: the former, which had been promoted by the Government, were now severely persecuted, and the part of the Anglican Communion which had been most completely Erastian now became the great witness against Erastianism.

For many years the Scottish Church was in communion with the English Non-Jurors. But there were also 'qualified chapels' in Scotland, which used the English Prayer Book, prayed for the House of Hanover, and were not under the Scottish bishops.

In 1788, at the death of Prince Charles Edward, the Scottish bishops formally recognized the House of Hanover, and the penal laws were gradually repealed. But by that time the Church had been reduced to 'the shadow of a shade'. There were only four bishops and about forty priests. Even most of the Highlanders had been lost because it was impossible to provide them with priests. Unlike the Romanists, the Scottish Church could not train priests on the Continent: ordinations were dangerous, when holding services with a congregation of more than five was punished with imprisonment. The old churches had been lost in 1689: many of those built since were destroyed by Cumberland's army. Many of the people had emigrated because of the 'Highland Clearances'. Nevertheless it was at this time that the Scottish Church gave America its first bishop, Samuel Seabury, Bishop of Connecticut, who, having failed to persuade the Eng-

lish bishops to consecrate him, was consecrated by the Scottish
bishops at Aberdeen, 14 November 1784.

Organization

Since then, the Scottish Church has been reorganized, and
spread all over the country. There are now seven dioceses, for
each of which a cathedral has been built, and about 300 priests.
No archbishops have been appointed since the Revolution: in
1720 the bishops decided to revert to the medieval custom of
electing a Primus. He is appointed for life: the Scottish bishop's
oath of obedience is given to the Synod of Bishops, and the
Primus is not a metropolitan. The Scottish Church does not
accept the popular 'denominational' theory: it claims formally to
be a branch ('province' would be a more correct word) of the
Catholic Church, and therefore, in the old Non-Juring phrase,
'the Catholique remnant of the Church of Scotland'. Since the
title 'Church of Scotland' belongs legally to the Presbyterians,
the adjective 'Episcopal' is accepted by the Scottish Church as
part of its title, but unwillingly, because, in the words of St.
Ignatius of Antioch, 'without bishops, priests, and deacons, the
name of a Church is not given'. The Episcopal Church is therefore in its own eyes the only genuine Church in Scotland and
claims to be the proper home of all Scottish Christians. (The
Roman Communion in Scotland, apart from some Highland
districts which never accepted the Reformation, is the Church of
the Irish immigrants after the famine of 1847. There was no
bishop of the Roman Communion in Scotland, after the Reformation, till 1695, and no hierarchy until 1878.)

The Scottish Church is made up of three elements, which are
not yet completely fused: first, the old Non-Juring congregations,
chiefly in the north, which are strictly orthodox in doctrine, but
dislike novelties in worship: second, the qualified chapels, which
have long since, with one or two exceptions, been absorbed into
the Scottish Church, and which with other congregations in the
south composed of English and Irish immigrants, represent a
more 'moderate' type of worship, and insist on the use of the
English liturgy: third, the Anglo-Catholic influence which has
spread across the border from England.

The Scottish Church has its own public school at Glenalmond,
and its own theological college at Edinburgh, which belong to the

same foundation: but many of its priests are trained in England. There is much passing to and fro across the border: the Scottish clergy is not nearly so sharply divided from the English as the Irish or even the Welsh clergy. The Scottish Canons, last revised in 1925, differ widely from the English Canons of 1604 and from the Irish Canons of 1877. There is nothing archaic in them, nothing which reminds us of King James I or Queen Victoria. The Provincial Synod is the supreme legislative authority, and the Episcopal Synod, consisting of the seven diocesan bishops, is the final court of appeal. The Provincial Synod consists of two chambers: the bishops constitute the First Chamber; the Second Chamber consists of the representatives of the clergy, together with the deans of all the dioceses, the Principal of the Theological College, and the Pantonian Professor of Theology. The Provincial Synod has no judicial powers, but it makes canons and authorizes the Prayer Book. The Episcopal Synod must meet every year: the Provincial Synod, whenever the Episcopal Synod chooses. There are also the Consultative Council and the Representative Church Council, which include lay representatives. The Consultative Council consists of the bishops, as many clerical representatives of each diocese as there are in the Provincial Synod, and an equal number of lay representatives. Its duty is to consult on any subject on which legislation is proposed, or seems desirable, and to make representations to the Episcopal Synod. The Representative Church Council is the organ of the Church for finance, but has nothing to do with doctrine or discipline.

Each diocese has its Diocesan Synod and Diocesan Council. The Diocesan Synod includes all priests in the diocese, and attendance is compulsory: absence without excuse is a punishable offence. The Bishop (in his absence, the Dean) presides, and his consent is necessary to all resolutions, as well as the vote of the majority. Any male communicant may be invited by the Bishop to address the Synod. It is the first court for the trial of priests and deacons, with appeal to the Episcopal Synod. It has no legislative powers: canons passed by the Provincial Synod are promulgated by each bishop in his diocese, and do not require the assent of the Diocesan Synod.

The Diocesan Council performs the same functions for the diocese as the Representative Church Council for the Province. Each bishop is elected by the priests of the diocese, together with one lay elector from each congregation, who must be a male communicant, at least twenty-four years old, and who is himself elected by the male communicants who are over twenty-one years old. The Diocesan Synod may raise objections to any lay elector as not properly qualified, and he may appeal to the Episcopal Synod. The bishop-elect must have the assent of at least the majority of the bishops. If no one has been elected within six months, the right of election passes to the Episcopal Synod for that turn. The right of patronage is in different hands, but in many cases the Vestry appoints: sometimes the Bishop.

The Scottish Church appears to be somewhat easy going. The canons are not enforced with rigid legalism, and disputes are rare. It is a very much smaller church than either the Irish or the Welsh Church. There is no tradition of connexion with the State, and the Scottish bishops are free from the legal impediments which formerly tied the hands of the English bishops. For this reason they have several times been able to consecrate bishops for foreign countries, who could not be consecrated in England for legal reasons. The most famous case is Samuel Seabury, Bishop for Connecticut, who has already been mentioned. Others were Michael Luscombe, who was consecrated to take charge of Anglican chaplaincies in Europe (1825): and Robert Kestell-Cornish, consecrated first Bishop of Madagascar in 1874.

The Scottish Church provides the fullest evidence that the Anglican system can live without any state support; for one hundred years it suffered persecution, and for fifty years more, severe disabilities. It receives no adventitious support from national history; it relies solely on the truth of its faith and order.

Worship and Life

The liturgical history of the Scottish Church is very interesting and important, but can only be briefly sketched here. After the Revolution, the English Prayer Book began to be used in Scotland, but the rejected liturgy of 1637 was reprinted in 1712, and authorized by the bishops in 1731. Thomas Rattray, Bishop of Dunkeld and Primus, wrote a book on the Eastern liturgies which was published posthumously in 1744, and had great influence on the Scottish clergy. The Scottish liturgy as at present arranged was first issued in 1735: it has been revised more than once, and the present liturgy dates from 1929. Unlike the English liturgy, which is based on the Prayer Book of 1552, the Scottish liturgy is derived from the Prayer Book of 1549 by a different descent, and shares with it the following features, which are found in all the ancient liturgies now in use, both eastern and western, but were removed from the 1552 Prayer Book through the influence of Bucer.

It contains an unbroken central prayer or canon, of which the Prayer for the Living and the Dead (for the Church Militant) is a part: an Anamnesis, or commemoration of the acts of redemption: and an Epiclesis, or invocation of the Holy Spirit (whether this exists in the Roman liturgy is disputed, but it is certainly found in all other ancient liturgies). But these are differently arranged in the Scottish and the 1549 liturgy: the Scottish order is, Sanctus, Ascription, Narrative of the Institution, Anamnesis, Epiclesis, Prayer of Oblation, Prayer for the Living and the Dead, Lord's Prayer: then the preparation for Communion follows; and 'Glory be to God on high', as in all Anglican liturgies since 1549, comes at the end. The American liturgy, through Seabury's influence, retains the principal features of the Scottish liturgy, and all other Anglican revisions have been influenced by it: so has even the Presbyterian liturgy in the *Book of Common Order*.

The English liturgy, and indeed the entire English Prayer Book, are fully authorized in the Scottish Church. In many churches both liturgies are used. The precise use of each congregation is fixed, and cannot be changed without the Bishop's consent. The rules governing this are rather elaborate, and are given in detail in Canon XXV, which safeguards bishop, priest, and congregation alike. Older forms of the Scottish liturgy are authorized in some places.

The Scottish Prayer Book contains many other interesting features. The Calendar includes a number of extra holy days, both red-letter and black-letter, which include the feasts of many Scottish saints. The lectionary is quite different from any English one, and is arranged for three years. The offices of Baptism, Marriage, and Burial resemble these in the Revised English Prayer Book of 1928. In Confirmation, signing with the Cross precedes the laying-on of hands. The Catechism contains three additional questions, on Confirmation. There are two additional litanies, and a form of Compline. The Athanasian Creed must be recited at least on Trinity Sunday, without omission.

S

The Thirty-Nine Articles are not printed in the Prayer Book, but every clergyman is required to assent to them together with the Prayer Book, and to promise submission to the tribunals of the Scottish Church, as a condition of being instituted or licensed. There is no special hymn book: but no hymn book, or particular hymn, may be used, which the Bishop has forbidden.

In Scotland, the Dean performs duties similar to those of an archdeacon: there is only one archdeacon, in Orkney. The priest in charge of a cathedral is called the Provost: but the Bishop is head of the cathedral, and has full rights there.

There are large areas where there are no churches or congregations of the Scottish Church, but its organization covers the whole country from Shetland to Galloway. All members of the Church of England and other Anglican Churches are regarded as being, when in Scotland, members of the Scottish Episcopal Church, bound by its laws and entitled to all its privileges.

The Scottish Church supports the great missionary societies, but it gives most of its attention to the two missions for which it is specially responsible, one in Nagpur, India, and one in Kaffraria, South Africa. Priests serving in the mission field retain all their rights in the dioceses from which they came.

II

THE CHURCH OF IRELAND

History

The history of the Church of Ireland is so different from that of the Church of England that a brief sketch of it is necessary to explain modern conditions. The English Church passed through one revolution, the Reformation: the Irish Church through two others, the acceptance of Roman order in the twelfth century, and disestablishment in the nineteenth.

Ireland was never conquered by the Romans, and its way of life continued till the seventeenth century. That is why it differs from all other European countries. St. Patrick organized the Church in the fifth century, and founded the See of Armagh, which has been the Primatial See ever since (except for a few years during the Reformation). For seven centuries after St. Patrick the Church of Ireland was mainly monastic and tribal, without dioceses or parishes. The bishops alone ordained, but the abbots governed. There is no parallel to this anomalous condition. But it was the golden age of the Church of Ireland; its missionaries evangelized Britain and half Europe, its schools gave the best education north of the Alps, its works of art are still famous.

The invasions of the Norsemen ruined Irish culture, and the Church fell into a deplorable condition. The Synods of Rathbreasil (1118) and Kells (1152) divided Ireland into four ecclesiastical provinces and twenty-five dioceses, placed the Church under the jurisdiction of Rome, and substituted Roman service-books for the old Gallican ones.

Immediately afterwards the Anglo-Normans under Henry II invaded Ireland. They never conquered the whole country, but they prevented it from developing into a national state. The laws, habits, and way of life of the Irish were too remote from those of the Normans for any fusion between them: but many Normans accepted the Irish way of life. There was for the next four centuries unceasing war in all parts of Ireland, which had no sovereign able to control the barons and the chiefs. Many bishops had to live by assisting diocesan bishops in England, because Ireland was so disturbed that they could not live in their dioceses. By the sixteenth century there was little religion left.

The bishops accepted Henry VIII's claim to independence of the Pope. But the changes made by the Reformation in doctrine and worship were not desired by anyone, Irish or English.

Elizabeth was forced to conquer the country. There were fifty independent chiefs, many of them with disputed titles, who could not be allowed to become instruments of Spanish intrigue. The English treated the Irish as their descendants treated the Red Indians: they confiscated the best of the land, drove the owners away, and settled 'plantations' of English colonists on it. The policy of the Irish was to continue, in an era of national states, the tribal life of a thousand years before: we may regret the destruction of that life, but it was inevitable. The wars were often wars of extermination, accompanied by every sort of atrocity on both sides. With the 'Flight of the Earls' in 1609, Ireland became a British colony: but the only permanent plantation was in Ulster, and the descendants of those Scottish colonists form the majority in Northern Ireland.

The bishops, who had returned to the Roman obedience under Mary, accepted the Reformation under Elizabeth, with two exceptions. The Irish episcopal succession through Curwen is independent of the English line through Parker. The organization of the Church, the dioceses, parishes, and cathedral chapters continued, though most of the cathedrals and churches were destroyed in the wars. The diocesan boundaries still represent the ancient tribal divisions, and are much older than the county boundaries. But the great majority of the people would not accept the new English services. The Prayer Book was not even translated into Irish, the only language of most of the people, till 1608, fifty years too late. The reformed clergy were mostly English and many were Calvinists, too Puritan for the English Church. The people associated the Reformation with their English conquerors, the new way of life, and the confiscation of the land. They deserted their parish churches for the services held by the recusant priests on the hills. The Counter-Reformation sent swarms of missionaries into the country, many of them Irishmen educated in France or Spain. They reconverted the bulk of the Irish people, which has ever since associated the religion of the Counter-Reformation with their culture and their political freedom. The Romanist bishops are the successors of the 'titulars' appointed by the Pope in Henry VIII's reign, most of whom never set foot in Ireland. The bishops of the Church of Ireland represent the ancient hierarchy.

Disestablishment and its effects

For nearly three centuries, the Church of Ireland was the Church of the English interest in Ireland, and was often used by the Government to Anglicize the Irish people: especially during the period of the ferocious penal laws, which followed the victorious campaign of William of Orange (still commemorated in Northern Ireland by a public holiday), in spite of the promise of religious freedom made by the Treaty of Limerick with which that campaign ended. The Church of Ireland was assimilated as closely as possible to the Church of England. The English Prayer Book was enforced by Acts of Uniformity in 1560 and 1662: the Thirty-Nine Articles were accepted by the Irish Synods in 1634 (after a period of Calvinism): the United Church of England and Ireland was formed in 1800. In 1827 the Romanist majority were given full rights of citizenship: in 1834 the first Reformed Parliament, without consulting the Church, suppressed ten of the twenty-two bishoprics, and reduced archbishoprics from four to two. The alarm caused by this was one of the causes of the Tractarian Movement. In 1870 the Church of Ireland was disestablished. For 150 years the Irish Provincial Synods had never been allowed to meet, in spite of repeated requests to both Whig and Tory governments. The Church of Ireland had no experience of self-government, and had not thought out the question of the nature of Church authority and the difference between it and civil authority. In 1870 the Provincial Synods met for the last time, and passed in general terms a resolution that the association of laymen with the government of the Church was desirable. This was required by the Act of Disestablishment. A General Convention was then held, consisting of the members of the Provincial Synods with twice as many lay representatives, all sitting together. This Convention drew up the new constitution of the Church. The legislative body is the General Synod, with two houses which sit together. The bishops form the Upper House, and the representatives of the clergy and laity, who may vote by orders, the Lower House. There are two laymen to each clergyman. The procedure is not synodical but is parliamentary, with first, second, and third readings. It is not clear whether the authority of the General Synod is derived from the old Provincial Synods, or from Parliament, or from the people direct. It appears to be a Church Parliament rather than what is historically called a Synod: it meets for one week every year, it is extremely efficient, and its authority is not disputed by anybody.

There is also a Diocesan Synod in each diocese, composed of all the clergy, and twice as many lay representatives. As some dioceses are united, a bishop may have more than one Diocesan Synod, and more than one cathedral, each with its Dean and Chapter. There are now fourteen united dioceses: two have been restored since 1872, Clogher and Connor. But there are twenty-one cathedral chapters and twenty-one diocesan synods. These are no legislative assemblies of bishops or clergy only: the laity have an equal share in deciding all questions. In this respect the Church of Ireland is unique among Anglican churches: but the strong anticlerical feeling prevalent at the time made this provision inevitable. Delicate and technical questions, such as reunion, which in England are decided by the Convocations, must in Ireland be discussed in an assembly containing hundreds of laymen, many of whom are necessarily ignorant and may be fiercely partisan. Women are not admitted to either the General or the Diocesan Synods. The judicial body is the Court of the General Synod consisting (where doctrine and worship are concerned) of three bishops and four lay judges who are not assessors, but have equal rights with the bishops. There is a diocesan court in each diocese, with an appeal to the Court of the General Synod. The latter is clearly intended to occupy the place of the Judicial Committee of the Privy Council before disestablishment.

The bishops are elected by the Diocesan Synods. A two-thirds majority of both orders is required: if they fail to agree, the House of Bishops appoints. There are special arrangements for the appointment of the Archbishop of Armagh. The rector of a parish is in most cases appointed by a Board of Nominators, consisting of the Bishop, three representatives of the diocese, of whom one must be a layman, and three representatives of the parish. Thus the laity always have a majority.

Doctrine and churchmanship

Calvinism was always stronger in the Irish than in the English Church, and was increased by the settlement of many French Protestant refugees, and by intermarriage with the Scottish Presbyterian colonists in the north: there are still many churchmen whose outlook is Presbyterian rather than Anglican. In 1872 the Evangelical Movement, which reached Ireland late, was at its height. The Tractarian Movement was only beginning to reach Ireland, but the scare caused by the early 'ritualists' aroused even greater alarm than in England.

One of the first steps taken by the General Synod was the revision of the Prayer Book and Canons. Thanks to Archbishop Trench and a section of the clergy, doctrinal changes which might have caused a schism were avoided: but the manner of worship then prevalent was strictly enforced by rubrics and canons. Though the Prayer Book was revised again in 1929 the liturgical development of the Church of Ireland has been permanently arrested. Not only elaborate ceremonial, but the eastward position, wafer bread, and lights on the altar ('except when necessary for giving light'), are forbidden, and so is any ceremony not expressly enjoined. Coloured stoles and the sign of the cross (except at Baptism) are forbidden. The result is that the Church of Ireland looks like a survival of mid-Victorian Anglicanism: and those of the clergy who find this irksome tend to go to England. The rules are strictly enforced, and there is a society which is always ready to prosecute anyone who breaks them. They cannot be changed except by a two-thirds majority in the General Synod, and any attempt to change them would be accompanied by a violent controversy which the responsible authorities are anxious to avoid. But the monochrome services do not mean that the development of thought is arrested. All the diversities of opinion found in the Church of England are also found in the Church of Ireland, though not in the same proportions: but they do not, as in England, affect the services.

All this is not due solely to conservatism or bigotry. The Church of Ireland, unlike all the other Anglican churches, is in what amounts to a state of siege. Its members are always aware subconsciously, and often consciously, of the presence of the aggressive Romanism of the majority of their countrymen. Personal relations are usually friendly: but the possibility of proselytizing and of mixed marriages of which the children are usually (but not invariably) brought up Romanists, constantly threatens the very existence of the Church. The difference between the two religions is not merely theological: it is social, cultural, and (though less than formerly) political. The Irish layman does not think of or call himself Anglican but 'Protestant', using the word in a sense now almost obsolete elsewhere: the religious difference affects his whole life in a way more characteristic of the East than of Western Europe. It is this difference which keeps him from sinking into what he regards as a lower civilization: he is therefore intensely opposed to anything which in his opinion tends to reduce it. This is the real explanation of Irish liturgical conservatism.

Though the Church of Ireland retains all the cathedrals and churches in use at the disestablishment, few of them are really ancient. The typical country church in Ireland is not a medieval building as in England, but a churchwarden gothic erection of the early nineteenth century. There is only one pre-Reformation parish church in Dublin: and only one, Carrickfergus, in the two dioceses of Connor and Down (in the extreme north-east,

around Belfast) which contains more church members than all
the other twelve put together. Some cathedrals, Cork, Waterford,
Belfast, Kilmore, are modern: most of the others, such as Armagh
and the two Dublin cathedrals, have had to be extensively
restored. The Irish churchman is therefore not usually reminded
by his surroundings in church of the mysterious beauty of the
Middle Ages. There is however a large number of ancient ruined
churches, usually very small, and situated in old churchyards
which are still used. They do not belong to the Church.

The most distinctive feature of work in the Irish Church is
that, except in Belfast, there are no unattached masses. Almost
everybody is a more or less practising member of some church.
Christianity is taken for granted as it certainly is not in Great
Britain. For instance, it is unnecessary to arrange confirmations
in the evening for working boys and girls. Anyone can always get
off work in order to be confirmed.

The clergy

The greater part of the clergy has been trained in the Divinity
School of Trinity College, Dublin, and many have not served
outside Ireland. Here again we find a survival of Victorian conditions: a century ago the Universities of Oxford and Cambridge
were considered to give sufficient training for ordination in
England. The Dublin Divinity School belongs to the Church of
Ireland, and its academic standards are higher than those required
of English candidates for ordination. Its professorships have for
generations been occupied by distinguished scholars.

But the absence of a theological college deprives most of the
Irish clergy of advantages which no university can bestow: a
thorough testing of vocation: training in devotional life and
habits: the experience of living in a small community separated
from the world and united by concentration on one purpose and
by a common vocation. The member of the university divinity
school, who has passed his examinations, has been morally blame-
less, and has been accepted by a bishop, proceeds to ordination
automatically. There is no daily devotional programme, such as
has been found so valuable in England, and no training in conducting services. The theological training itself appears a little
remote from life, and the absence of working people in large
numbers (for in Ireland they are only found in large numbers in

the north) increases this remoteness. But the Irish lay people are quite content, and are afraid of anything that seems to them an imitation of the Romanist seminary (being ignorant of the profound difference that among other things compulsory celibacy makes between the Roman and the Anglican college). There is a tendency to regard the ministry as a profession rather than as a vocation, and to oppose anything which increases the distinction between the clergy and the laity. This is encouraged by the method of appointment: applications are invited, as for business posts. The laymen, who form the majority in Boards of Nominators, are not accustomed to the idea that personal ambition and desire for 'promotion' are entirely out of place in a clergyman, however praiseworthy in a layman; that one cannot regard a post as one's vocation if one has tried to secure it; and that the responsibility and privilege of even the humblest 'steward of the mysteries' is so tremendous that the desire for a rosette or an apron appears childish in comparison with it. They assume that every curate wants a rectory, every rector a canonry, and every canon a bishopric.

The rubric which requires the clergy to recite Mattins and Evensong daily, in private if not in public, has been removed from the Irish Prayer Book. Retreats for the clergy, though not unknown, are still unusual. Week-day services are much fewer than in England, even in towns, and in the country often impossible. For the Irish country rector is usually in charge, not of a compact village, but of a large area in which the church members are widely scattered. The whole country is covered by the parochial system, but in the south and west the conditions sometimes approach those of the prairie. (I knew a rector who had three mission churches, each ten miles from the parish church, in different directions.) In the country there is often only one service on Sunday, and that at noon. Holy Communion must be celebrated at least once a month.

The Irish country rector's work differs widely from that of his English colleague. He must keep his people together, maintain such social life as is possible, and do his best to hinder emigration and mixed marriages. The great danger which threatens the Church of Ireland is that of being squeezed out of large areas, not by active opposition or persecution, but by slow pressure: every mixed marriage, every farm sold by a 'Protestant' to a

Romanist, may be a permanent loss. The disappearance of the minority from country districts would be a disaster to Ireland, for reasons which need not be specified here.

Finance

The money of the Church of Ireland is derived partly from what was left of the old endowments, including the life interests of the clergy at the time of disestablishment, which many of them handed over to the Church; partly of voluntary subscriptions since disestablishment. The Irish lay people are generous in support of their church, and the finance has been most efficiently organized. Each diocese has its own financial scheme: the Representative Church Body in Dublin acts as bank and every clergyman is paid by it quarterly. Every rector must get £400 a year and a free house. Curates are paid by the diocese: there is a minimum stipend, one consequence of which is that no one can be licensed as an 'honorary curate'. The curate's position is more secure than in England. It is not 'assistant priest wanted', but 'the curacy of so-and-so is vacant'. In the absence of the rector, the curate presides *ex officio* at the Select Vestry (corresponding to the English Parochial Church Council, but with wider powers). If a parish cannot produce the minimum stipend for a rector, with the aid of the diocesan funds, the rector becomes a 'priest-in-charge', appointed by the Bishop. The parish loses its share in appointing; and therefore it does all it can to avoid such a result.

Church life and worship

The number of church members in a parish is limited, often very small indeed, and there is little to be done for those who are not church members. Apart from Belfast, where the conditions are more like those of an English industrial town, the rector knows all his people personally; they expect to be frequently visited, and if they like their rector, will support him magnificently. Loyalty to the Church of Ireland is very strong: many who might not be thought specially devout will not hear a word of criticism of the Church.

At the same time, the Church of Ireland is very legal-minded, and that not only in liturgical matters. The question first asked in the Select Vestry about any proposal is whether it is 'legal'. Irish churchmen represent the historical defenders of English law: the law of the Church is known to everyone and is strictly enforced: the legal point of view seems to be universal. The Irish Prayer Book differs from the English Prayer Book chiefly in rubrics, and in the spirit with which it is used. In the Communion Service the only differences are the following:

1. Permission to use the Summary of the Law (but the Ten Commandments must be used once on Sundays and great festivals).
2. The Prayer for the King may be omitted, if there is any other prayer for him in the service (in the Prayer for the Church Militant, or at Mattins).
3. The usual ascriptions before and after the Gospel are permitted.
4. There are additional offertory sentences, including some for great festivals.
5. The words 'those who do not intend to communicate having had opportunity to withdraw' are inserted in a rubric.
6. The two post-communion prayers may both be said.
7. The people are (rightly) directed to stand up at 'Gloria in excelsis'.

The chief pecularity of the Irish Prayer Book is the Revised Psalter. Coverdale's English is retained, but meaningless sentences and mistranslations are corrected, e.g. 'Let not their precious balms break my head' (Psalm 141) becomes 'Let not my head refuse their precious balms'. The general result is admirable: having long used it in private, I should be glad to see it universal in England. The Psalter comes in a different place in the Prayer Book, immediately after 'Prayers and Thanksgivings'. The Collects, Epistles, and Gospels follow the Communion Service, and there are other changes in the order. The Athanasian Creed remains in the Prayer Book, between the Psalter and the Communion Service, but as there is no rubric prescribing its use it is little known to the laity.

There are no 'black-letter' days in the Calendar: but the Transfiguration and St. Patrick's Day are 'red-letter' days (the latter is a public holiday). The lectionary is the English lectionary of 1924, except the lessons from the Apocrypha, for which others are substituted. The omission of lessons from the Apocrypha, which appears to be inconsistent with Article VI, is one of the two points in which the Church of Ireland falls below Anglican standards: the other is the omission of the rubric requiring the clergy to say the daily offices. Both date from 1877, and both, strangely enough, reduce the reading of the Bible.

The Irish Prayer Book contains some additional services, such as the Order for the Institution of a Minister, which in Ireland always takes place in the church which he is to serve. Other admirable customs are the bestowal of a card, signed by the Bishop, on every person who is confirmed, and the thorough visitation by the Bishop, who sees the clergy of every parish personally, and examines their service books. There is an official hymn book, the *Irish Church Hymnal*, which is in use in most parishes, but is not compulsory. It contains some fine hymns which are little known in Great Britain, and many beautiful tunes by Irish composers. One section, the 'Hymns from Ancient Irish Sources', is especially valuable.

The Church's position and achievements

Recent political changes have not directly affected the Church. The boundary of Northern Ireland, one of the most inconvenient frontiers in Europe, cuts across four dioceses, because it follows the much later county divisions. But many of the landowners, who were formerly the main support of the Church, have left the country. The church population is much more concentrated than before in the two Belfast dioceses, Connor and Down, and is decreasing, more rapidly than the total population, in the rest of the island.

The Church of Ireland works very hard to educate all its children in their religion. It has its own elementary and secondary schools, and the Dublin Government gives every facility for Church of Ireland children to attend them, even where the distance is considerable. There is no 'undenominational' religious teaching. In Northern Ireland, the educational system is infected by English ideas, and is not so favourable to the religious bodies except when the voluntary schools are kept up.

The only important non-episcopal denominations in Ireland are the Presbyterians and the Methodists. They are chiefly confined to the North, where the Presbyterians are stronger than the Church of Ireland. In the South they hardly exist outside the towns. (Ireland is still largely a rural country.) They are not so sharply contrasted with the Church as in England; the common danger from Romanist pressure tends to unite all 'Protestants'. Intermarriage is common, and does not carry the political and, social consequences of intermarriage with Romanists. Few, if any,

Irish Church people think of the two cases as in any way similar. In some parishes, isolated Presbyterians or Methodists attend the parish church, and the rector finds it difficult to emphasize teaching peculiar to the Church, for fear of losing any of his small flock. This fact has some influence on the general tone of the Church.

Except the Trinity College missions in China and India, the Church of Ireland has no missions of its own. Overseas missions are keenly supported: the S.P.G. and C.M.S. are well organized throughout the country, and the smaller societies, the Church Missions to Jews, Universities' Mission to Central Africa, South American Missionary Society, etc., have their associations. Missionary meetings are a great feature of the week when the General Synod meets in Dublin. These and other Church Societies, such as the Mothers' Union, the Girls' Friendly Society, the Church Army, the Missions to Seamen, etc., are a strong link between the Church of Ireland and the other Anglican churches. The Moral Welfare Associations and the Church of Ireland Temperance Society correspond to their English namesakes, and the A.P.C.K. to the S.P.C.K. The Anglican and Eastern Churches Association has an Irish branch, of which the Primate of All Ireland is the patron. There are two religious communities for women in Dublin, the Community of St. Mary the Virgin and the Community of St. John the Evangelist: but none for men. The Irish Guild of the Church promotes interest in the Irish language (which is compulsorily taught in all schools under the Dublin Government), and has a church in Dublin, St. Finniom's, which is used solely for services in Irish.

The Church of Ireland has about half a million members, but its importance is much greater than its numbers imply, because most of its members belong to the more educated classes, and they are to be found among both the clergy and the laity, in every part of the Anglican world. They are usually well instructed in their religion and loyal to their Church: and they have produced a long list of leaders in every walk of life. To mention only recent names, Archbishops D'Arcy of Armagh, Bernard of Dublin, and Le Fanu of Perth have been among the most eminent Anglican prelates of our day. William Palmer, who wrote the *Origines Liturgicae* and the *Treatise of the Church*, was the most learned of the Tractarians; Robert Dolling, one of the most successful leaders of the later Anglo-Catholic Movement; Mrs. Alexander, whose husband was Archbishop of Armagh, and H. F. Lyte, the author of 'Abide with me' are among our most popular hymn-writers.

The Church of Ireland has a distinctive tradition without which the Anglican Communion would be much poorer. Various causes have in recent years increased the danger of its isolation. It is of the utmost importance for the Irish Church itself and for the whole of Christendom that it should take its full share in the main stream of Anglican development.

III

THE CHURCH IN WALES

History and organization

The Church in Wales is the church which was planted in Britain probably as early as A.D. 200, and from which St. Ninian went to Scotland and St. Patrick to Ireland. It had no share in the conversion of the English: and its organization, separate from the Church of England, remained until the twelfth century, when it became part of the Province of Canterbury. The Welsh received the Reformation unwillingly, but the Prayer Book and the Bible were soon translated into their language, and Wales did not become a second Ireland. The Methodist revival swept over Wales in the eighteenth century, and moved the nation profoundly. The social structure of the Welsh was different from anything in England at that time: the Welsh-speaking farmers and peasants were a strongly democratic society, divided sharply from the now Anglicized landowners, and from the bishops, who were at that period all English, and were often translated quickly to wealthier English sees. Calvinistic Methodist groups sprang up all over Wales, at first within the Church: but most of them separated from the Church in 1811, and the breach was made wider by the Industrial Revolution and by the growth of democracy. Agitation for the disestablishment of the Church became strong about 1885: the Parliament Act of 1911 swept away the power of the House of Lords to veto Disestablishment Bills: and an Act disestablishing the four Welsh dioceses was passed in September 1914, though because of the War it was not put into effect until 1920. Under this Act the Welsh dioceses ceased to share the privileges of the English dioceses; they lost all their ancient endowments, which were transferred to secular bodies, and were no longer allowed to receive anything from the Ecclesiastical Commissioners, or from Queen Anne's Bounty: all ecclesiastical corporations in Wales were dissolved, and ecclesiastical law ceased to be part of the civil law. The Welsh dioceses might no longer be represented in the Convocation of Canterbury.

Parishes beyond the boundaries of Wales and Monmouthshire were transferred to English dioceses: those which lay across the frontier were allowed to choose, and in every case they chose to belong to the Church of England and to retain their endowments. However, the Welsh Church retains many characteristic features of the English Church, of which it was a portion for 750 years, and which it resembles much more closely than the Irish and Scottish Churches do. I need not, therefore, mention anything which is the same in the Welsh Church as in the English.

During the years of respite, the Welsh bishops prepared the new constitution, with the help of their clergy and laity. With the consent of the Archbishop of Canterbury, who released the Welsh bishops from their oath of obedience to him, a new province of the Church was set up, and Alfred George Edwards, Bishop of St. Asaph, was elected Archbishop of Wales and Metropolitan. There is no metropolitan see: any of the diocesan bishops may be elected archbishop, but if he resigns his see, which is held together with the archbishopric, he ceases to be archbishop. Since 1920, two new dioceses have been formed, so that there are now six dioceses in the Province of Wales.

The six diocesan bishops constitute the ancient Provincial Synod, which retains all the canonical rights of such a synod. But the legislative organ of the Welsh Church is the Governing Body, which consists of three orders. The first order is the Provincial Synod, the six bishops. The second order consists of the deans and archdeacons, twenty-five elected clerical members from each diocese, and ten co-opted members, of whom five must be assistant curates. The third order consists of fifty lay members elected by each diocese, twenty co-opted members, and two life members. The orders sit together, but may vote separately.

The Representative Body is the legal holder of all the property of the Welsh Church. All Church property in Wales, except plate and furniture, was, under the Acts of Disestablishment, transferred either to secular bodies such as the University of Wales and the County Councils, or to the Commissioners of Church Temporalities in Wales. Even the cathedrals, churches, and parsonage houses could only be used by the clergy on sufferance until they were handed over by the Commissioners to the Representative Body, the formation of which was required by the Act. It is a body of trustees, and has no synodical or legislative functions.

The Representative Body consists of four classes: the diocesan bishops, *ex officio*: twelve elected members for each diocese, of whom four are clergymen and eight laymen; ten members nominated by the bishops: and two life members, both laymen.

The elected members of the Governing Body are elected by the Diocesan Conferences, clergymen by clergymen, and lay persons by lay persons. The elected members of the Representative Body are appointed in the same way, but in this case the voting is not by orders.

All members of the Diocesan Conferences must be communiants, but each Diocesan Conference settles for itself the number of its members and the method of their election, provided that these must not be more clerical members than lay members in any Diocesan Conference. The provision for the Ruridecanal Conference, Parochial Church Council, and annual meeting of electors (in Wales called the Easter Vestry) differs little from what is done in England: but there is no legal vestry open to all ratepayers, the churchwardens and sidesmen must be communiants, and the qualified electors, who are entitled to attend the Easter Vestry, must have been confirmed and admissible to communion (not merely, as in England, baptized and not members of any other religious body).

Women have the same rights as laymen at every level.

The State does not allow the Welsh Church to have any coercive jurisdiction: but recognizes that the laws of the Church existing in 1920, with any additions or alterations made, or hereafter to be made, by the Governing Body, are legally binding on all members of the Welsh Church as if they had contracted to observe them. Seven Acts of Parliament, of which the Public Worship Regulation Act is one, no longer apply to Wales: and the Welsh Church is not bound, in matters of faith, discipline, or ceremonial, by any decision of the English Courts, or of the Judicial Committee of the Privy Council. (For instance, it has been decided that, in spite of any judgment to the contrary, stone altars are legal in Wales.) The Church courts are the Archdeacon's, the Diocesan, the Provincial, the Special Provincial, and the Supreme Court. The Provincial Court is the final court in most cases: the laity as well as the clergy may be brought before it, for teaching false doctrine or for certain moral offences. It consists of four clerical and four lay judges, appointed by the Synod of Bishops.

The Special Provincial Court deals only with cases in which a bishop is involved. It consists of all the other bishops, and the lay judges who are members of the Provincial Court.

The Supreme Court deals only with charges against the Archbishop, and with appeals from the Special Provincial Court. Hitherto it has never been required to sit. Its constitution implies the interesting principle, not found elsewhere, that the Churches of the British Isles form a separate group or Exarchate:[1] for it consists of the Archbishops of Canterbury, York, Armagh, and Dublin, and the Primus of the Scottish Church, any of whom may appoint a bishop to take his place. There must also be four assessors, who have no vote. They are nominated by the President of the Court, but two of them must be lay members of the Special Provincial Court.

A bishop is chosen by the Electoral College, which consists of all the bishops, six clerical and six lay members from the diocese for which the candidate is being chosen, and three clerical and three lay members from each of the other Welsh dioceses. They meet in private, after a celebration of Holy Communion, and they vote by ballot. If within three days no candidate has received two-thirds of the votes given, the bishop is nominated by the Archbishop of Canterbury. The Archbishop of Wales is chosen from among the Welsh diocesan bishops, by an electoral college which consists of the six bishops with three clerical and three lay representatives of each diocese: if no one gets two-thirds of the votes, the Archbishop of Canterbury nominates the new archbishop. If one of the Welsh bishoprics is vacant, the archbishop cannot be elected until that bishopric is filled and its bishop

[1] Archbishop C. A. H. Green, *Constitution of the Church in Wales*, p. 227.

T

enthroned. The electoral college for the archbishopric meets in the Old Church at Llandrindod Wells.

Deans, archdeacons, canons, and prebendaries are appointed by the Bishop. Rural deans are chosen by the Bishop from a list of three sent in by the clergy of the deanery. Incumbents are appointed by the Bishop twice in seven turns, four times by the Diocesan Patronage Board, and once by the Provincial Patronage Board. (This system is felt by many to be unsatisfactory, but so far no better one has been found.) Anyone who endows a parish may be allowed to nominate the first incumbent, after which the appointment is made in the way just described.

Canons, or laws of the Church, are made by the Governing Body: the procedure is rather like that of Parliament. Hitherto very few canons have been made, and no liturgical changes. The Welsh clergyman is bound by the Prayer Book and Articles, precisely as in England. The Welsh Church has given no sanction, formal or informal, to the English Revised Prayer Book of 1928.

Education and the training of clergy

There are two theological colleges, St. David's College, Lampeter, which has power to grant degrees in Arts and Theology, and has a post-graduate section, and St. Michael's College, Llandaff, which is a post-graduate theological college. St. Deiniol's Library, Hawarden, is a centre where the clergy and others (not necessarily members of the Church) can stay for the purpose of study, and the Chantry, Monmouth, is a smaller foundation of the same kind for the clergy. These two institutions serve the whole Church: there is nothing like them in England, Scotland, or Ireland. Candidates for ordination are under the control of the Bishop and his 'Warden of Ordinands', who is the secretary of the Diocesan Training Committee, and who advises them in their choice of a title and in their course of study after ordination. Scholarships, exhibitions, and bursaries may be awarded to ordinands on certain conditions: they are to be held at one of the universities or at Lampeter, and afterwards at a theological college.

The language and church life

The Welsh language presents a problem which does not exist on a large scale elsewhere in the British Isles. In many parts of

Wales, though almost everyone can speak English, Welsh is the language of the home, the church, and the school: and through the influence of the University of Wales, there is a real literary revival in this ancient tongue. The Church has always made full provision for services in Welsh, and in many parishes, especially in the Diocese of Bangor and in Cardiganshire, there are no services in English (except in the summer for visitors). In very many others the services are duplicated to serve the needs of the speakers of both languages. Candidates for ordination are encouraged to use Welsh, and there are regular services for Welsh-speaking students at both Lampeter and Llandaff. The Welsh love pulpit oratory, and a good preacher in Welsh can still win great influence over their hearts: some people think that the Church might well pay more attention to this side of the training for ordination. Wales is celebrated for its hymns, and the Governing Body has made a grant towards the compilation of a new Welsh hymn book, the words of which have already been issued.

The Welsh Church has gained by disestablishment an advantage which had no parallel in Ireland or Scotland, and would not have any parallel in England if the English Church were disestablished. It is now no longer four dioceses of the Church of England, but a self-governing Welsh Church with its own Archbishop. It is still much the largest religious body in Wales, and it has, unlike the Irish and Scottish Churches, no rival as the historic Church of the Cymric (Welsh) nation, the 'Old Mother', as it is still called even by some outside its communion. It possesses all the ancient cathedrals and churches, and there is no parish in which it is not found. It has made great progress since disestablishment, which has given it freedom to elect its own bishops and to manage its own affairs, and has put an end to a long and exhausting political dispute. On the other hand, it is miserably poor: the Welsh dioceses were always the poorest part of the Church of England, and the rise of the cost of living has aggravated the difficulty caused by the loss of the endowments and of the help of Queen Anne's Bounty. The Welsh Church is also said to display a certain tendency to in-breeding, especially as the capacity to speak Welsh is useless outside Wales: and the system of patronage gives insufficient opportunities (in the opinion of some people), to the man of independent character, unusual gifts, or unpopular opinions. In the industrial districts there is now more enthusiasm among the people for politics than for religious revivalism, and the Church is confronted by a new set of problems. Nevertheless the Welsh Church is full of vigorous life, and though the period since disestablishment is still too short for us to be able to pronounce any final judgment on the result of that great constitutional change, the Church in Wales is regaining its ancient place as the Church of the Cymric nation.

XIV

THE MISSION OF THE CHURCH OF ENGLAND

by the REV. ROGER LLOYD, *Canon of Winchester Cathedral*

I

'What is the Church of England for?'

On 27 September 1873 E. W. Benson, at that time Chancellor of Lincoln and later Archbishop of Canterbury, was writing to encourage a friend to found a Brotherhood of Cathedral Missioners. 'I firmly believe', he wrote, 'that there is now no deed greater for the Church of England, which (so far as I can see) is now charged with the world's Christianity.'[1] It was a remarkable claim for a sober-minded man to make, but as the whole tenor of his teaching for the rest of his life showed, he meant just what he said, no more and no less. He did not pause in his letter to justify it. Twenty-seven years later, Dr. Hensley Henson, then Warden of St. Mary's Hospital, Ilford, always a great admirer of Benson as his frequency of quotation from him shows, took this phrase and gave it a new lease of life. He was editing a composite book called *Church Problems*, and he himself contributed the chapter on the Church of England, in which he wrote:

Events seem to be visibly converging to one result, and that an immense demand on the Church of the English people. . . . Archbishop Benson summed up the conviction which is forming in many minds when he declared his belief that the Church of England was 'now charged with the world's Christianity'.[2]

He then proceeded to give his reasons for supposing that this was so.

That is the end of the history of Benson's exact phrase, but the conception it so vividly crystallizes crops up again and again in the Christian thinking of England in the same period. Bishop

[1] A. C. Benson, *Edward White Benson* (Macmillan, 1899), Vol. i, p. 385.
[2] *Church Problems*, ed. H. H. Henson (Murray, 1900), pp. 25-6.

Westcott echoed it in his inaugural sermon to the Missionary Conference of the Anglican Communion in 1894:

There is a corporate Mission for Christ no less than a personal Mission. Nations are called as well as men; and surely England and the English Church have been called to an unmistakable office for the promoting of God's glory and the building up of his universal Church. . . . We can see the peculiar responsibility of England, the mother and the mistress of nations. . . . No call, no charge, could be more momentous.[1]

George Tyrell, while still a member of the Roman Catholic Church, was also sure that an immense destiny hung over the Church of England:

The compatibility of freedom and authority, of science and revelation, is surely a most essential and fundamental Catholic principle. Its application is the perennial problem. The Church which solves it first will sweep the world into its net. So far as, without attempting a logical synthesis, the Church of England has always preached, ultimately, respect for tradition and respect for conscience (moral and intellectual), and it is perhaps she who seems most likely to win the race.[2]

And so one might continue, for there would be little difficulty in extending this miniature anthology.

When the Victorians dreamed they were never afraid to do so on the grand scale. Their claims were large because their visions were great. The Church of England of that generation was a visionary Church. As a result, the people of England, in whose name it never hesitated to speak, flourished, for where the Church of a nation has no sense of its own greatness and no vision of its characteristic mission the Church will languish into the death of anaemia and the nation decay into senility. To-day we are much more sober, and we have very good reason to be. The sort of language the Victorian bishops used about the Church of England ceased to be fashionable by 1910, and since then has not been heard. We should not now dream of saying such things about the Anglican Communion as a whole, much less about the

---

[1] *Report*, pp. 3–4.
[2] Quoted by Dr. Cyril Garbett (Archbishop of York) in *The Claims of the Church of England* (Hodder and Stoughton, 1947), p. 45.

Provinces of Canterbury and York alone. The whole trend of modern missionary and evangelistic thinking in the Church of England is sober and realistic, and our statements of function are pitched in a minor key. We could not say now, 'The Church of England is charged with the world's Christianity' because it is quite evidently not true. In the same way we can no longer take on our lips the brave watchword of the Student Christian Movement in its early days, 'The Evangelization of the World in This Generation'. Too much has happened since then to allow us to make such claims. But if the Church of England is really to serve this generation, it must have its own contemporary vision to offer it, for in every age one function of the Church is to dream for the people. Archbishop Benson and his peers were all trying to answer a vital question: What is the Church of England for? We must also ask and answer it. The only possible justification for there being not one Church but many is if each one has its own characteristic contribution to make to the total mission to the world of the Catholic Church as a whole. What in the twentieth century is the characteristic contribution of the Church of England? Just what are we who serve it within the Provinces of Canterbury and York trying to do? Our answer will be our vision, but it will be no more than visionary unless it is built on actual knowledge of what the Church of England is and how it lives and worships.

II

The Church the Body of Christ

No answer to the question can be acceptable which is not related to St. Paul's great phrase, 'the Church is the Body of Christ'. Every Church which is worthy of the name so thinks of itself: if it did not it would have lost its salt. Every Church, and every province of every Church, believes it is a member or a limb of that whole Body, one family in the whole Body social of Christ on earth and beyond the earth. But all the Churches are not yet the same Church. Their several traditions, functions, ways of worshipping and ministering may be—and are—so many variations on that single theme, but they are not identical, not folded in the one great meadow. Thus they must express their divine calling and nature in various and different ways because all of them have their being and the areas of their competence in various localities. They inherit particular and separate historical traditions, and are built and sustained by particular peoples within the whole human family of God, each one of which has its own characteristics, climatic, historical, and cultural. Even within the Anglican Communion there are these wide differences, for from the Provinces of Canterbury and York has grown a Communion of Churches which is world-wide. But within these two Provinces (henceforward called the Church of England for the sake of convenience) there has never been a time, since the days of the great Caroline divines, when the Church was more sure than it is to-day that it is the Divine Society, and called by God to claim and better to deserve the fullness of the title—the Body of Christ. The whole trend of modern theology is concerned with the nature of the Church, and if the judgment of Dom Gregory Dix truly summarizes the dominant theological school —as it does—

. . . the topic of 'the Church' now bids fair to play in the intellectual history of Christendom in our twentieth century that dominant part which the topic of the Incarnation played in the fourth and fifth centuries [1]—

it is primarily the writings of the theologians of the Church of England [2] which have held it in forefront of the Church's consciousness. But while that is true, while it is the governing fact of the Church of England's thought about its nature and its function to-day, it is also true that the Church has, as given the circumstances of a disunited Christendom, it must have, its own peculiar ways of being the Divine Society in England, the primary area of its pastoral competence.

The Establishment

For many centuries the Church of England has been an Established Church, but established after its own manner. It is no creature of the State which gives to it this legal recognition and position of privilege, but it is free to 'maintain its own ways' subject to its acknowledgement of the Royal Supremacy. This position is summarized and defined by the new Canons Ecclesias-

---

[1] *Theology of Confirmation in Relation to Baptism* (Dacre Press, 1946), p. 5.
[2] Notably Hoskyns, Hebert, Dix, Thornton, Hodgson and others.

tical,[1] now before the Convocations, in these phrases, all of which are taken from the old Canons of 1603, and which, in the judgment of the Commission, need no revision:

> The Church of England, established according to the laws of this realm under the King's Majesty. . . . The Government of the Church of England under the King's Majesty by Archbishops, Bishops, Deans, Archdeacons, and the rest that bear office in the same. . . . We acknowledge that the King's Most Excellent Majesty, acting according to the laws of the realm, is the highest power under God in this kingdom, and has supreme authority over all persons in all causes, as well ecclesiastical as civil.[2]

Just as the blend of Catholicism and Protestantism in the Church of England is peculiarly baffling to Continental Christians, so the amalgam of privilege and freedom with an acceptance of the Royal Supremacy expressed in parliamentary decision is the astonishment of other churches, both those that are 'free' and those that are established. How well this arrangement works in the conditions of the twentieth century is not the purpose of this essay to inquire. There are many who think it does not work, and there is no doubt that the Church as a whole attaches a degree of importance to freedom which is higher than the value it sets on privilege or on the unique connexion with the State. On the whole it may be said that the Church's leaders are now clear that if the State should use the fact of establishment to encroach further on the Church's liberty of worship, then disestablishment would have to be claimed and the consequent disendowment accepted.[3]

But the Church is in fact established, and is thereby involved in four main responsibilities.

The Church and the churchless

First and most important of all, it must minister to all the people except those who refuse its ministrations by being active members of other churches. It therefore has the pastoral charge

---

[1] In 1939 a Commission was appointed to consider the Canons of 1603 and to revise them. It reported in 1947, and in its Report (*The Canon Law of the Church of England,* S.P.C.K.) drafted 134 Canons for the consideration first of the Convocations, and then of Parliament.

[2] Canons (of 1603) 3, 7, 1, 2. Proposed Canons of 1947, I, VI, X.

[3] See, e.g., Dr. Cyril Garbett, Archbishop of York, *The Claims of the Church of England,* pp. 196–9.

of two main groups of people, those who are definitely its own members and attend its services, and those who are members of no church and attend no services. Thus when a man is ordained a priest he is expressly reminded that his duty includes the seeking . . .

. . . for Christ's sheep that are dispersed abroad, and for his children who are in the midst of this naughty world, that they may be saved through Christ for ever.

And he is solemnly warned:

If it shall happen the same Church, or any member thereof, to take any hurt or hindrance by reason of your negligence, ye know the greatness of the fault, and also the horrible punishment that will ensue.

From out of the mists of antiquity has come down to us the rich and universally accepted idea of the English parish, with its church and its parson, as being at the service of all parishioners alike and all equally, whether formally members of the church or not. This the establishment has certified rather than invented, but it does guarantee the rights of all the people in their church, and it does tend to hold the Church to the recognition that its primary function is always pastoral and evangelistic. But it does this in such a way as to guard the moral freedom of both Church and people. For example, if a man wishes to marry a divorced woman he cannot claim the use of the parish church or the services of the vicar if he should conscientiously object to performing the marriage. On the other hand, if the man can find another priest to do it elsewhere, no one can forbid it.

There are of course many who argue that the idea of the Church of the nation at the service of all the citizens of the nation for Christ's sake is now no more than an ideal or a dream, and they reinforce their argument with rows of statistics to show how completely out of touch with any religion the greater part of the nation is. Their arguments are reinforced by voices within the Church which claim that she can only perform her true office to the people if there is such a closing of the Church's ranks as to make for a time the old idea impossible because it would involve not only a recognition but a definite exacerbation of the tension between the Church and the world. It is the requirement that all babies in the parish can claim baptism in the parish church as a right which now rubs skins most thin and consciences most tender, for their parents may have no intention whatever of bringing the babies up as Christians, and much less as churchpeople. That subject is a very sore place on the corporate conscience of the Church. It does not fall within the scope of this essay to pronounce judgment on that thorny problem. But just as it is right to point out that many churchmen no longer think that the idea of the Church of England at the service of all the people of England fits the facts of our situation, so it is true that the ideal (if it is one) is guaranteed by the establishment, and would be unlikely to survive its loss.

The Church and the community

Secondly, if a Church is established it follows that its ministrations to the people are not limited to the sphere of the strictly spiritual. It is responsible before God and Crown for the soul of England as a whole, for the Christianity of 'Englishness' as a corporate and national way of life, not less and not much more than for the separate individual soul of John Citizen and his family. The Church of England precisely because it is established has laid upon it the mission of baptizing the national culture, which means accepting a charge before God for the way the people live and work, their education, their housing, their getting and their spending. This, again, is hinted in the Ordinal, for when a bishop is consecrated he must declare his resolve to

. . . show yourself gentle, and be merciful for Christ's sake to poor and needy people, and to all strangers destitute of help;

and he is solemnly charged . . .

. . . be to the flock of Christ a shepherd, not a wolf; feed them, devour them not. Hold up the weak, heal the sick, bind up the broken, bring again the outcasts, seek the lost.

None of this can be thoroughly done if a bishop regards hygiene, social justice and secular administrations and systems as no business of his. Just because he is a bishop there can be for him no discernible boundary between sacred and secular, and because he is a bishop of an established Church he is legally protected in this ubiquity of charge and should logically be encouraged to

exercise it. It is very doubtful if such a portent as the tenure of
the Archbishoprics of York and Canterbury by William Temple
could have happened in a Church not established. Not only did
he say many uncomfortable and unpopular things but people
hearkened to them.

The Church and the State

Thirdly, the Church of England by being established has laid
upon it the charge of ministering to England as a whole, that is,
to the State. The outward and visible signs of this corporate
ministry are the official position of the Church in all great
national ceremonies, of which the coronation of the monarch is
the chief, and also the position which the Church has in Parliament. A proportion of the bishops are members of the House of
Lords by virtue of their office, and the chaplain of the House of
Commons is always an Anglican priest. But these outward and
visible signs are less important than the inward and spiritual
function of the Church towards the State which they symbolize.
It is a prophetic function—a duty to exhort and if need be to
rebuke the State, which means in practice the Government of the
day. Liberty of prophecy is always the beginning of redemption,
and a prophecy which has not redemption fully in view from the
beginning becomes either empty effusiveness or negative fault-
finding. A Church which has the legal standing of prophet in
ordinary to the nation has also the cure before God of the soul
of a whole people. Conversely, the nation which establishes a
Church acknowledges that there is such a thing as a national soul
which is other and more than the separate souls of its individual
citizens, that this national soul needs to be redeemed and saved,
and that Christ is its only Saviour. What puts the establishment
more in jeopardy than anything else is the fact that a majority of
the citizens appear not to believe this. But as long as the establishment lasts it gives the legal and logical basis for such adventures
as the bishops' intervention in the coal strike of 1926, and it was
in utter contradiction and defiance of this basic fact of the constitution of Church and State that the Archbishop of Canterbury
was refused a hearing on the wireless during the general strike of
1926. Correspondingly a national Church which hesitates to
rebuke the nation or the Government of the day when they do or
say things which can be shown to be clean contrary to the broad

faith of the Bible or the mind of Christ forfeits one of the bases of its own privileged position as established.

The Church as a society

The fourth great responsibility which the Church of England has is laid also upon all other churches, and it is derived from the Word of God and not from its established position. But the fact of establishment does as it were underline it. This is its duty to exhibit in its own domestic and interior life, and in experimentally verifiable form, the spectacle of what a divine society set to work out its destiny in a naughty world is actually like. The Church is to be a visible society of people gathered out of the world and yet living in it, which rules its life by standards and values which are other than and different from the standards and values of the world. When it does this, it becomes the embodied suggestion that current secularism is false and vulgar. The theological preoccupation of recent years with the problem of the Church's nature and its relation to the Gospel has brought this practical need of the Church's life well into the foreground of the Christian consciousness. There could be nothing more important because it was precisely by the power of their wonderful solution of this problem that the earliest generations of the Church forced the world of the Roman Empire to accept the Gospel. Although this is generally the duty of every church in the world, it is very specially the duty of an established church, which by the fact of establishment must work it out in circumstances more than ordinarily difficult, but also filled with more than ordinary opportunity. A church which is legally tied to the State and yet lives by a law of love which is higher than anything which the State demands of itself is in a fair way to do for the twentieth-century State what the early Church did for the Roman Empire. But it can do it only when it exhibits within itself the power of reform and adaptation to the point where both become indistinguishable from sacrifice.

An established church, then, is specially called to endure tension and to deal creatively with it. If it does the duty which acceptance of establishment lays upon it, it must constantly be in a state of some tension with the State which establishes it. If it tries to show to the citizens of the nation what an authentically divine society is really like, it is involved in tension within itself, since, by the very fact of being the national Church, it tends to carry an undue proportion of 'passengers', and they will resent the changes which are necessary in every generation if the Church is to be the divine society in and for that generation. But tension, properly understood, is not dismaying. It is, on the contrary, the very stuff of creativeness, and stagnation and death are where it is not. The secret of creative living is to find the right level of tautness and to keep the tension at that level. No one could deny that there is a great tension within the Church of England between its Catholic and Liberal wings; tension between the Church and the State over vital questions such as liberty of worship and the appointment of bishops, which, though at present masked, could burst or rupture at any moment; and tension again between the Church and the semi-secularized 'world' of England, which is evident wherever people talk of divorce. Within and without relationships are strained; and perhaps that is what they ought to be for the health of both sides. But the Church of England is a very mature church, to which in Canon Eric Abbott's vivid phrase, it is and it ought to be a strain to belong, because its very maturity has to operate in one of the rawest and most immature centuries of history. But maturity whether in churches or in families knows all about tension and how to deal wisely with it.

III

An indigenous and missionary Church

The blessing of churches is to be used by God. By the extent to which they have been and can still be used by God to spread His kingdom their health is estimated. No Christian should ask that his church be judged by some less exacting test, and no loyal child of the Church of England will doubt that, so judged, the hand of God has been stretched in blessing over it. For to use a technical term nowadays in high favour, the Church of England is certainly indigenous. The word describes two ecclesiastical conditions. An indigenous church must be genuinely native, worshipping in its own language, providing its own priesthood, governing itself, woven into the cultural pattern of the history of its own people. It must also be evangelistic at home and missionary overseas, reaching out to the ends of the earth and founding other Churches which, in their turn, themselves gradually become indigenous. The Church of England coming down to us from the time of Augustine of Canterbury, and wresting the first condition of an indigenous church out of the agonies of the Reformation, has since then fulfilled the second condition by giving birth to a notable family of churches all over the world. We call it the Anglican Communion, and it makes one of the three great ecclesiastical systems of Christendom. Geographically it is larger than the British Empire since it includes great blocks of Christians in the United States of America, and worshippers can make their communion at Anglican altars in many parts of the world where the British flag does not fly.

From China to Peru, and from the frozen lands of the Eskimo in northern Canada to the Falkland Islands, Anglican churches are found, and from all these lands bishops come to Lambeth Palace once in ten years to attend the Lambeth Conference of all the bishops of the Anglican Communion. This conference is the only visible symbol of the fact that the Anglican Communion is a world-wide Church, indigenous in every land to which it has penetrated. The conference begins with an inaugural act of worship in Westminster Abbey. An imaginary visitor, let us suppose, is standing in the Dean of Westminster's private gallery near the west end of the nave to see the long procession of bishops move into the choir for the service. Unless he is utterly insensitive, he cannot help but be moved and thrilled by the visible evidence of the vast extent, range, and variety of the Anglican Communion. The greatness of it is there before his very eyes, unfolding itself like a moving frieze. The mere colours of the bishops' skins, white and yellow, black and brown, would declare to him that his Church is a world-wide church, at work in every continent, and having outposts in every country. If this visitor were well enough versed he would see at once how few were the bishops of the English dioceses as compared to those of dioceses overseas. In the 1920 Lambeth Conference the bishops of England and their suffragans were a small minority in the procession. The Welsh, Scottish, Irish, and overseas dioceses sent as many bishops. Many came from the Empire Dominions, nineteen from Canada, three from New Zealand, twenty from Australia, twenty-three from Africa. India sent ten, China seven, and Japan three. From the lands designated East—Near East, Middle East, Far

East, came thirty. From the United States of America came fifty-two. These figures by no means exhaust the list. If the imaginary observer in the Dean's gallery knows his Anglican history he would perhaps reflect upon the astonishing fact that had there been a Lambeth Conference in 1820 not a tenth part of that number of Anglican bishops could have been there, since only within that narrow compass of time had the Anglican Church made claim in Christ's Name to souls of every land on earth.

Over that conference of bishops the Archbishop of Canterbury presides, and it is in his home that it is always held. For the heart and the nerve centre and the vital impulse of all that terrific endeavour is the two tiny provinces of Canterbury and York, the Church of England—a mother of churches indeed. A mother, yes—but not a mistress. For as children inherit traits and tendencies from their mother, and are free to accept or reject the other riches of character that she sets before them, so the Church of England has handed on to her daughter churches of the Anglican Communion a whole series of characteristics or 'notes'. They are Catholicity, Democracy, the Passion for Freedom, the Desire for Comprehensiveness, the High Sense of Pastoral Duty. Not every one of these is to be found in equal strength or the same proportion in every part of the Anglican Communion. But they are the doctrinal and qualitative marks of an Anglican Church, and every one of them is derived from the Provinces of Canterbury and York, and within this Church of England are still practised fully as and in perhaps a more creative relationship to each other than in any other church.

The notes of Anglicanism: the Quadrilateral

By every possible test the Church of England is a Catholic Church, and at the time of the Reformation it lost its Papalism (badly shaken for some centuries) not its Catholicism. Every where in the Book of Common Prayer it is described as Catholic and nowhere as Protestant. The outward and visible tests of a Catholic Church were stated in the Lambeth Quadrilateral by the Lambeth Conference of 1920. These tests are belief in the Bible as 'the rule and ultimate standard of faith', in the Nicene Creed as 'the sufficient statement of the Christian faith', in the biblical sacraments of Baptism and Holy Communion as 'expressing for all the corporate life of the whole fellowship in and with Christ', and in 'a ministry acknowledged by every part of the Church as possessing not only the inward call of the Spirit but also the commission of Christ and the authority of the whole body'. This last point of the Lambeth Quadrilateral, which is the one real stumbling block to unity between the Church of England and the Nonconformist Churches in England, is more and more strongly interpreted with every year that passes as pointing straight to the Apostolic Succession. There is to-day no note of a Catholic Church of which the Church of England is more conscious or is more determined to hold and keep unimpaired than the unbroken link of its bishops with the first apostles and with Christ who ordained them. This, in the phrase of the Bishop of Oxford, is the Essential Ministry[1]—essential because it is believed to enshrine the mind of our Lord and the will of God for His Church. What, asks the Bishop, is the true view?

In the minds of those who have combined to write this book it is simply this: The episcopate is the divinely ordained ministerial instrument for securing to the Church of God its continuous and organic unity, not as a club of like-minded worshippers or aspirants to holiness, but as a God-given city of salvation.[2]

This quotation takes a little precious space in a chapter all too short to fulfil its purpose of describing the Church of England as it is to-day. But it is more than worth that space because in ever-increasing numbers the clergy, and the laity too, hold that sentence to be the vital truth about the Church's ministry and hold it with passionate conviction. What a Church believes in the theological sphere has important practical consequences for its everyday life.

This belief that a Catholic Church must exhibit an organic unity in time, and that the essential expression of that unity is the episcopate in unbroken succession to Christ, does have a most important 'practical consequence' in the way the Church is organized. Its unit of charge and work and fellowship is the bishop in his diocese, and in the Church of England everything pivots around him as he sits on his throne in his cathedral. He it

---

[1] *The Apostolic Ministry: Essays on the History and the Doctrine of Episcopacy*, edited by K. E. Kirk, Bishop of Oxford (Hodder and Stoughton, 1946), p.9 and *passim*.

[2] Ibid., p. 8.

U

is who has the cure of souls; by his authority it is delegated to his vicars, the parish priests; all laymen who bear office in the diocese do so with his commission. This is the vital heart of Anglican worship and life and witness; and these bishops, with their awful charge, are gathered decennially in a loose federation to Lambeth to hold their conference under the chairmanship of the Archbishop of Canterbury. Nobody has ever defined precisely what authority the pronouncements of the Lambeth Conference have, but a Church which holds this Catholic view of the episcopal office cannot but view such pronouncements as possessing moral authority of a high order. But in England the King's Majesty is 'supreme in all causes and over all persons as well ecclesiastical as civil', and the Church of England holds this also to be true and scriptural; and these two seemingly contradictory principles are held together in the Church of England and combined with a deftness so astonishing in its success that not one member of the Church in a hundred is aware of any feat of balancing. But it is just this combination of Catholic principles with royal supremacy which delivers the English bishop (and his diocese) from prelacy and despotism. In our history the few bishops who have been tempted towards prelacy are precisely those who have not believed, or, if believing, have set no store by, the Catholic conception of their office and the apostolic succession of their ministry.

The instinct for democracy

In spirit the Church of England is profoundly democratic, but in its government, and especially in its ways of choosing and appointing men to hold office in it, it is a tempered democracy. Bishops are chosen by the Crown, and are accepted by the Dean and Chapter of the diocese, as also by the Archbishop of the province whose is the right to give or withhold consecration. Deans are appointed by the Crown, residentiary canons by either Crown or Bishop or Lord Chancellor. Incumbents are appointed by an immense variety of patrons, but every parish now has power to block the appointment of an unsuitable man. There has, however, lately been a great change in the democratic direction in the choosing of men to be candidates for ordination. Every young man who wants to offer himself for ordination must now attend a selection centre. It is generally a theological college, and he goes there for five days together with perhaps twenty others such as himself. Living with these twenty are the selectors, four or five in number and invariably including one or more laymen. By observation, by successive interviews with each one of the selectors, and in the atmosphere of the devotional life of the chapel, the selectors decide whether the young man's offer of himself as an ordination candidate should be called in, or whether it is his vocation to serve our Lord as a layman. Only when the young man has been thus selected by his peers is he recognized as an ordination candidate and admitted to a theological college, and not until then is he definitely accepted by a bishop (who of course may still reject him) as a candidate for ordination in his diocese. The same procedure is followed in the case of women who want to become recognized 'women workers' of the Church. It is a thoroughly democratic system and it works very well.

But the instinct for democracy in the English Church goes much deeper than that. It pierces to the roots, to the essential spiritual qualities of democracy, which secular 'democratic' systems of government so seldom exhibit. Democracy cannot grow and flourish without its roots, and these are a sense of human equality, a passion for freedom and the liberty of prophesying, a recognition of social responsibility, and a right valuation of the unique importance and sacred rights of personality of every individual soul. All of these are marks of the life of the Church of England to-day, as they have been from time immemorial, and all have been inherited by and are daily exhibited in the life of all Anglican Churches.

The Lambeth Conference is perhaps the best illustration of the Anglican instinct for equality and abhorrence of the demagogy which so quickly destroys equality in the name of equality. A few pages back an imaginary observer was placed in the Dean's Gallery at Westminster Abbey to watch the procession of the Anglican Episcopate at the inaugural service of the Lambeth Conference. The mere sight should be enough to dispel the common superstition that the bishop of some diocese of China or Ireland with an unpronounceable name is in some mysterious way the inferior of a Bishop of Manchester or Lincoln. If this observer were able to follow the bishops from the Abbey into the historic library of Lambeth Palace he would see with his own eyes a demonstration of Christian equality in the Spirit and Christian democracy in action. For there, day after day for six weeks, the bishops meet in actual and not merely theoretical equality. Their work is done in private: only its results are made public. None has any chance to act the demagogue. No bishop of an ancient and famous see can rest himself on the traditions and dignities of his diocese in his dealings with the bishop of a new see thousands of miles away with all its traditions still to create. Prestige counts for little; ability, character, wisdom, and a capacity for work count for much. These are just as likely to be found in Zanzibar or the Falkland Islands as in Barchester; and in fact if any single bishop could be said to have dominated a Lambeth Conference, it was Frank Weston of Zanzibar in 1920. The same spirit is often, though not invariably, found in the affairs of the parish, where the voice of sincerity and proved faithfulness will nearly always carry more weight than the voice of wealth and high birth unless it is equally sincere and proved. The Church of England is one of the few societies in which money does not talk, and a high level of culture does not override an uneducated but a faithful sincerity.

The passion for freedom
    The passion of the Church of England for freedom is so deep and steady that it talks about it very little, but its whole system is built upon the belief that the freer people are left the better work they will do. There is absolutely no attempt to regiment the laity, and it would be worse than useless to make one. The clergy, who have the freehold of their benefices and other offices, are to-day more completely free than any other functionaries the twentieth-century world can show. Their bishops cannot coerce them, society cannot reduce their rich individuality to a drab obedient average, and their people cannot starve them out if they say and do unpopular things. A few, a very few, take advantage of this virtual immunity from all the pressures which can so quickly be brought to bear on the members of every other profession. But, taking them by and large, the parochial clergy of the English Church have and live up to a standard of pastoral faithfulness which is probably higher than that of any other church in the world; and this they manage to maintain even when they hardly know where to turn for the next penny (as now so often happens) and when their hearts are near to breaking over the fact

that in big cities so few seem to want their ministrations. All this they do in absolute freedom, and indeed as a direct consequence of it.

Social responsibility

But democracy cannot long exist unless those who form it have a sense of social responsibility. The possession of this is an obligation laid upon us all by the Gospel itself, for its offer of salvation is made to communities and to society not less than to the individuals composing it. It is in fact quite improper to speak of 'The Social Gospel', for there is only 'The Gospel'. It cannot be said that throughout the centuries the Church of England has always shown its sense of social responsibility, or even much compassion for those whom a corrupt social order treats ill. That obligation is a part of its tradition, inherited from the Middle Ages and firmly pointed out whenever a bishop is consecrated, since he must answer Yes to the question:

Will you show yourself gentle, and be merciful for Christ's sake to poor and needy people, and to all strangers destitute of help?

But for a long period, from the time of John Locke to the time of Maurice and Kingsley, this charge of the Church was overlaid and forgotten. Since then, however, a new tradition has grown up through the tireless persuasions of those two men and those who came after them until to-day there is hardly anyone left in the Church who does not hold that evil social conditions and the whole maladjusted social order are very much the proper concern of the Church. Taught by Bishop Westcott of Durham modern bishops have not seldom intervened in obstinate strikes because they were hurting the economically weak. A whole Christian social philosophy has been steadily preached to the Church, and in this, too, bishops—Gore of Oxford and Temple of Canterbury —have done much to blaze the trail. The Church, acting through voluntary housing societies of the type created by Father Basil Jellicoe in North London, has played a very large part in the more worthy housing of the slum-dweller. In the days of heavy mass-unemployment it was the Church and its workers which was generally foremost in the difficult and exacting work of feeding the hungry, clothing the threadbare, and helping the unemployed to use their leisure more creatively. To all that must be added the fact that most of the really difficult social work, enterprises of moral welfare, spiritual ministration to condemned criminals, and the housing and training of destitute children, are generally left to the Church and the Church alone, and in this the Church of England has always borne a leading share. The change of climate in the last hundred years has been overwhelming. To-day few English churchmen are likely to be insensitive to the evils of bad housing, disease and poverty. Our danger now is that we may forget that these blemishes of a social order are far more likely to be found in the middle than in the working class, and that the new Moloch whom the Church may have to withstand is no longer the belted earl or the top-hatted capitalist but rather the apostle of planned efficiency, or sometimes the minister of State, or even the Trades Union leader, certainly the real magnate of our day. There are some words written in 1927 about the Church as a whole, which in 1947 are still luminously true of the Church of England:

It is seldom noted that even now the hardest works of mercy are still left to those whose devotion to Christ provides them both with the perseverance for the task and with the readiness to remain unknown and obscure in the doing of it. The worst wreckage of indulgence and sin can still be dealt with only by the Church's Homes of Mercy. The educational and medical care of backward races is still left to the Christian missionary. The bulk of such social work as is unpaid and voluntary is done demonstrably by people who 'go to Church'. And though in sentiment most people desire social reform it is still only the minister of Christ and his little band of helpers who live in the midst of conditions which others lament. [1]

Pastoral fidelity

Such is the vital tradition of the Church of England—a tradition alert and bright with daily use in the twentieth century. It is a pastoral tradition. Lecky has a passage somewhere to the effect that if you want to get to the heart of any society living or dead, you must first ask, what is its rudimentary virtue and what is its rudimentary vice? By that he means the virtue and the vice which are so commonplace within the society that nobody gets much credit for the one and everybody is apt to escape censure for the

---

[1] Eric Milner-White, Dean of York, in *Essays Catholic and Critical*, ed. E. G. Selwyn, Dean of Winchester (S.P.C.K., 1927), p. 325.

other. What, then, is the rudimentary virtue of the Church of England? It is to-day what it has always been, a fidelity to pastoral duty. Before all else the Church of England is a pastoral Church, and that is why the organization of the parochial system, with all the sense of universality which that implies, is the only mould in which it can really live and still be its characteristic self. It is no doubt true that in our day the parochial ministry is being and must be supplemented by many kinds of specialized ministries, works chaplaincies, diocesan youth chaplaincies, diocesan directors of education and the like. But all these are created to meet essentially pastoral needs which the parochial system cannot possibly meet, and in the end they justify their existence, and the taking away of priests from the parishes to man them, on pastoral grounds and on these alone. If an Anglican priest is a good and faithful pastor he does not get any special commendation for it because it is simply a virtue he shares with most others. But if he is a poor pastor he at once excites condemnation, and it is a label he will find it hard to live down.

A tradition of pastoral fidelity means more than a sense of responsibility to a flock: it means a refusal to think of them as a flock at all, but as so many individual sheep who compose a flock, and each one of whom is known to the shepherd by name, and thought of as an individual, and over whose rich and varied individuality he rejoices and would not for worlds have it pruned and tidied into some kind of statistical average. Shepherding is an art, but what makes it an art is that the approach to each sheep has to be different, because none are the same. It is true that the contemporary picture of the Church of England suggests at too many points that good and centralized organization can take the place of pastoral faithfulness, that it can drive on to the City of God by a short cut, for of course, it is infinitely easier and less laborious to organize than to shepherd. The picture, as I say, suggests it, with its increasingly centralized bureaucratic organization which takes more and more men away from their pastoral jobs to sit on committees in London. But it is only a suggestion as yet, not an actuality; and there has lately been a notable protest by the Archbishop of York against the legend that those who have to tend the machinery cannot be pastors. He should know. But the Anglican instinct to judge the effectiveness, in terms of the Kingdom of God, of any man who holds office in the Church by whether he is willing to give all the time that may be necessary to help forward one thoroughly obscure Christian soul is a sound instinct. And its corollary is not less sound, that work among individuals should take second place only to the public worship of God.

It is precisely this distinctive definition of pastoral duty in terms of individual need that makes this tradition of the Church of England profoundly democratic. More than that, it makes the Church which holds it 'a cause of democracy in other men', and a trustee and guardian of it over against so many secular systems of government which, while paying a tediously incessant lip-service to democracy are all the time using it to destroy itself by casting all their care on the collective at the expense of the individual. The real enemies of democracy are two, the tyrants and the planners: its friends are those who think of people one by one, and among them the chief is the Church. There, and there almost alone in the modern world, is a man or woman valued for what they are in themselves. In the Church, and only in the Church, is each separate child of God known by name and regarded as a sacred and imperishable end in himself.

This Anglican tradition that the highest of human relationships and privileges is seen in the pastor caring for his people, and knowing each one by name, is worthy of yet more treatment, quite apart from the bearing it has on the influence of the Church of England on the democratic idea. It is really the heart of the Church's whole ethos, and the best means of explaining her in any age. It explains both weaknesses and strengths, for out of the fundamental and ceaseless conviction that the Church must before all else be a pastoral Church, and therefore must always treat people as individuals rather than members of crowds, or social 'elements', or entries in a card-index system, arises a whole series of instinctive Anglican prejudices, standards of value. To this is to be traced the fact that the Church is always unenthusiastic about organization and not very impressed by numbers. To this is due the immovable distaste of the Church for publicity, which would always prefer to let the case go against her if the only defence involved calling public attention to her virtues and successes. The instinctive distrust of most Anglicans for the 'popular preacher' (though this is not invariable: nobody cavilled at Studdert-Kennedy or Dick Sheppard) is due to the same basic conviction. It comes out of the shrewd and generally accurate judgment that the more of a popular preacher a priest is the less individual pastoral work he is likely to be able to do. The real heroes of the Church are always the pastors, Herbert, Walton, Ken in one generation, and Lowder, Chavasse, Wainwright, or Winnington Ingram in another. During the centuries the Church of England has produced still greater giants, but it is to these, the saintly pastors, that Anglicans turn again and again as the years go by with unceasing affection. That they do so explains much about the Church they serve.

Comprehensiveness

To call attention to the fact that the Church of England is extremely comprehensive is to invite rough handling, for to not a few of her most loyal children the word is like a red rag to a bull. They wish, or say they wish, that it was a good deal less comprehensive, and ask how in the world a church which has any principles can possible keep within its fellowship the English Church Union, and the Union of Modern Churchmen, or the violent Protestant and the extreme Anglo-Catholic? They may well ask, but the fact is that it is done, and done successfully, though nobody quite knows how. None the less, any brief account of what the Church of England is cannot omit its note of comprehensiveness since that is one of the first things about it which strikes every outside observer. One of these, the Rev. K. L. Parry of the Congregational Church, has neatly expressed both the inescapable fact of Anglican comprehensiveness and the sense of bewilderment with which other Christians view it:

It cannot be disputed that the Church of England is a comprehensive Church, though what it is that holds it together I have never been able to discover.

That quotation occurs in a recent book on the problem of reunion, and the author of the book, who first quoted it, immediately answers the question:

I believe that the secret is its possession—blindly, often undogmatically, but loyally maintained—of continuity with the one undivided Church of Pentecost. That is an objective reality; even when it is unvalued it remains a potent fact.[1]

[1] H. Burn Murdoch, *Church Continuity and Unity* (Cambridge University Press, 1945), p. 179.

Still more recently the authors of the Report to the Archbishop of Canterbury called *Catholicity* have given an expanded form of just the same answer to the question:

The Anglican knows that wherever he worships throughout the Anglican Communion he will find the Holy Scriptures read and public worship conducted in the vulgar tongue; he will find the historic Creeds recited alike in the rite of Holy Baptism and in the Offices; he will find the Sacrament of Confirmation administered by the Bishop; and he will know that the celebrant at the Eucharist is a priest whom a Bishop, standing in the Apostolic Succession, has ordained. These things may be differently valued by churchmen, and even by theologians, but it is upon the constancy of these things in one single pattern, that the unity of the Anglican Communion rests. . . . It is by a principle of constancy in Scriptures, Creeds, Sacraments, and Apostolic Succession, that the Anglican Communion, for all the diversity within it, remains one.[2]

Now nobody would deny—certainly the present writer would not—that between the maintenance of the Apostolic Succession and the present comprehensiveness of the Church of England there is a real and inevitable connexion, though it may well be true that nobody can say precisely in what the connexion exists. To have the Succession is to be presented also with the large and charitable tolerance without which no comprehensiveness is possible: that, as the sources of the above quotations testify, is a perfectly Catholic judgment. But there is a still more obvious reason which is contained in the Anglican version of the Christian doctrine of personality as unique and sacred. The Church of England, as all know, contrives to keep all sorts of parties within itself, all sorts of oddities and freaks at unity in itself; and it so works upon them as gradually but successfully to draw out of them the rawness which causes them to quarrel, and instils into them the charity which enables all not only to live and worship together, but also to co-operate. In very few dioceses now is there any bitterness between the different parties, and in most there is real co-operation. It is difficult indeed to be a partisan for very long in the Anglican atmosphere, and one generation of a party's life is generally enough to draw the violence of partisanship out of it.

[2] *Catholicity* (Dacre Press, 1947), pp. 55-6.

Aversion from publicity

The Church, as we have seen, has an abiding passion for freedom, and knows well that the heart of freedom is a respect for personality. As a by-product of that it has also an instinctive aversion from publicity, especially individual publicity. In consequence its characteristic way of discharging its mission is to bring to bear upon the whole area of its competence the slow, steady, cumulative pressure of an essentially anonymous community, the parish priest and his people, not the famous Mr. X and the very few helpers out of his congregation who see eye to eye with him. The whole ethos of the Church of England is to rate the pressure of the average as more evangelistically potent by far in the long run than the specially heroic labours of the few giants, and in no Church in the world does the magic of a great name count for less. It is therefore specially difficult for any individualist, however strong his character, to impress himself so deeply on the Anglican consciousness as to draw away the mass of Anglican membership to follow him in his passionate partisanships. At the same time, however violent he may be, he is never or almost never, repudiated. Trials for heresy do not take place; and if, as is constantly happening, the more ardent spirits cannot refrain themselves from incessantly making every kind of public complaint and charge against the Church of their baptism, the charges are rarely answered, and they themselves are never silenced by authority. It must be most infuriating for them. Sooner or later, precisely because the freedom of the giant, the freak, and the rebel to express themselves after their own way is so completely respected, they themselves become subject to the cumulative pressure of the average, and their love and loyalty is won, and they themselves not stultified but made free of a larger loyalty and opportunity than could have come to them in any other way. And that is democracy—real democracy, the one form of social arrangement which, alike in Church and State and World, promises freedom and fulfilment to all.

IV

The Mission of the Church of England

We are now in a position to suggest an answer to the question asked in the first section of this essay. It was 'What is it that God wants the Anglican Communion in general (of which the Church of England is a vital part because the mother of all the parts) to do for Him in this present century?' The answer is, 'To uphold the Christian doctrine of man as free and personality as sacred in this century which, as it proceeds, subjects both to perhaps the most violent attack they have ever experienced.' It has been said, 'The forces of Satan are now massing for a last, desperate assault on Christ.' If this is so, there is no question as to the direction of their assault. It is an assault on everything that Christ attached to and Christians understand by the word Man. All churches the world over join in the defence, and in this they co-operate more and more. But the 'system' and the 'characteristic flavour' of the Church of England as Catholic and reformed, established and yet free, and setting a higher value on the average than on the exceptional, gives to it a central place in this warfare, and places it where the real fighting has to be done.

Fundamentally the Church is so organized as to make this mission as little difficult as possible, but superficially it is organized so as to magnify the difficulties of it. For there is a real difference between fundamental and superficial organization, and one of the reasons for our present discontents is that the superficial looms larger in our consciousness than does the fundamental. Where two or three churchpeople are gathered in talk over the affairs of the Church, the problem of its organization is certain sooner or later to come up for discussion and at that point the conversation is likely to take on an air of exasperation. Because it is this which churchpeople are now always discussing it cannot be omitted from any account of the Church of England to-day. But organization can only be discussed fruitfully when it is placed in the double context of agreement about the essential thing which the Church is trying to do, and agreement also about the relative importance of the instruments it must use to do it. This essay has argued that the essential thing the Church of England is trying to do in this century is to guard and to refound the Christian doctrine of man, and that the most effective of all the instruments it can use is what may be called pastoral work to sustain it, to quicken it, to provide for it the appropriate mould within which it can prosper and increase.

The question of organization

Now that is precisely what the fundamental organization of the Church does and the superficial organization is at present hampering. The fundamental organization is diocesan. The unit of the Church is the diocesan bishop with his priests, and their people and his, gathered round him. The parochial system hinges upon the diocese, and whatever may be said about the parochial system it remains potentially the most comprehensive and the simplest and most economical method of pastoral work which exists. It is also seminal in the sense that it quite easily gives birth to and keeps contact with specialized and non-parochial ministries to meet exceptional pastoral needs, as for example factory chaplaincies, moral welfare work, societies to promote social betterment, and the like. Such extra-parochial undertakings have always been and will always be essential because special and non-parochial pastoral needs must be met. But because they too are usually organized on a diocesan basis, and are subject to the diocesan bishop, they are part of the fundamental organization. Thus the principle of fundamental organization is clear: it is diocesan or local organization. Its method is also clear: it is flexible and economical.

Superficial organization is the 'extra' which is superimposed upon fundamental organization. It may be necessary, and often it is: 'superficial' is not necessarily a term of abuse. But its tendency is always towards centralization, and away from the proper diocesan pattern of a pastoral church, and its method is constantly, though not invariably, bureaucratic. That something very like this has happened in the Church during the last twenty years is evident. The Enabling Act of 1918 created the Church Assembly, which consists of all the diocesan bishops, all the archdeacons and the elected representatives of the clergy and laity. This was to be (and in fact is) the Church's parliament; and it has the power to suggest legislation to the House of Commons. But the promoters of that Act intended to make the new organization fundamental, and thus elected assemblies were made a matter of legal obligation for every diocese, every rural deanery, and every parish. This local organization has on the whole proved to be a blessing. By now the Diocesan Conference, the Ruridecanal Conference, and the Parochial Church Council have become an essential part of church life, and nobody has seriously suggested that the Church loses by having them. When we complain, as we constantly do, about the heavy top-hamper of organization which stultifies the Church of to-day, it is never the Diocesan Conference or the Parochial Church Council that we have in mind. They are local and fundamental. Nor is it of the Church Assembly as such that complaints are made. If it ceased to exist, it would be necessary to invent something else, because many of the things it does are vital to the pastoral ministry of the Church, and could not have been done by any other body or in any other way. The Church Assembly has done something to clear away from the impenetrable jungle of patronage its most stinking growths. It has produced the Clergy Pensions and the Dilapidations Measures. It has seriously tackled the thorny problem of the Church's colleges for training teachers, without which it would not be possible to provide Christian teachers in our schools or the State's. All these boons, and more besides, it has provided. All are vital to the pastoral ministry, and none could have been effectively carried through on a diocesan scale. But it also tends to draw more and more into the orbit of London the effective control of nearly all the non-parochial instruments of the pastoral ministry, providing central boards for moral welfare work, the supervision of ordination candidates, foreign missions, education, women's work and so on. All these living organizations are administered, or adjusted or added to, by an ever-increasing host of central committees which of necessity take more and more men and women away from their proper work for more and more weeks in every year, so that to-day a higher proportion of clergy and lay leaders of church life than ever before have to become administrators, and that precisely at the moment when the pastoral work among the individual people is more exacting and urgent than ever before. This organizing mania of bureaucratic centralization has fallen with almost crushing force upon the diocesan bishops, whose lives have indeed become an almost intolerable burden, and it is largely the Church Assembly that has made them so. That so many of them do somehow contrive still to be pastors more than administrators is undoubtedly a feat which partakes of the nature of the miraculous, but they pay a heavily disproportionate price to achieve it.

All this is an organizational failure, and it is by better organization rather than by no organization at all that it must be put right. The balance between fundamental or local and superficial or central organizing machinery has become badly maladjusted. The consequence is that the Church tends to fall a victim to the constant illusion of the secular State in supposing that if an enterprise (such as that of the evangelization of England) is well organized from some central office the vital part of the battle to achieve it has already been won. But it is not so. All that comes of this attempt to do the Church's work in the World's way is the vicious circle of over-stimulus, disappointment, and frustration. It was not thus that the early Church imposed its will upon the Roman Empire within three hundred years.

Such is the primary discontent of the Church at the present moment. From the Archbishop of Canterbury down to the fourteen-year-old boy or girl who was confirmed yesterday she longs to give herself wholly to her proper business of the cure of every soul God has given or will give her, but she finds it increasingly difficult to do this. Whether this can be done best in the spirit of 'Back to a Missionary Basis', or even (as some urge) 'Back to the Catacombs' remains to be seen. But it cannot be done at all until fundamental and superficial organization are properly adjusted.

In the meantime we have our immemorial traditions of hidden and unremarked faithfulness and devotion, and they burn brightly still. There are no more self-sacrificing and self-effacing workers for God's righteousness in the modern world than are to be found in the ranks of the Church of England. If this spirit can be set free to move at God's will through this whole iron age it may yet be redeemed, and men and women once more live free and satisfying lives.

SUMMARY AND CONCLUSION

by the BISHOP OF LONDON

The preceding chapters have, it is hoped, given the reader a comprehensive view of the Anglican Communion. Comprehensive it is, but not necessarily complete. There are at least two omissions which we must endeavour to rectify before proceeding to discuss our general conclusions.

Continental Churches

Only partial reference has hitherto been made to the Anglican churches on the continent of Europe. They are divided into two sections which are under different types of management. Those in Southern Europe, that is to say, in Spain, Portugal, Italy and Greece, together with the southern coast of France and islands of the Mediterranean form a separate diocese. The see-town is Gibraltar, and the Bishop takes his name from that centre, as has been explained in Chapter X.[1]

The chaplaincies in Northern and Central Europe, amounting to about eighty in all, have not been thus formed into a separate diocese, but are still part of the Diocese of London. This is the last relic of the arrangement by which at the instance of Archbishop Laud in the seventeenth century the Bishop of London was made responsible for all the overseas work of the Church of England. It is now the custom to place the care of these European chaplaincies in the hands of a suffragan bishop—the Bishop of Fulham. The area is administered almost as a separate diocese, with its own archdeacons and rural deans, but it has no cathedral or separate diocesan organizations, using still the cathedral and offices of the Diocese of London.

It may be added that in recent years there has been an American Bishop on the continent of Europe watching over the special interests of the American congregations.

Religious Communities

The other point of main interest that we have hitherto omitted,

[1] See p. 200.

except in one instance,[1] and by way of occasional reference else-where, is the very important section of Church activities comprised within the life and work of the Religious Communities. These have steadily mounted in importance during recent years. After the period of the Reformation community life actually ceased in the Church of England except for such small efforts as that of Nicholas Ferrar at Little Gidding in the seventeenth century. The modern revival of the Religious Life must be attributed to the influence of the Oxford Movement and more particularly to that of Dr. Pusey. The first community to be founded under this new influence came into existence in 1845, the very year of Newman's secession. Thus the monastic life in the modern Church of England is only just over a century old.

From references in the previous chapters, it will have been realized that the communities have spread into many different parts of the Anglican Communion. Mostly this has been by way of founding branch houses from some mother house in England, but there are Communities such as the Society of the Sacred Advent in Australia, and a native sisterhood in the Solomons, which are indigenous to the overseas Church. It is not however possible to give reliable statistics of membership. As no Communities publish their numbers it is not easy to form an accurate estimate of their growth. Some idea of their great expansion may be obtained from the fact that there are to-day in the Anglican Communion approximately fifty orders for women and nine for men.

Of the orders for women, six are entirely enclosed and devoted to the contemplative life. Most however are of a mixed character; falling roughly into three different categories. First there are those that undertake parochial work. Then there are missionary orders, which often control hospitals and convalescent homes, and there are finally teaching orders which run schools of all kinds. Several of the orders do not confine themselves to one particular activity, but combine parochial work at home and over-seas with the management of schools and hospitals. There are a number, of course, which give themselves especially to work among the less fortunate classes, and more particularly to girls who have been in moral difficulties or have passed through the police courts.

Of the orders for men, perhaps three call for particular mention

[1] See Chapter V, pp. 106-7.

x

because of their rather specially Anglican character. The Society of St. John the Evangelist (Cowley), founded in 1865, is specially missionary and educational; it not only has branch houses in India and South Africa, but it also has congregations in the United States and Canada. The Society of the Sacred Mission (Kelham) was founded in 1891, with the object of maintaining the spirit of devotion and self-forgetfulness in its members. Its principle task is the training of candidates for ordination, but it also does parochial and missionary work, especially in South Africa. The Community of the Resurrection (Mirfield) was founded by Charles Gore in 1892 for work of a pastoral, evangelical, literary and educational character. It has given two diocesans to the English Bench: the first Gore himself, who however was released from his vows on taking charge of his diocese; the other, Walter Howard Frere, who was in fact the second founder and who remained a full practising member of the Order during the whole period of his episcopate.

Three other Communities represent types of monastic life found in greater force elsewhere. There is the Society of St. Francis whose members live the life of Friars, and minister especially to the poor and destitute. There is the Oratory of the Good Shepherd, a Society of unmarried secular priests and laymen who live under a rule. Finally an Order of Benedictine Monks (Nashdom) has given evidence that it is able to combine community life with the pursuit of sacred learning and has enriched the life of the Anglican Communion with the contribution of real scholars.

Special Features—Effect of the Reformation

We can now turn to examine the special features of the Anglican Communion. We shall find that it exhibits to a degree unique in Christendom variety in unity. That unity is a very real fact. It is obviously true of course that every part of the Anglican Communion uses the same Bible, the same Creeds, the same Ministry, the same Sacraments. Those are evidences of the same underlying life in the one historic Body of Christ, and of the all-pervading presence of one Holy Spirit. But these may be common to other branches of Christendom, and they do not in themselves enable us to distinguish the peculiar characteristics of Anglican unity.

We get a little nearer to an appreciation of the difference if we emphasize the fact that all branches of the Anglican Communion use the vernacular in their worship. It is the aim everywhere, even in the remotest missionary field, to enable the members to worship in their own language. Missionary work has scarcely begun before Bible and Prayer Book are translated.

The mention of the Prayer Book reminds us of another common characteristic. Not all parts of the Anglican Communion use precisely the same Prayer Book, but all their forms of worship bear some obvious relation to the first English Prayer Book of 1549, and it is to the Book of Common Prayer that they all look back as the parent of their liturgy.

It follows from this that all the provinces bear upon them the marks of the Reformation. All alike share the same heritage of freedom from Papal jurisdiction and all of them enjoy a very large measure of self-government. It would require a separate treatise or at least a chapter to analyse the spirit of the Reformation and to draw out its leading features. But freedom of self-government, love of the Bible, use of the common tongue: these may all be taken as indications of that Reformation spirit which is common to all the provinces of the Anglican Communion.

It is quite true that the Reformation in England took a very different form from that which it assumed in other countries. It clung much more to the traditions of the past, particularly to the continuity of the Ministry, and showed much less willingness to dispense with liturgical forms and to imbibe that particular ascetic spirit which came to be known as puritanism. These marks are still distinctive of the Anglican Communion. Its Reformation tone is definitely that of England rather than that of the Continent.

It might even be said that Anglicans are in a sense more critical of the Reformation Movement as a whole than those sections of Christendom which derived their inspiration from the Continental Reformation. This rather detached attitude varies through every grade from an all but complete allegiance to a verbal, if not factual, repudiation. Nevertheless while the former extreme is still bound to recognize the difference between the English and Continental Reformations, the other is bound to recognize, however unwillingly, that the effects of the Reformation are strong upon it. Consequently the Reformation spirit in some degree may be taken as still characteristic of the whole Anglican Communion. It is quite definitely a 'Reformed' church.

Relation to State

This invariably involves a very real measure of freedom and independence on the part of the provinces, not merely from outside control but also from interference with each other. So far as outside control is concerned it might be alleged that the Papal jurisdiction has been replaced by that of the Monarch or of the State. That could nowhere have even the semblance of truth except in England. For only in England is any part of the Anglican Communion 'established'. How far the Church of England in this connexion does submit to State control is a vexed question and we must hope that it has been sufficiently dealt with in Chapter XIV. But at least it would be safe to say that even under the Establishment the Church of England is more free to manage its own affairs and to make its own appointments than it was in the time of the Papacy.

It would probably be true to say that the difference between establishment and non-establishment does not cause any sense of incongruity as one passes from the Church in England to the Church overseas, because almost everywhere there is a special relation between the Anglican Church and the government that can, without difficulty, be regarded as something distinctive. Anglicans are in no way accustomed to associate themselves with one political party. There was a time when they were derided as being 'the Conservative Party at prayer', but in our own day a leading publicist has upbraided the clergy for beoming 'Court Chaplains to King Demos'. The fact that they can be thus attacked from opposite positions gives the measure of their lack of party affiliation. Perhaps because of this reason, combined with their original Establishment, they have a more sophisticated approach to political questions than some of their colleagues. They do not normally encourage deputations to ministers of State, nor do they naturally act as a pressure group upon some government department.

The fact that in England the Bishops enjoy direct representation in the House of Lords has an effect far and wide over the Anglican Communion. The influence of the Episcopal Church of the United States in Government circles is probably all the greater because it is never pressed. In the Dominions it is probably true to say that Government circles instinctively feel a sympathy with and respect for the Anglican Communion which they do not always display to others even when those others are numerically stronger. This is not to say for one moment that Anglican dealings with the Government are necessarily more successful than those of other religious bodies. On the contrary, Anglicans have often enjoyed privileges won through the pressure of other religious bodies which their own more gentle measures would never have gained. Nevertheless this reciprocal attitude between the Church and State is worth noticing as a trait of Anglicanism. And it is quite consonant with freedom from State control.

A rather specialized illustration of the relation can be seen in the following extract from a statement by Pandit Nehru dealing with the position of Christians in India, although in this case the State is non-Christian and the Anglican Communion is not the only denomination involved:

It is notable that for the Christians 'India' is their natural and spontaneous outlook. The strength of the Christian position and its real power is in its non-communal outlook, its all-India outlook, if you like. This has been observed and envied by others. There is among the Christians, with all their faults, that 'something' which India needs now—a personal sense of liberation and a conscious appreciation of religious liberty. This quality of the Christian character and outlook needs no legal sanctions. The strength of the Christian position is the quality of the contribution the Christian can make to the new India.[1]

Constitution

Another example of the close relation between the Anglican Church and the secular government is to be seen in the way in which each national church tends to conduct its legislation on the lines familiar in its own country. In England where the law is not codified no attempt has been made to reduce ecclesiastical law to a code. Even the present proposal to revise the Canons expressly disclaims any intention to present the Church with a complete code. In other countries however where the secular law is codified each diocese generally has its own Book of Canons which takes 1603 for granted and incorporates on an equal footing every fresh

[1] From *The Discovery of India* (1946).

item of its own legislation. Such a Book of Canons thus carefully kept up to date is used as a comprehensive code, to be interpreted on the lines of an Act of Parliament, by which every detail of diocesan organization can be regulated.

So far as their relations with one another are concerned it is characteristic of Anglicans that the national churches and the provinces should have a large measure of autonomy. Indeed independence is so highly treasured that it might be questioned whether the diocese is not more definitely the unit of organization than the province. There are some dioceses which appear to stand on their own and to owe their allegiance to no Metropolitan. Although bishops of such sees would probably at their consecration take an oath of obedience to the Metropolitan who consecrated them, it would be assumed that their obedience would lapse when they entered the sphere of their own jurisdiction. Others, like Korea for instance, remain in obedience to Canterbury. Even when dioceses are grouped in provinces they still retain a very large measure of autonomy.

Similarly when provinces are grouped in national churches they do not forfeit their own independent status except at their own wish. The precise degree of dependence is regulated by their own canons, but generally the Metropolitan presides at the Provincial Synod, consecrates his suffragans and acts as referee. But there is no patriarch of the Anglican Communion, no one bishop or archbishop who can exercise control from a centre. The precedence that is accorded to the Archbishop of Canterbury is a matter of courtesy and he has no actual authority outside his own province, except in the case of the isolated dioceses already mentioned.

A closer inspection of the provincial constitutions reveals an almost infinite variety in detail. It would be true to say that no two provinces are exactly alike. This is partly due to the difference between established and non-established churches and partly due to the natural differences that arise when various groups of people organize separately their respective community life while consulting each other only irregularly. But it goes without saying that so far as constitution is concerned the presence or absence of a historic establishment does make a world of difference. In England the historical traditions have involved the Church in a whole set of legal institutions which are part and parcel of the

age-old life of the country. English unwillingness to part with
these traditions can be easily understood. It was no doubt the
very tenacity of the historic life of the people that formed one of
the major agents in holding them together during the two World
Wars. Historic precedent is not a thing which English people
easily jettison. Nevertheless modern conditions have imposed
upon them the necessity of providing swifter machinery, and
they have therefore followed the example of the non-established
churches overseas in acquiring new organs of legislation. The
result is that the English people enjoy or labour under a double
set of organizations, an old and a new. The old has not been
dropped, but it continues to function side by side with the new.
This has the advantage that if it were decided to disestablish the
Church in England there would be machinery all ready for carrying on independently of the State.

To that extent the old country has imitated the new. The
imitation however has not always been so close as it might have
been. The Church of England does not seem to have realized
that the self-government apparatus of the churches overseas is
linked fairly closely with financial provisions, and that privileges
are seldom accorded to a parish or a diocese without attaching
to them some financial responsibility. A parish for instance is
not usually allowed to choose its own rector unless it is prepared
to pay his stipend. Such provisions are vitally necessary in unendowed churches. In England the new machinery has been built
without much regard to these financial considerations. Consequently if disestablishment did come, and if it were accompanied
by a large measure of disendowment, there would be a very grave
financial crisis. The Church has not even now sufficient money
to meet its needs, and it would probably be altogether crippled
until it had time to recover from the first blow of disendowment.

Appointments

However at the moment we are not looking into the future,
but merely endeavouring to describe the variety that exists between the various constitutional arrangements of the Anglican
Communion. This variety can be seen very clearly in the number
of different methods by which bishops are appointed. In England
the part played by the Crown has already been mentioned.
Overseas the Crown has no part in the appointment of bishops.

Mostly they are elected either in open Synod or by committees specifically appointed for the purpose. Almost every variety of electoral method is employed. In some cases there is a straight vote, in others some form of proportional voting. In some cases speeches on behalf of the candidates are made. In other cases, such speeches are expressly forbidden, and there is allowed only a bare mention of the style and title of the person nominated.

It would be safe to say that nearly everyone is dissatisfied with the present methods of appointment. Overseas one finds clergy and laity alike saying over and over again how nice it would be if they could get rid of their popular election of bishops and have some method like that which prevails in England. In England the most vocal of the clergy and laity are loud in their denunciation of the present system, and say how much the dignity of the Church would be enhanced if it could enjoy some such freedom of election as is usual overseas. One who has been appointed under both methods may be forgiven if he states his own opinion that the English method is good provided that the deans and chapters can be relieved of the threat of *praemunire*. Elsewhere a small electoral committee would seem to be best, provided that its proceedings take place *in camera*.

Variety exists even after the bishop is appointed. In England the translation of a bishop from one see to another is very common, and nowadays most of the senior sees are held by men who have had previous experience as diocesans. In the Dominions translations may not be so common, but very often a bishop has had previous episcopal experience before he attains the dignity of an archbishopric. In America on the other hand translation is not allowed to full diocesan bishops although it may be permitted in the case of certain missionary bishops.

What looks like a definite contradiction is seen in the case of coadjutor bishops. In America they are appointed on the definite understanding that they have the right of succession. In Australia they are appointed on an equally strong understanding that they have no such right of succession. In England assistant bishops merely give whatever occasional help a diocesan may require.

The position of Suffragans is peculiar and varies. Strictly speaking every diocesan bishop is a suffragan of his Metropolitan, but in England the term is used of a bishop to whom a diocesan bishop gives a commission under seal to exercise such jurisdiction as he may think convenient. By an Act of Henry VIII the diocesan may name two persons to the King who chooses one and confers on him the title of Suffragan. Elsewhere Suffragans are appointed directly by the diocesan. In Canada the Suffragan occupies a rather different constitutional position from that which belongs to him elsewhere: there alone he is allowed to sit in the Upper House and to vote with the diocesan bishops. In England and elsewhere the diocesan bishops sit alone and the Suffragans only share the privileges of the House of Clergy. The fact that the diocesan does sit alone gives him in effect a right of veto over all legislation in his own diocese and is the constitutional foundation of his authority.

Similar divergencies can be seen in other aspects of Church organization. We have already pointed out that in some respects at least the province is the unit of organization. In England the two provinces of Canterbury and York have each their own separate Houses of Convocation. Their separateness however has recently been obscured to some extent by the fact that the Church Assembly acts as a common legislative body for the whole Church of the country, thus diminishing the importance of the provincial boundaries. In the Dominions the provinces are generally more obviously distinct than they are in England. In Australia, for instance, the provincial boundaries coincide roughly with those of the States, and the provinces follow closely the State organization, the Provincial Synod corresponding to the State Parliament while the General Synod corresponds to the Federal Parliament.

Even so it does not follow that all the provinces have reached precisely the same degree of development. Some carry their provincial organization further than others and have acquired actual power to pass legislation binding the dioceses, while others are little more than debating assemblies offering advice to the dioceses and having no power over them. In America the provinces are even less important. They are at the moment not much more than convenient areas for gathering together representatives from adjacent dioceses for mutual consultation. It is thought however by many Americans that there is room for considerable development in this respect, and many believe that the provincial organization will become more important as generations pass. This indeed would seem a logical proceeding if the United States become much more thickly populated. In that case there will be needed some provincial organization to stand between the dioceses and the General Convention.

The management of the dioceses varies to some extent from country to country. In some places there is a diocesan council elected by the Synod[1] which acts for Synod when Synod is not sitting. These councils are extremely important bodies, perhaps the most important in the whole Anglican constitution. The diocesan council is the effective governing body of the diocese. In England in place of the diocesan council there is a standing committee of the Diocesan Conference. Normally the standing committee is a much more numerous body than the diocesan council overseas, but paradoxically it has nothing like so much power. This is probably because it has not yet begun to assume or fully exercise the powers that properly belong to it. When the standing committees awake to their responsibilities and privileges they will no longer be content merely to arrange the business for the diocesan conferences, but they too will insist on being regarded as the effective governing body of the diocese. In England and elsewhere side by side with this council or standing committee there is generally a separate organization for managing the finances of the diocese (the Diocesan Board of Finance), which is separately appointed and has the right of direct report to the Diocesan Conference. It is possible that this may lead to some jockeying for position and to some jealousy between the two bodies, but logically it would seem inevitable that ultimately the diocesan council or the standing committee should exercise the full function of the Diocesan Synod or Conference when it is not in session.

The division of a diocese into archdeaconries and rural deaneries has not always been so thorough-going overseas as it is in England. In the more sparsely populated dioceses where there are very few clergy, the rural deans are hardly necessary, but in the more populous dioceses they are very valuable officials representing the clergy at the central headquarters and at the same time representing headquarters to the rank and file of the clergy. While the archdeacon is definitely the bishop's appointment and while the rural dean remains nominally so, the custom is gaining ground of allowing the clergy some voice in the choice of their rural dean.

[1] In this chapter the term synod is not used of Sacred Synod (i.e. clergy only) but of a conference of clergy and laity together.

It is obviously important that no rural dean should be appointed who is not *persona grata* to the clergy, otherwise his value as liaison officer between clergy and bishop will be greatly impaired. The existing variety in the means by which this desirable end is achieved, or at least sought, is a further illustration of the lack of constitutional uniformity to be found in the Anglican Communion.

Theological differences

In discussing our almost infinite variety it is inevitable that we should remember the differences in theological colour. Almost from the beginning of our separate history there has been a certain tension between those who emphasized the old Catholic traditions of the Church and others who stressed more strongly the different aspects of religious truth believed to have been recovered at the Reformation. There have been many modifications of this difference between High and Low or Catholic and Protestant. Sometimes they seem poles asunder and sometimes they shade off into each other. The relationship has been still further confused by the emergence of liberal thought which has cut right across the old division. It is sometimes suggested that liberalism is a distinct and separate type of theology, but that seems to be a mistake. There are Catholic liberals as well as Evangelical liberals, and while it is true that there are a few whose liberalism is so dominating a feature of their thought that they become modernists, normally the liberalism implies little more than a modern way of thinking about the literary composition of the Bible and the development of Christian doctrine. This type of thought is now almost universal, although there are a few fundamentalists both on the Protestant and on the Catholic side who will have no dealings with a scientific treatment of Christian history. However the majority are content to modulate their Catholicism or Evangelicalism with varying degrees of liberal thought, and they would probably hold that liberalism does not become modernism until the possibility of miracle is denied.

There are then in effect two, not three main schools of thought in the Anglican Communion. It is sometimes alleged that these are so fundamentally opposed to each other that they represent two different religions. On the other hand it might be said that the whole Anglican case rests on the belief that they are not two different religions but merely two aspects of the same fundamental Christianity. That it is difficult not to emphasize one side at the expense of the other goes without saying. Nevertheless at its first emergence as a distinct theological system Anglicanism did claim to be a synthesis of both. From time to time in subsequent history we have allowed one side to be obscured and have over-emphasized its opposite. At the present time both sides seem to be pressed so far as they will go within the limits of the Anglican formularies. It is therefore not quite so easy at this moment to say precisely in what the synthesis consists, but it may be that a new version of the old composition will presently appear which will give us a rounded theological system at a higher stage of development than that which has gone before.

It would be safe to say that the two strains of thought exist to some degree in almost every diocese of the Anglican Communion. They are evident in the differing types of ceremonial, in the varying extent to which sacraments are placed either towards the centre or towards the periphery of the Christian life, and in the shifting tendency to make either Sung Mattins or Sung Eucharist the more popular Sunday morning service. The first two of these points pass through many gradations, but the last is a fairly clear dividing line. However, even that is obscured where it is found possible to arrange a sung Parish Communion at an early hour. It is possible that this solution may be widely adopted in future in order to satisfy the tastes of both parties and to prevent divisions. In America, where 11 a.m. is still the almost universally observed hour of public worship, the proper solution may be more difficult to find.

Perhaps the most unfortunate dioceses from the point of view of the Church as a whole are those few in which differences of theological colour do not exist. A completely 'monochrome' diocese is not really a faithful reflection of the Anglican Communion and is therefore less easy to fit into the provincial or national background. Such dioceses have generally come into existence through the efforts of some single missionary society. When another society representing another point of view has established a diocese of an equally monochrome character side by side with the first it is not at all easy to build both into one provincial organization. East Africa has been the scene of our greatest failure in this respect so far, and it is there that we find it hardest to resist the reproach that Anglicanism is an attempt to reconcile two incompatible religions. However even there prospects are brightening, and our triumph will be the greater if we can show that dioceses springing up at either end of our theological scale can actually grow together.

The divisive effect of the missionary societies working in isolation gives additional point to the suggestion often made that they ought to give place to some organization representing the whole Church. America affords an instance of a national church which has been able centrally to take on responsibility for its missions. There are grave reasons why that cannot be done in England, some of which are indicated later in this chapter.

In the meantime we must notice that one great unifying influence is derived from those organizations of no party affiliation which spread around the world and pursue their aims in any diocese that is sufficiently fortunate to receive them. The Church Army, the Mothers' Union, the Church of England Mens' Society, the Girls' Friendly Society, each fulfil their beneficial activities in widely separated dioceses and so help to knit our whole life into one.

Liturgy

Variety in unity is strongly evidenced in the type of worship that prevails throughout the whole of Anglicanism. Most of the national churches have their own Prayer Book. Some, like Australia, have accepted completely the English standard, but even they have their own book of 'Occasional' Services. Elsewhere both Eucharist and choir office show many differences from the Book of Common Prayer. In a number of instances, as in America, the Scottish Prayer Book has been used as a common source side by side with the English. Elsewhere, as in South Africa, an effort has been made quite deliberately to improve on the technical attainment of the English book and to return nearer to the classical models, while in one instance at least the book of 1549 has been taken as the standard.

The result is that almost wherever you go you find differences in the mode of worship. Yet it is always obviously Anglican. The use of the vernacular is in itself enough to give the liturgical phrases an Anglican colour. Further the tones of the Prayer Book can always be discerned behind the living forms of worship.

There was a time when Anglicans found themselves resentful
and confused by any departure from the strict 'form and order'
of their book of 1662. But wider knowledge and growing experience have made them more sympathetic to local variations.
Probably not a few now find in such differences something that
adds life and colour to a common type of worship. Certainly
Anglicans are not now generally disposed to envy those who boast
that wherever they go they can always 'find precisely the same
form of service'. It is part of our sophistication and our world-
wide membership to feel at home with different versions of the
one fundamentally Anglican liturgy. Our tradition of worship is
alive not dead: it adapts itself to its environment. Consequently
this very variety makes, paradoxically enough, for our enhanced
unity. Witness what has already been said on this head in Chapter IX, on the West Indies.

Education

In few spheres does Anglicanism express itself more characteristically than in education. From its beginning as a separate communion it has regarded the training of the young as part of its
principal duty. The grammar schools were means by which it
strove to fulfil that task in the post-Reformation period. In the
early nineteenth century it was the most important purveyor of
elementary education in England. The awakening of the State
to a consciousness of its own duties in this respect has gradually
pushed the Church into the background, and when the new Act
has done its work it is possible that the Church of England will
retain only a mere fragment of its former influence in the elementary sphere.

By contrast we have maintained and even increased our
influence in the sphere of boarding schools (what is known in
England as Public School education). Many of the Church foundations which under boards of governors had begun to drift away
from Church influence have recently awakened to the importance
of a definitely Anglican atmosphere, and in consequence religious
education in the public schools has greatly benefited.

Curiously enough this seems to have set an example for our
churches overseas. Everywhere in America, in the Dominions,
and in the Colonies, you find splendid boarding schools founded
and managed by the Church. On the other hand primary schools

have not been so founded, or having been founded have been abandoned or handed over to the State.

There is of course a disadvantage in this. It is not merely that we lose the opportunity of bringing up a large proportion of our children in the Anglican tradition, but there is encouraged a suspicion of class distinction. No one would wish to decry the magnificent work done by Anglicans on behalf of young people who can afford to attend boarding schools, but one wishes that the benefits of our teaching could be more widely distributed among the less privileged children. The situation may become acute in England itself under the new Education Act. If the Church loses a large proportion of her primary schools Anglicanism may tend to become the religion of the well-to-do. One has heard this complaint already in Australia, and it is often alleged that class distinction is observable in the United States.

However in fairness it must be said that where Anglicans do not possess their own primary schools, they do at least attempt all possible expedients to make up for the deficiency. In some countries they have achieved the 'right of entry' so that their ministers or accredited teachers can go into the State schools and there give religious teaching to their own children. In some places this can be done during school hours; elsewhere it must be done outside the normal curriculum. Where both expedients fail, resort has to be made to Bible classes, Sunday schools, and weekday services in church. Nevertheless it is obvious that, however gallant an effort is made to use these various opportunities, nothing can really replace the full use of a school completely devoted to the interests of Church education.

Anglican influence in the higher flights of education is equally varied. The ancient universities in England, although they are no longer the close preserve of Anglicans, nevertheless maintain a strong Anglican flavour. The college chapels and their chaplains are of the Church of England and the ancient universities thus provide a magnificent opportunity for the Church's approach to youth. In the modern universities there is a different story to tell. In some instances they were founded with the definite intention of excluding religion or theological teaching. Practically everywhere this barrier has now been broken down. In most of the newer universities there are theological faculties, which are shared among the various denominations. In most of these universities, however, there are hostels which have been founded by Anglicans and are maintained in Anglican interests. This is the pattern which is generally followed in the Dominions, and there are some glorious institutions which have passed the stage of mere hostels, having become colleges and attained recognition as integral parts of their respective universities. Even in America Anglicans have not followed the example of other denominations in founding universities of their own, but have been rather content to let their young people become members of the great State or other institutions while endeavouring to watch over their spiritual interests from outside. Columbia, which was originally founded in close connexion with Trinity Church, New York, has ceased to display distinctly Episcopalian features, although the traces of its origin have not been entirely lost.

The education and training of the clergy follows much the same pattern throughout the Anglican Communion although there are variations on the one theme. The usual practice is to encourage ordinands to read for their degree at some university and then to spend some period in special training at a theological college or seminary. Some of our best seminaries are to be found in U.S.A. In England, Kelham tries to watch over the training of youths from a much younger age and to weld their whole education from school days to ordination into a unity. In some parts of the Mission Field where there are no such things as universities, candidates have to spend a long period as teachers and catechists with various stages of specialized training before they are ultimately admitted to Holy Orders.

On the whole the Anglican Communion has reason to be proud of its development of specialized theological education. It is not much more than a century since such technical training began to be regarded as necessary. The theological colleges that were then founded were as a rule the fruit of the zeal of some individual or group of persons: they did not result from the normal working of the organized machinery of the Church. The consequence is that still to-day many of them are really private concerns. In some instances, both in America and in the Dominions, dioceses or provinces have founded their own colleges and the whole Church in that area has thus very properly become responsible for the adequate training of its own clergy. The disadvantage of that method is that it results in a certain amount of inbreeding.

Clergy tend to remain in the neighbourhood where they were trained and there is not enough interchange among the dioceses. Nevertheless it has become increasingly the custom for the whole Church in each area to undertake this duty. Even in England the selection of ordination candidates, their examination, and to some extent the decision as to their training, is now in the hands of a central board. The effect is to equalize standards and to eliminate inadequacy. The danger is that it may grind down originality and produce monotony. So long however as some of the more brilliant students of the universities continue to respond to a vocation to the sacred ministry it is hardly likely that the Anglican clergy will be reduced to a dull level of mediocrity.

Missions

Not the least characteristic element of the Anglican Communion is to be found in its far-flung missions. No sooner does a church become well founded than it begins to send its agents to new fields. It is not always realized that the nineteenth century was the greatest period of Christian expansion, a triumph in which the Anglican Communion fully shared. This can be most exactly realized by comparing the seventy-five dioceses which represented the whole Anglican Communion in 1800 with the 320 that exist now. As Canon McLeod Campbell has pointed out in *Christian History in the Making*, during the former year only twelve of the seventy-five were outside the British Isles, ten in the United States and two in the rest of the world. In 1939 on the other hand, there were as many as 105 Anglican dioceses in the United States and 146 in the rest of the world outside the British Isles. During the same period the ranks of the native ministry have increased until they now embrace 2,000 clergy.

The means by which this expansion has been attained have sometimes seemed haphazard in the extreme. It was more by accident than carefully planned intent that we began to evangelize the natives of India. Much the same might be said of our work among the aborigines of Australia. Nearly always the first step has been due to the initiative of some specially zealous individual. For long there was no central organization at home to encourage him. He received his help from one or other of the missionary societies that had sprung up with the specific purpose of forwarding missionary work. As these societies represented different

Y

schools of thought there was sometimes rivalry between them. It was not often, as in the case of New Guinea, that an S.P.G. and a C.M.S. missionary joined hand in hand to found a new mission, although both societies have happily collaborated in China and Japan. Generally speaking the respective societies kept the work in their own hands until they grew much too powerful to give place to any other authority.

Efforts have been made from time to time to effect some kind of unity. In England there is a Central Missionary Church of the Church Assembly which endeavours to link together the work of the various societies and effects some sort of liaison between them. The United States has succeeded in making the whole Church responsible for its missionary work. Perhaps for this reason the missions of the Protestant Episcopal Church are better equipped than any others. Elsewhere it is generally thought that a good deal of interest would be lost if the societies ceased to keep their respective positions. People have become attached to their own society; they are familiar with its work and its workers; they understand and sympathize with its specific aims; they will contribute generously to the narrow but familiar purpose, while they will be lukewarm about an aim which is wider but less definite. This is a vexed question and one which will not easily be settled. The main point is that, however it is obtained, the fullest possible support for missionary work must be enlisted. The opportunities are great, but the difficulties arising from shortage of man-power and the rise of costs are also great. We shall need to strain every nerve if we are to mobilize our resources and take full advantage of our opportunities.

In the meantime we have to note that recent events have proved the capacity of the Anglican Communion to produce martyrs. Names as fully worthy to be honoured as those already in the calendar have been added to the Church's scroll of fame during the last few years. Indeed the history of missionary work shows a continued stream of heroism and self-sacrifice. Many have spent their strength in selfless devotion to their fellow men, while others have yielded their lives to the sword rather than betray the interests of their flocks. The Pacific, which has been the scene of some of the greatest martyrdoms of the nineteenth century, has seen the list notably increased during the past few years. If the blood of the martyrs is seed we may be sure that there will be a still further and more rapid expanse of the Church in the immediate future.

Social work

It is hardly necessary to describe in detail the vast amount of welfare work that is sponsored by the Anglican Communion. Such work inevitably takes on much the same characteristics by whatever Christian society it is performed. Hospitals, refuges, schools, almshouses, rest homes, asylums, are much the same wherever they are and by whatever agency they are conducted. More distinctive are the organizations like the Church of England Men's Society, the Mothers' Union, and the Girls' Friendly Society, which spread through England and the Dominions and tend to repeat themselves in parallel organizations in the United States.

There are however some differences in this respect between one national church and another. Australia for instance has developed the C.E.M.S. further than England has done. It has started two subsidiary organizations, the Church of England Young Men's Society and the Church of England Boys' Society. This development has a double effect: it provides a recruiting ground for the senior society and at the same time allows the C.E.M.S. to train leaders for youth and the C.E.Y.M.S. to train leaders for the youngest section. On the other hand in the United States and Canada a St. Andrew's Society performs much the same functions of binding together laymen for the service of the Church as the C.E.M.S. but it is thought by some to be an improvement in that its rules are more definite. If the Men's Society has flourished even more strongly in some of the Dominions than it has in the country of its birth, the Mothers' Union has found the going a little harder overseas. Both in America and in the Dominions the Woman's Auxiliary has banded women together in a very strong band of union to further the interests of their particular parishes. In very many instances they have raised the major part of the money necessary for running the machinery of the parish. This has given to the organization a practical purpose which has a very strong and indeed necessary appeal. It has not therefore been so easy to start branches of the Mothers' Union, which has for its main purpose the upholding of the ideal of marriage, and is not permitted to devote itself to the raising of money. This affords an interesting example of the way in which the needs of one national Church may differ from those of another. It suggests the value of consultation and co-operation between the different parts of the Anglican Communion before any effort is made to launch a would-be world-wide organization. Otherwise there is always a possibility that societies with somewhat similar aims spreading from one local church to another may find themselves in competition.

Organizations which arise more definitely out of the world-wide character of the Communion are such as deal specifically with seamen. The Missions to Seamen operates in many different parts of the British Empire. It was created in 1856 to promote the spiritual and temporal welfare of seamen in ports at home and overseas. A staff of clergy and lay readers works with the con-currence of the diocesan bishops whose licences they hold. Insti-tutes and hostels are maintained on shore in over a hundred stations at home and overseas. In the United States there is a parallel organization known as the Church Association for Sea-men's Work. It performs the same kind of function in promoting religious and philanthropic work amongst seamen, and its mag-nificent institution in New York is well known among sailors all the world over.

Another philanthropic task arising out of the world-wide spread of Anglicanism is the care of emigrants. Much valuable work of this kind is performed by the Church Army, but there is also the Church of England Advisory Council of Empire Settlement, which is the body recognized by the Church Assembly for migra-tion purposes. A skeleton organization was kept in being during the War period and is now ready to deal with the extensive migration which is expected to follow upon the resumption of peace. Corresponding organizations are maintained in the Dominions and it is possible for churchmen and churchwomen to be looked after when they leave their homes and settle in new countries. An especially valuable element of this work is its care for younger emigrants, who are carefully watched and assisted through their early difficulties until they have managed to make good in their new homes. In this way the Church shepherds its members, maintaining the age-old Christian duty of caring for the traveller, and enabling the Christian to realize that although he may be parted from his earthly home and family he is still surrounded by the love and care of the Family of God.

Nationalism

An interesting question arises about the extent to which Anglicanism is affected by racial and national characteristics. It might be expected that a Communion which lays such emphasis on national freedom and is in effect a union of national churches would display markedly distinctive features of a nationalist type. In reality it would not be altogether easy to point to such outstanding characteristics. As we have frequently mentioned there is variety in plenty, but this variety does not follow markedly national forms. It is always hoped that each nation will enrich the common apprehension of the faith with its own peculiar genius. There are indeed signs that Indian churchmen may bring their own deeply philosophical mentality to bear upon the explication of Christian doctrine. No doubt missionaries in Korea, China and Japan are conscious of a mode of apprehending the faith on the part of their converts which is not precisely that of practical and business-like Westerners. Certainly missionaries in the Pacific point with pride to the profound devotion and solemnity of their converts when they are engaged in public prayer, and many Westerners when they have been privileged to worship for the first time side by side with these children of the southern seas have gained a new insight into what a realization of God's presence may mean. But perhaps it is too early for anything to have arisen so distinctive as that essential mysticism which often illuminates the theology of the classical Eastern Christendom as contrasted with the more legal and logical theology of the West.

It is possible to distinguish varieties more clearly in the sphere of religious art. Every race has its own type of music, and even when Western religious music is introduced into the various parts of the Mission Field the natives generally tend to render it in a manner characteristic of themselves. So far there has been little compensating exchange by which the home Church could be enriched. In the architectural sphere there is a more obvious possibility of adaptation. Although the missionaries and settlers have taken with them their own type of church buildings so that often Christianity has been identified with pseudo-gothic, yet in many parts of the Anglican Communion experiments have been made in the appropriation of local forms for Christian purposes.

The cathedral at Dornakal is the best-known instance in point, although there are even more beautiful examples of the use of indigenous *motifs* in church buildings in Colombo and other parts of India. In the United States the 'colonial' style of architecture has provided some beautiful parish churches, but the Eastern States have preferred gothic styles for their cathedrals. The vast edifices in New York and Washington provide two of the best examples of modern gothic to be found outside Europe, although the unfinished cathedral at Brisbane will probably claim first place so far as the Southern Hemisphere is concerned.

In pictorial art there are happily many more signs of the influence of Native genius. From South Africa, India and the Mongolian countries there have already come some quite exquisite examples of Christian art that vie with the primitives of the classical West. It is much to be hoped that the Anglican Communion will inspire many more of its members to find expression for their native genius in many branches of Christian art. Already Maoris and Papuans have used their own characteristic furnishings and ornamentations to enrich ecclesiastical buildings, and the same might be said of most of the newer churches.

In the sphere of literature progress may be slower. The more backward races have had to be provided with an alphabet and a grammar. Often the first literature they have known has been the sacred scriptures and the liturgical services of the Church, but they already possess in every case a wealth of folk-lore and traditional tales. A great deal of that material could be sifted out, and used for religious and even for specifically Christian purposes. There is no why, as education spreads, a watch should not be kept for the ability of the story-teller to find expression in the production of an essentially Christian literature. In the English-speaking world it is not the representatives of the clergy who have at the moment the most popular appeal for religious readers. In days when T. S. Eliot, Dorothy Sayers, and C. S. Lewis command the attention of so wide a circle we have a special incentive to seek out particular ability among our lay converts and encourage them to consecrate the arts of the poet and story-teller to Christian uses.

Nationalism expresses itself in many other ways than these. Every organization that is carried from the Christian West into other parts of the world may be expected to be moulded according to the needs of the country into which it has been transplanted. Even religious communities may have a better chance of flourishing if they are indigenous and are not modelled too strictly upon lines that have been found suitable for conditions in the West. So far monastic orders for women have proved more tractable in this respect than those for men. The latter have sometimes perished prematurely because they could not free themselves from what proved to be the dead hand of the West. They have been too anxious to reproduce the precise conditions that prevail on the other side of the world. Life that no longer adapts itself to its environment ceases to be life. It is those institutions that have been able to learn most from their surroundings and to fit themselves most readily into the circumstances of their time and their area which have shown the most persistent vitality.

On the other hand it must be admitted that there is always a possibility that the nationalist element may prove too strong. In the early days of church history some national churches insisted so exaggeratedly upon their singularity as to cut themselves off from their environment and consequently became to a large extent atrophied. Continual watchfulness has to be exercised to prevent the same tragedy from being re-enacted. There have been recent movements of a nationalist kind in Japan and Egypt which have given rise to considerable anxiety. Among native races such as the Indians of America and the Maoris of New Zealand there have been corruptions of Christianity combined with an emphasis upon racialism that have broken the unity of the Church and done much harm. Where there is freedom there must always be danger. We cannot for that reason deny freedom; we must trust in the guidance of the Holy Spirit and exercise that eternal vigilance which is the price of liberty.

Reunion

This is not the place to enter into a discussion of the reunion movement, which is indeed the most marked feature of twentieth-century religious history, but at least a brief mention must be made of it here because of the outstanding part played by the Anglican Communion. The early history of Anglicanism did not give many signs of interest in this direction. The Church of England was unable to comprise within its bounds all the various types of Christian thought in its own country. Many attempts were made to accomplish this end but it could not include Romanists on the one side nor Puritans on the other. Nevertheless when it firmly established its own system it did from time to time make some approach to other bodies, both Continental Protestants and Eastern Orthodox, to say nothing of occasional discussions with Roman Catholics.

The modern Anglican effort towards the reunion of Christendom can be counted as beginning from the proposal in North America of 'the Quadrilateral' as the basis of union. Lambeth was in a favourable position to open up negotiations on such terms. Anglicanism, because of its special history, had an interest both in the old historic churches of Christendom and also in the newer post-Reformation churches. It was able to hold out a hand to either side. The most noteworthy and indeed epoch-making effort to do this was made by the Lambeth Conference of 1920. It was recognized that the greatest obstacle to reunion was the inability of the churches to accept each other's sacraments; and they were not acceptable because there was no agreed ministry to provide them. The Lambeth Fathers therefore offered to submit themselves to the laying-on of hands by the ordaining authorities of any other church with which general agreement had been made provided that their ministers were prepared in their turn to submit to the laying-on of hands by our bishops. This attempt to create a mutually acceptable ministry proved abortive, but it drew the attention of the whole world in the most striking way to the need and practicability of reunion, and to Anglican sincerity in striving to arrive at agreement.

Under this kind of impulse, which seems to have been felt spontaneously in other quarters, considerable progress has been made. Naturally like has drawn to like. The various Methodist bodies have united with each other and the same has been true of various sections of Presbyterianism. In Canada different types of Free Churches have combined to form a United Church of Canada. The Anglican Church, true to its history, has made terms with representatives both of the Catholic and Evangelical traditions. It is now in full communion with the Old Catholics of Europe and America and it has also shared in the episcopal consecrations of the national Church of Sweden. Very close agreement has been reached with various Orthodox Churches and there is good hope that the ties may be drawn closer still. A more adventurous effort, which has involved some dioceses (it is hoped only temporarily) in separation from the Anglican Communion in order to unite with local sections of the Free Churches, is the creation of a United Church of South India.

Side by side with progress towards actual reunion there has been immense advance in co-operation between the various sections of Christendom. This has developed into what is known as the Oecumenical Movement, represented by a World Council of Churches which includes practically every type of Christian except the Roman Catholic. The British Council of Churches encourages and effects similar collaboration in Britain and there are parallel bodies in other parts of the world. In the Oecumenical Movement Anglicans have taken an important part, and again their position of friendship with both the ancient and the modern churches has enabled them to render conspicuous service.

The theoretical and practical steps by which the cause of union may be advanced form a recurrent concern at each Lambeth Conference, and there are many who believe that under divine providence the main destiny of Anglicanism may be found in a call to act as a mediating influence among the disparate sections of Christendom. It is indeed one of the major reasons why every nerve must be strained to maintain and develop the Anglican synthesis. If by any chance the Anglican Communion could not hold together, the clock would be set back 500 years. If on the other hand we can maintain our positon and prove that it is the source of vitally creative power we shall by God's mercy perform a service of unique importance to Christendom and assist materially towards the fulfilment of our Lord's own prayer, *ut omnes unum sint.*

Spirit and Life

In conclusion we must inquire wherein consists the inmost essence of Anglicanism. What is the life (as distinct from the constitution) that holds the vast Communion together? What is the spirit, the tone and the temper of mind that it displays?

1. The characteristic most obvious to the outsider is its comprehensiveness. There is probably no Christian society which unites within its fold so many diverse shades of belief. Two generations ago this was recognized by most of its members as its greatest virtue. To-day we are apt to be more conscious of the

dangers of comprehensiveness. Those who have little liking for Anglicanism complain it is essentially illogical and that it really endeavours to hold together two irreconcilable religions. Too many of its own adherents are inclined to listen to these disparaging voices and to allow their confidence in the validity of their own position to be weakened.

Yet if the New Testament is to be taken as a standard there can be little doubt that Anglicanism is closer to its spirit and indeed to its practice than those who try to narrow down the limits of strict orthodoxy. Modern reading of the foundation documents makes us aware that within their pages are to be found not one but several embryonic theological systems. Indeed each of the leading writers seems to have developed his own characteristic scheme of Christian teaching. It was only in the later history of Christian doctrine that schemes became more closely articulated and endeavoured to claim the whole field for themselves against all comers.

It is therefore still possible for Anglicans to take pride in their comprehensiveness. They may be assured that a vast proportion of other Christians look at their unique freedom with considerable longing. That there must be limits to comprehensiveness goes without saying, and indeed over and over again in its history Anglicanism has had to insist upon those limits. But whether we like it or not comprehensiveness is an obvious characteristic of Anglicanism, and if it is denied the very *raison d'être* of Anglicanism is lost.

2. Next must be noticed the typical Anglican restraint. This is not merely due to the English character or to the national genius for understatement. It is equally obvious in the Episcopal Church of America as compared with its neighbours, and in Anglican missions overseas as compared with the corybantic religions which form their environment.

Everything concerned with Anglicanism, whether its intellectual type of piety or the severe beauty of its churches or the simple dignity of its ceremonial, speaks of the same restraint. Indeed the term 'simple dignity' has itself become so widely used in connexion with Anglican worship as to become an amusing cliché. Nevertheless it is quite expressive of the good order which is preserved within the churches. Sometimes this may appear to lead to aloofness and frigidity. The worshippers in many a little

Bethel miss the intimacy and warmth of their customary services when they find themselves in a great Anglican parish church or cathedral. Attempts are made from time to time to break down the austerity of Anglican services. It may be true that we could do with more colour in our buildings and more warmth in our devotions. Both these qualities have to some extent been supplied in recent years and there may well be more to come. At the same time it is extremely unlikely that the traditional restraint will be altogether lost, and classical severity will undoubtedly remain one of the main characteristics of Anglicanism.

3. This may to some extent spring from the typical Anglican regard for learning. There are other churches that produce great doctors of theology. It is indeed sometimes said that Anglicanism, has not produced theologians of the highest order. The general tendency has been to encourage a wide range of study, and classical scholarship has flourished perhaps more than other types of learning among Anglicans. Many fields however have been widely explored, and it is generally admitted that the compliment, 'clerus Anglicanus stupor mundi' has been well deserved.

It is a question whether Anglicans are losing their reputation for learning. It is true that great attention is given in these days to the technical training of ordinands for the precise work they have to do in the ministry. It was undoubtedly high time that such a development should take place. But that does not mean that there are none whose wider scholarship befits them to carry on the great traditions of the past. It is not many years since an editor of the *English Historical Review* told the present writer that whenever he had a book on an out-of-the-way subject to review, he had to send it to some country parson. While that spirit remains among the clergy, Anglicans can still regard the love of learning as one of their main characteristics.

4. The wholehearted use of the Bible is another example of the Anglican spirit. All Christians of course use the Bible and there are probably many who devote more time to private reading of it than the typical Anglican. But there is no church in Christendom that devotes more time to its public reading. The daily round of services provides for the monthly repetition of the Psalter, the yearly reading of the Old Testament, the half-yearly reading of the New Testament, and not infrequent lections from the Apocrypha. Ever since the Reformation and the time when the

vernacular Bible was chained in the churches for everyone to read who could not afford to buy a copy for use at home, the Bible as a whole has been familiar to members of the English Church. We unite with the ancient churches of Christendom in the regular lections at the Eucharist and the recitation of the Psalter, and we unite with the post-Reformation churches in readings from the Old and New Testament at Morning and Evening Prayer. Our people have good reason to know their Bible.

This has given a specific character to Anglican religion, but except in rare instances it has never degenerated into a Biblicism which makes of the Bible a fetish and turns Christianity simply into the religion of a book. There is a wholesomeness and a freshness about the Anglican use of the Bible which prevents us from being satisfied with the mere quotation of proof texts. The spread of modern knowledge has encouraged readers to aim at finding out what is the general lesson conveyed by each writer of each book. But even without this more scholarly approach the Anglican has generally tended to rest his case upon the whole Bible. Nevertheless he has always been a New Testament rather than an Old Testament Christian. His recognition of the superior authority of the New Testament and his use of tradition have given him an essentially sound approach to the whole Bible, which has reflected itself in the calmness of his attitude as contrasted with the fanaticism and bigotry of some who have used the Bible as an idolatrous object of worship rather than a guide to spiritual knowledge.

5. Again Anglicanism is a sacramental religion. This is abundantly true although there is a wide variety in attempts to explain the nature of the sacraments. The growing frequency of Communion, the present efforts to fence about the administration of Baptism, the care with which preparation is made for Confirmation; all these signs point the same moral, to say nothing of the more general recourse to Absolution and the spasmodic use of Unction.

There is of course a difference in the extent to which Anglicans use the sacraments as there is in the extent to which their theologians regard them as fundamental to Christian practice. Some put them in the centre and some on the circumference of their life and thought. But to every type of Anglican they are necessary: they are of the *esse* and not merely the *bene esse* of Church life. Although the minimum requirement for the laity is three Communions a year, in practically every church where a priest is available the Eucharist is celebrated each Sunday and Saint's Day and in many it is celebrated every day. It is this sacramental life of the Church that forms its chief attraction in the eyes of many Nonconformist ministers.

6. Another characteristic that proves very attractive to those outside its pale is the ordered round of daily worship. Many whose chapels are closed from one Sunday to the next would welcome the opportunity not only of private prayer in the open church but also of joining in the official public prayer and worship of the Church day by day. Indeed many are happily following our example in this respect.

An American view of this influence, written by an acute observer who is not an Anglican, can be seen in Dr. W. L. Sperry's *Religion in America*:

The Episcopal Church knows better than many other Protestant Churches how to greet and to meet the crowds in the city streets, at a mid-day service in Lent. . . . Simple liturgical services, an open door, when far too many other church doors are closed and locked, the encouragement of private devotions at any and all hours of the day, useful manuals for devotions, the patent lack of all class distinctions and the presence of a sincerely intended catholicity in the services of cathedrals and pro-cathedrals—all these are marks of vitality, sincerity and imagination (pp. 111, 113).

7. Finally there is the mark of a deep-seated moralism, which to those who know it best, is perhaps the most distinctive feature of Anglicanism. It can be realized most clearly if we reflect that by common consent the most constant form of heresy in England is Pelagianism. That heresy indeed is indigenous in this country and has repeatedly shown itself in the national character from the fifth century to the present time. What is sometimes known as 'public school religion', the religion whose ideal is the Christian gentleman with the gentleman rather more prominent than the Christian, is a modern version of the old tendency.

When the trait is not so strongly developed we still get an emphasis on works at the expense of much else which is characteristically Anglican. Of the three supreme qualities: goodness, truth and beauty, the Anglican has no doubt that the first is the most important. This certainly makes predestinarian Calvinism quite alien to him and puts Orthodox mysticism quite beyond his grasp. 'By their fruits ye shall know them' is a favourite text, and an accepted aphorism is: 'It is character and character alone that can truly save us'. The hardest doctrine to bring home to an Anglican is the priority of faith over works. Even his religious revivals are strongly moralistic. The Evangelical Revival soon found its most popular expression in works of charity, and the supreme object of the Catholic Revival was not churchliness but holiness. Above everything the Anglican wants to be good, and his strongest temptation is to regard his religion as a mere means to that end.

Anglicanism is thus something of a layman's religion, with all the emphasis on essentials and the disregard of niceties that characterize the unprofessional layman. For better or worse it has planted ethical principles deep in the heart of our people. It has made the Anglican's character respected and his word honoured the world over.

Moralism, daily worship, sacramentalism, the Bible, learning, restraint, comprehensiveness, these are the notes that seem most characteristic of the inner life of the Anglican Communion. They most clearly mark the quality of that vital energy which has carried the Gospel into many corners of the earth, inspired settlers and natives to establish fresh branches of the one Society, and expressed itself in the varied yet essentially similar constitutions that have been described in the preceding pages. The result in its totality is immensely impressive. It covers the globe, but its unity is symbolized at Lambeth; its roots are in ancient history, but its organization is fitted to modern needs; it reveres orthodoxy, but it baptizes into Christ the newest thought and the most recent science. Its position is peculiar and perhaps unique: but for that very reason its influence may still prove of paramount importance for the future of the Church and the welfare of the world.

BIBLIOGRAPHY

CHAPTER I

P. HEYLYN, *Cyprianus Anglicus*. (London) 1668. (A Life of Archbishop Laud.)

J. HACKETT, *Scrinia Reserata*. (London) 1693. (A Life of Archbishop Williams.)

W. R. W. STEPHENS and W. HUNT (Editors), *A History of the English Church*. (Macmillan, London). 1899–1910. (Especially Vols. V, VI, and VII: for the general historical background.)

NORMAN SYKES, *Edmund Gibson*. (Clarendon Press, Oxford) 1926. (For American affairs.)

R. D. MIDDLETON, *Dr. Routh*. (O.U.P., London) 1938.

M. CREIGHTON, *The Church and the Nation*. (Longmans, London) 1901. (Especially pp. 156–215 and 248–69: for the medieval background and the abolition of Roman jurisdiction.)

The Book of Common Prayer. (Tractates 'Concerning the Service of the Church' and 'Of Ceremonies', with the Ordinal and the Thirty-Nine Articles.)

CHAPTER II

Books by Episcopalians:

W. W. MANROSS, *A History of the American Episcopal Church*. (Morehouse Publishing Co., New York and Milwaukee) 1935.

Constitution and Canons for the Government of the Protestant Episcopal Church in America. Latest edition 1946.

The Living Church Annual. (Morehouse Gorham Co., New York.) Annually. (Current statistics, clergy directory, institutions, etc.)

Current reports and pamphlets on the work of the National Council, Woman's Auxiliary, etc. (Council's office, 281 Fourth Avenue, New York, N.Y.)

E. L. PARSONS and B. H. JONES, *The American Prayer Book: Its Origins and Principles*. (C. Scribner's Sons, New York) 1937.

'*As others see us*':

W. L. SPERRY, *Religion in America*. (Cambridge University Press, London, and Macmillan, New York) 1945.

GEORGE HEDLEY, *The Christian Heritage in America*. (Macmillan, New York) 1946.

CHAPTER III

General. (There is no up-to-date and generally informative work.)

J. LANGTRY, *History of the Church in Eastern Canada and New-foundland*. (S.P.C.K., London) 1892.

C. W. VERNON, *The Old Church in the New Dominion*. (S.P.C.K., London) 1929.

C. W. VERNON (Editor), *Our Church in Canada: A Series of Sketches of its History and Mission*. (Restoration Fund of the Church in Canada, Toronto) 1933.

H. P. THOMPSON, *Canadian Journey*. (S.P.G. and S.P.C.K., London) 1939.

F. M. BUFFETT, *The Story of the Church in Newfoundland*. (General Board of Religious Education, Toronto) n.d.

C. L. FORSTER, *The Church in the Arctic*. (S.P.G. and S.P.C.K., London) 1937.

Biography:

W. B. HEENEY and others, *Leaders of the Canadian Church*. Second Series. (Musson Book Co., Toronto) 1920.

J. W. LYDEKKER, *Life and Letters of Charles Inglis*. (S.P.C.K., London) 1936.

CHAPTER IV

A. H. HAMILTON BAYNES, *South Africa*. (Mowbray, London) 1908.

C. LEWIS and G. E. EDWARDS, *Historical Records of the Church of the Province of South Africa*. (S.P.C.K., London.)

OSMUND VICTOR, *The Salient of South Africa*. (S.P.G., London) 1931.

B. T. PAGE, *The Harvest of Good Hope*. (S.P.C.K., London) 1947.

AUDREY BROOKE, *Robert Gray*. (Oxford University Press, London and Cape Town) 1947.

CHAPTER V

The two essential books are:

EYRE CHATTERTON, *A History of the Church of England in India.* (S.P.C.K., London) 1924.

C. J. GRIMES, *Towards an Indian Church.* (S.P.C.K., London) 1946.

An immense amount of information on all subjects connected with the life of the Indian Church can be found in:

E. STOCK, *History of the C.M.S.* (C.M.S., London) 1899–1916. 4 vols.

Another important compilation is:

C. F. PASCOE (Editor), *Two Hundred Years of the S.P.G.* (S.P.G., London) 1901.

Lives of the outstanding bishops of the Church of India have been written. Those of Bishops Middleton, Heber, and Daniel Wilson of Calcutta are most important. Reference may also be made to CAROL GRAHAM, *Azariah of Dornakal.* (S.C.M. Press, London) 1946.

CHAPTER VI

F. T. WHITTINGTON and F. A. MICKLEM, *Life of William Grant Broughton.* (Angus and Robertson, Sydney) 1936.

R. G. BOODLE, *Life of William Tyrrell.* (Wells, Gardner & Co., London) 1881.

C. T. DIMONT and F. DE W. BATTY, *St. Clair Donaldson.* (Faber and Faber, London) 1939. (Certain chapters.)

W. K. HANCOCK, *Australia.* (Ernest Benn, London) 1930.

A. E. DAVID, *Australia.* (Mowbray, London) 1908.

J. W. S. TOMLIN, *Australia's Greatest Need.* (S.P.G., London) 1914.

Official Year Books of the Commonwealth of Australia.

Professor Hancock's book deals with Australia generally; those by Archdeacon David and Canon Tomlin deal with the Australian Church. Two books dealing with the work of the Bush Brotherhoods may also be mentioned:

CHARLES H. S. MATTHEWS, *A Parson in the Australian Bush.* (S.P.C.K., London. New edition) 1926.

B. P. ROBIN, *The Sundowner.* (S.P.C.K., London) 1922.

z

Chapter VII

Unfortunately there is no recent history of the Church in New Zealand, but information on the period up to 1910 may be found in:

LOUISE CREIGHTON, *G. A. Selwyn, D.D., Bishop of New Zealand and Lichfield.* (S.P.G., London) 1923.

HENRY JACOBS, *New Zealand.* (Colonial Church Histories Series.) (S.P.C.K., London) 1887.

H. T. PURCHAS, *History of the English Church in New Zealand.* (Sampson Low, London) 1914.

Each diocese publishes an annual Year Book and the *Proceedings of the General Synod* are published triennally, and contain the Constitutions and Canons of the Church.

Each diocese used to publish its own diocesan paper but the four dioceses of the North Island and Christchurch Diocese now unite in a monthly publication known as *Church and People*.

Chapter VIII

China:

FRANK L. NORRIS, *China.* (Handbooks of English Church Expansion.) (Mowbray, London) 1908.

GWENDOLIN R. BARCLAY and others, *The Way of Partnership— With the C.M.S. in China.* (C.M.S., London) 1937.

V. K. SHEBBEARE, *China.* (S.P.G., London) 1933.

VIRGINIA E. HUNTINGTON, *Along the Great Rivers.* (National Council of the Protestant Episcopal Church, New York) 1940.

GILBERT BARKER, *Changing Scene in China.* (S.C.M. Press, London) 1946.

MICHAEL BRUCE, *Opportunity in China.* (S.P.C.K., London) 1947.

Japan:

MARION H. BICKERSTETH, *Japan.* (Handbooks of English Church Expansion.) (Mowbray, London) 1907.

The Church in Post-War Japan. Report of the Anglican Commission to the Nippon Sei Ko Kwai. (Press and Publications Board of the Church Assembly, London) 1946.

C. K. SANSBURY, *Japan.* (The War and After Series.) (S.P.G.) London) 1947.

Korea:

MARK NAPIER TROLLOPE, *The Church in Corea*. (Mowbray, London) 1915.

CONSTANCE TROLLOPE, *Mark Napier Trollope*. (S.P.C.K., London) 1936.

CHAPTER IX

A. CALDECOTT, *The Church in the West Indies*. (Colonial Church Histories Series.) (S.P.C.K., London) 1898.

J. B. ELLIS, *The Diocese of Jamaica*. (S.P.C.K., London) 1913.

ROSCOW SHEDDEN, *Ups and Downs of a West Indian Diocese*. (Mowbray, London, and Morehouse Publishing Co., Milwaukee) 1927. (On the Diocese of Nassau.)

T. H. BINDLEY, *Annals of Codrington College, Barbados*, 1710–1910. (The West India Committee, London) 1911.

There seems to be no up-to-date account of the Church of the Province but for the West Indian background, with some reference to the part of religion in the history, see:

LORD OLIVIER, *Jamaica, The Blessed Island*. (Faber and Faber, London) 1936.

CHAPTER X

B. J. KIDD, *The Churches of Eastern Christendom*. (Faith Press, London) 1927.

W. R. W. STEPHENS and W. HUNT (Editors), *A History of the English Church*. (Macmillan, London) 1899–1910. Vol. VIII, *The English Church in the Nineteenth Century*, by F. Warre Cornish, Part I, pp. 264–70 and Part II, pp. 358–9.

W. A. WIGRAM, *History of the Monophysite Separation*. (Faith Press, London) 1922.

ADRIAN FORTESCUE, *The Lesser Eastern Churches*. (Catholic Truth Society, London) 1913.

CHAPTER XI

There is a lack of comprehensive or general books on the subject of the chapter. The books mentioned in the footnotes are:

A. R. TUCKER, *Eighteen Years in Uganda and East Africa*. (Edward Arnold, London) 1908;

and for the diocesan constitutions:

W. R. LOWTHER CLARKE, *Constitutional Church Government*. (S.P.C.K., London) 1924.

Reference may also be made to:

EDWIN W. SMITH, *Knowing the African*. (Lutterworth Press, London) 1947.

G. W. BROOMFIELD, *Colour Conflict: Race Relations in Africa*. (Edinburgh House Press, London) 1943.

CHAPTER XII

SIR FRANK SWETTENHAM, *British Malaya*. (John Lane, London) 1908.

CHARLOTTE E. FERGUSON-DAVIE, *In Rubber Lands*. (S.P.G., London) 1921.

R. COUPLAND, *Sir Stamford Raffles*. (O.U.P., London) 1926.

C. J. BUNYON, *Memoirs of Bishop McDougall*. (Longmans, London) 1889.

L. B. CURREY, *Borneo*. (S.P.G., London) 1933.

ERNEST PARRY, *Borneo Essays*. (Richard Jackson, London) 1924.

CHAPTER XIII

Scotland:

The Scottish Prayer Book. (Cambridge University Press) 1929.

Code of Canons of the Scottish Episcopal Church. (Cambridge University Press) 1929.

ANTHONY MITCHELL, *Scotland's Church*. (David Winter, Dundee) 1933.

M. E. M. DONALDSON, *Scotland's Suppressed History*. (John Murray, London) 1935.

LEIGHTON PULLAN, *Religion Since the Reformation*. (Clarendon Press, Oxford) 1923. (Chapter VI.)

Ireland:

Irish Prayer Book and Canons. (A.P.C.K., Dublin) 1929.

Constitution of the Church of Ireland. (Hodges & Figgis, Dublin) 1926.

W. ALISON PHILLIPS (Editor), *History of the Church of Ireland*. (O.U.P., London, 3 vols.) 1933.

H. E. PATTON, *Fifty Years of Disestablishment*. (A.P.C.K., Dublin) 1922.

GODFREY DAY and H. E. PATTON, *Cathedrals of the Church of Ireland*. (S.P.C.K., London) 1932.

HENRY HOLLOWAY, *The Reformation in Ireland*. (S.P.C.K,, London) 1919.

Wales:

C. A. H. GREEN, *The Setting of the Constitution of the Church in Wales*. (Sweet & Maxwell, London) 1937.

J. W. JAMES, *A Church History of Wales*. (A. H. Stockwell, Ilfracombe) 1945.

Official Handbook of the Church in Wales. (Representative Body of the Church in Wales, Cardiff) 1939.

CHAPTER XIV

CYRIL GARBETT, *The Claims of the Church of England*. (Hodder & Stoughton, London) 1947.

H. HENSLEY HENSON, *The Church of England*. (Cambridge University Press) 1939.

K. E. KIRK and others, *The Apostolic Ministry*. (Hodder & Stoughton, London) 1946.

S. C. CARPENTER, *Church and People*, 1789–1889. (S.P.C.K., London) 1933.

ROGER LLOYD, *The Church in the Twentieth Century*. (Longmans, London) 1946.

INDEX

Aberdeen, 254, 256

Aborigines, Australian, 135, 136, 323

Absolution, Sacrament of, *see* Confession

Abyssinia, Church of, 208

Accra, Diocese, 214, 215, 217, 228

Achimota College (Gold Coast), 232

Adelaide, Diocese, 116, 117, 119

Africa, East, 17, 214–5, 223–4, 225, 318–9; *and see* 214–39 *passim*

Africa, North, *see* North Africa, Diocese

Africa, South, *see* South Africa

Africa, tropical, Church in, 214–39, *and see* Africa, East, *and* Africa, West; Australian missions in, 136; N.Z. missions in, 156

Africa, West, 17, 214, 224, 231, 232, 235, 236; *and see* 214–39 *passim*

Alaska, Church in, 34, 35

Alexander, Mrs. C. F., 272

Alexander, Michael (Bishop of Jerusalem 1841–6), 205

America, *see* United States

Anglican and Eastern Churches Association, 271

Anglican Communion, characteristics of, 172, 282, 308–36; definition of, vii–ix, 219; general, 65, 83, 161, 230, 260, 272, 289, 306

Anglicanism, viii; genesis of, 1–9, 330; extension of, 9–17, 289; character of, 17–21, 93, 185–9, 215–6, 238, 245–248, 251, 255, 290–305, 308–36

Anglo-catholicism, 35, 39, 42, 43, 55, 122, 256, 272, 299

Anking, Diocese, 162

Antigua, Diocese, 192, 193

Aotearoa, Suffragan Bishopric of, 150

Apostolic Succession, 4, 73–4, 291, 292, 300

Archbishops, Metropolitans, Presiding Bishops, etc., appointment of, 53–4, 275; sees of, xii, 16, 53, 117, 143–4, 193, 273. *See also* 169

Archdeacons, office of, 316

Architecture of churches, 43, 61, 91, 105, 108, 232, 251, 327–8, 332

Armagh, See of, 260, 266, 275

Armenian Church, 201, 211

Art, ecclesiastical, 328

Articles, the XXXIX, 3, 213, 219, 260, 262, 276; Article VI, 269; XI, 7; XVII, 7; XXXIV, 120, 185, cf. 23

Assam, Diocese, 77

Association for Promoting Christian Knowledge (Dublin), 271

Assyrian Church, 209, 210, 212

Auckland, See and Diocese, 16, 138, 139, 143, 148, 152, 153; St. John's College, 139

Australia, Church in, viii, 16, 115–37, 156, 160 n., 289, 314, 321, 325

Australian College of Theology, 126, 127–8

Azariah, V. S. (Bishop of Dornakal 1912–44), 80, 90

Bangor, Diocese, 277

Baptism, doctrine, 21, 172, 255; practice, 171, 182, 186, 220, 238, 247, 254, 284–5, 290, 300, 308, 334; rite, 259, 265, 300

Barbados, Diocese, 11, 16, 192, 193, 194; Codrington College, 192, 197

Barclay, J. (Bishop of Jerusalem 1879–81), 206

Barker, F. (Bishop of Sydney 1854–84), 123

Belfast, 266, 268, 270

Benson, E. W. (Archbishop of Canterbury 1883–96), 206, 279, 281

Berkeley, George (Bishop of Cloyne 1734–53), 11–12

Berkeley Divinity School (U.S.A.), 12

Bermuda, 12, 48

Bernard, J. H. (Archbishop of Dublin 1915–19), 271

Bible, the, viii, 19–20, 65, 245–6, 308, 333–4

Bible Churchmen's Missionary Society, 160 n., 162, 164, 166, 168, 172, 174

Bishops, appointment of, xii, 27, 54, 84–6, 87, 102–3, 169, 194–5, 222, 257–8, 264, 275, 288, 292, 313–4; Missionary Bishops, 25, 27, 54, 103, 169; Suffragan or Assistant Bishops, 28, 118, 314–5

Bishops, Assistant, xii, 314

Bishops, Co-adjutor, position of, xii, 29, 118, 314

Bishops, Houses of, in Australia, 118, 121; Canada, 53, 54; China, 159, 169; India (Episcopal Synod), 86–7; Ireland, 263; Japan, 176, 178, 179, 181; Scotland, 256, 257, 258; South Africa, 98; Wales, 273, 275;

345